JAMES CAMPBELL

James Campbell was born in Glasgow in 1951. From 1978 to 1982 he was Editor of the *New Edinburgh Review*. He is the author of, among other books, *Talking at the Gates: A Life of James Baldwin* and, most recently, *Paris Interzone: Richard Wright, Lolita, Boris Vian and others on the Left Bank*. He lives in London where he works for the *Times Literary Supplement*.

The Picador Book of

Blues and Jazz

EDITED BY JAMES CAMPBELL

PICADOR

First published 1995 by Picador

This edition published 1996 by Picador
an imprint of Macmillan Publishers Ltd
25 Eccleston Place, London SW1W 9NF
and Basingstoke

Associated companies throughout the world

ISBN 0 330 34445 5

The acknowledgements on pages 391–6 constitute an extension of
this copyright page

1 3 5 7 9 8 6 4 2

A CIP catalogue record for this book is available from
the British Library

Typeset by CentraCet Limited, Cambridge
Printed and bound in Great Britain by
Mackays of Chatham plc, Chatham, Kent

Contents

JAMES CAMPBELL

Introduction

Writing to Gertrude Stein in Paris at the end of the Second World War, the novelist Richard Wright, then in New York, said he had heard that a point of solidarity between black and white soldiers in the segregated forces in Europe was 'Negro hot music'. Jazz, Wright suggested to Stein, seemed to be 'a sort of password'. He went on to tell Stein that when he was growing up in Mississippi, his grandmother had forbidden the playing of swing records on the family phonograph. In her devout mind, blues and jazz were associated with the wrong kind of person and the wrong kind of activity – a self-protective respectability not uncommon among the black population in the South. Wright himself grew up with the understanding that this music belonged to the inferior part of a race that was struggling to pull itself upwards. But when he went north to Chicago, 'white boys would corner me and tell me the deep meanings buried in a solo trumpet'.

Wright was heartened by these cross-cultural dialogues, which suggested that the racial cauldron could yet become a melting-pot. The African-American in his song – no matter if the song had words or not, whether it was uttered by a man or a woman, played on a Steinway or a homemade guitar – was endlessly posing the question: 'What did I do / to be so black and blue?' And the white boys who buttonholed Richard Wright, to talk about the 'deep meanings' encoded in the music, suggested that this question, and the history which prompted it, affected them too, even if they were not fully aware of it.

White boys have been searching for words to express what they hear in a trumpet solo, or in the metallic jangle of a country-blues guitar, ever since. Usually, the trumpeter is black, but not always. Likewise, the critic is more often than not white. Some of the best jazz has resulted from the complicity of black musicians and white composers (Irving Berlin, Jerome Kern, George Gershwin and others). Miles Davis, often fiercely 'black' in his attitude to the world at large, had a particular love for, and talent for playing, 'standards' – pop songs – by such composers. One of his most fruitful partnerships was with a white orchestrator, Gil Evans (who called his son Miles). When asked to name his influences, Davis would often start with the name of Frank Sinatra ('he taught me how to phrase'). Ray Charles, starting out as a blues singer in the early fifties, achieved wide popularity in the next decade singing country-and-western songs such as 'Georgia on My Mind' (composer: Hoagy Carmichael) and 'Your Cheatin' Heart' (Hank Williams), though infused with the feeling of the music – blues and gospel – with which he was raised.

One could continue at length in this vein, varying the theme with justified complaints by black artists about exploitative white managers and stolen copyrights; but always returning to the refrain: the blues is a melting-pot, and jazz, ruled over by a black prime minister with a solo trumpet, is a universal democracy.

There is more than one way of phrasing it, of course. During a conversation with the anthropologist Margaret Mead in 1970, James Baldwin related how, one day in London, his brother had got into 'a small argument' with a black Englishman who had assumed an air of superiority in the face of the two Americans. 'David said, "I don't care if all that is true. I come to London and I don't hear your island songs. I go to Stockholm and I don't hear your island songs. But no matter where I go in the world, I hear Aretha Franklin."'

This 'small argument' leaves quite a lot out of account – the power of the promotions departments of American record companies, for one thing – but it still makes an important point. The music that began 'on the auction-block', as Baldwin puts it in the essay in this book, has become the Esperanto of the global village – whether you call it blues, jazz, swing, soul, gospel, R&B or rock and roll (and if you think rock and roll began with Elvis Presley, read Gary Giddens's essay here).

If Baldwin faltered in attempting to unearth the roots of this music, then it would be reckless of me to try to do so; but I would raise my hand in order to make one small point in the democratic commons of jazz which is apt to be overlooked: while gospel and the blues, and eventually jazz, came out of slavery, and the slaves came from Africa, the slavers – or a significant number of them – came originally from Britain, as did the plantation owners to whom they auctioned their cargo.

Many of the variants of American folk music – bluegrass, country, Appalachian – have roots in Scottish, English and Irish folk traditions (the melting-pot is deeper than we think). They changed, naturally, according to native influences and as a result of encountering one another, over time developing local characteristics and variations. This is as true of Negro folk-song as it is for other branches of American music. In this case, the native influence was that of the Africans and their descendants who grafted the harmonic and rhythmic elements of tribal songs and shouts on to the hymns and ballads which they heard all around them on the plantation. African rhythm made the music black. Slavery and its legacy made it blue.

I was first alerted to the deep meanings buried in a blue note when in my teens and listening to records by Robert Johnson, Lightnin' Hopkins, Blind Boy Fuller and others, in between mixing with fiddlers, squeeze-box players, bodhran-beaters, pipers, jews-harpists and other assorted Scottish folk musicians who met to play each night of the week in a Glasgow pub called the Scotia Bar. There were many good guitarists and singers among them, too, but the first bluesman I had the opportunity to hear in person was Son House, the venerable Mississippi Delta singer, who visited Scotland at the end of the sixties. House had known Robert Johnson in his youth. If he did not match Johnson's weird, hell-driven intensity, he still struck the chords on his National steel guitar with the same authority: a mixture of lamentation and sensuality, the outcome of a life lived with loss, violence, sexual betrayal, close acquaintance with the Devil, and faith in the cosmic forces of retribution – all the elements of the Scottish ballads, in short, which were audible every night in the tiny backroom of the Scotia Bar.

The standard verse-form of the twelve-bar blues – AAB – can be traced to the repetitions of the rhythmical work-song, which also provided the subject-matter of many blues (chain-gangs, violence, remorse), but it is also found in old Scottish and English songs, such as 'Lord Randal', 'The Bonnie Lass o' Fyvie-O' and 'The Ballad of Pretty Polly':

> Polly, pretty Polly, won't you come along with me,
> Polly, pretty Polly, won't you come along with me;
> Before we get married, some new love to see.

As with all ballads, the date of this is unknown, but it was probably being sung before the first African was brought to the New World.

The black poet and folklorist Sterling Brown has made the same point, indicating the songs 'Barbara Allen', 'The Briary Bush' and 'Lord Lovell' as 'examples of traditional ballads that the Negro has helped to preserve'. Brown also noted that the lullaby 'Froggy went-a-courtin'', often thought of as being a Negro folk-song, 'first appeared in London in 1580 as "A Moste Strange Weddinge of the Frogge and the Mouse"'. Brown pointed out that the lines

> Who's gonna shoe to yo' little feet
> Who's gonna glove yo' hand

from the exemplary Negro ballad 'John Henry', 'have come down the long years from the old Scottish ballad called "The Lass of Roch Royal"'. (The lines Brown is referring to are 'O wha will shoe my fair foot, / And wha will glove my han'?'.)

The poetry of the ballads is superior to that of the blues, for one clearly definable reason: they are older, and therefore have benefited from time's pruning and shaping. Both musically and emotionally, on the other hand, the blues – especially when taken together with jazz – form a richer resource. Of the many reasons why this should be so one need only mention the historical events which produced the blues, which, taken together with the irony that infuses them, lend the music what might be called a bitter modernity; equally important is the vast recorded archive to which we have access, starting from the 1920s. We know nothing about the men and women who composed the ballads, and little about how they sung them. But we are intimately familiar with the broad musical range of those who sing the blues.

This cross-fertilization surely helps to explain the popularity of blues and blues-derived music among the British ever since Elvis Presley borrowed 'That's Alright Mama' from Arthur 'Big Boy' Crudup and recorded it in 1954. I doubt whether, say, an indigenous African musician would have affected the Scottish audience that night the way Son House did, although we might have responded to the melodic and rhythmic surfaces of the music, just as at the time we were enjoying the ragas of Ravi Shankar, in total ignorance of their technical, formal and even ritual subtleties. The powerful grip which the blues took on us came from a recognition that some of the roots of this bewildering, but none the less haunting, folk music were earthed in our own folk tradition.

Some, but not all. What sets black American music apart from other folk musics is the circumstances of its creation, which is what gives it its sense of urgency. And as certain parts of the border ballads drifted over the ocean and 'down the long years' to settle in early Negro folk-song, so this urgency – the sense of freedom – has carried back over the water, keeping time with our own time.

The slave sang the song in order to make himself free, in the inner realm enfolded by his music. He also sang to appeal to his Maker: to 'talk about Jesus', to ask Him to 'tell old Pharaoh / to let my people go', or to remind himself that 'He will never let go your hand'. His modern descendant, the jazz musician, living in an existential world, makes a peculiarly modern bid for liberty. He speaks of loss, but in telling of his loss, he finds a voice – the mark of the true jazzman is that you can recognize him from the opening bar – and in the voice his identity.

It is not surprising that *le be-bop* enjoyed a vogue in postwar, newly liberated St-Germain-des-Prés, from where Gertrude Stein, seeing the black GIs on the streets, wrote to ask Richard Wright what they were thinking. The solo trumpeter was the existentialist credo made flesh. 'Man is nothing else but what he makes of himself,' Sartre wrote; and 'Man simply is'. The jazz musician, improvising his freedom nightly, his notations a personal poetics of *Angst*, was 'man-simply-is' *par excellence*.

In the 1980s, I used to make annual autumn visits to Poland, as a guest of the Warsaw jazz festival, 'Jazz Jamboree'. These were the days of generals in government and martial law on the streets, but for some reason the long-standing Jazz Jamboree suffered only one suspension, in 1982, before being allowed to resume. In 1984, the festival coincided with a major political event, the kidnapping of the priest, Father Jerzy Popiełuszko, who had been snatched from the street and, though we didn't know it until the festival was over, murdered by police on the orders of high office. Father Popiełuszko had been closely associated with the Solidarity movement, and many of the festival's Western invitees received a lesson then in how, in an unfree society, people might seek a private freedom in some hitherto concealed compartment of the mind.

The tension of the day-to-day events pulsed through the intervals between concerts, and even through the concerts themselves. For in my imagination, at least, what was happening on the stage was connected to the immediate concerns of the moment. On the festival Sunday, together with thousands of Poles, I attended a vigil at the church of Father Popiełuszko in a Warsaw suburb. It was poignant, and ironic, to go directly from there to a concert given by Ornette Coleman, one of the originators of 'free' jazz, or Ray Charles – 'The world is in an uproar / the danger zone is everywhere' – in the Salla Congressowa, a giant wedding-cake of Socialist architecture imposed on the Poles by a hated dictator, Stalin, at the end of the Second World War. When American friends began to say, quite casually but convincingly, that the money for this lavish 'jamboree' came largely from the cultural wing of the American intelligence services ('You think Ray Charles would take a cheque in zlotys?'), the ironies started criss-crossing so fast that my sense of irony couldn't keep up. Sure enough, some years later, at the moment when the Iron Curtain finally parted and the peoples of Eastern Europe entered the nominally free world, the dollars which had kept the Jazz Jamboree going were no longer available – reserved, it would seem, for different causes.

In 'Red Music', included here, the Czech novelist (and tenor saxophonist) Josef Škvorecký tells a related story, from closer and more menacing quarters. When Goebbels decreed that the 'Judeo-Negroid' swing sounds were potentially harmful to the master race, then in the process of formation, Škvorecký and his band transformed 'St Louis Blues' into 'The Song of Rešetova Lhota' ('I'm on my way . . . to see my Aryan folk . . .') and carried on playing.

In time, the Nazis were replaced by the Communists, who took their tempo from Maxim Gorky's 'The Music of the Degenerate', and who decided that the capitalist noise (they didn't see the irony that this American music had an anti-American bass pattern) had no place in the ideal society. The music was banned all over again.

Jazz was not silenced as a result – on the contrary, as an

underground art, a sort of *samizdat* of the soundwaves, it only assumed greater significance for its performers and audience. There is no more potent example of the equation between jazz and freedom in the modern European experience than the story told by Eric Vogel, a member of two orchestras – the Ghetto Swingers and the Kille Dillers – which played in the concentration camps, where several of their members perished.

The history of this music is told most vividly in the music itself, of course, and sometimes the written history has let the music down. The biographies and autobiographies of great performers are often 'as told to' yarns, plump with tales of early hardship and wild nights on Fifty-Second Street when all the girls were good-time girls and nobody slept. Usually, they lack the introspection necessary to convey the feeling which is abundantly present in their authors' own playing, and on the whole I have left them out of this anthology.

In the early stages of compilation I was asked by someone what I was looking for in a piece that would make it worthy of inclusion. I replied that it should be 'unusual', which is simple but also sufficient. To elaborate only slightly, I felt that an item – whether a poem, an essay, an interview, a letter or a newspaper clipping – should not only be well written but also evocative of the social context from which both it and the music which governs it emerge. My ears pricked up at the sound of Richard Wright's 'deep meaning', whether it was found in the words of the ex-slave Solomon Northup describing musical life on a plantation, or Ralph Ellison courteously dismembering the politically slanted analyses of LeRoi Jones, or in the chain-gang rhythms of Sterling Brown's poem 'Southern Road'.

Among the memoirs which passed my test are Art Pepper's *Straight Life* – one of the best books about jazz ever written – the opening pages of Charles Mingus's *Beneath the Underdog*, in which Mingus fences unguardedly with his psychiatrist, and Mike Zwerin's *Close Enough for Jazz*, the autobiography of a trombonist written by an excellent journalist (the two being one and the same). The direct route into this book, in short, was through good writing. I have tried to be generous in range and eclectic in taste, without aspiring to be in any way comprehensive (that would require several more volumes). Where it is thought to be helpful, introductory remarks and dates have been provided; otherwise the pieces are left unencumbered.

The roughly chronological arrangement of the material was the simplest option available, but it was chosen after some reflection, as the best way of allowing the story – or this part of the story – to unfold by itself. The earliest item included here was published in 1741, the most recent exactly two hundred and fifty years later. This is 'the *beat*' which, as James Baldwin writes, 'recognizes, changes, and conquers time'.

Runaway: Eighteenth-century
Slave Advertisements

The columns of colonial newspapers frequently contained advertisements offering slaves for sale, and also gave notice of runaways. Such notices often included details of musical skills, which revealed, among other things, the instruments most commonly played by slaves.

RUN AWAY the 3rd Instant December from Combahee Ferry, a middle-sized Negro Fellow named Sam; had on when he went away a Negro Cloth Jacket died with red oak bark with Mohair Buttons, and a new Hat, can play upon the violin, and pretends he was born free in Virginia. Whoever apprehends the said Fellow shall have twenty pounds reward on Delivery either to the Work House in Charleston or to me at Combahee Ferry.

Alexander Moon

[*South Carolina Gazette*, 26 December 1741]

Whereas Cambridge, a Negro Man belonging to James Oliver of Boston doth absent himself sometimes from his Master: SAID NEGRO PLAYS WELL UPON A FLUTE, AND NOT SO WELL ON A VIOLIN. This is to desire all Masters and Heads of Families not to suffer said Negro to come into their Houses to teach their Prentices or Servants to play, nor on any other Accounts. All Masters of Vessels are also forbid to have anything to do with him on any Account, as they may answer it in the Law. N. B. Said Negro is to be sold: Enquire of said Oliver.

[*Boston Evening Post*, 24 October 1743]

RUN AWAY from the Pelham Privateer – Thomas Ebsery, born in Jamaica, a tall slim Fellow hard of Hearing; he beats a Drum very well and is well known amongst the Negroes in Charles Town having been here before with Captain Abrasher. Whoever apprehends the said Negro shall have 5 lb. Reward by applying to Reid and Kennan.

[*South Carolina Gazette*, 15 April, 1745]

RAN-away from Capt. Joseph Hale of Newbury, a Negro Man named *Cato*, the 6th Instant, about 22 Years of Age, short and small, SPEAKS GOOD ENGLISH AND CAN READ AND WRITE, understands farming Work carry'd with him a striped homespun Jacket and Breeches, and Trousers, and an outer Coat and Jacket of home-made Cloth, two Pair of Shoes, sometimes wears a black Wigg, has a smooth Face, a sly Look, TOOK WITH A VIOLIN, AND CAN PLAY WELL THEREON. Had with him three Linnen Shirts, home-made pretty fine yarn Stockings. Whoever shall bring said Negro to his Master or secure him so that he may have him again shall have *five Pounds* Reward and all necessary Charges paid by me.

Joseph Hale, Newbury, July 8th, 1745
[*Boston Gazette or Weekly Journal*, 9 July 1745]

RUN AWAY from the subscriber in Amelia, in the year 1766, a black Virginia born Negro fellow named Sambo, about 6 ft high, about 32 years old. He makes fiddles, and can play upon the fiddle, and work at the carpenter's trade.

[*Virginia Gazette*, 18 August 1768]

RUN AWAY – a Negro man, named Zack, about 20 years of age, 5 feet 7 or 8 inches high, slender built, sprightly walk, has lost the sight of his left eye, born in Connecticut, speaks good English, plays on the fife and German flute; had a fife with him; had on a coat, waistcoat and overalls of light-colored homemade bearskin, round hat, and shoes; carried with him a new green broadcloth coat striped cotton waistcoat, fustian overalls, namkeen do. [ditto], white cotton stockings, thread do., several shirts and other clothing.

Samuel Barber

[*Poughkeepsie Journal*, 6 January 1796]

Five Dollars Reward

Absented himself from the subscriber about the 10th of April, a likely young NEGRO FELLOW named CAROLINA, he has always been accustomed to wait in the house; he was seen in the city about ten days ago, dressed in a sailor jacket and trowsers. CAROLINA plays remarkably well on the violin.

The above reward will be paid to any person delivering him to the Master of the Work-House or at No 11 East Bay.

All Masters of vessels and others are hereby cautioned against carrying said Negro out of the State, as they will, on conviction, be prosecuted to the utmost rigor of the law.

June 13.   Robert Smith

[*City Gazette and Daily Advertiser*, 30 July 1799]

WILLIAM F. ALLEN

The Voices of the Coloured People . . .

The voices of the coloured people have a peculiar quality that nothing can imitate; and the intonations and delicate variations of even one singer cannot be reproduced on paper. And I despair of conveying any notion of a number singing together, especially in a complicated shout, like 'I can't stay behind, my Lord!', or 'Turn, sinner, turn, O!'. There is no singing in *parts*, as we understand it, and yet no two appear to be singing the same thing – the leading singer starts the words of each verse, often improvising, and the others, who 'base' him, as it is called, strike in with the refrain, or even join in the solo, when the words are familiar. When the 'base' begins, the leader often stops, leaving the rest of his words to be guessed at, or it may be they are taken up by one of the other singers. And the 'basers' themselves seem to follow their own whims, beginning when they please and leaving off when they please, striking an octave above or below (in case they have pitched the tune too high) or hitting some other note that chords, so as to produce the effect of a marvellous complication and variety, and yet with the most perfect time, and rarely with any discord. And what makes it all the harder to unravel a thread of melody out of this strange network is that, like birds, they seem not infrequently to strike sounds that cannot be precisely represented by the gamut, and abound in 'slides from one note to another, and turns and cadences not in articulated notes'.

1867

FANNY KEMBLE

Slave Singers

The English actress and singer Fanny Kemble lived on a plantation on the Georgia coast with her American husband during the winter of 1838–39. Her journal, published twenty-five years later, contained some vivid descriptions of the music she heard sung by the slaves there.

Mr M— sat in the middle of a perfect chaos of such freight; and as the boat pushed off, and the steersmen took her into the stream, the men at the oars set up a chorus, which they continued to chant in unison with each other, and in time with their stroke, till the voices were heard no more from the distance. I believe I have mentioned to you before the peculiar characteristics of this veritable Negro minstrelsy – how they all sing in unison, having never, it appears, attempted or heard anything like part singing. Their voices seem oftener tenor than any other quality, and the tune and time they keep something quite wonderful; such truth of intonation and accent would make almost any music agreeable. That which I have heard these people sing is often plaintive and pretty, but almost always has some resemblance to tunes with which they must have become acquainted through the instrumentality of white men; their overseers or masters whistling Scotch or Irish airs, of which they have reproduced these *rifacciamenti* . . . the tune with which Mr M—'s rowers started him off down the Altahama, as I stood on the steps to see him off, was a very distinct descendant of 'Coming Through The Rye' . . .

I have heard that many of the masters and overseers prohibit melancholy tunes or words, and encourage nothing but cheerful music and senseless words, deprecating the effect of sadder strains upon the slaves, whose peculiar musical sensibility might be expected to make them especially excitable by any songs of a plaintive character, and having reference to their particular hardships.

. . . My daily voyages up and down the river have introduced me to a great variety of new, musical performances of our boatmen, who invariably, when the rowing is not too hard, moving up or down with the tide, accompany the stroke of their oars with the sound of their voices. I told you formerly that I thought I could trace distinctly some popular national melody with which I was familiar in almost all of their songs; but I have been quite at a loss to discover any such foundation for many that I have heard lately, and which appeared to me extraordinarily wild and unaccountable. The way in which the chorus strikes in with the burden, between each phrase of the melody chanted by a single voice, is very curious and effective, especially with the rhythm of the rowlocks for accompaniment.

SOLOMON NORTHUP

Music on the Plantation

The only respite from constant labour the slave has through the whole year, is during the Christmas holidays. . . . It is the time of feasting, and frolicking, and fiddling – the carnival season with the children of bondage. They are the only days when they are allowed a little restricted liberty, and heartily indeed do they enjoy it.

It is the custom for one planter to give a 'Christmas supper', inviting the slaves from neighbouring plantations to join his own on the occasion; for instance, one year it is given by Epps, the next by Marshall, the next by Hawkins, and so on. Usually from three to five hundred are assembled, coming together on foot, in carts, on horseback, on mules, riding double and triple. . . .

Then, too, 'of all days i' the year', they array themselves in their best attire. The cotton coat has been washed clean, the stump of a tallow candle has been applied to the shoes, and if so fortunate as to possess a rimless or a crownless hat, it is placed jauntily on the head. They are welcomed with equal cordiality, however, if they come bare-headed and bare-footed to the feast. . . .

The table is spread in the open air, and loaded with varieties of meat and piles of vegetables. Bacon and corn meal at such times are dispensed with. . . .

When the viands have disappeared, and the hungry maws of the children of toil are satisfied, then, next in the order of amusement, is the Christmas dance. My business on these gala days always was to play on the violin. The African race is a music-loving one, proverbially; and many there were among my fellow-bondsmen whose organs of tune were strikingly developed, and who could thumb the banjo with dexterity; but at the expense of appearing egotistical, I must, nevertheless, declare, that I was considered the Ole Bull of Bayou Boeuf. My master often received letters, some-times from a distance of ten miles, requesting him to send me to play at a ball or festival of the whites. He received his compensation, and usually I also returned with many picayunes jingling in my pockets – the extra contributions of those to whose delight I had administered. In this manner I became more acquainted than I otherwise would, up and down the bayou. The young men and maidens of Holmesville always knew there was to be a jollification somewhere, whenever Platt Epps was seen passing through the town with his fiddle in his hand. 'Where are you going now, Platt?' and 'What is coming off tonight, Platt?' would be interrogatories issuing from every door and window, and many a time when there was no special hurry, yielding to pressing importunities, Platt would draw his bow, and sitting astride his mule, perhaps, discourse musically to a crowd of delighted children, gathered around him in the street.

Alas! had it not been for my beloved violin, I scarcely can conceive how I could have endured the long years of bondage. It introduced me to great houses – relieved me of many days' labour in the field – supplied me with conveniences for my cabin – with pipes and tobacco, and extra pairs of shoes . . . gave me an honoured seat at the yearly feasts, and secured the loudest and heartiest welcome of them all at the Christmas dance. The Christmas dance! Oh, ye pleasure-seeking sons and daughters of idleness, who moved with measured step, listless and snail-like, through the slow winding cotillion, if ye wish to look upon the celerity, if not the 'poetry of motion' – upon genuine happiness, rampant and unrestrained – go down to Louisiana and see the slaves dancing in the starlight of a Christmas night. . . .

One 'set' off another takes its place, he or she remaining on the floor longest receiving the most uproarious commendation, and so the dancing continues until broad daylight. It does not cease with the sound of the fiddle, but in that case they set up a music peculiar to themselves. This is called 'patting', accompanied with one of those unmeaning songs, composed rather for its adaptation to a certain tune or measure, than for the purpose of expressing any distinct idea. The patting is performed by striking the hands on the knees, then striking the hands together, then striking the right shoulder with one hand, the left with the other – all the while keeping time with the feet, and singing, perhaps, this song:

> Harper's creek and roarin' ribber,
> Thar, my dear, we'll live forebber;
> Den we'll go to de Ingin Nation,
> All I want in dis creation,
> Is pretty little wife and big plantation.
>
> *Chorus* Up dat oak and down dat ribber,
>   Two overseers and one little nigger

Or, if these words are not adapted to the time called for, it may be that 'Old Hog Eye' *is* – a rather solemn and startling specimen of versification, not, however, to be appreciated unless heard at the South. It runneth as follows:

> Who's been here since I've been gone?
> Pretty little gal wid a josey on.
>   Hog eye!
>   Old Hog Eye!
>   And Hosey too!
> Never see de like since I was born,
> Here comes a little gal wid a josey on
>   Hog eye!
>   Old Hog Eye!
>   And Hosey too!

Or, maybe the following, perhaps, equally nonsensical, but full of melody, nevertheless, as it flows from the negro's mouth:

> Ebo Dick and Jurdan's Jo,
> Them two niggers stole my yo'.
> *Chorus* Hop Jim along,
>   Walk Jim along,
>   Talk Jim along, &c.
> 'Old black Dan, as black as tar,
> He dam glad he was not dar.
>   Hop Jim along &c.

During the remaining holidays succeeding Christmas, they are provided with passes, and permitted to go where they please within a limited distance, or they may remain and labour on the plantation, in which case they are paid for it. It is very rarely, however, that the latter alternative is accepted. They may be seen at these times hurrying in all directions, as happy looking mortals as can be found on the face of the earth. They are different beings from what they are in the field; the temporary relaxation, the brief deliverance from fear, and from the lash, producing an entire metamorphosis in their appearance and demeanour.

1853

THOMAS W. HIGGINSON

Collecting Negro Spirituals

During the Civil War, Thomas W. Higginson served as a colonel in command of the first slave regiment to be mustered into the service of the Union army, the South Carolina Volunteers. His interest in folk music led him to collect the songs he heard sung by the ex-slaves.

The war brought to some of us, besides its direct experiences, many a strange fulfilment of dreams of other days. For instance, the present writer had been a faithful student of the Scottish ballads, and had always envied Sir Walter [Scott] the delight of tracing them out amid their own heather, and of writing them down piecemeal from the lips of aged crones. It was a strange enjoyment, therefore, to be suddenly brought into the midst of a kindred world of unwritten songs, as simple and indigenous as the Border Minstrelsy, more uniformly plaintive, almost always more quaint, and often as essentially poetic. . . .

Often in the starlit evening I have returned from some lonely ride by the swift river, or on the plover-haunted barrens, and, entering the camp, have silently approached some glimmering fire, round which the dusky figures moved in the rhythmical barbaric dance the negroes call a 'shout', chanting, often harshly, but always in the most perfect time, some monotonous refrain. Writing down in the darkness, as I best could, – perhaps with my hand in the safe covert of my pocket, – the words of the song, I have afterwards carried it to my tent, like some captured bird or insect, and then, after examination, put it by. Or, summoning one of the men at some period of leisure, – Corporal Robert Sutton, for instance, whose iron memory held all the details of a song as if it were a ford or a forest, – I have completed the new specimen by supplying the absent parts. The music I could only retain by ear, and though the more common strains were repeated often enough to fix their impression, there were others that occurred only once or twice. . . .

The favourite song in camp was the following, – sung with no accompaniment but the measured clapping of hands and the clatter of many feet. It was sung perhaps twice as often as any other. This was partly due to the fact that it properly consisted of a chorus alone, with which the verses of other songs might be combined at random.

Hold Your Light

> Hold your light, Brudder Robert, –
>   Hold your light,
> Hold your light on Canaan's shore.
>
> What make ole Satan for follow me so?
> Satan ain't got nothin' for do wid me.
>   Hold your light,
>   Hold your light,
> Hold your light on Canaan's shore.

This would be sung for half an hour at a time, perhaps each person present being named in turn. It seemed the simplest primitive type of 'spiritual'. The next in popularity was almost as elementary, and, like this, named successively each one of the circle. It was, however, much more resounding and convivial in its music.

Bound to Go

> Jordan River, I'm bound to go,
>   Bound to go, bound to go, –
> Jordan River, I'm bound to go,
>   And bid 'em fare ye well.
>
> My Brudder Robert, I'm bound to go,
>   Bound to go, &c.
>
> My Sister Lucy, I'm bound to go,
>   Bound to go, &c.

Sometimes it was 'tink 'em' (think them) 'fare ye well'. The *ye* was so detached that I thought at first it was 'very' or 'vary well'.

Another picturesque song, which seemed immensely popular, was at first very bewildering to me. I could not make out the first words of the chorus, and called it the 'Romandàr', being reminded of some Romaic song which I had formerly heard. That association quite fell in with the Orientalism of the new tent-life.

Room in There

> O, my mudder is gone! my mudder is gone!
> My mudder is gone into heaven, my Lord!
>> I can't stay behind!
> Dere's room in dar, room in dar,
> Room in dar, in de heaven, my Lord!
>> I can't stay behind!
> Can't stay behind, my dear,
>> I can't stay behind!
>
> O, my fader is gone! &c.
>
> O, de angels are gone! &c.
>
> O, I'se been on de road! I'se been on de road!
> I'se been on de road into heaven, my Lord!
>> I can't stay behind!
> O, room in dar, room in dar,
> Room in dar, in de heaven, my Lord!
>> I can't stay behind!

By this time every man within hearing, from oldest to youngest, would be wriggling and shuffling, as if through some magic piper's bewitchment; for even those who at first affected contemptuous indifference would be drawn into the vortex ere long.

Next to these in popularity ranked a class of songs belonging emphatically to the Church Militant, and available for camp purposes with very little strain upon their symbolism. This, for instance, had a true companion-in-arms heartiness about it, not impaired by the feminine invocation at the end.

Hail Mary

> One more valiant soldier here,
>> One more valiant soldier here,
> One more valiant soldier here,
>> To help me bear de cross.
> O hail, Mary, hail!
>> Hail, Mary, hail!
> Hail, Mary, hail!
>> To help me bear de cross.

. . . Almost all their songs were thoroughly religious in their tone, however quaint their expression, and were in a minor key, both as to words and music. The attitude is always the same, and, as a commentary on the life of the race, is infinitely pathetic. Nothing but patience for this life, – nothing but triumph in the next. Sometimes the present predominates, sometimes the future; but the combination is always implied. In the following, for instance, we hear simply the patience.

This World Almost Done

Brudder, keep your lamp trimmin' and a-burnin',
Keep your lamp trimmin' and a-burnin',
Keep your lamp trimmin' and a-burnin',
   For dis world most done.
So keep your lamp, &c.
   Dis world most done.

But in the next, the final reward of patience is proclaimed as plaintively.

I Want to Go Home

Dere's no rain to wet you,
   O, yes, I want to go home.
Dere's no sun to burn you,
   O, yes, I want to go home;
O, push along, believers,
   O, yes, &c.
Dere's no hard trials,
   O, yes, &c.
Dere's no whips a-crackin',
   O, yes, &c.
My brudder on de wayside,
   O, yes, &c.
O, push along, my brudder,
   O, yes, &c.
Where dere's no stormy weather,
   O, yes, &c.
Dere's no tribulation,
   O, yes, &c.

This next was a boat-song, and timed well with the tug of the oar.

The Coming Day

I want to go to Canaan,
I want to go to Canaan,
I want to go to Canaan,
    To meet 'em at de comin' day.
O, remember, let me go to Canaan, (*Thrice.*)
    To meet 'em, &c.
O, brudder, let me go to Canaan, (*Thrice.*)
    To meet 'em, &c.
My brudder, you – oh! – remember, (*Thrice.*)
    To meet 'em at de comin' day.

The following begins with a startling affirmation, yet the last line quite outdoes the first. This, too, was a capital boat-song.

One More River

O, Jordan bank was a great old bank,
    Dere ain't but one more river to cross.
We have some valiant soldier here,
    Dere ain't, &c.
O, Jordan stream will never run dry,
    Dere ain't, &c.
Dere's a hill on my leff, and he catch on my right,
    Dere ain't but one more river to cross.

I could get no explanation of this last riddle, except, 'Dat mean, if you go on de leff, go to 'struction, and if you go on de right, go to God, for sure.'

In others, more of spiritual conflict is implied, as in this next.

The Dying Lamb Poetry

I wants to go where Moses trod,
    O de dying Lamb!
For Moses gone to de promised land,
    O de dying Lamb!
To drink from springs dat never run dry,
    O, &c.
Cry O my Lord!
    O, &c.
Before I'll stay in hell one day,
    O, &c.

I'm in hopes to pray my sins away,
  O, &c.
Cry O my Lord!
  O, &c.
Brudder Moses promised for be dar too,
  O, &c.
To drink from streams dat never run dry,
  O de dying Lamb!

In the next, the conflict is at its height, and the lurid imagery of the Apocalypse is brought to bear. This book, with the books of Moses, constituted their Bible; all that lay between, even the narratives of the life of Jesus, they hardly cared to read or to hear.

Down in the Valley

We'll run and never tire,
We'll run and never tire,
We'll run and never tire,
  Jesus set poor sinners free.
Way down in de valley,
  Who will rise and go with me?
You've heern talk of Jesus,
  Who set poor sinners free.

De lightin' and de flashin'
  De lightin' and de flashin',
  De lightin' and de flashin',
  Jesus set poor sinners free.
I can't stand the fire. (*Thrice.*)
  Jesus set poor sinners free,
De green trees a-flamin'. (*Thrice.*)
  Jesus set poor sinners free,
    Way down in de valley,
      Who will rise and go with me?
    You've heern talk of Jesus
      Who set poor sinners free.

'De valley' and 'de lonesome valley' were familiar words in their religious experience. To descend into that region implied the same process with the 'anxious-seat' of the camp-meeting. When a young girl was supposed to enter it, she bound a handkerchief by a peculiar knot over her head, and made it a point of honour not to change a single garment till the day of her baptism, so that she was sure of being in physical readiness for the cleansing rite, whatever her spiritual mood might be. More than once, in noticing a damsel thus mystically kerchiefed, I have asked some dusky attendant its meaning, and have received the unfailing answer, – framed with their usual indifference to the genders of pronouns, – 'He in de lonesome valley, sa.'

PAUL LAURENCE DUNBAR

When Malindy Sings

G'way an' quit dat noise, Miss Lucy –
    Put dat music book away;
What's de use to keep on tryin'?
    Ef you practise twell you're grey,
You cain't sta't no notes a-flyin'
    Like de ones dat rants and rings
F'om de kitchen to de big woods
    When Malindy sings.

You ain't got de nachel o'gans
    Fu' to make de soun' come right,
You ain't got de tu'ns an' twistin's
    Fu' to make it sweet an' light.
Tell you one thing now, Miss Lucy,
    An' I'm tellin' you fu' true,
When hit comes to raal right singin',
    'Tain't no easy thing to do.

Easy 'nough fu' folks to hollah,
    Lookin' at de lines an' dots,
When dey ain't no one kin sence it,
    An' de chune comes in in spots;
But fu' real melojous music,
    Dat jes' strikes yo' hawt and clings,
Jes' you stan' an' listen wif me,
    When Malindy sings.

Ain't you nevah heerd Malindy?
    Blessed soul, take up de cross!
Look heah, ain't you jokin', honey?
    Well, you don't know what you los'.
Y'ought to heah dat gal a-wa'blin',

Robins, la'ks an' all dem things,
Heish dey moufs an' hides dey faces
    When Malindy sings.

Fiddlin' man, jes' stop his fiddlin',
    Lay his fiddle on de she'f;
Mockin'-bird quit tryin' to whistle,
    'Cause he jes' so shamed hisse'f.
Folks a-playin' on de banjo,
    Draps dey fingahs on de strings –
Bless yo' soul – fu'gits to move 'em,
    When Malindy sings.

She jes' spreads huh mouf and hollahs,
    'Come to Jesus', twell you heah
Sinnahs' tremblin' steps and voices,
    Timid-like a-drawin' neah;
Den she tu'ns to 'Rock of Ages',
    Simply to de cross she clings,
An' you fin' yo' teahs a drappin',
    When Malindy sings.

Who dat says dat humble praises
    Wif de Master nevah counts?
Heish yo' mouf, I heah dat music,
    Ez hit rises up an' mounts –
Floatin' by de hills an' valleys,
    Way above dis buryin' sod,
Ez hit makes its way in glory
    To de very gates of God!

Oh, hits sweetah dan de music
    Of an edicated band;
And hits dearah dan de battle's
    Song o' triumph in de lan'.
It seems holier dan evenin'
    When de solemn chu'ch bell rings,
Ez I sit an' ca'mly listen
    While Malindy sings.

Towsah, stop dat ba'kin' heah me!
  Mandy, make dat chile keep still;
Don't you heah de echoes callin'
  F'om de valley to de hill.
Let me listen, I can heah it,
  Th'oo de bresh of angel's wings,
Sof' an' sweet, 'Swing Low, Sweet Chariot',
  Ez Malindy sings.

1895

W. E. B. DuBois

Of the Sorrow Songs

> I walk through the churchyard
>   To lay this body down;
> I know moon-rise, I know star-rise;
> I walk in the moonlight, I walk in the starlight;
> I'll lie in the grave and stretch out my arms,
> I'll go to judgment in the evening of the day,
> And my soul and thy soul shall meet that say,
>   When I lay this body down.

What are these songs, and what do they mean? I know little of music and can say nothing in technical phrase, but I know something of men, and knowing them, I know that these songs are the articulate message of the slave to the world. They tell us in these eager days that life was joyous to the black slave, careless and happy. I can easily believe this of some, of many. But not all the past South, though it rose from the dead, can gainsay the heart-touching witness of these songs. They are the music of an unhappy people, of the children of disappointment; they tell of death and suffering and unvoiced longing toward a truer world, of misty wanderings and hidden ways.

The songs are indeed the siftings of centuries; the music is far more ancient than the words, and in it we can trace here and there signs of development. My grandfather's grandmother was seized by an evil Dutch trader two centuries ago; and coming to the valleys of the Hudson and Housatonic, black, little, and lithe, she shivered and shrank in the harsh north winds, looked longingly at the hills, and often crooned a heathen melody to the child between her knees, thus:

Do ba - na co - ba, ge - ne me, ge - ne me!

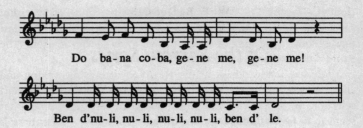

Do ba-na co-ba, ge-ne me, ge-ne me!

Ben d'nu-li, nu-li, nu-li, nu-li, ben d' le.

The child sang it to his children and they to their children's children, and so two hundred years it has travelled down to us and we sing it to our children, knowing as little as our fathers what its words may mean, but knowing well the meaning of its music.

This was primitive African music; it may be seen in larger form in the strange chant which heralds 'The Coming of John':

> 'You may bury me in the East,
> You may bury me in the West,
> But I'll hear the trumpet sound in that morning',

– the voice of exile.

Ten master songs, more or less, one may pluck from this forest of melody – songs of undoubted Negro origin and wide popular currency, and songs peculiarly characteristic of the slave. One of these I have just mentioned. Another is 'Nobody knows the trouble I've seen'. When, struck with a sudden poverty, the United States refused to fulfil its promises of land to the freedmen, a brigadier-general went down to the Sea Islands to carry the news. An old woman on the outskirts of the throng began singing this song; all the mass joined with her, swaying. And the soldier wept.

The third song is the cradle-song of death which all men know, – 'Swing low, sweet chariot', – whose bars begin the life story of 'Alexander Crummell'. Then there is the song of many waters, 'Roll, Jordan, roll,' a mighty chorus with minor cadences. There were many songs of the fugitive like that which opens 'The Wings of Atalanta', and the more familiar 'Been a-listening'. The seventh is the song of the End and the Beginning – 'My Lord, what a mourning! when the stars begin to fall'; a strain of this is placed before 'The Dawn of Freedom'. The song of groping – 'My way's

cloudy' – begins 'The Meaning of Progress'; the ninth is 'Wrestlin'
Jacob, the day is a-breaking,' – a pæan of hopeful strife. The last
master song is the song of songs – 'Steal away', – sprung from 'The
Faith of the Fathers'.

There are many others of the Negro folk-songs as striking and
characteristic as these; and others I am sure could easily make a
selection on more scientific principles. There are, too, songs that
seem to be a step removed from the more primitive types: there is
the maze-like medley, 'Bright sparkles', one phrase of which heads
'The Black Belt'; the Easter carol, 'Dust, dust and ashes'; the dirge,
'My mother's took her flight and gone home'; and that burst of
melody hovering over 'The Passing of the First-Born' – 'I hope my
mother will be there in that beautiful world on high'.

These represent a third step in the development of the slave song,
of which 'You may bury me in the East' is the first, and songs like
'March on' and 'Steal away' are the second. The first is African
music, the second Afro-American, while the third is a blending of
Negro music with the music heard in the foster land. The result is
still distinctively Negro and the method of blending original, but the
elements are both Negro and Caucasian. One might go further and
find a fourth step in this development, where the songs of white
America have been distinctively influenced by the slave songs or
have incorporated whole phrases of Negro melody, as 'Swanee
River' and 'Old Black Joe'. Side by side, too, with the growth has
gone the debasements and imitations – the Negro 'minstrel' songs,
many of the 'gospel' hymns, and some of the contemporary 'coon'
songs, – a mass of music in which the novice may easily lose himself
and never find the real Negro melodies.

In these songs, as I have said, the slave spoke to the world. Such
a message is naturally veiled and half articulate. Words and music
have lost each other and new and cant phrases of a dimly understood
theology have displaced the older sentiment. Once in a while we
catch a strange word of an unknown tongue, as the 'Mighty Myo',
which figures as a river of death; more often slight words or mere
doggerel are joined to music of singular sweetness. Purely secular
songs are few in number, partly because many of them were turned
into hymns by a change of words, partly because the frolics were
seldom heard by the stranger, and the music less often caught. Of

nearly all the songs, however, the music is distinctly sorrowful. The ten master songs I have mentioned tell in word and music of trouble and exile, of strife and hiding; they grope toward some unseen power and sigh for rest in the End.

The words that are left to us are not without interest, and, cleared of evident dross, they conceal much of real poetry and meaning beneath conventional theology and unmeaning rhapsody. Like all primitive folk, the slave stood near to Nature's heart. Life was a 'rough and rolling sea' like the brown Atlantic of the Sea Islands; the 'Wilderness' was the home of God, and the 'lonesome valley' led to the way of life. 'Winter'll soon be over', was the picture of life and death to a tropical imagination. The sudden wild thunder-storms of the South awed and impressed the Negroes, – at times the rumbling seemed to them 'mournful', at times imperious:

> 'My Lord calls me,
> He calls me by the thunder,
> The trumpet sounds it in my soul.'

The monotonous toil and exposure is painted in many words. One sees the ploughmen in the hot, moist furrow, singing:

> 'Dere's no rain to wet you,
> Dere's no sun to burn you,
> Oh, push along, believer,
> I want to go home.'

The bowed and bent old man cries, with thrice-repeated wail:

> 'O Lord, keep me from sinking down,'

and he rebukes the devil of doubt who can whisper:

> 'Jesus is dead and God's gone away.'

Yet the soul-hunger is there, the restlessness of the savage, the wail of the wanderer, and the plaint is put in one little phrase:

My soul wants some-thing that's new, that's new

Over the inner thoughts of the slaves and their relations one with
another the shadow of fear ever hung, so that we get but glimpses
here and there, and also with them, eloquent omissions and silences.
Mother and child are sung, but seldom father; fugitive and weary
wanderer call for pity and affection, but there is little of wooing and
wedding; the rocks and the mountains are well known, but home is
unknown. Strange blending of love and helplessness signs through
the refrain:

> 'Yonder 's my old mudder,
> Been waggin' at de hill so long;
> 'Bout time she cross over,
> Git home bime-by.'

Elsewhere comes the cry of the 'motherless' and the 'Farewell,
farewell, my only child'.

Love-songs are scarce and fall into two categories – the frivolous
and light, and the sad. Of deep successful love there is ominous
silence, and in one of the oldest of these songs there is a depth of
history and meaning:

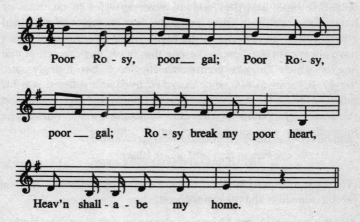

Poor Ro - sy, poor— gal; Poor Ro - sy,
poor — gal; Ro - sy break my poor heart,
Heav'n shall - a - be my home.

A black woman said of the song, 'It can't be sung without a full
heart and a troubled sperrit.' The same voice sings here that sings in
the German folk-song:

> 'Jetz Geh i' an's brunele, trink' aber net.'

Of death the Negro showed little fear, but talked of it familiarly
and even fondly as simply a crossing of the waters, perhaps – who
knows? – back to his ancient forests again. Later days transfigured
his fatalism, and amid the dust and dirt the toiler sang:

> 'Dust, dust and ashes, fly over my grave,
> But the Lord shall bear my spirit home.'

The things evidently borrowed from the surrounding world
undergo characteristic change when they enter the mouth of the
slave. Especially is this true of Bible phrases. 'Weep, O captive
daughter of Zion', is quaintly turned into 'Zion, weep-a-low', and
the wheels of Ezekiel are turned every way in the mystic dreaming
of the slave, till he says:

> 'There's a little wheel a-turnin' in-a-my heart.'

As in olden time, the words of these hymns were improvised by
some leading minstrel of the religious band. The circumstances of
the gathering, however, the rhythm of the songs, and the limitations
of allowable thought, confined the poetry for the most part to single
or double lines, and they seldom were expanded to quatrains or
longer tales, although there are some few examples of sustained
efforts, chiefly paraphrases of the Bible. Three short series of verses
have always attracted me, – the one that heads this chapter, of one
line of which Thomas Wentworth Higginson has fittingly said,
'Never, it seems to me, since man first lived and suffered was his
infinite longing for peace uttered more plaintively.' The second and
third are descriptions of the Last Judgment, – the one a late
improvisation, with some traces of outside influence:

> 'Oh, the stars in the elements are falling,
> And the moon drips away into blood,
> And the ransomed of the Lord are returning unto God,
> Blessed be the name of the Lord.'

And the other earlier and homelier picture from the low coast lands:

> 'Michael, haul the boat ashore,
> Then you'll hear the horn they blow,
> Then you'll hear the trumpet sound,
> Trumpet sound the world around,

> Trumpet sound for rich and poor,
> Trumpet sound the Jubilee,
> Trumpet sound for you and me.'

Through all the sorrow of the Sorrow Songs there breathes a hope – a faith in the ultimate justice of things. The minor cadences of despair change often to triumph and calm confidence. Sometimes it is faith in life, sometimes a faith in death, sometimes assurance of boundless justice in some fair world beyond. But whichever it is, the meaning is always clear: that sometime, somewhere, men will judge men by their souls and not by their skins. . . .

Your country? How came it yours? Before the Pilgrims landed we were here. Here we have brought our three gifts and mingled them with yours: a gift of story and song – soft, stirring melody in an ill-harmonized and unmelodious land; the gift of sweat and brawn to beat back the wilderness, conquer the soil, and lay the foundations of this vast economic empire two hundred years earlier than your weak hands could have done it; the third, a gift of the Spirit. Around us the history of the land has centred for thrice a hundred years; out of the nation's heart we have called all that was best to throttle and subdue all that was worst; fire and blood, prayer and sacrifice, have billowed over this people, and they have found peace only in the altars of the God of Right. Nor has our gift of the Spirit been merely passive. Actively we have woven ourselves with the very warp and woof of this nation, – we fought their battles, shared their sorrow, mingled our blood with theirs, and generation after generation have pleaded with a headstrong, careless people to despise not Justice, Mercy, and Truth, lest the nation be smitten with a curse. Our song, our toil, our cheer, and warning have been given to this nation in blood-brotherhood. Are not these gifts worth the giving? Is not this work and striving? Would America have been America without her Negro people?

1903

S. BRUNSON CAMPBELL

I Was Scott Joplin's Pupil

S. Brunson Campbell, Scott Joplin's only white pupil, was named by him 'the Ragtime Kid'. At the end of the nineteenth century, he was playing piano in Wild West saloons, in one of which the bartender claimed to own 'the bullet that killed Jesse James'. This account was written later.

El Reno was sure a wild town during those days, with lots of gun fights, and on top of that the soldiers from Fort El Reno, when they had gotten around too much liquor would shoot up the town and the 'red-light' district once in a while. Everyone seemed to be making money hand over fist, so I decided to make myself some easy money too. At every saloon that had a piano in it I would step in and play a few ragtime pieces and pick up a few dollars from the customers. . . .

Playing ragtime was an exciting life. I met and played for many notable people: Teddy Roosevelt, Bill Cody (Buffalo Bill), Gordon Lillie (Pawnee Bill), Governor Ferguson of Indian Territory, George Evans (Honey Boy Evans), Lew Dockstader, the great minstrel man. These last were mostly auditions. Salary differences kept me from signing contracts with them as a featured ragtime piano act. I realized later that I had made the greatest mistake of my life in not doing so. I also played ragtime for famous outlaws and other men, such as Frank Jones, Cole Younger, Emmet Dalton, Henry Starr, Old Bat Masterson, Bud Ledbetter, Heck Thomas, and many others including the famous Hobo A#1, who was in reality a railroad detective.

There is an old proverb, Arabian, I believe, to the effect that a man's fate is hung around his neck like a collar that cannot be removed, which amounts to saying we all have a destiny we cannot lose. It was my destiny to become one of the pioneer ragtime pianists of the 1890s.

It was in 1898 that fate introduced me to Negro ragtime. A friend and I ran away to Oklahoma City to a celebration being held there. We became separated and I wandered into the Armstrong-Byrd music store and began to play some of the popular tunes of the day. A crowd gathered to listen, encouraged me with applause and called for more. After a time a young mulatto, light complexioned, dressed to perfection and smiling pleasantly, came forward. He placed a pen-and-ink manuscript of music in front of me entitled 'Maple Leaf Rag', by Scott Joplin. I played it and he seemed impressed. (He afterwards told me I had made two mistakes.) He turned out to be Otis Saunders, a fine pianist and ragtime composer, a pal of Scott Joplin and one of ragtime's first pioneers. I learned from him that Joplin was then living in Sedalia and that he, Saunders, was joining him there in a few days.

I returned home, but a roaming propensity and a newly awakened interest in ragtime prompted me to run away again. This time I headed for Sedalia and after riding in boxcars, cattle cars, and 'blind baggage', I finally reached there and lost no time seeking out Otis Saunders and Scott Joplin, who was playing piano in a tavern there. At Saunders's request, I played for Joplin. They both thought I played fine piano and Joplin agreed to teach me his style of ragtime. He taught me how to play his first four rags, the 'Original Rags', 'Maple Leaf Rag', 'Sun Flower Slow Drag', and 'Swipesy Cake Walk'. I was the first white pianist to play and master his famous 'Maple Leaf'.

I became a kid ragtime pianist, the 'Original Ragtime Kid' of the nineties, and met almost all of the early Negro pianists and composers of ragtime. . . .

Sedalia was a wide-open town in those days, with saloons, gambling houses, dancehalls, a red-light district, and it was in these places the pianists could be found selling their musical wares. Two very popular clubs were the Maple Leaf and the 400 Special Club, run by the Williams brothers, friends of Joplin. . . .

It was Scott Joplin over at Sedalia who set the true ragtime pattern in 1897 with 'Original Rags'. This was published in 1899 by Carl Hoffman of Kansas City. If that rag did not convince the critics that Joplin was the 'ragtime master', then his next did, for it was his famous 'Maple Leaf Rag' of 1899. It became the 'classic' of all rags and today it is the most beloved of the Ragtime Era. Ragtime was the Negro's music, but it was the white man who made it popular. They first heard it in the Negro districts of Sedalia, Kansas City, and Saint Louis. They invited the Negro pianist into their homes to play for their parties and dances, and with the publication of Joplin's 'Maple Leaf' ragtime spread like wild fire to all corners of the globe.

None of the original pianists played ragtime the way it was written. They played their own style. Some played march time, fast time, slow time, and some played ragtime blues style. But none of them lost the melody and if you knew the player and heard him a block away you could name him by his ragtime style.

Scott Joplin named me the 'Ragtime Kid' after he had taught me to play his first four rags, and as I was leaving him and Sedalia to return to my home in Kansas he gave me a bright, new, shiny half dollar and called my attention to the date on it. 'Kid,' he said, 'this half dollar is dated 1897, the year I wrote my first rag. Carry it for good luck and as you go through life it will always be a reminder of your early ragtime days here at Sedalia.' There was a strange look in his eyes which I shall never forget.

Well, I carried that half dollar as a good luck pocket piece as Joplin suggested. Then in 1903 I met another pianist in a midwestern city and we became chums. One day we decided to go frog hunting down at the river near by. We got into a friendly argument as to who was the best shot, so I took my silver dollar and placed it in a crack on top of a fence post as a target. We measured off and my friend fired and missed. I shot and hit it dead centre. The impact of the bullet really put it out of shape, so on our return to the city I went to a blacksmith shop and with a hammer reshaped it as best I could and then carried it as a pocket piece as before. But one day I somehow spent it.

Years later I married and moved to California. On 1 May 1930, a customer came into my place of business and paid for a purchase with the same silver half dollar I had used for a target 27 years before. My lucky piece had returned to me. I could hardly believe my eyes, but there it was – right in my hand.

JAMES EDWIN CAMPBELL

Mobile-Buck

O, come erlong, come erlong,
    Wut's de use er hol'in back;
O, hit it strong, er hit it strong,
    Mek de ol' flo' ben' an' crack.
O, hoop tee doo, uh, hoop tee doo!
Dat's de way ter knock it froo.
      Right erlong, right erlong,
    Slide de lef' foot right erlong.
      Hoop tee doo, O, hoop tee doo,
    See, my lub, I dawnce ter you.
      Ho, boy! Ho, boy!
    Well done, meh lady!

O, slide erlong, slide erlong –
    Fas'ah wid dat pattin', Sam!
Dar's music in dis lef' heel's song,
    Mis'ah right foot, doan' you sham!
O, hoop tee doo, oh, hoop tee doo!
Straight erlong I dawnce ter you.
      Slide erlong, slide erlong,
    Mek dat right foot hit it strong.
      Hoop tee do, O, hoop tee doo,
    See, my lub, I dawnce ter you.
      Ho, boy! Ho, boy!
    Well done, meh lady!

Author's footnote: 'The above is an attempt to catch the shuffling, jerky rhythm of the famous negro dance, the Mobile-Buck. The author has watched by the hour the negro roustabouts of Ohio and Mississippi river steamboats "buck" against each other, to use their own expression. One roustabout called on by the crew steps out and begins the shuffle.

Suddenly he makes a tremendous slide forward on one foot, like the swift stroke of a skater, while with the other foot he beats a perfect tattoo. Each dancer in succession tries to outdo his predecessor, while all are cheered on by the comments and laughter of their rude but picturesque audience.'

1887

WILLIAM FERRIS

Work-songs

Though work chants have largely disappeared their sounds can still be heard in Parchman State Penitentiary at Camp B, near Lambert, where black prison gangs sing work chants as they cut wood and hoe cotton. Their leader calls a phrase and a refrain is repeated by workers in a call and response pattern which can continue indefinitely. When a tree is cut or the hoers reach the end of a row, the caller signals the end of his chant by crying 'Mud! Mud! Mud!'

Parchman work chants often speak of escape. One declares, 'Take this hammer, take it to the sergeant. Tell him I'm gone,' and its verses describe how a prisoner 'made it across' the Sunflower River, which borders the prison, so that bloodhounds could not follow him. As axes or hoes fall on each beat, other verses declare love for women with names like 'Rosie'.

> Boat up the river turning around and around.
> I said her fly wheel knocking 'Bama bound.
> I said her fly wheel knocking, well, 'Bama bound.

> *Chorus*
> Oh Rosie,
> Well, oh Lord Gal.
> Oh Rosie.
> Oh Lord Gal.

> Said I'll cut your kindling, Gal, I'll build your fire.
> I'll tote your water from that boggy biar [bayou].
> Said I would do your cooking but I don't know how.

> *Chorus*
> Said Rosie, Rosie, Gal will you be mine?
> Said I won't do nothing but wash and iron.
> Said gal you just do what I tell you to do.
> Said I'll be true to you, you know, well true to you.

Chorus

Said Woman, Woman, you don't know my name.
I'm the same grand rascal stole the watch and chain.
I'm the same grand rascal want to be your man.
I'm the same grand rascal used to hold your hand.

Chorus

Well you won't write me, you won't come and see.
Say you won't write me, you won't send no word.
Said I get my news from the mocking bird.
Said I get my news from that mocking bird.
'Mud! Mud! Mud!'

Work chants also direct railroad crews who line heavy steel tracks. When workers lift tracks a caller directs their moves. Railroad construction has specialized jobs, and a caller on the 'tamping crew' uses chants which would not be appropriate for the 'line crew' which lays rails. The weight of steel tracks makes it essential that every man work together. An individual's failure to do so places more strain on the rest of the crew or, even worse, may cause a fatal accident. Cal Taylor led work crews in the Mississippi Delta for fifty years and explains how on each beat the crew slowly moved heavy rails into position:

When you're lining track you say:

> Oh, up and down the road I go,
> skipping and diving for my forty-four.
> Ha ha, way over.
> Ha ha, way over.
> Poor boys, pull together.
> Track'll line much better.
> Whoa!

Then we might say for the next track:

> Oh, I got a letter from Haggis Town.
> East St Louis was burning down.
> Ha ha, way over.
> Ha ha, way over.
> Poor boys, pull together.

Track'll line much better.
Whoa!

There's a lot more verses for track lining, but most of 'em got bad stuff in 'em. If you don't care I'll put them on there too.

Oh, talking about a pretty girl, you oughta see mine.
Great big titties and a broad behind.
Ha ha, way over.
Ha ha, way over.
Poor boys, pull together.
Track'll line much better.
Whoa!

STERLING BROWN

Southern Road

Swing dat hammer – hunh –
Steady, bo';
Swing dat hammer – hunh –
Steady, bo';
Ain't no rush, bebby,
Long ways to go.

Burner tore his – hunh –
Black heart away;
Burner tore his – hunh –
Black heart away;
Got me life, bebby,
An' a day.

Gal's on Fifth Street – hunh –
Son done gone;
Gal's on Fifth Street – hunh –
Son done gone;
Wife's in de ward, bebby,
Babe's not bo'n.

My old man died – hunh –
Cussin' me;
My ole man died – hunh –
Cussin' me;
Ole lady rocks, bebby,
Huh misery.

Doubleshackled – hunh –
Guard behin';
Doubleshackled – hunh –
Guard behin';

Ball an' chain, bebby,
On my min'.

White man tells me – hunh –
Damn yo' soul;
White man tells me – hunh –
Damn yo' soul;
Got no need, bebby,
To be tole.

Chain gang nevah – hunh –
Let me go;
Chain gang nevah – hunh –
Let me go;
Po' los' boy, bebby,
Evahmo'. . . .

1929

PAUL OLIVER

Henry Ford Blues

In 1914 the continual flow of immigrants from Europe to the United States ceased and the northern industrialists, whose work was expanding with the demands of impending war, required cheap labour in quantity. Restricted immigration still operated in the 1960s, but by then it had no major influence on the national economy; during the years of World War I when the stream of European unskilled labourers was halted there was an acute labour shortage in the industrial North. Recruitment officers were sent south to draw workers from the plantations, and special freight cars were chartered to bring them to the North. Many of the labour officers were literally tarred and feathered or expelled from southern towns and villages at the point of a gun, and Blacks who left the plantations were forced back by county sheriffs who implemented hastily drawn laws designed to stem the tide of migrant coloured workers. The extreme was reached in Macon, Georgia, where a labour agent was required to pay a licence fee of $25,000 to operate, and only then if he had the recommendations of twenty-five businessmen, ten ministers, and ten manufacturers of goods. Elsewhere, heavy fees were demanded and operating agents were put into jail. Though they were often technically in debt through the perniciousness of share cropping, countless numbers of Blacks left the country farms that had been their whole world for their entire lives and, having little or no conception of northern urban life, prepared to face the risks involved in the hopes of a better future.

The cessation of the influx of European immigrants into the United States coincided with Henry Ford's pronouncement, in 1914, that none of his workers would earn less than five dollars per day, and it was in that year also that he commenced to employ Blacks on his assembly lines. As his huge plants in Detroit continued to expand and more workers were taken on, the news reached the

remotest corners of the South and attracted men who had been
living in penury. Blind Blake, who followed them, sang on their
behalf.

> I'm goin' to Detroit, get myself a good job, (*twice*)
> Tried to stay around here with the starvation mob.
>
> I'm goin' to get a job, up there in Mr Ford's place, (*twice*)
> Stop these eatless days from starin' me in the face.
>
> When I start to makin' money, she don't need to come around,
>   (*twice*)
> 'Cause I don't want her now, Lord, I'm Detroit bound.
>
> Because they got wild women in Detroit, that's all I want
>   to see, (*twice*)
> Wild women and bad whisky would make a fool out of me.

The pictures that the recruiting men painted were bright and
colourful, and to many a southern Black with his limited experience
and his folk ways, the prospect of work in the North was infinitely
attractive. If he questioned the employers' motives or stopped to
consider what his ultimate destiny might be, he was too familiar
with poverty and exploitation to let the thoughts deter him long.
Ford, it is alleged, with a long and distasteful history of anti-Semitism
in his industrial dealings, had his reasons for employing black
workers. He put considerable sums of money in the black 'Urban
League', paid good wages to his southern employees, and used them
to block the organization of labour unions within his firm. As the
unions gained strength he employed more Blacks, but few were
aware of these motives, though Bob Campbell's woman clearly
suspected them.

> I'm goin' to Detroit, build myself a job,
> Say, I'm goin' to Detroit, I'm gonna get myself a job.
> I'm tired of layin' around here workin' on the starvation farm.
>
> Say, I'm goin' down there and get me a job now, working in
>   Mr Ford's place, (*twice*)
> Say, that woman tol' me last night, that 'you cannot even
>   stand Mr Ford's ways'.
>
> Say I know my dog, baby when I hear him bark, (*twice*)
> And I know my woman if I feel her in the dark.

> Say, you better stop your woman from smilin' in my face
>   (*twice*)
> Woman, if you keep on a-smilin' I'm sure gonna take your
>   place.

In his latter verses Campbell expressed his distrust by analogy. But when the eruptions between Ford and the unions came to a head in the mid-thirties, it was to the unions that the Blacks gave their votes. In the ensuing years, nevertheless, there were many in all parts of the country who had good reason to be glad of the dependability of Henry Ford's products, and in particular the celebrated 'Model T' when, like, 'Sleepy' John Estes, they could afford to purchase one of the ancient and out-of-date models.

> Well, well, when you feed in the winter, please throw your
>   wire over in the bin, (*twice*)
> Well, well, papa, next spring, eeh-yeah, I won't wreck up my
>   T-Model again.
>
> Well, well, a T-Model Ford, I say is a poor man's friend, (*twice*)
> Well, well, it will help you out, yeah when your money is
>   thin.
>
> Well, one thing about a T-Model, you don't have to shift no gear,
>   (*twice*)
> Well, well, just lay down your brake and feed the gas, eeh-
>   yeah, and the stuff is here. . . .

Woman's Blues

The majority of blues singers are men, and the 'trouble in mind' of which the blues speak is largely trouble seen from a man's point of view; this despite the fact that the stars of the early recording era – Bessie Smith, Ma Rainey – were women. There are many little-known 'woman's blues'. This selection comes from a 1926 anthology of 'Negro workaday songs'.

Dem Longin', Wantin' Blues

I loves dat bully, he sho' looks good to me,
I always do what he wants me to.
Den he don't seem satisfied.
I got de blues,
Yes, Saro, I's got dem wantin' blues,
Dem longin', wantin' blues.

He don't send me no hearin',
I know another gal's dere an' I's fearin'.
He don't seem satisfied.
Now I got de blues,
Yes, Lawd, I got dem wantin' blues,
Dem longin', wantin' blues.

I Don't Love Him No Mo'

If I don't come back,
If I don't come back,
Put de cop on dat
Black man's track.

He's a rough-neck black,
Keep de p'liceman on his track,

Put 'im in de jail house,
Keep 'im dere.
I don't love him no mo',
So I don't care.

Dere's a Lizzie After My Man

Dere's a Lizzie after my man,
Dere's a Lizzie after my man;
She git 'im if she can,
'Cause I kotch her holdin' his han',
Dis-a mawnin', dis evenin' more 'n late.

Her face am powdered white,
Her face am powdered white;
Her hair am greasy an' slick,
On my man she try to work 'er trick,
Dis-a mawnin', dis evenin' more 'n soon.

She comed 'roun' to my do',
She comed 'roun' to my do';
Den I ripped offen her skirt,
Den I tore offen his shirt,
Dis-a mawnin', dis evenin', more 'n soon.

Worried Anyhow

When de man dat I love says
He didn't want me no mo',
I thought it was de hardest word
I ever heard befo'.

When de blues overtake you,
I's can't beat a deal,
If it wusn't fer my mother
An' de man I loves.

I give myself to de sick
An' my soul to de God above.
If you quit me, daddy,

It won't worry me now,
Because when we are together
I am worried anyhow.

Dere's Misery in Dis Lan'

I got a man an' a sweetheart, too,
I got a man an' a sweetheart, too,
I got a man an' a sweetheart, too,
Dere's misery in dis lan', dis lan'.

Can't please my man an' my sweetheart, too,
Can't please my man an' my sweetheart, too,
Can't please my man an' my sweetheart, too,
Dere's misery in dis lan', dis lan'.

My man makes money an' my sweetheart makes none,
My man makes money an' my sweetheart makes none,
My man makes money an' my sweetheart makes none,
Dere's misery in dis lan', dis lan'.

My sweetheart makes love an' my man makes none,
My sweetheart makes love an' my man makes none,
My sweetheart makes love an' my man makes none,
Dere's misery in dis lan', dis lan'.

Dat Chocolate Man

I ain't never goin' to be satisfied,
All day an' night I cried.
Dat big Bill o' mine he hide
From me, yes, from me.

My ol' haid it's weary,
My ol' heart it's dreary
For dat chocolate man.

I wonder where dat slim Bill's gone,
I can't do nothin' but set an' mo'n.

Dat big Bill stray from me,
Yes, he stray from me.

My bed it's lonesome an' col',
I can't sleep to save my soul.
Dat big Bill o' mine,
He's got dat yaller gal.

My ol' haid it's achin',
My ol' heart it's breakin'
For dat chocolate man.

I Done Sol' My Soul to the Devil

I done sol' my soul,
Done sol' it to de devil,
An' my heart done turned to stone.
I got a lot o' gol',
Got it from de devil,
Because he won't let me alone.

He says he can make me happy
An' give me back my man
If you follow me in sin,
An' I was so blue he took me in.
Look what a fool I am.

Done sol' my soul,
Done sol' it to the devil,
An' my heart done turned to stone.

I live down in de valley
By a hornet's nest,
Where de lions, bears, and tigers
Come to take deir rest.

Occupied

Coon, coon, coon, great big yaller coon,
He sets all night jis' outern my do'.

He says, 'Please lemme res' dere jis' once mo','
But, Lawd, it's occupied,
But, Lawd, it's occupied.

Dat coon'd be hot if he knowed de troof,
Dat a chocolate-drop lef' over de roof.
But he wanta come in once mo'
An' be occupied,
An' be occupied.

I Got Another Daddy

Leavin' here, I sho' don't wanta go.
Goin' up de country,
Brown-skin, I can't carry you.

Don't write me no letters,
Dont' sen' me no word,
I got another daddy
To take your place.

DOC REESE

Prison Blues

The folk musicologist and field-recorder Alan Lomax met Doc Reese as a result of his recording work in southern prison farms. When Lomax urged him to write his story, Doc Reese complied, delivering an account which is, as Lomax remarked, 'written as freshly as if English had never before been used for literary purposes'.

> I was born on the 13th, I'm my mother's only son,
> I was born on the 13th, I'm my mother's only son,
> Out of all the money in the world, I swear I ain't had none.
>
> I'm the unlucky one, no matter how I try,
> I'm the unlucky one, no matter how I try,
> I took the plane for California, landed in Shanghai.
>
> I have no schooling, I'm just another fool in town,
> I have no schooling, I'm just another fool in town,
> The first day I started to school, the sucker, it burnt down.

Often I ponder why I was born black and was forced to undergo so many unjust and unequal things. I feel and I always have felt that, regardless of what I did, mine would be a position of servitude. There was a craving in me, however, that forced me to try to break into a place of comfort, by any means. Stealing was my way.

It was not that I had failed to get proper guidance as to the great evil that this crime actually was, nor was I void of the knowledge of the punishment that would follow, nor did I ever think that I would be able to get around the law. I was imbued with a spirit of vengeance. I felt somewhat elated to have taken something from the white man. I felt I was merely evening up the score. Even if the law did place me in prison I felt justified because, to me, the law was warped to suit the fancies of the white man, whether I was being justly treated by it or no. What I thought was proven wrong to me, but as I thought, many others think, 'deep in the heart of the Delta'.

I worked at a drugstore in the coloured section and, when this store was looted of all the goods on the shelves, I was arrested. Although I had nothing to do with this crime and although I had never before been arrested and had no record at all, I was taken to the investigation cell and blackjacked in an attempt to extort a confession from me. Every ounce of third degree-ism was used against me. Finally, I was released, but with a black mark on my record and my inward feelings enraged. I had not been out of jail a day when an ex-convict made me an offer that was to be my undoing. I was to be turnover man for a gang. This suited me fine, for it would give me the chance to retaliate for the brutal treatment I had suffered.

The gang did a thriving business of looting cafés and I had little trouble in turning over the loot, which was mostly cigarettes. Six months later, when I had just reached the age of seventeen, I was apprehended with a large stock of stolen goods on my hands. They brought the whole gang in for investigation and placed us in separate cells. I managed to get a note to the rest of my boys advising them not to talk. I told them I would take all the blame.

The officers stood me on a brick all night, twisted my arms until they were sore, pressed a pencil under my nose until the pencil broke, but still couldn't get me to clear their books – that is, spill the goods on my buddies. My buddies were released and I was billed and transferred to the county jail to await grand-jury action. . . .

> I'm not talking to one,
> I'm not talking to two,
> I'm talking to the judge
> And the prosecutor, too.
>
> Jump in your places
> Like mules in their traces
> And let's get back!
>
> This jim has broke in, so the court is called,
> So each one line up against the wall!

. . . I was indicted on four separate counts. Each one of them was a burglary committed on the same night at about the same hour in different neighbourhoods of town. Just how I managed all those crimes without an accomplice will always be a mystery to me. On the day of my trial I pleaded guilty and asked for the mercy of the court. The mercy was a sentence of twelve years. I left the courtroom pondering what fate held in store for me. What would the prison make of me? Would I ever walk out in the free world again?

My cell mate in the county jail, where we were waiting for transfer to the pen, was a wrinkled-up old fellow named Uncle Frank. Uncle Frank was stooped over from work and mean enough, I believe, to steal the pennies off a dead man's eyes. Some of the boys called him One-Wing Frank on account of him missing one hand, and he told me how he lost his hand:

'When I first went down on the river, I tried to work hard and make it in the way they told me, but, shuh, man, they'd beat you anyhow. Look like to me they took delight in it. They beat on me till one day I run off. In my young days I could run, man! And I outrun all the dogs and the hosses they sent after me.

'But I was foolish, too. I got clean away into the next county, then I stole me some clothes and went to town and got drunk wid one of the pretty big-hipped gals. What did she do but turn me in. They took me on back to the farm and whipped me till I was raw as beef. Right then I made up my mind that I wouldn't work no mo. So the next day out in the bottom, I knocked this joe, a permanent one.' One-Wing held up his stub arm. 'Yeah, I never did no more heavy work after I chopped off this hand.'

After hearing Uncle Frank's story, dark thoughts used to come rolling through my mind as I lay in my cell at night. Then one morning I heard chains rattling down the corridor of the jail and somebody hollered that Uncle Bud had come and Black Betty was waiting.

Now you must know that in red-heifer times a man by the name of Bud Russell operated the transfer wagon that collected the prisoners from all over the state and brought them to the pen. They called him Uncle Bud and they sang many songs about him.

> Yonder comes Bud Russell,
> How do you know?
> I know him by his big hat
> And his forty-four.
>
> He walks into the jailhouse
> With his chains in his hand,

I heard him tell the captain,
'I'm the transfer man.'

They used to sing that song to Uncle Bud's face. They sang a different song behind his back:

Uncle Bud, Uncle Bud was a man like this,
Couldn't get a woman, he'd use his fist.

Uncle Bud had corn that never been shucked,
Uncle Bud had gals that never been ——.

So ever after on, they call any man that operates the wagon 'Uncle Bud', no matter what his name is. In place of Black Maria, we call Uncle Bud's old wagon Black Betty.

Uncle Bud had come and Black Betty was waiting! It seemed to me as if my whole body had turned cold as ice. I got up off my bunk and couldn't seem to get my feet down on the floor. Could hear my joints crack whenever I took a step. We were called out in the corridor and they gave us a necktie – a long chain with a Regent lock for the knot in every necktie. Thus I marched out of that jail and into the black, wire-enclosed truck, where Uncle Bud stood watching with his sub-machine-gun under his elbow. When we started, I peeped through a heavy black wire grating to tell my old hometown goodbye. We were a full chain – eighteen men, two white women, and one coloured woman.

At two o'clock the same afternoon we rolled up to the walls. This was the main unit of the prison system with the hospital, the shoe shop, the place where they made automobile licence tags, the school, the trusty shack, the auditorium, the dining-room, the big steel dormitory, and also the death house. The building had old-fashioned towers and funny-shaped windows all over it. Maybe it looked good at one time, but now it seemed to me all black and smoky and greasy like an old kerosene stove. When walked in, I felt I had walked into a big pair of black jaws and they had closed down behind me.

They stripped us, fingerprinted us, and gave us a bath and a medical examination. We were allowed to keep only our belts and our money was placed to our account for us to draw on whenever we wanted. Most of us were issued white duck clothes. To the escapees and parole violators they gave stripes. Then they marched us to our sleeping quarters. The reception committee was waiting.

'Hey, there, old Big Head!' I didn't turn around, because I didn't know they were talking to me.

'Yes, I mean you.' This time the jim tapped me on the shoulder. 'We gonna call you Big Head because you got a head as big as a punkin and empty as a gourd.'

Like every man who enters the prison, I now had my convict alias. The boys christen you as soon as they see you or as soon as they latch on to you. And that name is likely to stick to you until you leave the prison. I tried to grin at the man.

'Well, Big Head – if you know how to talk – where did you fall from?'

'Houston.'

'How much time you doin?'

'Twelve years.'

'That's schoolboy time. I could do that in my shirt-tail and never show my black behind.'

'How much time do you have?' I asked him. His name, I found out later, was Iron Jaw. He was a man that liked to talk.

'I have a hundred and twenty-five years for a number of crimes. . . . Well, Big Head, you ain't gonna be lonesome. They's enough boys here from Houston to work all the farms in the river bottoms.'

The bell in the tower rang and we got in line and marched into the dining-room. To my surprise the scaugh was all right. I asked Iron Jaw, 'Do they feed this way all the time?'

'Here in the walls they do. The members of the prison board come here a lot. But when you get down on those farms in the Brazos bottoms, you may never see a decent meal for months. The farms are rotten – rotten sleeping and eating, rotten hard work, and rotten bosses. Bout all you can do is gamble.'

'Well, that's gonna be hard on me because I don't gamble. Don't have any luck.'

'That's good, cause you can't win in the pen. These guys can outcheat the devil. After the lights go off at ten, come on over to my bunk and we'll talk.'

At the time I thought Iron Jaw looked at me in a funny way, but

I told myself that I was feeling jumpy. So after lights I went to his bunk and we began to chat. Right off he asked me, 'Did you have a wife in the streets, old Big Head?'

'Yes, I've got a wife and one kid about two months old.'

'Well, what do you think she's doing tonight?'

'I don't know. Hope she's thinking about me.'

'More likely she's out with Joe the Grinder, if she's like the other gals.'

'She wouldn't do that, I don't believe.'

'Man, you think she's gonna wait for you twelve flat years?'

'Maybe I'll get parole,' I muttered. I was feeling low in my mind by now and I wished I never had come to talk to this man who seemed to want to torture me with thoughts of home. As he went on talking, I began to think he had been well named, for his voice rang like iron.

'We all have that hope when we first come down here, but we soon find out we are the forgotten men. I had some broads promise they would be true to me when I first fell, but, since the months turned into years, those promises is forgot and the letters have stopped coming.'

I started to get up and walk away from Iron Jaw's bunk, but he grabbed my arm. His voice became more friendly, 'Did you see that slick cat sitting across from us in the dining-room with all those starched clothes on?'

'Yeah.'

'He is really making it easy here. He's a gal-boy we call Rosetta.'

'What's a gal-boy do?'

'What does a woman do in the streets?' Iron Jaw asked me.

'You mean wash and cook?'

'Women do more than that, you know as well as I do. Haven't you ever heard of a punk?'

I said I had.

'Well, Rosetta is a punk, and you have him just like you would your wife.'

'You mean he has what my wife has?'

'Something just as good and when you have him, you won't ever have any use for a woman again. Now listen, Big Head, I can help you a lot while you're here. I have some good connections and

I can keep you from going to the farm. Besides, I can let you have all the dough you need, if you will be my gal-boy. Would you like that?'

It was my first day in prison and I didn't want trouble with any man. I spoke just as easy and quiet as I could: 'I'll tell you, Iron Jaw, I never hold any hard feelings for what a man thinks or does, but, when I was born, I was a man-child. When I get low enough to take my mother's place, I will jump in my own ass and break my damn neck.'

The day I left the walls on transfer to the farm I was worried, but I was glad to get away from Iron Jaw's looks. I had been afraid all the time he would try to do some dirty deed and get me in trouble. As we neared the farms, we looked through the dust flying up from the wheels of the big truck and could hear the men singing:

> Black Betty's in the bottom,
> Let your hammer ring,
> Black Betty's in the bottom,
> Let your hammer ring.

Squads of men were scattered out across one of the biggest cotton fields you ever saw. The rows ran straight away from the road until they came together in the distance and wiggled in the heat from that old hot broiling sun. 'It is a burning hell,' I thought.

'Christ, man, that don't look like no farm. Mo like a garden,' the boy next to me remarked.

It looked like the people had crumbled up the clods by hand. The song of the hoe squads got louder. The convicts were chopping all together, and when they'd raise those hoes, the blades would catch the sun and twinkle like a rainbow. The rainbow came falling down as the men struck in time to the song:

> Black Betty's in the bottom,
> I can hear her roar,
> She's bringing some po sucker
> With an achin soul.

> She'll bring you here and leave you,
> Let your hammer ring,
> For a hundred summers,
> Let your hammer ring.

> Black Betty's got a baby,
> Let your hammer ring,
> Damn thing's gone crazy,
> Let your hammer ring,
> Dipped its head in gravy,
> Let your hammer ring.

They carried us to the building, where we were unchained. The guard on the truck gave our papers to the building steward and we were assigned to tank number three. The tanks were big and high dormitory rooms with four rows of bunks in three tiers. One end of each of the tanks faces on the picket and these ends are closed off by big black steel pipes that run from floor to ceiling. Steel doors open into the picket and there the guards and the building tenders stand watch with their clubs and guns.

A large, black, smooth-skinned, gross-talking Negro met us at the door. This was the building tender for tank three and he had an expression on his face just exactly like an old coon your dog has got cornered up in a wire fence. He turned out to be as mean as he looked. He ordered us to sit down. One of the boys took his time about it and the building tender slapped him to the floor.

'When I tell you to do anything, I mean do it, understand?' He looked at us with a wolfish smile. 'Where'd you come from, boy?' he asked a slim guy standing next to me.

'I'm from the capital.'

'I guess since you fell out the governor's mansion you come down here to run everything, but get this straight. The cap'un run the farm and I run this tank. There ain't but three ways that you can make it here. They are hard ass, suck ass, or haul ass. If you gonna hard ass, you gotta have an iron ass, a brass belly, and a heart of steel, because we been practising on hard guys for years and we know how to crack you. To suck ass, you got to be an ace sucker; you gotta look like you enjoy it. If you gonna haul ass, you better be ready to outrun the shit eaters and swim the big muddy river.'

This man was a convict like me, and probably had more time than I did. He turned to Joe, one of my fall buddies, and said, 'Where'd you come from, old yellow gal. I bet you're fine and

I'm gonna have you for my boy.' He laughed like a wolf while he ran his hand over Joe's legs. And what he said came true. The first night we were in the tank he came to Joe's bunk and Joe pushed him off. The next day the building tender, Old Love they called him, claimed Joe had broken a rule and he beat Joe down to the floor with his club. He kept on beating him and putting him up for punishment with the captain till Joe gave in. From then on, until he got tired of him, Old Love made things easy for Joe. That boy turned punk for true. He *made* him into a gal-boy. To me, this is the worst thing about prison life. Everyone knows it goes on – warden, captain, guards and all – yet nobody does anything about it.

Old Love went on talking to Joe: 'How much time do you have?'

'Two years.'

'Two years? You won't even find out where the captain s——! What did you steal?'

'I was sent up for assault and attempt.'

'I know assault and attempt. Assault on some white man's window and attempt to steal what he had on the inside. You can assault and attempt here on the weeds and Johnson grass in this good captain's cotton . . . Now, Shorty, what's your story?'

'I'm from Dallas with a double fan [ten years – two hands]. I tried to do away with all the weed out there.'

'So you're a sniffer! Well, you can't sniff here unless you want to use alfalfa . . . Now listen, you bulls, my rules are simple. No loud talking, no spitting on the floor, bathe often, git offa your bunk when the bell rings in the morning, and don't forgit to make it up when you git off it. Holler "Alley Boss" when you want to get up at night and don't leave your bunk until the night man give you the word to go ahead on. In the morning, the captain will tell you which squad to catch, and then you'll go to the fields.'

We were assigned to our bunks and the rest of the day was passed in talk about the streets with the sick boys who were staying in the building. About six-thirty the turnkey drug his keys across the bars to notify the picket boss that the squads were coming in from the fields. This picket boss was a big brute with a look like Dillinger in his bloodshot eyes and a potbelly that hung almost down to his knees. We called him Dough Belly behind his back.

'Number one plough, boss!' yelled the turnkey.

'That's right,' Dough Belly hollered back.

'Number two plough, boss.'

'Let um come.'

'Twenty of um, boss. Captain say put this un in the hospital.'

'I got um.'

And so the squads were checked into the tanks. The men were wet with sweat down to their socks. Their faces were dusty and their eyelashes hung with dirt. They were cursing a steady curse till the building sounded like a big nest of mad bumblebees. As many of the 'victs as could ripped off their dirty clothes and rushed to the showers in the rear of the tanks. One young bull sat down on the bunk opposite me and began to look at me the way a cow looks at a new gate.

'My name's Fast Black,' he told me. 'What do they call you?'

I told him my name. 'Well, how're things on the streets?' he inquired. 'Is the jims and janes still knockin theirself out?'

'The streets are on the beam and the janes on the ball. The jims are on the cut as sharp as tacks each and every day.'

'That sounds fine, man.' Fast Black smiled. 'I'm down here wrestling with a long stretch and it's knockin me, but I'll be out there some sweet day afterwhile. . . . Now look here, after supper we'll have a talk and I'll wise you up to what goes on around this place.'

I thought about Iron Jaw and I mumbled something. This Fast Black looked like an all-right jim, but then how could I be sure?

We fell in line with our hands on the right shoulders of the men just ahead of us and marched in to supper. There I got my first taste of prison-farm scaugh. The best you could say about it was that there was a plenty – slices of coarse bread, slabs of hog meat, piles of vegetables cooked tasteless – stuff like that. The rest I will tell you in a prison song I learned:

> You wake up in the morning
> When the ding-dong ring,
> Go marchin to the table,
> See the same damn things.
> It's on the table,
> Knife, fork, and pan.

> If you say anything about it
> You're in trouble with the man.

After supper, they had mail call and opened the commissary. Some of the boys marched off for school. Then in an hour Old Love hollered, 'Let's ride um,' meaning we should get in our bunks. We mounted and I heard Fast Black whisper, 'Hey, want to know why they call me Fast Black?'

'Uh-huh.'

'It's because I'm so dark, old Big Head.'

'Listen, if you're a friend, call me Doc, will ya?'

'Okay, Doc.'

'Tell me about the squads, Fast Black. Which one is the best to get on?'

'Them squads is all hard if the boss don't like you. Talk humble and don't grumble; act like your head's been bored for the simples; then maybe your boss won't ride you. Now here's the way the squads is laid out.

'There's number one hoe squad, where they put all the hard asses and haul asses. They make that squad *roll*. They have to set the pace for the rest of the squads in the field. Try to work um so hard they'll make a break, then they can lay the punishment on um. Number two hoe squad moves a little slower but must stay on the tail of number one. They push number one if it ever drag ass in the field. Number three is gen'ally the easy squad and do easy jobs, like shucking corn. Number four is boys who ain't well and can't keep up, but they make um work anyhow because they so tough to handle in the building. Number five is called the "pull-do's" because they got to be pulled to make um do *any* work. Some are cripple. Some just contrary. They the last to get to the field, riding while the rest of us trots ahead of the boss's horse.'

> You shoulda been on the river, nineteen and nine,
> Number one was runnin, number two was flyin,
> Number three was hollerin, number four was cryin,
> Number five was draggin, and the pull-do's dyin.
> Why don't you wake up, dead man, help me drive my row?
> My row is so grassy, I can't hardly go.

They have murdered my partner, plan on killin me.
If I get my chance, buddy, I'm gonna try to run free.

The next morning I was assigned to number four hoe squad, same as my new buddy, Fast Black. I felt good till I saw our boss. The men called him old Easter Rabbit because he didn't have but one big long tooth in front of his face and when he chewed his tobacco his ears wiggled just like a rabbit eating. But that was the only thing about him that resembled a rabbit. The rest of him was part snake and part bear. He had a high whiny voice and more words of profanity than the Japs have rice.

'Just don't never talk nothin where he can see your lips movin,' Fast Black told me while we were trotting to the woods ahead of old Easter Rabbit's horse. 'That old devil's about half deaf and he'll think you're cussing at *him*.'

After we got out in the bottoms, Easter Rabbit called me over to his horse. 'Well, high-pockets, I guess you've come down from Huntsville to tell us how to run this farm.'

'No sir.'

'What's that you say, god damn your black soul?' he said. 'Don't mumble at me.'

'No, boss, I just wants to get along,' I said very loud.

'Well, you can get along, if you watch yourself,' he said. 'But, goddammit, if you get tough, I can get a whole lot tougher. What'd *you* do in the streets, old nigger?'

'Worked in cafés, shine parlours – whatever I could find,' I said.

'Well, you gonna get some blisters on those soft hands of yours now, you soft-bellied bastard,' he whined. 'And the only shoes you'll get to shine are mine. You can start right now.'

Easter Rabbit gave me a kick with the toe of his boot. 'Now I want you to walk down there and take a look at that river. Anytime things get too hot for you here, you can always try to swim across,' he grinned.

I stood and looked at the old Red Brazos. It was swift and wide and full of drift logs, tangles and mudholes. A million ideas swept through my mind while the men sang this song:

> I was standing on the river when the ship passed by,
> I looked and saw my mother, turned my head and cried.
>
> If I ever do get wounded and pass away,
> You can tell my people these are the things I say –
>
> Give my clothes to my sister, give Papa my diamond ring,
> Give my shoes to my sister, don't give my wife a doggone
>   thing.
> If my mother don't want my body, cast it in the deep blue sea
> Where the catfish and the alligators can fight over me.

We kept on down into the bottom, deep down in there where the sun don't never shine because the woods are so thick and heavy. The boys say the trees down there look like old ghosts standing in some lonesome graveyard. We grouped up, four men to a tree.

'Old Big Head, you watch us strike a few times,' said Bad Eye, a bulky guy who had been on the river for sixteen years and had natural life for murder, 'and then you come on in. You strike with Gizzard Lips and I'll strike with Butter Bowl.'

Those guys could make an axe do tricks. Alternate men around the tree struck together, in a steady rhythm: 'Blam-lam, blam-lam, blam-lam.' On the upstroke they'd twirl their axe helves round in their palms so those double-bitted heads would flash like diamonds in the sunshine. I fell in with Gizzard Lips and Bad Eye began to sing:

> Why don't you ring, old hammer?
>   Hammer ring,
> Ring-ho, ring-ho,
>   Hammer ring.

We all sung the 'hammer ring' and Gizzard Lips began to 'preach' to his diamond, which is what he called his axe.

> I'm gonna preach to my diamond,
>   Hammer ring,
> If you walk, I'll ride yuh,
>   Hammer ring,
> And if you ride, I'll drive yuh,
>   Hammer ring,
> Cause I'm a number one driver,
>   Hammer ring,

> The axes is a-walkin,
>   Hammer ring,
> The chipses is a-talkin,
>   Hammer ring,
> Looky, looky yonder,
>   Hammer ring,
> I think I see sperrits,
>   Hammer ring,
> A-walkin in the timber,
>   Hammer ring.

Every man in our squad was striking to the rhythm of Bad Eye's song. Every man was swinging on that hot beat of his. The blood was running warm in my veins and I felt lifted up like I have in church sometime. There wasn't any more Easter Rabbit, no more bullying building tender, no more prisoners – just that old live oak and the axes biting them big chips and the song rising right through those dark woods up to the blue sky. About the time old Bad Eye began to talk about the 'sperrits in the timber', I heard somebody holler, 'Timbohhhhh——'

That long, lonesome holler nearly scared me to death. I looked up in time to see one of those big live oak trees come crashing down – whoomp! The ground shook when it hit.

By eleven o'clock there was a b   patch of sunshine in those dark bottoms where we had been working. Also, breakfast had begun to seem about a day ago. My little guts felt as if they were about to be eaten up by my big guts. Fast Black was the first one to see the wagon coming with our dinner, or 'johnny', and he began to holler:

> Believe I spied the johnny, believe I spied the johnny,
> Believe I spied the johnny, God Almighty God knows.
>
> Coming over yonder, coming over yonder,
> Coming over yonder, oh my Lordy.
>
> She's rockin dead easy, she's rockin dead easy.
> She's rockin dead easy, God Almighty God knows.

When the wagon got to the johnny grounds, plates were laid out on the ground in rows. Each convict got down by his own plate. The pots were passed along the lines and we ate, with the guards eating and sitting in a big circle around the edge of the johnny ground.

Johnny lasts an hour in winter and two in the summer. Dice games usually take place as soon as dinner is over, and those who do not participate get with their friends and venture into the streets of the past.

'Getting over here by old Big Head, boss!' Bad Eye hollered to the johnny boss.

'Go ahead, old Bad Eye, but I don't want to hear too damn much noise out of you,' replied the boss. Bad Eye slid along the ground until he was in our crowd. 'You from Houston?' he asked as soon as I was near.

'Yeah.'

'How much time they give you?'

'I got twelve years for my silly little game. It was all right at first, but looks like it'll be hell at the close.'

'You can make it, if you try,' he encouraged me.

'That's right, Doc,' said Fast Black. 'Just keep your mouth shut and your asshole open and you can roll right on.'

'It don't make no diffunce whether you got a long time or a short one,' said a voice behind us. 'You a dead man anyhow soon's you come down on these farms.' It was Butter Bowl talking. He was a short chubby fellow, and this was the first time I heard him say a word all morning. 'Naw, hell, it don't make no diffunce. After all this mess, you won't care whether you live or die.' He looked at me and his eyes looked like a dead man's eyes. They caused a cold chill to run down my spine. 'We in a dead man's hole,' he muttered like he was talking to himself. . . .

The next morning Old Love, the building tender, woke up on the wrong side of the bed and began to roar just like a lion. He had lost a lot of money in a crap game the night before and he was raging.

'Come off those damn bunks, tighten them damn sheets, and fold them blankets right. I don't want to hear a goddam sound out of any of you. Whose damn bunk is this?' he yelled as he stood by my bunk.

'It's mine,' I said, half afraid.

'You're a new nigger, ain't you?'

'Uh-huh.'

'Well, if I have to tell you about this bunk again, I'll put so many knots on your damn head you won't be able to put that damn head of yours through that damn door.'

I went to makin the bed over again, and he walked down the aisle and stopped at Butter Bowl's bunk. 'Get your sorry ass over here, old Butter Bowl. You may do what you want to out there in the fields and cuss the bosses, but in here you gonna make your damn bunk up.'

Butter Bowl came, walking slowly, and, as he approached his bunk, Old Love let him have it. He hit him on the right side of the head and the blow rang through the entire building. Now, Butter Bowl never had building trouble before. He had been respected as a man and avoided by the tenders. When Old Love hit him, he put his hands up to his head, half dazed, with the blood running in his eyes. He saw Love reaching for his dirk and he turned and ran up the alley with Love right on his heels, cutting him at every step. He ran to the back of the building, snatched the top off a commode, and whirled just in time to let Love have it against his head. The top shattered and a sharp piece stuck into Love's head. Love lost his dirk and club and Butter Bowl began to beat him down to the floor, growling, 'You low-down, belly-crawling bastard, you been fooling with us too long. This time you grabbed the wrong man.'

By this time the assistant building tender had grabbed his club and was rushing to help Old Love. As he moved in, Gizzard Lips rose to Butter Bowl's defence. Gizzard Lips was a small Negro, about five feet four inches tall, weighing about one hundred and forty pounds, but he was tough as a boot and didn't take any fooling with. He came up with a curse on his lips, 'You ratty trusties ain't gonna beat that boy up for nothin without first havin hell outa me.'

He went in with his six-inch chin gleaming. The building tenders were in a panic and Dough Belly, the picket boss, was shouting, 'Old Love, Old Love! Bring him up front and I'll shoot him.' The fight was raging. Gizzard Lips stabbed Old Love. The assistant building tender clubbed Gizzard Lips. Butter Bowl was hitting like a V-8 Ford and was as bloody as a butcher. Old Love was growing weak from the loss of so much blood.

The turnkey let the building tenders off tank number two and this put the odds against the two 'victs. They were beaten down to the floor and dragged to the front, where they were kicked insensible. All were taken to the emergency room and given first aid and then to the hospital, where they were sewn up. On the fourth day Love and Butter Bowl died, and Gizzard Lips was charged with murder and ninety-nine years were added to his life sentence.

I was filled with fear and hatred of this place and all I had seen. My friends, Fast Black and Bad Eye, seemed to have deserted me. They didn't want to talk. We just kept our heads down and walked like dead men. . . .

We rolled on under that sun. Old Bad Eye began to sing. It was the first time he'd sung since Butter Bowl had been murdered.

> My mama called me, Lawd, Lawd, Lawd,
> And I answered, 'Ma'am.'
> 'Ain't you tired of rollin, O Lawd, Lawd,
> For that big-hat man?'
>
> My pappy called me, Lawd, Lawd, Lawd,
> And I answered, 'Suh.'
> 'If you tired of rollin, O Lawd, Lawd,
> What you stay there fuh?'
>
> My sister called me, Lawd, Lawd, Lawd,
> But I ain't got long,
> 'Just a few more summers, O Lawd, Lawd,
> And I'll be gone.'
>
> Well, they's some in the buildin, Lawd, Lawd, Lawd,
> Some on the farm,
> Some in the graveyard, O Lawd, Lawd,
> And some goin home.

Somehow that mournful old song crept into my ears, and I began to sing, too. I knew Bad Eye was talking to me. Talking to the rest of us. I knew he'd made a lifetime sentence and was subject to parole this year. He was telling us that if he could make it, we could, too. You could hear us for a mile. We made a big sound that rolled over that old green cotton field like a big wind, rising. All the guards rode with their guns out that day.

On the johnny grounds Fast Black got to talking about hauling ass. He was trying to get me to go with him. 'We can outrun anything they got on this river. Ain't no use in staying here and getting killed. Might as well die trying to get away.'

Bad Eye listened and didn't say much at first. Then he began to talk to us and we listened because he was an old 'vict and knew the ropes. 'They ain't no use tryin to beat the system,' he said. 'I tried it every way I know. Only thing to do is to throw your time the way they tell you to and then leave out of this southern country. Lissen what I tell you now. I know. I been through all of it.' . . .

'Raise um up, you sorry bastards,' hollered Easter Rabbit. We grabbed our hoes and went back to the field. Now, as everybody knows, conversation is not permitted the convicts while they're working. But in our songs we had a way to talk right on. Today it was old Bad Eye giving good advice to me and my friend Fast Black. He was singin the song about old Rattler, the fastest dog they ever had on the Brazos.

> Early one Sunday mornin,
>   Here, Rattler, here,
> Captain called the dog sergeant,
>   Here, Rattler, here.
>
> He ran so fast till he looked like a streak,
> You should have seen that dog a-workin his feet.
>
> The Texas Special was a-runnin downhill,
> But Rattler pass it like it was standin still.
>
> Soon as he heard old Rattler's cry,
> Old Beatum wished for wings to fly.
>
> Here, Rattler,
>   Here, Rattler, here,
> Here, Rattler,
>   Here, Rattler, here.

'Just the same,' Fast Black told me when we were washing up for supper, 'I'm gonna make it for the river just as soon as I can. You might as well come with me.'

Right then I wasn't studying about trying to outrun those dogs, but something happened to change my mind. The new tender, named Creepin Jesus, who was put in Old Love's place on tank three, asked me did I want to be schoolteacher for the camp. That would mean I wouldn't have to go in the field no more. No more

Easter Rabbit. No more hard rolling under the barrels of a shotgun. But the way Creepin Jesus looked at me when he made the proposition, I knew what *he* wanted. So I told him I didn't have enough education to teach.

Creepin Jesus was no bully like Old Love. He was worse. He *kept* after me. He pestered me to death. I made like I didn't know what he meant, but every day I felt more like telling Fast Black I'd go along with him when he made his break.

One night I woke up and felt a hand under my mattress. It was Creepin Jesus. He jerked his hand out and held up a homemade dirk, the kind the prisoners sometimes manage to make and hide around theirself for protection. If they find one of those daggers on you, you're *bound* to be in trouble.

'All right, old Doc,' Creepin Jesus said right low, so he wouldn't wake nobody, 'I got the goods on you this time. What do you say? Want to be my boy and have me forget this? Or want me to turn you in?'

Just about that time a great big pair of hands slipped around that building tender's throat and cut his wind off short. Fast Black had grabbed him. Before I knew what was going on, Bad Eye snatched the dirk out of Creepin Jesus' hand and placed the point right over his heart. 'Don't move, you rotten son-of-a-bitch, or I'll cut your heart out,' Bad Eye told him. 'I oughta kill you now, but I give you a chance. Leave Doc alone and forget about this dirk or get ready to die. You gonna do like I tell you?'

Creepin Jesus couldn't say nothing, so he sort of waggled his head up and down. 'And get this, you slimy bastard,' Bad Eye say. 'If you spill to the white man, I'll get to you somehow and kill you deader than hell. I might go, but I'll carry you with me. Understand?'

Creepin Jesus nodded his head again, so Fast Black and Bad Eye let him go. He didn't even look around. Went down that aisle like a lizard looking for his hole. My two buddies mounted their bunks and nobody even turned over. It was like a nightmare that hadn't even been dreamt. Creepin Jesus never did so much as speak to me again. Fact was, he got himself transferred to tank number one the next week.

He didn't forget Bad Eye, though. He paid him back, at least I will always think it was him did the dirty deed. Bad Eye had a life sentence. He'd served sixteen years of it and had earned ten years good time. That meant he could be paroled, because nineteen years on any sentence, if a man have a good record, make him eligible for clemency. The Prison Board had sent the investigator to interview him and this man had sent in a favourable report on Bad Eye. Bad Eye was looking every day for his pardon to come from the governor. He was always humming the old song about

> I'm gwine away to leave, my time ain't long,
> The man gonna call and I'm goin home.
> Then I'll be done all my grievin, whoopin, holl'in, an cryin,
> Then I'll be done all my studyin about my great long time.

Then one day in cane-cutting time they called him out of our squad and placed him in number one hoe, the squad that led the rest. When Bad Eye ask him, the captain mumbled something about needing all his best men in number one squad. So that morning Bad Eye left us. Later he told us what had happened.

The boss on number one squad was the man Bad Eye had slipped away from that time he'd made it to the river. He still held a grudge against Bad Eye. When they got to the field, this boss said to Bad Eye, 'Well, old nigger, I notice the board's been out to see you.'

'Yassuh, boss, after sixteen years on this old river, I think it's about time.'

'What you gonna do when you git out?'

'I dunno, boss. I think I move to Kansas City and git me a job. I hear times is good up there in the war.'

'Don't build your dreams too high,' said the boss, 'you might be disappointed.'

That night, when the squads were checked in the building, Bad Eye was ordered to get on the barrel, and for what no one knew. When he later secured his record, he found he had been 'impolite'. A letter from the board told him that, since his record was not clear, his case would be reconsidered later on.

Bad Eye won't talk to anybody, no more'n to ask for his victuals. He just stares ahead of him all day like he was seeing ghosts. Fast Black is making ready for the day when he's going to try and run out from under those shotguns. He wants me to be his buddy and go with him, and I can't see much reason why I shouldn't. Every day we slop through the cold mud down between the cane rows. The cane leaves cut our hands to the bone. The northers blow right through our cotton convicts' stripes. Not far away the big muddy river flows through the bottoms, the barrier between us and everything we want and love. None of us knows whether we shall cross it in this life or in the next. . . . Some days when the winter rain whips across the field, I can hear my friend Bad Eye talk to the river. And all us prisoners heist the song behind him. Maybe our folks will hear it when the wind goes moaning by.

> Little boy, little boy, how did you git so long?
> Must of killed your rider in the high sheriff's arms.

> Little boy, little boy, you should have stayed home,
> Picked up chips for your mammy, blowed your daddy's horn.

Ain't No More Cane

In a poor, shabby room in the coloured section of Houston, a thin, worn man sat holding a guitar, playing a little on the strings, looking out of the window. It was a dull winter day, a heavy wind swirling the dust across the yard. There was a railroad behind the houses, and a few children were playing on the rails, shivering in their thin coats.

'There's a song my cousin learned when he was out on the farm.' He was talking partly to me and partly to a friend of his, sitting in the shadows behind him. 'Smokey Hogg got a little of it, but there hasn't been nobody done it right.' Then he began singing:

> You ought to been on the Brazos in 1910,
> Bud Russell drove pretty women like he done ugly men. . . .

He was singing one of the most famous work-songs of the Texas penitentiary farms, 'Ain't No More Cane on this Brazos'. His eyes were closed, he was singing quietly:

> My mamma called me, I answered, 'Mam?'
> She said, 'Son, you tired of working?'
> I said, 'Mama, I sure am.'

He sat a moment, thinking of the hot, dusty summers on the flat cotton lands along the Brazos River, thinking of the convict gangs singing as they worked, the guards circling them slowly, a shotgun across the saddle.

> You ought to been on the Brazos in 1904,
> You could find a dead man on every turnin' row. . . .

He shook his head; then he began to sing parts of the song again, playing his guitar a little. He stopped to drink some gin out of a bottle under the chair. He drank nearly a half pint of raw gin, using the metal cap of the bottle for a glass. His friend looked over and smiled, 'He's getting it now.' The singer went over two or three runs on the guitar; then he nodded and began singing:

> Uumh, big Brazos, here I come,
> Uumh, big Brazos, here I come.
> It' hard doing time for another man when there ain't a thing poor
>   Lightnin' done.

> You ought to been on the Brazos in 1910,
> Bud Russell drove pretty women just like he done ugly men.
> Uumh, big Brazos, oh lord yes, here I come.
> Figure on doing time for someone else, when there ain't a
>   thing poor Lightnin' done.

> My mama called me, I answered, 'Mam?'
> She said, 'Son, you tired of working?'
> I said, 'Mama, I sure am.'
> My pappa called me, I answered, 'Sir?'
> 'If you're tired of workin' what the hell you going to stay
>   here for?'

> I couldn't . . . uumh . . .
> I just couldn't help myself.
> You know a man can't help but feel bad, when he's doing time
>   for someone else.

The man was named 'Lightnin'' Hopkins, from outside of Centerville, Texas. 'Ain't No More Cane on this Brazos' was a song he had heard when he was a young man, working in the fields. His own song was a reshaping and reworking of the old work-song into something intensely personal and expressive. He had changed it into a blues.

Back Water Blues

(as sung by Bessie Smith)

When it rained five days and the skies turned dark as night
When it rained five days and the skies turned dark as night
Then trouble taken place, in the lowlands at night

I woke up this morning, can't even get outa my door
I woke up this morning, can't even get outa my door
There's enough trouble to make a poor girl wonder where
     she want to go

Then they rowed a little boat about five miles 'cross the pond
Then they rowed a little boat about five miles 'cross the pond
I packed all my clothes, throwed 'em in, and they rowed me
     along

When it thunders and lightning, and the wind begin to blow
When it thunders and lightning, and the wind begin to blow
There's thousands of people, ain't got no place to go

Then I went and stood up on some high old lonesome hill
Then I went and stood up on some high old lonesome hill
And looked down on the house, where I used to live

Backwater blues done caused me to pack my things and go
Backwater blues done caused me to pack my things and go
'Cause my house fell down and I can't live there no more

Mmmmm, I can't move no more
Mmmmm, I can't move no more
They ain't no place for a poor old girl to go

CHRIS ALBERTSON

The Death of Bessie Smith

'Blues Singers' Queen' Dead

MEMPHIS, Sept. 26 (AP). – Show folk on Beale Street mourned today the death of Bessie Smith, 50, 'queen' of blues singers, who was killed in an automobile accident. In 1917 Bessie sang the blues in a Beale Street show house, attracted attention of Eastern theatrical agents and was soon famous. Broadway welcomed her. She made many phonograph recordings. Two weeks ago she returned to Memphis to join the 'Broadway Rastus' show on Beale Street. Early today an automobile in which she was riding overturned.

The New York Times, 27 September 1937

The Associated Press report of Bessie's death that appeared in white newspapers across the country was brief and inaccurate, but it represented more attention than the white press had ever given Bessie in her lifetime.

Stories in the black press were more detailed and, of course, more prominent, but no more accurate. The Chicago *Defender* ran a headline across the top of its front page: BESSIE SMITH, BLUES SINGER, KILLED. Capsule biographies and accounts of Bessie's final hours were wildly contradictory. It was obvious that reporters knew little about Bessie's life and even less about how it ended.

Her funeral a week and a half later inspired more write-ups and photos in newspapers that for six years had all but forgotten her existence. There were fragmentary and inaccurate references to the accident – most papers merely pointed out that it had occurred – but there were long stories describing Bessie's accomplishments, real and imagined: the *Afro-American* told its readers Bessie had made 1,023 records for Columbia, 'including many with accompaniments by white orchestras', and that she had spent seventy-five thousand

dollars cash in the course of a few weeks; the Philadelphia *Tribune*
claimed she 'pulled the Columbia Recording Company back to its
feet after it had collapsed on the verge of bankruptcy' and that
George Gershwin 'refused to write the final score of *Porgy and Bess*
until he had sought her opinion'.

The widespread controversy over the circumstances surrounding
Bessie's death did not arise until the following month, when *Down
Beat* magazine printed an article by John Hammond. Hammond's
story, under the provocative heading 'Did Bessie Smith Bleed to
Death While Waiting for Medical Aid?', contained the first published
hint that Bessie might have been the victim of southern racism:

> A particularly disagreeable story as to the details of her death
> has just been received from members of Chick Webb's orchestra,
> who were in Memphis soon after the disaster. It seems that Bessie
> was riding in a car which crashed into a truck parked along the
> side of the road. One of her arms was nearly severed, but aside
> from that there was no other serious injury, according to these
> informants. Some time elapsed before a doctor was summoned to
> the scene, but finally she was picked up by a medico and driven
> to the leading Memphis hospital. On the way this car was involved
> in some minor mishap, which further delayed medical attention.
> When finally she did arrive at the hospital she was refused
> treatment because of her colour and bled to death while waiting
> for attention.
>
> Realizing that such tales can be magnified greatly in the telling,
> I would like to get confirmation from some Memphis citizens who
> were on the spot at the time. If the story is true it is but another
> example of disgraceful conditions in a certain section of our
> country already responsible for the killing and maiming of legit-
> imate union organizers. Of the particular city of Memphis I am
> prepared to believe almost anything, since its mayor and chief of
> police publicly urged the use of violence against organizers of the
> CIO a few weeks ago.

Hammond ended his extraordinary piece with an ill-timed pitch
– the first harvest of Bessie Smith's death was about to be reaped:

> Be that as it may, the UHCA [United Hot Clubs of America] is
> busy sponsoring a special Bessie Smith memorial album . . . the
> album will be released by Brunswick-Columbia around the middle

of November with pictures of the performers and details about each of the discs. Take it from one who cherished all the records that this will be the best buy of the year in music.

There had been plenty of talk in jazz circles about racial injustice in connection with Bessie's death (the black press, usually quick to point out incidents of racial injustice, carried no such story in connection with Bessie Smith's death until after the publication of Hammond's *Down Beat* piece), but the *Down Beat* article spread the rumours far afield and – Hammond's admitted lack of evidence notwithstanding – gave them credence.

Considering the temper of the times and Hammond's involvement in what was then a very disorganized and far from popular fight for the civil rights of black people, the irony of Bessie's dying at the hands of southern bigotry provided the perfect *cause célèbre*. From a writer's point of view it made a fascinating story: Bessie Smith, the great blues singer who had moved millions of southerners to tears with her songs of misery, killed by southern prejudice.

Thirty-four years later John Hammond admits with some embarrassment that his article was based entirely on hearsay and that a few phone calls, made at the time, might have curbed the circulating rumours. Once the article appeared, however, it was too late to change the story; people refused to accept any other version.

The attack on Memphis in Hammond's article drew angry protests from the city's hospital authorities. In response *Down Beat* published a second article stating that Bessie had been taken directly to the black hospital in Clarksdale, Mississippi, where she had died due to loss of blood. There was no mention of her having been refused admittance to a white hospital, but no one paid attention when this contradictory story was published.

Twenty years later, in the 17 October 1957, issue of *Down Beat*, the late George Hoefer noted that the truth about the accident and its aftermath was still being ignored by writers. He quoted the Hammond article and set the record straight; once again, it made little difference. In 1960 Edward Albee's play *The Death of Bessie Smith* opened in West Berlin; based on the same rumours that had inspired the Hammond article – and perhaps on the article itself – it perpetuated the myth. Bessie Smith became better known for the way in which she had allegedly died than for what she had done in life.

Richard Morgan, who survived the accident, died around 1943. No reporter ever asked him what actually happened on the morning of 26 September 1937. Only he could have described the circumstances that led to the accident.[1] The highway patrolmen who handled the case were reported dead by the mid-fifties, and if there are any records of the accident in the files of the Clarksdale Police Department, they seem unwilling to make them public – letters of inquiry remain unanswered.

Virtually nothing would be known of the circumstances leading up to Bessie Smith's death were it not for the arrival on the scene, moments after the accident occurred, of Dr Hugh Smith and his fishing partner, Henry Broughton. Mr Broughton has long since died, without anyone's having interviewed him, but Dr Smith – referred to by *Down Beat* only as 'a Memphis surgeon who came upon the scene of the accident and attended Bessie Smith' – was contacted by that magazine in the early 1940s for a published interview. Further details of Dr Smith's recollections appeared in a 1969 *Esquire* article entitled 'The True Death of Bessie Smith', but that piece revealed little more than the fact that Dr Smith was still alive, and contained such misinformation as the detail that Bessie's car was travelling north instead of south.

We will never know the whole story, but the truth probably lies somewhere between the two following accounts based on Dr Smith's detailed recollections for this book, and a 1938 interview with Jack Gee, Jr.

Smith and Broughton were in the habit of leaving Memphis around one o'clock every other Sunday morning and driving south into Mississippi for two or three hours to go fishing in a lake there before daybreak.

On Sunday, 26 September 1937, they left home at one-thirty and headed down Route 61 as usual. Dr Smith had just finished his training at the Campbell Clinic and was recently married. To

---

1. The only other person who might have shed some light on the circumstances, the driver of the truck, has never been found or identified. Morgan's account of the accident was only given to the family. It appears at the end of this chapter.

celebrate he had traded in his old Model-A Ford for a small new Chevrolet. The fishing tackle was on the back seat and the weather conditions seemed perfect: a warm, humid night, no moon, no wind stirring.

They were about seventy miles south of Memphis when they spotted something on the road ahead. Dr Smith had been driving at fifty to fifty-five miles per hour, but now he slowed down and stopped fifty feet from the wreck of a big car, lying on its left side diagonally across the narrow highway. Illuminated by the bright headlights of Dr Smith's car was the large figure of Bessie Smith, lying lifeless in the middle of the road. A man moved out of the darkness, waving his arms frantically as he approached the doctor's car – it was Richard Morgan, who was unhurt. In the distance Dr Smith could see a pair of red tail-lights disappearing into the night, heading in the direction of Clarksdale.

The tail-lights belonged to the truck Bessie's car had struck; in previous accounts it has been described as belonging to the National Biscuit Company or the U-Needa-Biscuit Company, but Dr Smith believes it was a truck leased to the US Post Office during the week and used to deliver the Memphis *Commercial Appeal* on Sundays.

According to information Dr Smith received in the days following the accident, the driver, fearing that his tyres were overheated, had pulled up and parked on the side of the road. The shoulders were only two feet wide on this particular stretch, so it was impossible for him to pull completely off the road. Most of the truck had to rest in the right lane, making it necessary for any passing car to pull into the northbound lane. The truckdriver checked his tyres, found them to be all right, and climbed back into the cab of his vehicle. He had just started moving at the time of the impact.

Dr Smith's theory of how the accident happened is certainly a plausible one:

> If you've ever driven down a two-lane highway in the middle of the night, you know that it's almost impossible to estimate the distance of a pair of tail-lights – they can be a mile, four miles, or four hundred and forty yards away. I would assume Richard Morgan realized there was a truck up there, but didn't realize that his depth perception extended only to his headlights. . . . It would be natural to assume he expected those tail-lights to be moving at

about forty-five to sixty miles per hour down the highway when, in fact, the truck had just pulled back on the highway and hadn't gone two hundred and twenty yards at the time of the accident. So the tail-lights and the depth perception all came together just at the instant that Richard Morgan realized he was about to plough into the back of a slowly moving truck on the east side of the highway.

From the skid marks, I don't think there is any question that he tried to go to the left side of the truck and miss it, but at the same time he applied his brakes, which made it go into a skid and probably almost a 90° angle at the time of impact. It ricocheted backwards and then flopped on its left side. The impact of Morgan's car was on Bessie Smith's side and she had 'side-swipe' injuries.[2]

So one of two things happened. Either she was asleep with her entire arm out of the car, or else just the point of her elbow was out of the car – I suspect that was true – and it hit the tailgate of the truck as the top of Bessie's old Packard was sheared off. It was a real old car, for instead of a metal roof or metal struts supporting the roof, it was all wood – it was literally splintered like an old piece of dead kindling wood.

Dr Smith jumped out of his car, rushed toward Bessie, and began a preliminary examination:

All the bones around the elbow were completely shattered; there was a complete circumferential interruption of soft tissues about the elbow, except, miraculously – despite the fact that she had almost had her forearm torn loose from her upper arm at the elbow – the three nerves were intact, lying there like telephone wires. The two major vessels, the artery and the nerve were intact. What that boils down to is that haemorrhage from the arm did not cause Bessie Smith's death.

It was a horrible mess, lying out there in the open with maybe half a pint of blood on the highway. But if that had been her only

---

2. Many Mississippi roads, built during the Depression, were so narrow that two wide trucks could barely pass each other. Drivers often rode with an elbow protruding from the car's window, and it was not unusual for the bed of a passing truck to hit the elbow of a driver going in the opposite direction. These were called 'side-swipe' injuries – usually a combination of a compound fracture dislocation of the wrist, with bones of the forearm broken, and the elbow itself completely crushed.

injury, she would have survived – there's no question in my mind about this at all. In this day and time we might even have saved her arm, but in that day and time there wouldn't have been any question; you'd just amputate, she'd have a seven-inch stump below the shoulder and probably be out of the hospital in twelve or fourteen days. However, that was not the case – she had sustained severe crushing injuries to her entire right side.

I don't recall if Bessie Smith ever uttered a word, I don't think she answered any questions. She was moaning and groaning from excruciating pain and she was having a lot of trouble getting her breath. She was just breathing on the left side of her chest, all the ribs on her right side had been crushed pretty bad, and she probably had some interabdominal injuries. She was probably bleeding in her abdomen, because it was very stiff and rigid.

Whether or not she had a head injury is a moot question, she wasn't conscious enough to talk. In the available light and without tools, I could not examine her pupils – at this stage it would have been too early to know if she had an intercranial haemorrhage, but she did have only minor head lacerations. Suffice it to say that Bessie Smith was in very critical condition.

As Richard Morgan watched in silence, Mr Broughton and Dr Smith moved Bessie onto the road's grassy shoulder. They covered the major wound with a clean handkerchief, and Dr Smith asked his friend to go to a house some five hundred feet off the road and call an ambulance. About ten minutes had elapsed since the accident, and another fifteen passed before Mr Broughton returned. By this time Bessie was in shock.

The scene of the accident was still quiet; a few crickets and the voices of the two men seemed loud in the humid night. Richard Morgan, who had remained quite calm, just stood there – there was nothing he could do to help Bessie at this point. It has been suggested that Morgan was intoxicated at the time of the accident, but Dr Smith recalls that he was completely sober.

As time passed without a sign of an ambulance, Dr Smith suggested that they remove the fishing tackle from the back seat of his car and take Bessie into Clarksdale. They had almost finished putting the tackle in the car's trunk when they heard the distant sound of another car approaching at high speed. Dr Smith's car was in the middle of the road, making it impossible for the approaching car to pass on either side, and it didn't sound as if it were slowing down. At Broughton's suggestion, Dr Smith climbed onto the left running board of his car and proceeded to blink his lights manually as a warning to the other driver:

> I'll never forget this as long as I live. Mr Broughton was on the right side hollering 'Smith, you'd better jump – he ain't checkin'.' Well, I jumped and Broughton jumped just as this car barrelled into the back of my car at about fifty miles per hour. It drove my car straight into the wrecked Bessie Smith car and made a real pretzel out of it – it was a total loss. He ricocheted off the rear of my car and went into the ditch to the right. He barely missed Mr Broughton and Bessie Smith.

Riding in that car was a young white couple who had obviously been partying. Dr Smith had his hands full:

> Now, my God, we had three patients on our hands. A young lady, curled up under the instrument panel on the right, screamed at the top of her voice, hysterical, scared to death. There was a man draped over the steering wheel, which had broken off completely. Well, we got them out in the grass and started to check them. As far as I could tell, the young lady didn't have any major injuries, but the man had a chest injury and that was about all. It turned out later that he had multiple fractures of the ribs, but fortunately he didn't have any lung injury, he wasn't in shock and he wasn't critical.

Dr Smith was examining the young couple when an ambulance, a deputy sheriff, and several officers of the law appeared on the scene. They carried Bessie to the ambulance, and Richard Morgan accompanied her in it to Clarksdale. Almost simultaneously a second ambulance arrived and picked up the injured couple.

One of the ambulances had been summoned by Broughton. The other, it turned out, had been sent at the request of the truck driver, who had gone straight to Clarksdale and reported the accident.

It is at this point that the story of Bessie's death becomes controversial: was she refused admittance to a white hospital? After answering that question with an emphatic no, Dr Smith explains:

> The Bessie Smith ambulance would *not* have gone to a white hospital, you can forget that. Down in the Deep South cotton

country, no coloured ambulance driver, or white driver, would even have thought of putting a coloured person off in a hospital for white folks. In Clarksdale, in 1937, a town of twelve to fifteen thousand people, there were two hospitals – one white and one coloured – and they weren't half a mile apart. I suspect the driver drove just as straight as he could to the coloured hospital.

The driver of the ambulance, Willie George Miller – a black man – confirmed this twenty years later. He remembered taking Bessie straight to the G. T. Thomas Hospital, Clarksdale's black hospital. He also claimed that Bessie was dead on arrival. 'I can't remember for certain,' he told a reporter, 'but I don't think she died instantly. But she did die within a few minutes after putting her in the ambulance, before we could get her to the hospital.'

That part of Miller's statement is almost certainly true. According to the official death certificate issued by the Mississippi State Board of Health, Bessie Smith died in Ward 1 of the Afro-American Hospital, 615 Sunflower Avenue, Clarksdale, 26 September, 1937, at 11.30 a.m. 'The principal cause of death and related causes of importance in order of onset were as follows: *Shock. Possibly internal injuries. Compound, comminuted fractures of rt. humerus, radius and ulna.* Contributory causes of importance not related to principal cause: *Rt. humerus, radius and ulna*. Name of operation: *Amputation rt. arm.*'

As Dr Smith points out, in 1937 it took an hour to draw a pint of blood from a donor. Then, too, both Clarksdale hospitals were country hospitals, neither of which was as well equipped as the ones in larger cities, like Memphis. Given the same situation today, says Smith, Bessie would have stood only a fifty-fifty chance of surviving the accident – she certainly would never have been able to sing again.

Of course, none of this can excuse the neglect on the part of the truck driver, who should have transported Bessie to a hospital at once, nor Dr Smith's failure to do so in his own car before wasting time summoning an ambulance.

Much later Dr Smith found out who the woman he had attended that night in Mississippi was. The name Bessie Smith meant nothing to him in 1937,[3] and he did not see Hammond's article when it first

---

3. A strange fact, considering that Dr Smith even then was a part-time jazz pianist with a Fats Waller-inspired style.

appeared. Not long after it was brought to his attention, he found himself in New York on a business trip, and decided to look up Frank Walker. 'I wanted to give him the full details as to what actually happened down there in Mississippi,' Dr Smith recalls. 'Well, he wasn't very interested and I could tell that he couldn't care less about Bessie – and that was the end of that.'

Richard Morgan may well have coloured his account of what happened at the scene of the accident and in the hours that followed. Some members of the family felt he was holding something back. 'He used to talk about Bessie, and he'd start crying,' says Maud Smith. 'I never would ask him exactly what happened, but there were many times when he would start crying in my company. Richard and Bessie were *very* close, he was good for her, and he was never the same after she died. Richard sent for me before he passed, but I wasn't able to come to him in time – he said he had something to tell me, but I have no idea what that could have been.'

Rather than rely on his memory, Jack Gee, Jr., produces a newspaper clipping from an early 1938 issue of the *Afro-American* to give his version of his mother's death. It is, he says, based in part on Richard Morgan's account to the family.

'My mother and her chauffeur were on their way to Clarksdale, Mississippi, where she was to fill a singing engagement. It was on Saturday night, September 25. About 3 a.m., Sunday, just ten miles out of Clarksdale, her car ran into a parked truck belonging to the National Biscuit Company, which was standing on the side of the narrow highway without any lights.

'Before the chauffeur, Richard Morgan, had a chance to stop, or turn out, he ran into the left corner of the truck, wedging my mother between the truck and the car.

'Her left arm was cut almost off, and was hanging just by the skin. She was knocked unconscious. Moore (*sic*) jumped out of the car and went up to the driver of the truck, a white man, and said: 'What have you done? Pull up your truck.' The truck driver pulled up, but pulled away and had to be run down by State troopers and arrested. He was released on bail and is still free.

'A white physician, a Dr Smith, came along about this time. He stopped to administer first aid, while Moore (*sic*) hiked to town to get an ambulance. My mother was still unconscious.

'While the doctor was administering first-aid to my mother,

another motorist came along and hit his car. A white woman passenger in the car was hurt in this second accident. One of the spectators asked the doctor why he didn't take my mother to town in his car, but he replied that his car would get too bloody.

'About this time Morgan came back with the ambulance. As the men were about to take the stretcher out to take my mother, somebody in the crowd said: 'Wait, let's see what's the matter with this white woman first.' The doctor then administered first-aid to the white woman, and then put her in the ambulance, and sent her back to town. Morgan protested but could do nothing.

'We have never found out accurately yet how my mother was taken back to town, but we do know that she was first taken to a white hospital, which refused to administer first-aid or take her in. She was then taken to the Afro-American Hospital, a coloured institution. This hospital didn't have the proper equipment with which to operate. Physicians had to run all over town to get the proper equipment.

'It was about 11.30 a.m. before they administered ether to her. She died at 11.45 a.m. No reason was given as to why she died, but we know clearly that she died from loss of blood and neglect. I believe that if the ambulance had taken my mother back to town, as it was proper for the doctor to have instructed the driver, since the ambulance was sent for her case, she might be alive today.'

GREGORY R. STAATS

Sexual Imagery in the Blues

The prominence of sexual themes within blues music is an important example of how blues musicians have not only developed a special symbolic language for their transmission but have also experienced mutual understanding with the listening audience, as demonstrated by their popularity and commercial success. Consequently, sexual themes and imagery still predominate in many of the verses of blues compositions today and remain valued by contemporary bluesmen using the traditional sexual symbolism. Samuel Charters states that even though there is occasional difficulty in understanding the sexual imagery of the blues, there is little use of the double meaning. Thus 'easy rider', by a fairly common consensus among blues singers, refers to a physical relationship between lovers.

Similarly, the popular phrase 'tight like that' may also refer to the physical union of lovers or may be used as a description of hard times or difficulties. The following verses suggest how this expression may be used in a sexual manner.

> Two times three is six,
> Three times three is nine,
> You give me some of yours,
> And I'll give you some of mine.
> > Cause it's tight like that, yes, yes,
> > Cause it's tight like that, yes, yes,
> > Hear me talkin' to you,
> > Yes, it's tight like that.
> Say I got a key,
> Shines like gold,
> All the women tell me
> It satisfies their soul,
> > Cause it's tight like that . . .

As an expression of hard times, 'tight like that' may be used as follows:

> Going away, mama,
> Won't be back 'til fall.
> Times don't get better
> Won't be back at all
>   It's tight like that . . .

These are just a few of the expressions commonly used in the sexual imagery of the blues. Sexual image analogies may come from other areas of everyday life as well.

Sexual images have come from cooking and baking, automobiles, and various types of animals. From the area of cooking and baking some common terms are 'jelly roll' and 'biscuits'. Consider Hogman Maxey's 'Rock Me, Mama'.

> Roll me, mama, like you roll roll yo' dough, (Repeat)
> Oh, I want you to roll me, roll me over slow.

Another example can be found in Butch Cage and Willie B. Thomas's 'Jelly Roll':

> Reason why grandpa like grandma so,
> Same sweet jelly she had a hundred years ago.

The term 'jelly roll' is a familiar blues phrase which arises from the motion of sexual intercourse. Peg Leg Howell sings in his 'New Jelly Roll Blues' in 1927,

> I never been to church and I never been to school,
> Come down to jelly I'm a jelly-rollin' fool,
> I got a sweet jelly to satisfy my worried soul,
> I like to have my jelly and I like to have my fun.

We frequently find that a lover admires his 'jelly bean' and the way she can 'jello' and prides himself on being a good 'jelly roll baker'. A desirable young girl is likely to be called a 'biscuit', while a good lover is a 'biscuit roller'.

The automobile has also been used extensively for sexual imagery by blues performers. One of the best examples of this theme can be found in Robert Johnson's most commercially successful recording, 'Terraplane Blues'.

> I said I flashed your lights, mama, your horn won't even blow,
>   (Repeat)

> There's a short in this connection, ooh well babe, way down
>   below.
> I'm goin' h'ist your hood mama, I'm boun' to check your oil,
>   (Repeat)
> I got a woman that I'm lovin' way down in Arkansas.
> Now you know the coils ain't even buzzin', your little
>   generator won't get the spark,
> All in bad condition, you gotta have these batteries charged,
> I'm cryin' please, don't do me wrong,
> Who's been drivin' my Terraplane now, for you since I been
>   gone?
> I'm goin' to get deep down in this connection, keep on
>   tangling with your wires (Repeat)
> And when I mash down on your little starter, then your spark plug
>   will give me fire.

Other examples of the use of the automobile for sexual imagery can be seen in such works as Virginia Liston's 'Rolls-Royce Papa', Sonny Boy Williamson's 'My Little Machine', Joe McCoy's 'One More Greasin'', Charlie McCoy's 'Valves Need Grinding', Lightnin' Slim's 'My Starter Won't Work', and Memphis Minnie's 'Me and My Chauffeur Blues'. Memphis Minnie's 'Me and My Chauffeur Blues' creates a situation where the female is symbolized as a automobile while her lover is depicted as the chauffeur:

> Won't you be my chauffeur (Repeat)
> I want some one to drive me,
> Downtown.
> Baby driver so easy, I can't turn him down.
> But I don't want him, (Repeat)
> To be riding these girls, (Repeat)
> A-round
> You know I'm gonna steal me a pistol,
> Shoot my chauffeur down.

Within a few months of Victoria Spivey recording 'Black Snake Blues', Blind Lemon Jefferson recorded the first of three versions of 'That Black Snake Moan' and within a year he recorded 'Black Snake Dream'. Victoria Spivey also made other recordings of the original song, along with a version titled 'Garter Snake Blues'. Other uses of the black snake metaphor may be found in titles such as

Rosa Henderson's 'Black Snake Blues', Joshua White's 'Lazy Black Snake', Tallahassee Tight's 'Black Snake Blues', Blind Boy Fuller's 'Black Snakin' Jiver', Roosevelt Sykes 'Jet Black Snake', John Henry Howard's 'Black Snake', and Peggy Walker's 'Blacksnake Wiggle'.

Black snakes have not been the only animal used as a sexual symbol in blues music. Hogs and cows have been also utilized for this purpose. According to Charters, a man may be described in the rural imagery as a 'ground hog' or as a 'rooting ground hog'. For Little Son Jackson, a ground hog is one who tries to take advantage of other men's wives.

> There's a ground hog rooting, rooting in the next door yard,
> Ain't nothing can stop him, unless the ground get real hard.
> If I catch a hog in my yard just before day,
> I'm going to get my double barrelled shotgun and drive that hog
>   away.

Another example of this symbolism can be found in Bo Carter's 'Tush Hog Blues':

> Mama, can't you hear this tush hog rootin' roun' your front
>   door? (Repeat)
> But if you give him what you promised him, mama, he won't
>   have to root no more.
> I roots so long, mama, done rooted a hole through your door,
>   (Repeat)
> But if you give him what you promised him, mama, I won't have
>   to root no more.
> Can't you hear this tush hog gruntin' all around you hole?
>   (Repeat)
> But if you give him what you promised him, mama, he will
>   soon be gone.

Examples of bovine comparisons can be found in Sleepy John Estes's 'Milkcow Blues', Bill Weldon's 'What's the Matter With My Milk Cow (She Won't Stand Still)', and Robert Johnson's 'Milkcow's Calf Blues'. Charters explains that often rural imagery depicts the woman as a milk cow. A verse which demonstrates this application is as follows.

> If you see my milk cow, won't you send her home,
> If you see my milk cow, won't you please send her home.
> I ain't had no milk since she been gone.

Black Ace used the mixed metaphor 'pigmeat heifer' in his 'Lowing Heifer' recorded in 1937.

> I been a mighty good bull cow, Oh Lord, but I got to go,
>> (Repeat)
> I found me a pigmeat heifer, I can tell by the way she lows.
> She lows all night long, you can hear her for a solid mile, (Repeat)
> I can't stand to hear her low, I cried jes' like a chile.
> Whoa babe, your bull cow got to go, (Repeat)
> I can't stay here no longer, she calls me when she lows.
> Mama, I'm gone, with a horn long as your right arm, (Repeat)
> And when I get to hookin, I'll have me a brand new happy home.
> Good-bye, good-bye, an' I don't see you no mo', (Repeat)
> Just remember me at night, when you hear mammy's heifer low.

Black snake themes have been used to refer to male genitalia. Other objects may be put to symbolic use to refer to female genitalia as well. One popularly used object put to such a purpose is the petunia flower.

The term 'sweet patuni' has been much used as a vaginal image by blues performers, because, according to Paul Oliver, it comes from the form of the petunia flower. Originally a traditional song, it has been recorded many times under such variations as Ora Alexander's 'I'm Wild About My Patootie', Monkey Joe Colemen's 'Sweet Patuna Stomp', Curley Weaver's 'Sweet Patunia', Willie Baker's 'Sweet Patunia Blues', Lucille Bogan's 'Sweet Patunia', Little David's 'Original Sweet Patuni (Patootie Blues)', among others. An early recording by Curley Weaver, 'Sweet Patunia', is a more cautious version.

> I got a gal, lives down by the jail,
> Sign on the door 'Sweet Patuni for Sale',
> I'm wild about my 'tuni, only thing I breathe,
> Lord I'm wild about my 'tuni, only thing I breathe,
> Sweet patuni, gonna carry me to my grave.

Willie Baker, after three recording sessions in 1929, finally released a version of 'Sweet Patunia Blues':

> Well I woke up this mornin' 'bout half pas' four,
> Long tall gal rappin' at my door.
> She was singin', 'Sweet patuni, only thing I crave, (Repeat)
> Well sweet patuni gonna carry me to my grave.'
> If all the 'tunis were brought to a test,
> A long tall gal would swing it the best,
> Now I'm wild about my 'tuni, only thing I crave, (Repeat)
> Well sweet patuni, goin' to carry me to my grave.

A good example of how a sexual theme has been carried on by blues performers is given by the various applications of the term 'shave 'em dry' (an expression indicating intercourse without preliminary lovemaking). This theme seems to have been as favoured among female singers as the sweet petunia had been favoured by male singers. Gertrude Ma Rainey recorded the first version, 'Shave 'Em Dry', in 1924, Papa Charlie Jackson followed a year later with 'Shave 'Em Dry'. In 1930 James Boodle-It Wiggins recorded 'Gotta Shave 'Em Dry', which was followed some years later by Lil Johnson's recording of 'New Shave 'Em Dry' in 1936. In Lucille Bogan's version of 'Shave 'em Dry', recorded in 1935, she sings:

> I ain't rough, I ain't tough,
> I'm just a stomp-down roller and I like to strut my stuff,
> Talkin' 'bout shave 'em, mama's gonna shave 'em dry,
> And if you don't know, mama's gonna learn you how.
> I met a man lived down the way,
> He had so much money until I had to say,
> Talkin' 'bout shave 'em, mama's gonna shave 'em dry,
> And if you don't know, mama's gonna learn you how.
> If you meet your man an' he tell you a lie,
> Just pull out your razor and shave him dry,
> Talkin' 'bout shave 'em, mama's gonna shave him dry,
> 'Cause I don't want no man to tell me no dirty lie.

As Oliver writes in *The Blues Tradition*:

Offensive terms were thinly veiled and doubtlessly amused the readers of record catalogues as they saw listed 'Dirty Mother For You' by Shufflin' Sam and His Rhythm. 'Dirty Mother For You' was a laboured way of writing a phrase which, when spoken rapidly, sounded more like 'Dirty Mother Fuyer'. In turn this was a euphemistic elision of the palatal 'ck' in the expletive 'mother fucker'.

Memphis Minnie first recorded 'Dirty Mother For You' accompanied by Charlie Segar in January 1935, for Decca Records to the tune of a Huddie Ledbetter (Leadbelly) song, 'Noted Rider'.

> I ain't no doctor but I'm a doctor's wife,
> You better come to see me if you want me to save your life,
> He's a dirty mother fuyer, he don't mean me no good,
> He got drunk this mornin', woke up the neighbourhood.

A year after Memphis Minnie's recording, Roosevelt Sykes, her pianist, made a version to another tune and titled it 'Dirty Mother For You' which was recorded by Decca in February 1936.

> Mama, I got a hot dog and it ain't cold,
> It's just right to fit your roll,
> It's a fittin' mother fuyer don't you know,
> I'm a hungry mother fuyer don't you know,
> I'm a dirty mother fuyer and I won't tell you no lie.

In September 1936, Washboard Sam made another version of 'Dirty Mother For You'. Although many singers have recorded other versions on this theme, Oliver maintains it was Roosevelt Sykes's record which fixed the form of the song.

RALPH ELLISON

Blues People

In his Introduction to *Blues People* LeRoi Jones advises us to approach the work as

> . . . a strictly theoretical endeavor. Theoretical, in that none of the questions it poses can be said to have been answered definitely or for all time (sic!), etc. In fact, the whole book proposes more questions than it will answer. The only questions it will properly move to answer have, I think, been answered already within the patterns of American life. We need only give these patterns serious scrutiny and draw certain permissible conclusions.

It is a useful warning and one hopes that it will be regarded by those jazz publicists who have the quite irresponsible habit of sweeping up any novel pronouncement written about jazz and slapping it upon the first available record liner as the latest insight into the mysteries of American Negro expression.

Jones would take his subject seriously – as the best of jazz critics have always done – and he himself should be so taken. He has attempted to place the blues within the context of a total culture and to see this native art form through the disciplines of sociology, anthropology and (though he seriously underrates its importance in the creating of a viable theory) history, and he spells out explicitly his assumptions concerning the relation between the blues, the people who created them and the larger American culture. Although I find several of his assumptions questionable, this is valuable in itself. It would be well if all jazz critics did likewise; not only would it expose those who have no business in the field, but it would sharpen the thinking of the few who have something enlightening to contribute. *Blues People*, like much that is written by Negro Americans at the present moment, takes on an inevitable resonance from the Freedom Movement, but it is in itself character-ized by a straining for a note of militancy which is, to say the least, distracting. Its introductory mood of scholarly analysis frequently shatters into a dissonance of accusation, and one gets the impression that while Jones wants to perform a crucial task which he feels *someone* should take on – as indeed someone should – he is frustrated by the restraint demanded of the critical pen and would like to pick up a club.

Perhaps this explains why Jones, who is also a poet and editor of a poetry magazine, gives little attention to the blues as lyric, as a form of poetry. He appears to be attracted to the blues for what he believes they tell us of the sociology of Negro American identity and attitude. Thus, after beginning with the circumstances in which he sees their origin, he considers the ultimate values of American society:

> The Negro as slave is one thing. The Negro as American is quite another. But the *path* the slave took to 'citizenship' is what I want to look at. And I make my analogy through the slave citizen's music – through the music that is most closely associated with him: blues and a later, but parallel, development, jazz. And it seems to me that if the Negro represents, or is symbolic of, something in and about the nature of American culture, this certainly should be revealed by his characteristic music. . . . I am saying that if the music of the Negro in America, in all its permutations, is subjected to a socio-anthropological as well as musical scrutiny, something about the essential nature of the Negro's existence in this country ought to be revealed, as well as something about the essential nature of this country, i.e., society as a whole. . . .

The tremendous burden of sociology which Jones would place upon this body of music is enough to give even the blues the blues. At one point he tells us that 'the one peculiar reference to the drastic change in the Negro from slavery to 'citizenship' is in his music'. And later with more precision, he states:

> . . . The point I want to make most evident here is that I cite the beginning of the blues as one beginning of American Negroes. Or, let me say, the reaction and subsequent relation of the Negro's experience in this country in *his* English is one beginning of the Negro's conscious appearance on the American scene.

No one could quarrel with Mr Jones's stress upon beginnings. In 1833, two hundred and fourteen years after the first Africans were brought to these shores as slaves, a certain Mrs Lydia Maria Child, a leading member of the American Anti-Slavery Society, published a paper entitled: *An Appeal in Favor of that Class of Americans Called Africans*. I am uncertain to what extent it actually reveals Mrs Child's ideas concerning the complex relationship between time, place, cultural and/or national identity and race, but her title sounds like a fine bit of contemporary ironic *signifying* – 'signifying' here meaning, in the unwritten dictionary of American Negro usage, 'rhetorical understatements'. It tells us much of the thinking of her opposition, and it reminds us that as late as the 1890s, a time when Negro composers, singers, dancers and comedians dominated the American musical stage, popular Negro songs (including James Weldon Johnson's 'Under the Bamboo Tree', now immortalized by T. S. Eliot) were commonly referred to as 'Ethiopian Airs'.

Perhaps more than any other people, Americans have been locked in a deadly struggle with time, with history. We've fled the past and trained ourselves to suppress, if not forget, troublesome details of the national memory, and a great part of our optimism, like our progress, has been bought at the cost of ignoring the processes through which we've arrived at any given moment in our national existence. We've fought continuously with one another over who and what we are, and with the exception of the Negro, over who and what is American. Jones is aware of this and, although he embarrasses his own argument, his emphasis is to the point.

For it would seem that while Negroes have been undergoing a process of 'Americanization' from a time preceding the birth of this nation – including the fusing of their blood lines with other non-African strains, there has persisted a stubborn confusion as to their American identity. Somehow it was assumed that the Negroes, of all the diverse American peoples, would remain unaffected by the climate, the weather, the political circumstances – from which not even slaves were exempt – the social structures, the national manners, the modes of production and the tides of the market, the national ideals, the conflicts of values, the rising and falling of national morale, or the complex give and take of acculturalization which was undergone by all others who found their existence within the American democracy. This confusion still persists and it is Mr Jones's concern with it which gives *Blues People* a claim upon our attention.

Mr Jones sees the American Negro as the product of a series of transformations, starting with the enslaved African, who became the Afro-American slave, who became the American slave, who became, in turn, the highly qualified 'citizen' whom we know today. The slave began by regarding himself as enslaved African, during the time when he still spoke his native language, or remembered it, practised such aspects of his native religion as were possible and expressed himself musically in modes which were essentially African. These cultural traits became transmuted as the African lost consciousness of his African background, and his music, his religion, his language and his speech gradually became that of the American Negro. His sacred music became the spirituals, his work-songs and dance music became the blues and primitive jazz, and his religion became a form of Afro-American Christianity. With the end of slavery Jones sees the development of jazz and the blues as results of the more varied forms of experience made available to the freedman. By the twentieth century the blues divided and became, on the one hand, a professionalized form of entertainment, while remaining, on the other, a form of folklore.

By which I suppose he means that some Negroes remained in the country and sang a crude form of the blues, while others went to the city, became more sophisticated, and paid to hear Ma Rainey, Bessie, or some of the other Smith girls sing them in night-clubs or theatres. Jones gets this mixed up with ideas of social class – middle-class Negroes, whatever that term actually means, and light-skinned Negroes, or those Negroes corrupted by what Jones calls 'White' culture – preferring the 'classic' blues, and black, uncorrupted, country Negroes preferring 'country blues'.

For as with his music, so with the Negro. As Negroes became 'middle-class' they rejected their tradition and themselves. '. . . they wanted any self which the mainstream dictated, and the mainstream *always* dictated. And this black middle class, in turn, tried always to dictate that self, or this image of a whiter Negro, to the poorer, blacker Negroes.'

One would get the impression that there was a rigid correlation between colour, education, income and the Negro's preference in music. But what are we to say of a white-skinned Negro with brown freckles who owns sixteen oil wells sunk in a piece of Texas land once farmed by his ex-slave parents who were a blue-eyed, white-skinned, red-headed (kinky) Negro woman from Virginia and a blue-gummed, black-skinned, curly-haired Negro male from Mississippi, and who not only sang bass in a Holy Roller church, played the market and voted Republican but collected blues recordings and was a walking depository of blues tradition? Jones's theory no more allows for the existence of such a Negro than it allows for himself; but that 'concord of sensibilities' which has been defined as the meaning of culture, allows for much more variety than Jones would admit.

Much the same could be said of Jones's treatment of the jazz during the 1930s, when he claims its broader acceptance (i.e., its economic 'success' as entertainment) led to a dilution, to the loss of much of its 'black' character which caused a certain group of rebellious Negro musicians to create the 'anti-mainstream' jazz style called bebop.

Jones sees bop as a conscious gesture of separatism, ignoring the fact that the creators of the style were seeking, whatever their musical intentions – and they were the least political of men – a fresh form of entertainment which would allow them their fair share of the entertainment market, which had been dominated by whites during the swing era. And although the boppers were reacting, at least in part, to the high artistic achievement of Armstrong, Hawkins, Basie and Ellington (all Negroes, all masters of the blues–jazz tradition), Jones sees their music as a recognition of his contention 'that when you are black in a society where black is an extreme liability [it] is one thing, but to understand that it is the society which is lacking and is impossibly deformed because of this lack, and not *yourself*, isolates you even more from that society'.

Perhaps. But today nothing succeeds like rebellion (which Jones as a 'beat' poet should know) and while a few boppers went to Europe to escape, or became Muslims, others took the usual tours for the State Department. Whether this makes *them* 'middle-class' in Jones's eyes I can't say, but his assertions – which are fine as personal statement – are not in keeping with the facts; his theory flounders before that complex of human motives which makes human history, and which is so characteristic of the American Negro.

Read as a record of an earnest young man's attempt to come to grips with his predicament as Negro American during a most turbulent period of our history, *Blues People* may be worth the reader's time. Taken as a theory of American Negro culture, it can only contribute more confusion than clarity. For Jones has stumbled over that ironic obstacle which lies in the path of any who would fashion a theory of American Negro culture while ignoring the intricate network of connections which binds Negroes to the larger society. To do so is to attempt a delicate brain surgery with a switchblade. And it is possible that any viable theory of Negro American culture obligates us to fashion a more adequate theory of American culture as a whole. The heel bone is, after all, connected, through its various linkages, to the head bone. Attempt a serious evaluation of our national morality and up jumps the so-called Negro problem. Attempt to discuss jazz as a hermetic expression of Negro sensibility and immediately we must consider what the 'mainstream' of American music really is.

Here political categories are apt to confuse, for while Negro slaves were socially, politically and economically separate (but only in a special sense even here), they were, in a cultural sense, much closer than Jones's theory allows him to admit.

'A slave', writes Jones, 'cannot be a man.' But what, one might ask, of those moments when he feels his metabolism aroused by the rising of the sap in spring? What of his identity among other slaves? With his wife? And isn't it closer to the truth that far from considering themselves only in terms of that abstraction, 'a slave', the enslaved really thought of themselves as *men* who had been unjustly enslaved? And isn't the true answer to Mr Jones's question, 'What are you going to be when you grow up?' not, as he gives it, 'a slave' but most probably a coachman, a teamster, a cook, the best damned steward on the Mississippi, the best jockey in Kentucky, a butler, a farmer, a stud, or hopefully, a free man! Slavery was a most vicious system and those who endured and survived it a tough people, but it was *not* (and this is important for Negroes to remember for the sake of their own sense of who and what their grandparents were) a state of absolute repression.

A slave was, to the extent that he was a *musician*, one who expressed himself in music, a man who realized himself in the world of sound. Thus, while he might stand in awe before the superior technical ability of a white musician, and while he was forced to recognize a superior social status, he would never feel awed before the music which the technique of the white musician made available. His attitude as 'musician' would lead him to seek to possess the music expressed through the technique, but until he could do so he would hum, whistle, sing or play the tunes to the best of his ability on any available instrument. And it was, indeed, out of the tension between desire and ability that the techniques of jazz emerged. This was likewise true of American Negro choral singing. For this, no literary explanation, no cultural analyses, no political slogans – indeed, not even a high degree of social or political freedom – was required. For the art – the blues, the spirituals, the jazz, the dance – was what we had in place of freedom.

Technique was then, as today, the key to creative freedom, but before this came a will toward expression. Thus, Jones's theory to the contrary, Negro musicians have never, as a group, felt alienated from any music sounded within their hearing, and it is my theory that it would be impossible to pinpoint the time when they were not shaping what Jones calls the mainstream of American music. Indeed, what group of musicians has made more of the sound of the American experience? Nor am I confining my statement to the sound of the slave experience, but am saying that the most authoritative rendering of America in music is that of American Negroes.

For as I see it, from the days of their introduction into the colonies, Negroes have taken, with the ruthlessness of those without articulate investments in cultural styles, whatever they could of European music, making of it that which would, when blended with the cultural tendencies inherited from Africa, express their own sense of life – while rejecting the rest. Perhaps this is only another way of saying that whatever the degree of injustice and inequality sustained by the slaves, American culture was, even before the official founding of the nation, pluralistic; and it was the African's origin in cultures in which art was highly functional which gave him an edge in shaping the music and dance of this nation.

The question of social and cultural snobbery is important here. The effectiveness of Negro music and dance is first recorded in the journals and letters of travellers but it is important to remember that they saw and understood only that which they were prepared to accept. Thus a Negro dancing a courtly dance appeared comic from the outside simply because the dancer was a slave. But to the Negro dancing it – and there is ample evidence that he danced it well – burlesque or satire might have been the point, which might have been difficult for a white observer to even imagine. During the 1870s Lafcadio Hearn reports that the best singers of Irish songs, in Irish dialect, were Negro dock workers in Cincinnati, and advertisements from slavery days described escaped slaves who spoke in Scottish dialect. The master artisans of the South were slaves, and white Americans have been walking Negro walks, talking Negro flavoured talk (and prizing it when spoken by Southern belles), dancing Negro dances and singing Negro melodies far too long to talk of a 'mainstream' of American culture to which they are alien.

Jones attempts to impose an ideology upon this cultural complexity, and this might be useful if he knew enough of the related subjects to make it interesting. But his version of the blues lacks a sense of the excitement and surprise of men living in the world – of enslaved and politically weak men successfully imposing their values upon a powerful society through song and dance.

The blues speak to us simultaneously of the tragic and the comic aspects of the human condition and they express a profound sense of life shared by many Negro Americans precisely because their lives have combined these modes. This has been the heritage of a people who for hundreds of years could not celebrate birth or dignify death and whose need to live despite the dehumanizing pressures of slavery developed an endless capacity for laughing at their painful experiences. This is a group experience shared by many Negroes, and any effective study of the blues would treat them first as poetry and as ritual. Jones makes a distinction between classic and country blues, the one being entertainment and the other folklore. But the distinction is false. Classic blues were both entertainment *and* a form of folklore. When they were sung professionally in theatres, they were entertainment; when danced to in the form of recordings or used as a means of transmitting the traditional verses and their wisdom, they were folklore. There are levels of time and function involved here, and the blues which might be used in one place as entertainment (as gospel music is now being used in night-clubs and on theatre stages) might be put to a ritual use in another. Bessie Smith might have been a 'blues queen' to the society at large, but within the tighter Negro community where the blues were part of a total way of life, and a major expression of an attitude toward life, she was a priestess, a celebrant who affirmed the values of the group and man's ability to deal with chaos.

It is unfortunate that Jones thought it necessary to ignore the aesthetic nature of the blues in order to make his ideological point, for he might have come much closer had he considered the blues not as politics but as art. This would have still required the disciplines of anthropology and sociology – but as practised by Constance Rourke, who was well aware of how much of American cultural expression is Negro. And he could learn much from the Cambridge School's discoveries of the connection between poetry, drama and ritual as a means of analysing how the blues function in their proper environment. Simple taste should have led Jones to Stanley Edgar Hyman's work on the blues instead of Paul Oliver's sadly misdirected effort.

For the blues are not primarily concerned with civil rights or obvious political protest; they are an art form and thus a transcendence of those conditions created within the Negro community by the denial of social justice. As such they are one of the techniques through which Negroes have survived and kept their courage during that long period when many whites assumed, as some still assume, they were afraid.

Much has been made of the fact that *Blues People* is one of the few books by a Negro to treat the subject. Unfortunately for those who expect that Negroes would have a special insight into this mysterious art, this is not enough. Here, too, the critical intelligence must perform the difficult task which only it can perform.

DONALD M. MARQUIS

Forming the Buddy Bolden Band

In legend, Buddy Bolden is the first significant jazzman, even though no recordings of his music exist. Little was known about his life either, except that he played cornet in New Orleans at the end of the last century, and died in a mental hospital, until Donald Marquis wrote In Search of Buddy Bolden *in 1978.*

Most information indicates that Buddy developed his style in the small string band playing for dances and parties, rather than apprenticing in parades. He did play in a few parades as a sideman with other bands, and he sometimes used a pick-up group for the larger parades when fifteen or twenty bands were out at the same time, but he did not have a regular brass band. His brass band personnel, such as it was, changed often. The fact that very few people remember much about Bolden's street music career makes it seem a rather insignificant part of his musical development. A few did mention seeing Buddy in parades and others mentioned marching with him, but their recollections were somewhat hazy. Papa John Joseph had seen Buddy play with the Holmes band in Lutcher that one time, but Louis Jones didn't remember ever seeing him play a parade. Jones's observations were generally accurate, but because he was not much of a second-liner (parade follower) he would not have been on the parade routes when Buddy did indeed march.

Bolden's string band personnel was not too stable those first few years. Much experimenting was done and if someone did not like the way Buddy played, or vice-versa, he left. Given Bolden's personality we can be sure he was looking for a novel approach – something to gain the crowd and sway the applause when he competed with other bands. His efforts took the form of playing 'wide-open' on the cornet and of playing in up-tempo or ragging the hymns, street songs, and dance tunes to create a musical sound that people were unfamiliar with. This style did not catch on immediately and the Creoles scornfully called it honky-tonk music. But Buddy kept working, and he began to gain followers.

By 1897 the style and membership of the band was taking a definite shape. They began to get jobs that were no longer in the 'kid' category. Although their sound was alien to some, it had an appeal, especially to a liberated, post-Civil War generation of young blacks. According to Louis Jones, Bolden played both by note and by ear and he liked to please the audience. Having a great ear he could hear another band play and after practising their piece between dances was able to duplicate it by the end of the evening. As he matured musically, he would listen to a number, memorize it instrument by instrument, then teach the parts to the others. Some of the musicians who played with him during this time were William 'Red' Warner, who periodically substituted on clarinet, and Bill Willigan, John McMurray, Cornelius Tillman, and Frank Jackson, all of whom played drums at one time or another. Wallace Collins added his tuba when the band went on the street. Later in 1897 Bolden realized the possibilities of putting more brass band sound on the bandstand and got Willie Cornish with him on valve trombone. Cornish, however, left shortly to serve in the Spanish–American War.

A few people remembered Bolden's band in its earlier days. Zue Robertson, who later played with the Original Creole Band, said he saw Bolden play before the 1898 Spanish–American war. One number he remembered was 'Ride On, King', a spiritual in which 'Bolden would blow so hard, he actually blew the tuning slide out of his cornet and it would land twenty feet away.' If it were not a physical impossibility this would have been a good gimmick, and it is an indication of the legendary power with which Buddy blew the horn. It would by no means be the last seemingly impossible description of Bolden's assault on his instrument. Another story came from Ray Lopez, later a renowned band leader, who recalled hearing Bolden's band play for the embarkation of a Negro regiment bound for Cuba during the Spanish–American War. As the ship moved away the band played 'Home, Sweet Home', and some of the men on board were so overcome by nostalgia they jumped off and swam to shore.

An intriguing mystery grew up around the possibility that this early Bolden band had made a cylinder recording. In 1939 Willie Cornish told *Jazzmen* editor Charles E. Smith that the cylinder had been made before 1898, and Smith, along with Orin Blackstone and Bill Russell, began an extensive search for it. Their leads met frustrating dead ends; in a 1957 *Saturday Review* article Smith concluded that the cylinder would never be found. The search had been revived temporarily in 1951 through an article by Tom Sancton in *The Second Line*, with the magazine offering a hundred-dollar reward for information, but this effort, too, was fruitless.

MICHAEL ONDAATJE

Coming through Slaughter

Two years before Donald Marquis ended his research, Michael Ondaatje wrote a poetic novel about 'King' Bolden. The two approaches could not be more different. In this extract, the novelist imagines Bolden's demise.

Interviewer: To get back to Buddy Bolden—
John Joseph: Uh-huh.
Interviewer: He lost his mind, I heard.
John Joseph: He lost his mind, yeah, he died in the bug house.
Interviewer: Yes, that's what I heard.
John Joseph: That's right, he died out there.

Travelling again. Home to nightmare.

The earth brown. Rubbing my brain against the cold window of the bus. I was sent travelling my career on fire and so cruise home again now.

Come. We must go deeper with no justice and no jokes.

All my life I seemed to be a parcel on a bus. I am the famous fucker. I am the famous barber. I am the famous cornet player. Read the labels. The labels are coming home.

Charlie Dablayes Brass Band

The Diamond Stone Brass Band

The Old Columbis Brass Band

Frank Welch Brass Band

The Old Excelsior Brass Band

The Algiers and Pacific Brass Band

Kid Allen's Father's Brass Band

George McCullon's Brass Band

And so many no name street bands
. . . according to Bunk Johnson.

So in the public parade he went mad into silence.

This was April 1907, after his return, after staying with his wife and Cornish, saying *sure* he would play again, had met and spoken to Henry Allen and would play with his band in the weekend parade. Henry Allen snr's Brass Band.

The music begins two blocks north of Marais Street at noon. All of Henry Allen's Band including Bolden turn onto Iberville and move south. After about half a mile his music separates from the band, and though the whole procession is still together Bolden is now stained untouchable, powerful, an 8 ball in their midst. Till he is spinning round and round, crazy, at the Liberty–Iberville connect.

By eleven that morning people who had heard Bolden was going to play had already arrived, stretching from Villiere down to Franklin. Brought lunches and tin flasks and children. Some bands broke engagements, some returned from towns over sixty miles away. All they knew was that Bolden had come back looking good. He was in town four days before the parade.

On Tuesday night he had come in by bus from Webb's place. A small bag held his cornet and a few clothes. He had no money so he walked the twenty-five blocks to 2527 First Street where he had last lived. He tapped on the door and Cornish opened it. Frozen. Only two months earlier Cornish had moved in with Bolden's wife. Almost fainting. Buddy put his arm around Cornish's waist and hugged him, then walked past him into the living-room and fell back in a chair exhausted. He was very tired from the walk, the tension of possibly running into other people. The city too hot after living at the lake. Sitting he let the bag slide from his fingers.

Where's Nora?
She's gone out for food. She'll be back soon.
Good.
Jesus, Buddy. Nearly two years, we all thought—
No that's ok Willy, I don't care.

He was sitting there not looking at Cornish but up at the ceiling, his hands outstretched his elbows resting on the arms of the chair. A long silence. Cornish thought this is the longest time I've ever been with him without talking. You never saw Bolden thinking, lots of people said that. He thought by being in motion. Always talk, snatches of song, as if his brain had been a fishbowl.

Let me go look for her.
Ok Willy.

He sat on the steps waiting for Nora. As she came up to him he asked her to sit with him.

I haven't got time, Willy, let's go in.

Dragging her down next to him and putting an arm around her so he was as close to her as possible.

Listen, he's back. Buddy's back.

Her whole body relaxing.

Where is he now?
Inside. In his chair.
Come on let's go in.
Do you want to go alone?
No let's go in, both of us Willy.

She had never been a shadow. Before they married, while she worked at Lula White's, she had been popular and public. She had played Bolden's games, knew his extra sex. When they were alone together it was still a crowded room. She had been fascinated with him. She brought short cuts to his arguments and at times cleared away the chaos he embraced. She walked inside now with Willy holding her hand. She saw him sitting down, head back, but eyes glancing at the door as it opened. Bolden not moving at all and she, with groceries under her arm, not moving either.

The three of them entered a calm long conversation. They talked in the style of a married couple joined by a third person who was catalyst and audience. And Buddy watched her large hip as she lay on the floor of the room, the hill of cloth, and he came into her dress like a burglar without words in the family style they had formed years ago, with some humour now but not too much humour. Sitting against her body and unbuttoning the layers of cloth to see the dark gold body and bending down to smell her skin and touching with his face through the flesh the buried bones in her chest. Writhed his face against her small breasts. Her skirt still on, her blouse not taken off but apart and his rough cheek scraping her skin, not going near her face which he had explored so much from across the room, earlier. When Cornish had still been there.

They lay there without words. Moving all over her chest and arms and armpits and stomach as if placing mines on her with his mouth and then leaned up and looked at her body glistening with his own spit. Together closing up her skirt, slipping the buttons back into their holes so she was dressed again. Not going further because it was friendship that had to be guarded, that they both wanted. The diamond had to love the earth it passed along the way, every speck and angle of the other's history, for the diamond had been earth too.

So Cornish lives with her. Willy, who wanted to be left alone but became the doctor for everyone's troubles. Sweet William. Nothing ambitious on the valve trombone but being the only one able to read music he brought us new music from the north that we perverted cheerfully into our own style. Willy, straight as a good fence all his life, none to match his virtue. Since I've been home I watch him and Nora in the room. The air around them is empty so I see them clear. They are for me no longer in a landscape, they are not in the street they walk over, the chairs disappear under them. They are complete and exact and final. No longer the every-second change I saw before but like statues of personality now. Through my one-dimensional eye. I left the other in the other home, Robin flying off with it into her cloud. So I see Willy and Nora as they are and always will be and I hunger to be as still as them, my brain tying me up in this chair. Locked inside the frame, boiled down in love and anger into dynamo that cannot move except on itself.

DAVID BOULTON

Early Ideas on the Origin of the Word 'Jazz'

In an attempt to provide an explanation of the origin of the word 'jazz', the *Negro Year Book* for 1918 published a statement made by James Reese Europe, 'acknowledged King of Jazz', which became the source of much early British (and American) speculation on the subject. Europe credited the name to a dance-combination known as Razz's Band, a group of

> truly extraordinary composition. It consisted of a baritone horn, a trombone, a cornet and an instrument made out of the chinaberry tree. This instrument is something like the clarinet and is made by the Southern Negroes themselves. . . . The four musicians of Razz's Band had no idea at all of what they were playing; they improvided [*sic*] as they went along, but such was their innate sense of rhythm that they produced something that was very taking. From the small cafés of New Orleans they graduated to the St Charles Hotel, and after a time to the Winter Gardens in New York, where they appeared, however, only a few days, the individual musicians being grabbed up by various orchestras in the city. Somehow in the passage of time Razz's Band got changed into Jazz's Band, and from this corruption arose the term 'Jazz'.

Yet more unlikely is the explanation tentatively offered by London's *Dancing Times* in the November 1917 issue, when Negro jazz was still quite unknown in England. The 'nigger bands', it was suggested, borrowed the term from the mining camps in the American West, where it was said to be in common use as a slang expression. But of all theories, the most fantastic was that put forward, again by the *Dancing Times* (February 1920), as follows:

> The word 'Dios', which is Portuguese for God, was picked up by English sailors at Indian ports, and when they went to China

in the 17th century, they carried the word with them. With the dental softened, this became 'Joss'. The Celestials adopted the word and it was gradually absorbed into their language with a religious meaning such as Joss House, Joss Stick, etc. In San Francisco a Chinese Colony was formed at the beginning of the last century, and as John Chinaman could not bring a Joss Orchestra, he improvised one. The 'Frisco Chinatown Joss Orchestra made a great appeal to the niggers, who improvised again. Now a nigger will say Jazz for Joss. Bands were formed and sent on circuit, and finally Jazz music found its way east to New York and finally to London.

This article was accompanied by a photograph of one such Chinese band over the caption THE ORIGIN OF JAZZ.

MAXIM GORKY

The Music of the Degenerate

... The stillness of this night, permitting the mind to rest from the
various if paltry grievances of the day's work, seems to whisper to
the soul of a solemn music of the universal labour of great and small,
a magnificent song of a new history – a song boldly raised by the
working people of my country.

Then, all of a sudden, in the sensitive stillness resounds the dry
knocking of an idiotic hammer – one, two, three, ten, twenty strokes
and after them – as a splash of mud in clear transparent water, there
come with a crash, a wild whistle, screeches, rumbling, wailing,
howling, the snorting of a metal pig, the cry of a donkey, the
amorous quacking of a monstrous frog. All this insulting chaos of
mad sounds is submitted to an imperceptible rhythm and after
listening for one, two minutes to those wails, one begins unwillingly
to imagine that this is an orchestra of maniacs, stricken with sexual
mania and directed by a man-stallion who brandishes a huge genetic
member.

That is the radio – one of the greatest discoveries of science, one
of the mysteries wrested by it from nature, hypocritically silent. It is
the radio in a neighbouring hotel, bringing consolation to a world
grown gross, the world of birds of prey – transporting to them on air
the tune of a new foxtrot executed by a negro orchestra. It is the
music of grossness. To its rhythm in all the magnificent 'cabarets' of
a cultured continent the degenerate, with cynical fluctuations of the
hips, pollute, simulate, the fecundation of woman by man.

From time immemorial the poets of all nations, all epochs, have
lavished their creative power in ennobling this act, adorning it,
making it worthy of man that in this he should not be on a plane
with the goat, bull, or boar. Hundreds, thousands of beautiful poems
have been composed in praise of love – an emotion which has ever
been potent in stimulating the creative powers of men and women.
Through the force of love man has become a being far more social

than the cleverest of animals. Poetry expressing a matter-of-fact, healthy, active romanticism in sex relationship has had great educative and social importance for humanity.

Love and hunger govern the world, said Schiller. Love, as the basis of culture, hunger as that of civilization. Then came an overgrown vampire, a parasite living on the labour of others, a semi-man with the motto: 'After me the deluge', and with his thick feet he tramples all that has been created by the finest nervous tissue of great artists, the illuminators of the working classes.

He, the gross, does not need woman as a friend and human being; she is for him a mere tool of pleasure, unless she is as much a bird of prey as he is himself. As a mother she is of no use to him, for although he is fond of power, children are an impediment to him. Power, too, seems necessary to him only for foxtrotting and the latter has become a necessity because a man grown porcine is already a poor male. Love for him is – depravity, and not, as it was, mere appetite. In the world of the gross, homosexual love acquires an epidemic character. The evolution of grossness is – degeneration.

It is the evolution from the charm of a minuet and the passionate vitality of a waltz, to the cynicism of a foxtrot with the convulsions of the Charleston; from Mozart and Beethoven to the jazz of the negroes who undoubtedly laugh in their sleeves seeing how their white masters evolve towards a savagery which the negroes of America are leaving behind them more and more rapidly. 'Culture is declining', cry those who would like to see prevail over the working man, the prestige of grossness. The proletariat threatens to do away with culture! Its constituents cry and lie, for they cannot remain blind to the fact that it is the universal herd of the bestial which is trampling culture; they cannot fail to understand that the proletariat is the only force capable of saving culture, of fathoming and widening it.

The monstrous bass throws out English words; a wild horn wails piercingly, reminding one of the cries of a raving camel; a drum drones; a nasty little pipe sizzles, tearing at one's ears; the saxophone emits its quacking nasal sound. Swaying, fleshly hips, thousands of heavy feet, tread and shuffle.

The music of the degenerate ends finally with a deafening thud, as though a case of pottery had been flung from the skies to the earth. Again limpid stillness reigns around me and my thoughts return home; the peasant Vassily Kucheriavenko writes to me from there: 'Before, in our village we used to have one school for three hundred houses; now we have three, a co-operative society, three red "corners", a club, a library, a reading-room, various groups; we have a wall-newspaper, we subscribe to countless reviews, papers, books. In the evenings – from white-haired old men to red pioneers – the clubs are crammed with all kinds of people. Lately an old woman of seventy-two died; before her death she used to say she would have loved to join the union of young communists had she not been so old. Why had it all begun so late, she said! She begged to be buried in the Soviet manner, with the flag. She went to all the meetings, walking many versts, and was like a girl.—Recently in an American review, *Asia*, there was an article about all this, with photographs.'

She is a curious person, that old grandmother. Of course: 'One grandam will not make culture', as the proverb says, but how many do I know of such, let us say, amusing cases of rejuvenation of the ancient peasant, all pointing to one conclusion: the Russian nation is growing young.

How fine it is to be working and living in our time!

Translated by Marie Budberg, 1929

S. FREDERICK STARR

Jazz Comes to Revolutionary Russia

The barriers to the free flow of new cultural forms into the Soviet Union in the 1920s were formidable but by no means insurmountable. In jazz, they could be overcome by anyone capable of developing a convincing explanation of why this outlandish music should be fostered under the new Communist regime and of somehow securing all the necessary instruments and music. The person who accomplished both these feats was the Russian Futurist poet, Dadaist, Surrealist, editor and dancer but non-musician, Valentin Parnakh. Thanks to Parnakh, Russia had the distinction of being one of the few European countries – along with independent Estonia – in which jazz was first introduced by a native son, rather than by a touring American group.

Born to a Jewish family in the south of Russia, Parnakh followed the parade of pre-World War I émigrés to Europe and, after tossing about Spain for a while, arrived in Paris in 1913. He was a striking figure. Friends in Paris recall him being short and extremely frail, 'like a jockey, like a leaf'. His slight frame was sustained largely by coffee which he imbibed in Paris cafés and at the small Rue Callot apartment of the émigré painters Mikhail Larionov and Natalia Goncharova. A surviving sketch by Picasso depicts him as handsome, but contemporaries recall his head being too large and perched constantly at an unnatural angle. Memoirs devote far more attention to his strange dance movements than to his poetical work.

Parnakh's first exposure to jazz was a performance by Louis Mitchell's Jazz Kings at the Trocadero in Paris in July 1921. Later that year he heard other touring American groups in Berlin. The café and dance hall settings were important. For Parnakh, jazz was above all dance music, a vehicle for the fox trot and the shimmy. In jazz, this ungainly poet found a physically liberating rhythm that could make the common man an artist and, in the process, drive decadent classical ballet from the stage. This is how Parnakh saw his mission in Russia.

Parnakh carefully laid the groundwork for a crusade on behalf of jazz before departing for Russia. He placed articles on 'The New Dances' and 'The Jazz Band', in *Veshch*, an avant-garde émigré journal that was well known and respected in Russia. The new American dances, he argued, embodied the spirit of postwar 'détente' (he actually used the word) and translated the life of modern man into linear, mechanistic but free movement, just as the nineteenth century's unfocused yearnings had coalesced in the swimming movement of the waltz. 'All these dances are therefore the expression of a jazz orchestra, of a music of dissonances, syncopations, crashes, soaring brasses, shrieking ratchets, whistles, howls, and alarm sirens all sounding like an alternating current of electricity,' Parnakh explained in his essay on 'The Jazz Band'. However limited Parnakh's knowledge of music, he clearly knew less about electricity! In this same essay the word 'jazz' appears in Russian for the first time. But Parnakh did not dwell on its musical qualities. Instead, he stressed the visual aspects of the new music. The bass drum must be lighted with an electric light, and the horn players must gyrate with their instruments. When Mitchell's bandsmen performed a New Orleans-style second-line strut through the Trocadero, Parnakh was in ecstasy. A jazz band plays for dancing, but the band itself also dances: it is a 'mimetic orchestra'.

Parnakh arrived in Moscow in the summer of 1922 with a collection of the necessary instruments. Immediately, he began pressing his campaign in the Soviet press. In several fresh attacks he argued that jazz is a distillation of modern man's movements and manners. He compared the movements of Mitchell's pianist on his stool at the Elite Café with what he imagined Chopin's movements to have been, and praised the freedom of the former. The key to jazz dance and music, Parnakh argued, is its 'eccentricity', the vibrant energy and motion released by the granting of boundless individual freedom to each participant.

Why did Parnakh believe that Moscow was ready for his crusade of emancipation? Much had changed since the bleak Civil War years 1918–20. Lenin, realizing that the peasantry was solidly opposed to bolshevism and that the Bolsheviks themselves possessed neither the numbers nor the skills to manage the economy, took a giant step backward to state capitalism. The New Economic Policy (NEP), proclaimed in 1921, enabled the new regime to consolidate its control while permitting both entrepreneurs and labour unions to pursue their own interests, so long as they did not collide with those of the government. Exhausted by war, revolution, and civil strife, urban Russia breathed a sigh of relief. Olivier's Hermitage, a Moscow restaurant and garden famed for its variety shows and its mayonnaise, reopened in the autumn of 1921. Crooked Jimmy's, another cabaret theatre that had survived the turmoil since 1918, expanded its programmes. And when the Aquarium Gardens reopened in Petrograd a sign at the door proclaimed 'Everything as Before'. In 1917 Russians had sung the 'Marseillaise'; by 1922 they were crooning Yuri Miliutin's pop hit 'The Sound of Nocturnal Marseilles'. . . .

The blond-haired poet set about organizing what became known as 'The First Eccentric Orchestra of the Russian Soviet Federated Socialist Republic – Valentin Parnakh's Jazz Band'. The ensemble consisted of a piano, banjo, drums, xylophone, and two violins. The first concert was announced for Sunday, 1 October 1922, in the auditorium of the State Institute for Theatrical Art in Moscow. . . .

What did Russia's first jazz band sound like? Only a few tantalizing hints have survived. Parnakh himself speaks of the melodic line but makes no reference to polyphony. He speaks also of American melodies, suggesting that he had brought a few arrangements from Paris. Improvisation, of course, was out of the question, and remained so in Russia for another decade. The entire stress was on the syncopated rhythms created by the drums, banjo, and xylophone. Parnakh also speaks of dissonances produced by the saxophone, suggesting bent notes. These must have sounded rather strange, since the handful of Russian sax players all used a tight, classical embouchure until the visit of Sidney Bechet in 1926, and hence could produce neither a convincing glissando nor a relaxed vibrato. Parnakh's 'jazz', then, consisted of American popular songs accompanied by a syncopated rhythm band.

This was enough to stun the audience. The Petrograd conductor Nikolai Malko came away from the performance convinced that jazz would open up new areas of musical timbre for composers of the future. The theatre critic Vladimir Fedorov also judged the event a success and went so far as to declare that Parnakh's shimmy, fox-trot, and two-steps 'might provide an excellent means of enlivening dancehalls and organizing the free time of labour'. . . .

What jazz initially lacked in audience support it made up through backing from the Soviet government. *Glavlit*, the censorship organ within the Commissariat of Public Enlightenment, regularly approved Western foxtrots and 'waltz-Bostons' for publication. The Commissar of Agriculture hired Parnakh's group to perform at the 1923 'First All Union Exhibition of Agriculture and Cottage Indus-tries', and the Communist International called on Parnakh to enter-tain foreign comrades at its congress on the occasion of the fifth anniversary of the Bolshevik Revolution in November 1922. A French Communist who attended the meeting described 'a formi-dable band thundering away, crude and noisy'. Except for the Original Dixieland Jazz Band's performance at the 1918 London ball in honour of the forthcoming opening of peace negotiations at Versailles, this was probably the first appearance of a jazz band at any state occasion.

Three years after the Russians' first clumsy attempts to imitate jazz, the Soviet government's newspapers were criticizing a Harlem band for being insufficiently hot. Such published sentiments reveal the deep change in Russia since the Civil War. Through a stupendous reconstruction effort, Russians had gotten their economy back on the move. Prewar levels of production had been attained again in most industries, and cities had regained their vitality. Dramatic new buildings, some in the Constructivist style, were rising in Moscow and the partial renewal of international tourism gave the city a cosmopolitan air that had been absent. Ideological zeal was decidedly out of fashion.

Lenin had died on 21 January 1924, after a prolonged illness. With the Father of the Revolution dead and embalmed, the younger generation could take its oedipal revenge. Night-clubs boomed, privately owned boutiques poured out flapper fashions, and in the workers' capital there appeared a breed of young people with

seemingly nothing to do all day. A series of novels, beginning with
Sergei Malashkin's *The Moon on the Right Side*, a literary *cause célèbre*
in 1926, documented the degeneracy of youth in lurid detail. The
stories of members of *Komsomol* (the Young Communist League)
engaging in orgies of alcohol and drugs were not far off the mark.
Everyone knew that powerful marijuana from Central Asia was
readily available at the Sukharevka Market, and that the suspension
in 1925 of the liquor prohibition law Nicholas II had foolishly
introduced in 1914 had put vodka within easy reach of anyone with
a rouble to spare.

The apparent idleness of youth bothered moralists and con-
founded sociologists. The country's leading pollster, Sergei Strumilin,
surveyed high school and college students, as well as young factory
workers, in order to find out how they spent their days. None
reported more than a few hours of free time each week. Yet to all
appearances there were large numbers of young men and women
with time on their hands.

By 1926 the desire to revert to the pre-revolutionary fashions in
popular culture was dead. Nor did the Party's Civil War songs and
agitmuzyk hold much attraction. Even the true believers' journal, *For
Proletarian Music,* had to admit that young people and workers found
the ideological potboilers 'dull, deadly, and grey'. Earnest researchers
attempted to elicit the true tastes of the nation's popular audiences.
Their conclusion: neither folk-songs nor the tired diet of hits from
light operas satisfied anyone.

The researchers needed only to have perused the sheet music ads
of the State Press (*Giz*) to learn what the public wanted: Matvei
Blanter's 'John Gray', 'Aero-Foxtrot', 'I am Billy', or 'Eccentric
Dances'; M. Nikolaevsky's 'Miss Evelyn Foxtrot'; Lev Drizo's 'Yes!
We Killed the Bottle'; 'The Hypnosis Tango'; and Yuri Miliutin's
foxtrot 'Harry and Barry'. Russia was foxtrotting to Communism,
and when the official publishers couldn't meet the demand for new
foxtrot melodies, the writers published them on their own, often
engaging the best designers to do the covers. Even young Dmitri
Shostakovich, the shining star of musical Leningrad, arranged Vin-
cent Youmans's 'Tea for Two' as a foxtrot for symphonic orchestra
called 'Tahiti Trot'.

Down Beat: *Front Page*

The jazz magazine Down Beat *was founded in Chicago in 1933, during the Swing era. Originally, its format was that of a broadsheet, with front-page news stories and feature articles inside. Here is a typical assembly of lead stories from an early issue (December 1937). Note the follow-up piece on the death of Bessie Smith, correcting the suggestion by John Hammond in an earlier issue that she had bled to death after having been turned away from a whites-only hospital.*

"SWING TO BE PART OF U.S. SYMPHONY!" P.W.

By Carl Cons

Chicago, Ill. – Condemned by critics of the "God damn" school for taking the "guts" out of swing, and commended by the literati for refining it, Paul Whiteman, former "King of Jazz," says Swing will one day form an important part in American Symphony Music . . .

. . . And that the future American musical organization will be a 40-piece brass and woodwind choir!

A New Organ to Express American Music

"American is dynamic and the virility of the brasses express her spirit," declared Paul. "But the great 'melting pot' of her emotions needs contrast and a richer tone color."

And because the strings do not balance the brasses, Whiteman has eliminated the violin and is seeking tonal blends in the woodwind family.

"There may be a place, too, for the electronic instruments. America has made great progress and the brilliant new instruments may widen the tonal possibilities of musical execution to heights hitherto unknown.

"The Therman, the Hammond Organ, the electrically amplified string instruments, have not yet been intelligently used or properly blended with the instruments we already employ.

"Melting Pot' of Instruments"

"It's all an experiment, of course, but I do know America has its own message, and I think a new organ of musical expression and typically American will evolve from this 'melting pot of instruments'."

Whiteman's present conception of this is a 40-piece brass and woodwind choir with doubles that will give him the rich tonal flavoring of 35 saxes, a dozen oboes or flutes, a half dozen brasses, English horns, bassoons, clarinets, French horns, etc.

"It would be the ideal all-American

band," says Paul, "composed of men who can 'swing' and yet are good enough musicians to play Wagner or anything in brass band literature."

Whiteman's present band is a nucleus for this mythical American band and it is with this idea in mind that each new musician is added.

'It's the 'Hot' Guys Who Are Really Corny!"

Called corny on many an occasion because he treated many jazz themes in a semi-symphonic style,

(Modulate to Page 18)

"GET OUT OF TOWN OR ELSE" NON-UNION MEN WARNED

Cops Guard Hotels On Tip "Gorillas" Were Imported

LOCAL OFFICIALS TO RESIGN

By Harry Knotts

Baltimore, Md. – Acting on a "tip" that gorillas and strong-arm muggs were being imported, Baltimore Hotel managers recently asked for police protection. As a result, it wasn't unusual to find several cops and plainclothesmen on hand when Baltimore nite-clubbers visited one of the seven strike-bound hotels.

At the Lord Baltimore, Bob Stanley, who had been imported to play in the Florentine Room, reported that while he had not been threatened, the boys in his band had received numerous telephone calls warning them "to get out of town, or else!" One of Bob's men came out of the hotel one day to find that someone had tampered with his car. No serious damage had been done except to the tires, which had been punctured, evidently with an ice pick. Another incident early in November marked the first action on part of strong-arm men who, several local "gates" intimate, were being hired by

the local union. Eddie Norwood, a local non-union leader, was reported to have been beaten up by thugs who called at his home and warned him against playing in the Lord Baltimore hotel. Norwood was apparently afraid to talk, as he would make no statement to the press. However, boys in his band confirmed the report and vouched for its authenticity.

Local No. 40 denied any responsibility for either the Norwood attack or for threats made to non-union men. Oscar Apple, president of the local union, discounted reports of gorillas being imported as "ridiculous." "The Musician's Union," he said, "has been a peaceful organization for more years than I can remember."

Imported non-union musicians were instructed to sit tight and it was strongly hinted in local circles that the present administration of Local No. 40 would resign in the near future because of pressure brought to bear by Hotel Men's Association and the press. Public sentiment in Balto has never been with the local and the members seemed to feel that a new administration was needed.

Local No. 40 finally cleaned house the end of November, with Business Manager Edgar Hunt and Secretary Elmer Martin planning to resign, while President Oscar Apple stayed on the job. All members who had been expelled or suspended were reinstated with cancellation of their fines.

Nazi Musicians Swallow Own Medicine

Nazi musicians were forced to swallow their own medicine with the publication of the official program for the 1938 Salzburg music festival recently.

Conductor Arturo Toscanini has been working on a grudge for three years, ever since Wilhelm Furtwaengler, Prussian state opera director, appeared at the Nazi-controlled Bayreuth festival. Toscanini's protests have finally resulted in omission of Furtwaengler's name from the Salzburg festival programs.

Southern Whites Did Not Turn Dying Bessie Away

Memphis, Tenn. – Bessie did not bleed to death from lack of medical attention. According to a prominent Memphis surgeon who reached the scene a few minutes after Bessie's car crashed into the back of a truck, the accident occurred near Coahoma, a small town near Clarksdale, Miss. The surgeon, even though an ambulance had already been summoned, saw that she was bleeding to death and attempted to put her in the back of his car. While he was trying to pick her up (she weighed 200 lbs.) another car going about 50 miles an hour rammed into the back of his car and completely demolished it.

However, about five minutes later the ambulance arrived and she was rushed to the negro hospital in Clarksdale where one of the town's best doctors immediately amputated her arm. She died a few minutes later *in the hospital* but undoubtedly more from internal injuries than loss of blood.

Ku Klux Klan Wrecks Nite Club

Miami, Fla. – Self-appointed vice squad for the shady hinterlands of Miami, select members of the city's Ku Klux Klan wrecked the La Paloma night club middle of November, then "ordered" it to stay closed.

Same day that grand dragon of the Klan for Florida denied Klansmen had made the raid, Miami Klansmen proudly admitted the raid (but refused to give names!) and promised they would see to it that the club stayed dark.

Day after the raid Carrol King, master of the club, announced a gala re-opening for that evening. Later in the day he retracted, said that necessary repairs would delay re-opening.

King charged that the "righteous" raiders had beaten entertainers and waitresses, wrecked the club's interior and furniture, pilfered $360 in cash, half a dozen rifles and shotguns, and a gold watch from the office of Al Youst, club owner. Klansmen denied the charges.

Deputy sheriffs raided and closed the spot Nov. 27 after its re-opening, but two days later County Solicitor Robert R. Taylor gave Manager Al Youst permission to re-open. Said he could find no basis for sheriff's charges against Youst and employees.

SHERIFF CHASES DON BESTOR INTO A BOILER ROOM

Joliet, Ill. – "Play-Don" Bestor's former wife let her temperature rise late in November when alimony didn't arrive when she wanted it. Joliet cops, writ in hand, set out to jerk Bestor from the orchestra pit of Joliet's Rialto Theater. Bestor waxed a bit warm himself, scooted for the theater boiler room where cops, hot on the trail, found him hiding.

Bestor's temperature slowly declined as he reclined in the city cooler and two days later he gave up his room there, after turning over to the ex-ball and chain $3,000 worth of life insurance to keep their 16-year-old son.

Ex-spouse Hattie C. Catton had been promised $600 by court order here, to be paid by Dec. 13, but got jittery when she suspected Bestor planned getting out of court's jurisdiction before payment deadline. She has another $1600 coming to her between now and Dec., 1938.

Throw A Tear-Gas Bomb at Fritz Kreisler

Ann Arbor, Mich. – A tear-gas bomb exploded during recital of Fritz Kreisler, violinist, at University of Michigan Nov. 29. Of audience of 5000, many fled to escape fumes. Kreisler carried on after five-minute recess.

Mezzrow's Half-Negro, Half-White Band Closes

New York, N. Y. – Once again the experiment to combine whites and Negroes in a single band has proved a failure. The Harlem Uproar House in New York City, the scene of this latest effort, closed its doors after exactly eleven nights of jam by Mezz Mezzrow's "Fourteen Disciples of Swing."

The band which had such white and colored jam men as Zutty Singleton, Max Kaminsky, Eugene Sedric, Frank Newton and others who were recruited from in and out of town failed to draw at all and has completely broken up since the closing of the Uproar House.

This is the second time that Mezzrow has failed in his attempt to produce a successful mixed band. About four years ago he rehearsed a band on the coast which started out with only one or two colored men, the plan being to add more later as the public became used to the new idea. Bud Freeman, Joe Sullivan, and Pee Wee Russell were among those present. After a few weeks of rehearsals with no prospective jobs in sight the band disbanded without actually having tested the idea.

Girl Vocalist Suffers Fracture of the Skull

Milwaukee, Wis. – Arlene Lederman, feminine accordionist with Casper Reda band, suffered a skull fracture and other members of the band were shaken and bruised, in a head-on collision near Dodgeville, Wis., Thanksgiving Day.

The Reda unit were enroute to Guttenberg, Ia. Maestro Reda claims the other car hit them while trying to pass a car.

GUNTHER SCHULLER

Louis Armstrong: The First Great Soloist

When on 28 June 1928 Louis Armstrong unleashed the spectacular cascading phrases of the introduction to 'West End Blues', he established the general stylistic direction of jazz for several decades to come. Beyond that, this performance also made quite clear that jazz could never again revert to being solely an entertainment or folk music. The clarion call of 'West End Blues' served notice that jazz had the potential capacity to compete with the highest order of previously known musical expression. Though nurtured by the crass entertainment and night-club world of the Prohibition era, Armstrong's music transcended this context and its implications. This was music for music's sake, not for the first time in jazz, to be sure, but never before in such a brilliant and unequivocal form. The beauties of this music were those of any great, compelling musical experience: expressive fervour, intense artistic commitment, and an intuitive sense for structural logic, combined with superior instrumental skill. By whatever definition of art – be it abstract, sophisticated, virtuosic, emotionally expressive, structurally perfect – Armstrong's music qualified. Like any profoundly creative innovation, 'West End Blues' summarized the past and predicted the future. But such moments in the history of music by their very brilliance also tend to push into the background the many preparatory steps that lead up to the masterpiece. Certainly, 'West End Blues' was not without its antecedents. It did not suddenly spring full-blown from Armstrong's head. Its conception was assembled, bit by bit, over a period of four or five years, and it is extremely instructive to study the process by which Armstrong accumulated his personal style, his 'bag' as the jazz musician would put it.

Armstrong's recording activity in the years 1926–29 was so prolific that the jazz analyst's task is both easy and difficult. On the one hand, the recordings give an exhaustive, almost day-by-day documentation of Louis's progress. On the other hand, he recorded so much, under so many varying circumstances and pressures, recorded such a variety of material with the indiscriminate abandon in which only a genius can afford to indulge, that the task of gaining a comprehensive view, in purely statistical terms, is formidable. The wonder of it all is that Armstrong, irrespective of what or with whom he recorded, maintained an astonishingly high degree of inventiveness and musical integrity, at least until the early 1930s, when he did succumb to the sheer weight of his success and its attendant commercial pressures.

In Oliver's Creole Jazz Band we have already observed the twenty-three-year-old cornet player skilfully treading the fine line between the functional requirements of second cornet to King Oliver and his own burgeoning solo tendencies. In even these earliest Armstrong recordings, tiny phrase-cells began to appear and recur, which seen in retrospect, became the stand-by devices of his solos. This is not to say that they were mere mechanically delivered clichés. They were for the most part original with Louis (a few seem to have come from Bunk Johnson and Oliver), and they were fundamental manifestations of Armstrong's particular brand of lyricism. They became the pivotal points upon which a solo was constructed, and through the years they were expanded in expressive scope and function until entire solos could be constructed from them.[1]

Armstrong's emergence as a soloist coincides with his joining the Fletcher Henderson band in New York. Here Louis could test his creative and instrumental abilities in a less fettered context than that provided by Oliver's orchestra. In fact, Henderson – who was already one of the leaders in setting the post-New Orleans jazz style, through his emphasis on soloists and arrangements, sometimes of a fairly sophisticated nature – hired young Louis specifically to be his featured soloist. This provided the perfect opportunity for Louis to develop his musical identity, to eliminate that which was of secondary quality or imitative, and to refine the personal ingredients of his maturing style.

1. The process of developing a few motivic traits into a personal style can be observed in every great jazz artist, whether it be Armstrong, Parker, Monk, or Lester Young.

In listening to the Henderson band recordings made between October 1924 and October 1925, one is amazed at the disparity in quality between Armstrong's superior work and that of his colleagues in the band. Even Louis's most conservative solos are comparative triumphs of style and conception. This fact is the more impressive when we consider that his colleagues included such men as Coleman Hawkins, Charlie Green, and Buster Bailey, and the entire band consisted of the best jazz musicians money could buy. And yet the level of inspiration jumps when Armstrong enters with a solo and drops when the ensemble returns. This is especially painful when Louis's solos are juxtaposed abruptly with the trumpet lead-work of Elmer Chambers or Howard Scott (as, for example, in 'Mandy, Make Up Your Mind'). The light, airy, open quality of Louis's solos, the elegance of tone, and the easy swing of his beat, freeze suddenly into stiff, stodgy, jerky rhythms and a grey undistinguished tone quality.

What is it that distinguishes Louis from the rest? Why does an Armstrong solo stand out like a mountain peak over its neighbouring foothills? There are four salient features, none of which, to my mind, take priority, but which are instead inseparable elements of a single total conception: (1) his superior choice of notes and the resultant shape of his lines; (2) his incomparable basic quality of tone; (3) his equally incomparable sense of swing, that is, the sureness with which notes are placed in the time continuum and the remarkably varied attack and release properties of his phrasing; (4) and, perhaps his most individual contribution, the subtly varied repertory of vibratos and shakes with which Armstrong colours and embellishes individual notes. The importance of the last fact cannot be emphasized enough, since it gives an Armstrong solo that peculiar sense of inner drive and forward momentum. Armstrong was incapable of not swinging. Even if we isolate a single quarter note from the context of a phrase, we can clearly hear the forward thrust of that note, and in it we recognize the unmistakable Armstrong personality. It is as if such notes wish to burst out of the confines of their rhythmic placement. They wish to do more than a single note can do; they wish to express the exuberance of an entire phrase.

A Vocabulary of Swing Terms

alligator (1) a swing fan who plays no instrument. (2) a musician who frequents places where orchestras are playing.

balloon lungs pertaining to a brass man with plenty of wind or power.

barn a ballroom without acoustics.

barrel-house (1) swing music played in a 'dirty and lowdown' style. (2) a method of playing which permits every man to swing out for himself, allowing great freedom to the soloist.

barrel-house spot a small, intimate night-club where musicians gather.

baton weaver a band leader.

battle axe trumpet.

belly fiddle guitar.

blackstick clarinet.

bleed all choruses no introduction, no verse, no change of key; just choruses.

bogie man a critic.

bounce prominent rhythm.

brass blaster trumpeter or trombonist.

break a hot phrase by a solo instrument, usually occurring in the 7th and 8th and 15th and 16th measures of a hot chorus.

break it down get hot; swing it; go to town.

bring down (1) a mental let-down. (2) music played in such bad taste as to kill the enthusiasm of other players or to disappoint listeners.

canary girl vocalist.

cats (1) musicians in a swing orchestra. (2) people who like swing music.

coffee-and-cake money enough to barely cover expenses.

collegiate a very slow style of playing swing music.

commercial appealing to popular taste.

corn (1) music in bad taste. (2) outmoded music.

corny (1) outmoded style using freakish effects to call attention to one's self. (2) a more precise meaning of corny might be as follows: not stupid, not old-fashioned, but too stupid to know or not caring when one is being old-fashioned.

coupling the other side of a phonograph record.

dime-grind palace a dancehall with 10c-a-dance attraction.

dirty and lowdown pertaining to swing music played in a powerful, primitive style.

disc or **disk** a phonograph record.

Dixieland a style of playing used by orchestras from about 1915 to 1920, recently revived, and in which trumpet, trombone, and clarinet assume great importance as the solo and lead ensemble instruments.

dog house string bass.

drive notes ensemble chords that indicate change of key.

eighty-eight (88) piano.

frisking whiskers (1) tuning up. (2) getting in the mood.

gate word of greeting between musicians.

get off start to swing.

give out play from the heart.

gliss sliding from one note to another.

gobble pipe saxophone.

gob stick clarinet.

going up the Golden Stairs up before the union trial board.

groan box accordion.

growl a lowdown tone played by brass.

guinea's harp guitar.

gut scraper a violinist.

hep-cat (1) a swing devotee who is 'hep' or alert to the most authoritative information. (2) a swing musician.

herring farm a mountain resort.

hide drums.

hot circle or **hot plate** hot phonograph record by a swing band.

hot man a musician who plays swing music well.

ickie one who does not understand swing music.

icky straight and sweet.

ink slinger an arranger.

in the groove (1) playing genuine swing. (2) carried away by the music.

iron horn trumpet, cornet.

jam to improvise against a rhythmic background.

jam session informal gathering at which musicians play for their own pleasure, without leadership or score.

jig a coloured musician.

jitterbug a swing fan (not a true swing music lover) who expresses his fondness for swing music by eccentric dancing or emotional gestures and gyrations.

jive (1) to fool. (2) the language of swing.

jive artist an elegant nothing; a ham who sells out.

Joe Below a musician who pays less than union scale.

joint a small night-spot where musicians play all night for a 'kitty,' or for very meagre wages.

kicking out very free; improvising.

kitty a receptacle into which patrons of a joint toss tips for the musicians.

knocked out so inspired by the music as to be oblivious of everything but the music being played.

know where beat is to understand swing.

lick a hot phrase in rhythm.

licorice stick a clarinet.

lift inspiration.

liver lips strong, tough lips (refers to trumpet players).

lollypop band a sweet band.

long hair a symphony man; one who likes classical music.

meal ticket one's instrument.

Mickey Mouse music a very simple kind of music, using trick musical effect, played by commercial bands. It is kept simple enough so that anyone can understand it, and is held in contempt by swing musicians.

monkey hurdler organist.

mothbox a piano.

mugging heavy swinging with heavy beat.

mugging lightly soft, staccato swinging.

muggles marijuana.

name band a nationally known band, not necessarily good.

nitery a night-club.

old man a band leader.

one-in-a-bar and live forever a bass player.

one-nighter a one-night stand or engagement.

open cold to play an engagement without any advance publicity.

out of this world *par excellence*, incredibly good.

paper man a musician who plays by note only, just as the music is written.

peckhorn a mellophone.

pipe a saxophone.

platter a phonograph record.

plumbing a trumpet.

pop a popular tune.

pops a word of greeting between musicians.

pressing equivalent of 'edition' with reference to phonograph records.

pretzel a French horn.

prima donna a temperamental musician.

quiver bells vibraharp or vibraphone.

rhythm on the bounce see **lift**.

ricky-tick corn.

ride to play effortlessly, but with intensely rhythmic phrasing.

rideman the musician in each section of the orchestra who plays the hot solos.

rock-crusher an accordion.

rooty-toot corn.

rug-cutter a swing dancer.

salon man a legitimate musician.

satchelmouth see **liver lips**.

saw box a cello.

scat singer vocalist who sings rhythmically, but without using accepted English words; most frequent expressions are da, lee, la – and the like.

schmalz, schmaltz sweet, sentimental, straight.

schmooey schmalz.

screwball (1) an eccentric musician. (2) unrestrained playing.

send to arouse the emotions with swing music.

sender (1) a musician capable of playing good hot solos. (2) a performance that pleases swing fans.

sent to be thrilled emotionally by a performance.

shag a form of dance inspired by swing music.

sideman any musician in the band except the leader.

sit in voluntarily to join someone else's band temporarily, playing for the pleasure in it.

skin-beater a drummer.

skins drums.

slip horn a trombone.

slush pump a trombone.

smear to play with glissando.

sock chorus an intensely rhythmic chorus, usually played as the finale.

solid really good.

spook a white musician.

spots notes.

squeaker a violinist.

stick-waver a band leader.

strictly union corny.

sugar band a sweet band.

suitcase drums.

swing the latest name for hot jazz music; more freely used as a term applied to all popular jazz.

swing man a swing musician.

swing out to embellish a melody in rhythm.

tea hound one who smokes marijuana.

tin ear one who does not like swing music.

viper a marijuana smoker.

voodoo boilers drums.

wah-wah a brass effect secured by favouring the bell of a horn with a mute.

warden the secretary of the union.

wax a disc to make a recording.

weed marijuana.

whacky wild, unrestrained, applied to swing music.

wire a radio outlet.

woodpile a xylophone.

woodshed a place for a private rehearsal, often used as a verb, meaning to practise in private.

1939

NORMAN SULLIVAN

Real Musician

Q Are you a musician, Mr Snipeworthy?

A Yes, I'm a gate with a . . .

Q A gate?

A Yeah. I can swing way out wide. I'm a gate with a solid send of jive.

Q A solid send of what?

A Jive. The stuff that's mellow. It sends you right out of this world if you've got an alligator ear.

Q Not so fast, Mr Snipeworthy. I don't understand.

A An alligator ear is what hep-cats have got. It means you know good music, you're not an icky.

Q And why were you speeding on Main Street?

A I was going after a dotmaker to keep a date to make a platter.

Q Stop! Confine yourself to English. What is a dotmaker?

A A guy who writes musical arrangements. We was hurryin' to make a platter – I mean to cut the wax – that is, make a record. Well, just then the solid-beat man . . .

Q Hold on! The solid-beat man?

A The drummer. He looked at his watch and saw we was late. We'd been to a little E-flat meetin' . . .

Q An E-flat meetin'. What's that?

A Just a little unimportant engagement, your honour. Where the band can't ride because it's mostly paper-men.

Q What are they?

A Guys who just play the notes. Some of 'em can play maybe an honest trumpet, but not a go trumpet, see? Not real dixieland.

Q You are a member of a good band?

A Oh sure, we can really send. We really get ridin' and lick our whiskers. We go right into it and jubit.

Q Jubit?

A Yeah, kick it, break it down. We're murderistic. We beat you right down to your socks, send you swing-happy. Your honour, we just dream it up.

Q Well, I'm letting you go, but don't do any more speeding in this town. I realize you probably couldn't read our road signs, written in English. Case dismissed.

1938

Dope

It was that flashy, sawed-off runt of a jockey named Patrick who made a viper out of me after Leon Rappolo failed. Back in the Arrowhead Inn, where I first met Patrick, he told me he was going to New Orleans and would be back one day with some marijuana, real golden-leaf. He asked me did I want some of the stuff, and coming up tough I said sure, bring me some, I'd like to try it. When Patrick marched into the Martinique one night I began to look for the nearest exit, but it was too late. 'Hi ya, boy,' he said with a grin bigger than he was hisself, 'let's you and me go to the can, I got something for you.' That men's room might have been a death house, the way I kept curving away from it, but this muta-mad Tom Thumb latched on to me like a ball-and-chain and steered me straight inside.

As soon as we were alone he pulled out a gang of cigarettes and handed them to me. They were as fat as ordinary cigarettes but were rolled in brown wheatstraw paper. We both lit up and I got halfway through mine, hoping they would break the news to mother gently, before he stopped me. 'Hey,' he said, 'take it easy, kid. You want to knock yourself out?'

I didn't feel a thing and I told him so. 'Do you know one thing?' he said. 'You ain't even smokin' it right. You got to hold that muggle so that it barely touches your lips, see, then draw in air around it. Say *tfff, tfff*, only breathe in when you say it. Then don't blow it out right away, you got to give the stuff a chance.' He had a tricky look in his eye that I didn't go for at all. The last time I saw that kind of look it was on a district attorney's mug, and it caused me a lot of inconvenience.

After I finished the weed I went back to the bandstand. Everything seemed normal and I began to play as usual. I passed a stick of gauge around for the other boys to smoke, and we started a set.

The first thing I noticed was that I began to hear my saxophone as though it was inside my head, but I couldn't hear much of the band in back of me, although I knew they were there. All the other instruments sounded like they were way off in the distance; I got the same sensation you'd get if you stuffed your ears with cotton and talked out loud. Then I began to feel the vibrations of the reed much more pronounced against my lip, and my head buzzed like a loudspeaker. I found I was slurring much better and putting just the right feeling into my phrases – I was really coming on. All the notes came easing out of my horn like they'd already been made up, greased and stuffed into the bell, so all I had to do was blow a little and send them on their way, one right after the other, never missing, never behind time, all without an ounce of effort. The phrases seemed to have more continuity to them and I was sticking to the theme without ever going tangent. I felt I could go on playing for years without running out of ideas and energy. There wasn't any struggle; it was all made-to-order and suddenly there wasn't a sour note or a discord in the world that could bother me. I began to feel very happy and sure of myself. With my loaded horn I could take all the fist-swinging, evil things in the world and bring them together in perfect harmony, spreading peace and joy and relaxation to all the keyed-up and punchy people everywhere. I began to preach my millenniums on my horn, leading all the sinners on to glory.

The other guys in the band were giggling and making cracks, but I couldn't talk with my mouthpiece between my lips, so I closed my eyes and drifted out to the audience with my music. The people were going crazy over the subtle changes in our playing; they couldn't dig what was happening but some kind of electricity was crackling in the air and it made them all glow and jump. Every so often I opened my eyes and found myself looking straight into a girl's face right in front of the bandstand, swinging there like a pendulum. She was an attractive, rose-complexioned chick, with wind-blown honey-coloured hair, and her flushed face was all twisted up with glee. That convulsed face of hers stirred up big waves of laughter in my stomach, waves that kept breaking loose and spreading up to my head, shaking my whole frame. I had to close my eyes fast to keep from exploding with the joy.

It's a funny thing about marijuana – when you first begin smoking it you see things in a wonderful soothing, easygoing new light. All of a sudden the world is stripped of its dirty grey shrouds and becomes one big bellyful of giggles, a spherical laugh, bathed in brilliant, sparkling colours that hit you like a heatwave. Nothing leaves you cold any more; there's a humorous tickle and great meaning in the least little thing, the twitch of somebody's little finger or the click of a beer glass. All your pores open like funnels, your nerve-ends stretch their mouths wide, hungry and thirsty for new sights and sounds and sensations; and every sensation, when it comes, is the most exciting one you've ever had. You can't get enough of anything – you want to gobble up the whole goddamned universe just for an appetizer. Them first kicks are a killer, Jim.

Suppose you're the critical and analytical type, always ripping things to pieces, tearing the covers off and being disgusted by what you find under the sheet. Well, under the influence of muta you don't lose your surgical touch exactly, but you don't come up evil and grimy about it. You still see what you saw before but in a different, more tolerant way, through rose-coloured glasses, and things that would have irritated you before just tickle you. Everything is good for a laugh; the wrinkles get ironed out of your face and you forget what a frown is, you just want to hold on to your belly and roar till the tears come. Some women especially, instead of being nasty and mean just go off bellowing until hysteria comes on. All the larceny kind of dissolves out of them – they relax and grin from ear to ear, and get right on the ground floor with you. Maybe no power on earth can work out a lasting armistice in that eternal battle of the sexes, but muggles are the one thing I know that can even bring about an overnight order to 'Cease firing'.

Tea puts a musician in a real masterly sphere, and that's why so many jazzmen have used it. You look down on the other members of the band like an old mother hen surveying her brood of chicks; if one of them hits a sour note or comes up with a bad modulation, you just smile tolerantly and figure, oh well, he'll learn, it'll be better next time, give the guy a chance. Pretty soon you find yourself helping him out, trying to put him on the right track. The most terrific thing is this, that all the while you're playing, really getting off, your own accompaniment keeps flashing through your head, just like you were a one-man band. You hear the basic tones of the theme and keep up your pattern of improvisation without ever getting tangled up, giving out with a uniform sequence all the way. Nothing can mess up. You hear everything at once and you hear it right. When you get that feeling of power and sureness, you're in a solid groove.

You know how jittery, got-to-be-moving people in the city always get up in the subway train two minutes before they arrive at the station? Their nerves are on edge; they're watching the clock, thinking about schedules, full of that high-powered mile-a-minute jive. Well, when you've picked up on some gauge that clock just stretches its arms, yawns, and dozes off. The whole world slows down and gets drowsy. You wait until the train stops dead and the doors slide open, then you get up and stroll out in slow motion, like a sleep-walker with a long night ahead of him and no appointments to keep. You've got all the time in the world. What's the rush, buddy? Take-it-easy, that's the play, it's bound to sweeten it all the way.

I kept on blowing, with my eyes glued shut, and then a strange thing happened. All of a sudden somebody was screaming in a choked, high-pitched voice, like she was being strangled, 'Stop it, you're killing me! Stop! I can't stand it!' When I opened my eyes it seemed like all the people on the dance floor were melted down into one solid, mesmerized mass; it was an overstuffed sardine-can of an audience, packed in an olive-oil trance. The people were all pasted together, looking up at the band with hypnotic eyes and swaying – at first I saw just a lot of shining eyes bobbing lazily on top of a rolling sea of flesh. But off to one side there was discord, breaking the spell. An entertainer, one of the girls who did a couple of vocals and specialized in a suggestive dance routine, was having a ball all to herself. She had cut loose from her partner and was throwing herself around like a snake with the hives. The rhythm really had this queen; her eyes almost jumped out of their sockets and the cords in her neck stood out stiff and hard like ropes. What she was doing with the rest of her anatomy isn't discussed in mixed company.

'Don't do that!' she yelled. 'Don't do that to me!' When she wasn't shouting her head off she just moaned way down in her soundbox, like an owl gargling.

Then with one flying leap she sailed up on the bandstand, pulled her dress up to her neck, and began to dance. I don't know if dance is the right word for what she did – she didn't move her feet hardly at all, although she moved practically everything else. She went through her whole routine, bumps and grinds and shakes and breaks, making up new twists as she went along, and I mean twists. A bandstand was sure the wrong place to do what she was trying to do that night. All the time she kept screaming, 'Cut it out! It's murder!' but her body wasn't saying so.

It was a frantic scene, like a nightmare walking, and it got wilder because all the excitement made us come on like gangbusters to accompany this palsy-bug routine. Patrick and his gang of vipers were getting their kicks – the gauge they picked up on was really in there, and it had them treetop tall, mellow as a cello. Monkey Pollack stood in the back, moving a little less than a petrified tree, only his big lips shaking like meatballs with the chills, and the Ragtime Cowboy Jew was staring through the clouds of smoke as though he was watching a coyote do a toe-dance. That girl must have been powered with Diesel engines, the way she kept on going. The sweat was rolling down her screwed-up face like her pores were faucets, leaving streaks of mascara in the thick rouge. She would have made a scarecrow do a nip-up and a flip.

The tension kept puffing up like an overstuffed balloon, and finally it broke. There was the sharp crack of pistol shots ringing through the sweat and strain. Fear clamped down over the sea of faces like a mask, and the swaying suddenly stopped.

It was only Mac, our gunplayful cowboy bartender. Whenever he got worked up he would whip out his pistols and fire at the ceiling, catching the breaks in our music. The excitement that night was too much for him and to ease his nerves he was taking potshots at the electric bulbs, with a slap-happy grin on his kisser. Every time he pulled the trigger another Mazda crossed the Great Divide – he may have been punchy but his trigger finger didn't know about it.

The girl collapsed then, as though somebody had yanked the backbone right out of her body. She fell to the floor like a hunk of putty and lay in a heap, quivering and making those funny noises way down in her throat. They carried her upstairs and put her to bed, and I guess she woke up about six weeks later. Music sure hath charms, all right, but what it does to the savage breast isn't always according to the books.

The bandstand was only a foot high but when I went to step down it took me a year to find the floor, it seemed so far away. I was sailing through the clouds, flapping my free-wheeling wings, and leaving the stand was like stepping off into space. Twelve months later my foot struck solid ground with a jolt, but the other one stayed up there on those lovely soft clouds, and I almost fell flat on my face. There was a roar of laughter from Patrick's table and I began to feel self-conscious and nauseous at the same time. I flew to the men's room and got there just in time. Patrick came in and started to laugh at me.

'What's the matter, kid?' he said. 'You not feeling so good?' At that moment I was up in a plane, soaring around the sky, with a buzz-saw in my head. Up and around we went, saying nuts to Newton and all his fancy laws of gravitation, but suddenly we went into a nosedive and I came down to earth, sock. Ouch. My head went spattering off in more directions than a hand grenade. Patrick put a cold towel to my temples and I snapped out of it. After sitting down for a while I was all right.

When I went back to the stand I still heard all my music amplified, as though my ear was built right into the horn. The evening rolled away before I knew it. When the entertainers sang I accompanied them on the piano, and from the way they kept glancing up at me I could tell they felt the harmonies I was inventing behind them without any effort at all. The notes kept sliding out of my horn like bubbles in seltzer water. My control over the vibrations of my tones was perfect, and I got a terrific lift from the richness of the music, the bigness of it. The notes eased out like lava running down a mountain, slow and sure and steaming. It was good.

The Swing Era: Big Bands, Big Money, and the Breakdown of Some Racial Barriers

In the mid-fifties, Nat Hentoff and Nat Shapiro compiled a book, **Hear Me Talkin' to Ya,** *with the subtitle, 'The story of jazz by the men who made it'. The reminiscence in this extract ranges from Benny Goodman forgetting the names of the players in his own band, to Roy Eldridge being refused entry to a club where he was actually top of the bill.*

BENNY GOODMAN: When the band started, we didn't have any special ambition or goal, and we didn't know what it was exactly that made the band sound the way it did. But it was work, and detail – and arrangements. Why, do you know, when a new arrangement would come in, it would be an occasion. We couldn't wait to get started on it, and we'd work for three or four hours on it right away. And *know* if it wasn't ready. We'd play it for a few nights before letting it go over the air, for instance. When a new arrangement by 'Smack' or Jimmy Mundy would come in, we'd work on it, and if we liked it, you'd be sure to hear some of the guys say, 'C'mon, let's play it again.'

When we started the band, the only purpose we had was to play music, and Gene Krupa, Teddy, Hampton, Jess, Hymie, and the rest, they had a purpose. It was their life, it was important to them.

A lot of guys today, they don't know what they want, do they? Maybe I don't either. But something happens when you find out that what you're doing is no longer music – that it's become entertainment. It's a subtle thing and affects what you're playing. Your whole attitude changes.

As far as I'm concerned, the most important or the most exciting thing that ever happened with the band was when we opened at the Palomar in Los Angeles. (When was it – 1935?) We had just laid a big egg in Denver and were pretty low. And we figured that the further west we went, the worse it would get. Before we hit LA we played a few one-nighters, one in San Francisco that wasn't too bad. When we opened at the Palomar we had a 'what've we got to lose' attitude and decided to let loose and shoot the works with our best things like 'Sugar Foot Stomp', 'Sometimes I'm Happy', and others. Actually though, we was almost scared to play.

From the moment I kicked them off, the boys dug in with some of the best playing I'd heard since we left New York. I don't know what it was, but the crowd went wild, and then – boom!

That was the real beginning.

DICK CLARK: We were all sort of scared and worried until that night at the Palomar, and never really got going until that night. Then it happened, and it's great to feel that I was there and had a part in it. Though now I'm glad to be settled down, in radio and recording work, I can thank Benny for that too.

GENE KRUPA: Had Benny thrown in the towel before his first great triumphs at the Palomar in Los Angeles and the Congress in Chicago, there's little doubt but what many of us who have enjoyed success, prominence, and considerable financial reward since the late 1930s would have ever attained these heights.

Benny built himself a band playing musicians' music, but didn't shoot over the heads of the public. It took the people time, but once they grasped the Goodman musical sermon, they easily understood, accepted, and followed. Being a part of this band was the fulfilment of a dream for any young musician. It allowed us to play the way we honestly wanted to play, with good pay and before huge, appreciative audiences. In the days before the Goodman era, we played that way, too, but in smaller bands with no similar success, or in sessions held in empty halls with no one to appreciate our efforts but the fellows playing the other instruments.

For all that Benny did for music, for jazz, for musicians, and for me, I, for one, doff my cap in a salute of sincere appreciation.

BENNY GOODMAN: By the time we finished our job in *The Big Broadcast of 1937*, which was made in summer of 1936, we had a pretty good idea that the public for real jazz was a big one, and growing all the time. Even when we opened at the Pennsylvania, some of the people around the hotel were sceptical, saying the band was too loud. After the band was set in the room and the crowds started to come and keep on coming, we didn't hear much more comment on the band being loud. But I don't think that any of us realized how strong a hold it had on the youngsters until a certain day in March 1937.

We had undertaken a double at the Paramount Theatre in New York in addition to playing our job at the Pennsylvania, with no expectation that we would do more than fair business. After all, our only previous theatre bookings had been something less than sensational. So when we arrived at the theatre for an early morning rehearsal before the first show and found a couple of hundred kids lined up in front of the box office at about 7 a.m., we couldn't help feeling that every one of our most loyal supporters in the five boroughs was already on hand.

However, this wasn't a patch on what happened even before we got on stage. All through the showing of the picture, the folks backstage said there were noises and whistling coming through from the house as Claudette Colbert did her stuff in *Maid of Salem*. The theatre was completely full an hour before we were supposed to go on, and when we finally came up on the rising platform, the noise sounded like Times Square on New Year's Eve. That reception topped anything we had known up to that time, and because we felt it was spontaneous and genuine, we got a tremendous kick out of it.

However, we didn't know half the story until we got off the stage and were back in our dressing-rooms. It seems that my manager, Willard Alexander, was sitting in the mezzanine with Bob Weitman, the manager of the Paramount. They got the same thrill out of this enthusiasm that we did, up to the point where a couple of youngsters got up and started to shag in the aisles. Then a few more started to climb over the rail towards the orchestra, and Bob jumped up and rushed out, yelling, 'Somebody's going to get hurt there any minute. There'll be a panic.'

He ran down the steps to the back of the orchestra, and as soon as the ushers saw him they snapped to attention and started saluting.

'The hell with that,' he shouted. 'Get down there and stop those kids from killing themselves!'

As he went from aisle to aisle to get the ushers organized, he had to go through this same routine of being saluted by each one before he could get things under control.

By three o'clock in the afternoon, eleven thousand five hundred people had paid their way into the theatre, and the total for the first day's attendance was twenty-two thousand. Another thing about that first day which caused talk around the theatre was this: The total for the day's sale at the candy counter was nine hundred dollars – which is some kind of a record, too.

It was during this engagement that we found out what this particular sort of success means. We played five shows a day at the Paramount, beginning around ten-thirty in the morning, and in between the two evening shows, we did our usual stint at the Pennsylvania, going back there after the last show (about ten-thirty) to finish up the dance session, until 2 a.m. Then, of course, there was the radio commercial once a week, with the special rehearsals that go with it. There was also the problem of moving the stuff up to the studio, which in our case was the CBS Radio Theatre at Broadway and 53rd Street. Just how we managed to stand up under that grind, I don't know – except that once you get into that groove, you just keep on going.

Right after this we got the first taste of what comes with being a really successful band. I didn't have any more love for one-nighters than I had before, but that summer we filled a schedule of bookings that lasted almost two months, and we never played the same town twice. As a matter of fact, we finished up with a string of thirty consecutive dates on as many nights, in the middle of a broiling Midwest July.

Travelling with a band on tour is the next thing I can think of to moving a circus. There's the music to be taken care of, the instruments to be checked, the trunks and other baggage to keep in line, all of which was in the care of a general handyman, porter, and looker-outer. In our organization he was an efficient fellow by the name of Peewee Monte, who had made a career out of nursing bands. Later it was Popsie Randolph.

But there also had to be someone on hand to manage the actual work of making hotel arrangements for the men, taking care of the transportation, ironing out the difficulties that come with the promoters in the various halls and pavilions that we played, acting as contact man for the press, and generally doing all the things that I couldn't possibly do myself.

On a typical one-nighter around the New York territory, we travelled in a Greyhound bus that stayed with us throughout the entire tour. Generally it rolled up to the place late in the afternoon and if we hadn't been there before, we had to find out about the P.A. (the public address system) and hook up the one we carried along, if the permanent installation wasn't any good. Then the stands had to be set up and the music laid out – and in most places, some kind of a rope or a guard-rail put around the stand so that we could work without stepping on the fingers of the kids that hung around the band.

By this time, Hymie Schertzer's nose for corn-beef had led him, without fail, to the best place in town for his favourite food, and a few of the boys went along with him. The rest of us picked out some likely-looking place for the kind of food we wanted, and got through with the meal just in time to change our clothes and get on the bandstand. The crowd started coming in, the requests started piling up, and another job was under way.

We played right through until about one o'clock, with the trio and quartet coming out for a session around midnight. What happened after that depended on the distance to the next booking. If the jump was a fairly short one, say two hundred miles or so, we spent the night at a hotel in the same town, and made the trip the following day. If it was closer to three hundred or anything up to four hundred, we piled into the bus when the job was finished, and made the jump at night, when we could make better time, and allow for any incidents that might come up on the trip. That brought us into the next town around nine or ten o'clock in the morning – and after eight hours bumping around in a bus, trying to catch a few winks of sleep, the only thing you wanted to do was crawl into bed at the hotel, and get some sleep before it was time to go to work again. There are more towns in America that I have only seen after dark than I would care to think about.

It was while we were out on the Coast that we engaged Martha Tilton. After Helen Ward left us, we had been trying out various girl singers, some of them well known, others that weren't. But none of them could sing with the band like Helen did, and it wasn't until we heard Martha that we found what we were looking for. Martha was a hard worker and improved consistently when she was with us, and really had a personality that everybody liked.

Of course, when Teddy Wilson joined us and later, Lionel Hampton, there was talk about the problems of presenting a band with a mixed group like the trio and the quartet. However, I found few places where the crowds were not wonderfully responsive to Lionel and Teddy. Most of the people who listened to us appreciated what swell musicians these boys are, and recognized that what they did was something that was just unique, that nobody played piano or vibes just the way they did.

About the only unpleasantness that we ever had in this connection happened in this same summer of 1937. It was after we finished *Hollywood Hotel* and were working our way back east by way of the southern route, stopping off for a couple of weeks to play a big fair in the south-west. We opened to a fine crowd, and through the first day or two everything was swell.

But we noticed about the second day, that a couple of city police on duty around the place didn't like the attention that Lionel and Teddy were getting. They didn't say anything, but every time one of the kids came up and asked either of them for an autograph (naturally calling them 'Mr Hampton' or 'Mr Wilson') they'd act nasty, because it seems that isn't done in their circles.

On the third night, after we had finished a session with the quartet, one of the guests thought he'd express his appreciation by sending some champagne back to Lionel. As he got to the stage door, one of these officers stopped him and said, 'Where you goin' with that?'

The waiter answered, 'It's for Mr Hampton.'

'The hell with that stuff,' this guy yelled, and flung out his arm, knocking the tray, glasses, ice, and champagne out of the waiter's hand.

Well, we were up against it. We didn't want to complain because the fellow might have gotten some of his boyfriends together and really made trouble for us – and at the same time, we couldn't stand for any jive like this.

Luckily, one of the boys was friendly with a local police official (who happened to be a jazz fan) and he went to him confidentially that night and told him what was happening. He came right back with Leonard, walked up to this officer (who knew well enough who he was, because he had made a name for himself all over the south-west by capturing Bonny Parker and Pretty-boy Floyd), grabbed him by the shoulder, and said, 'Get the hell off these grounds and stay off. And if any of your pals have an idea to start trouble here, I'll see to it that you're kicked off the force.'

Jumping around the way we did, playing for every kind of audience in the most varied places, we got a reaction that represented a pretty good cross-section of opinion. I know that for a lot of people that came to hear us, the quartet was a special kick – and when we played, nobody cared much what colours or races were represented just so long as we played good music. That's the way it should be.

I know, for example, that our 1938 concert in Carnegie Hall would have lost a lot if we didn't have the cooperation of fellows like Johnny Hodges, who is by far the greatest man on alto sax that I ever heard, or Harry Carney, who is just about the same on baritone, or Cootie Williams, whose trumpet playing is like nobody else's. Then in the jam session, we had such other great coloured players as Lester Young, who is one of my favourite musicians, that swell guitar player, Freddie Greene, Count Basie on piano, and Buck Clayton to play his own particular kind of trumpet, with Walter Page doing wonderful things on bass.

Actually that jam session was a real thrill – not the way it worked out in the concert unfortunately, because it is always a difficult thing to know how such a set-up will turn out on any particular occasion – but when the boys first came together, just to try things out, a few days before. There was Count, with his hat on the back of his head, picking notes at the piano; Johnny Hodges (in a sweater, I think); bashful Harry Carney, hiding behind his baritone; and all the rest, sitting down with Gene, Harry James, and Vernon Brown (who plays fine hot trombone) from my band. I went down in the Hall to get an idea of how it sounded, but before they had done more than five or six choruses on 'Honeysuckle Rose', the thing was jumping so much that I had to rush up and get in on it. We probably would have kept on playing all night if there hadn't been jobs waiting for us.

That night at Carnegie was a great experience, because it represented something – a group of musicians going on that stage and playing tunes by Gershwin and Berlin and Kern in arrangements by Fletcher and Edgar Sampson, getting up and playing the choruses the way they wanted to, each of them just being himself – and holding the attention of all those people for two hours and a half.

One thing I found out is that there wasn't much difference in the people you played for, east or west. They wanted to hear the same tunes when they were new, or the same standbys they'd heard on the air, or the things we'd made records of. 'Sing Sing Sing' (which we started doing back at the Palomar on our second trip there in 1936) was still a big thing, and no one-nighter was complete without it . . . they wanted 'Big John Special', 'One O'clock Jump', 'King Porter', 'Blue Skies', or the quartet doing 'I Got Rhythm', and, of course, 'Don't Be That Way'.

Pretty soon, people and places became pretty much a blur. You start thinking (if you ever get a chance to) – was it in Cincinnati that Bud Freeman played those three terrific choruses on the 'Yam', each one better than the last? Was it in Scranton that Lionel sat in on 'Sing Sing Sing' and gave that tough old set-up the workout of its life, or was it in Buffalo? Was it in Detroit that we first started doing these descending trumpet runs in the last chorus of 'One O'clock Jump' (so that everybody started referring to it as 'Two O'clock Jump') or was it in Philadelphia?

JOHNNY GUARNIERI: I'm probably the best guy to tell about those swing days because I'm probably the only one who was ever sober. When I joined Benny Goodman, it was like a fulfilment of a beautiful dream for me. It was what I had lived and worked for, and, because I was a sober individual and wasn't involved in rivalries, drinking, narcotics, money problems, and such, like some of the other musicians, I enjoyed every minute of it. It was all very vital and absorbing, including the travelling. In fact, I can say that I've had more fun than anybody in this business.

When I first joined Benny, he called me 'Fletcher' for three months before he could remember my name. And then he told me I was the worst piano player he'd had since Frankie Froeba. He didn't like my so-called 'imitating' other pianists. I'll tell you, though, both Lionel Hampton and Charlie Christian would tell me, 'Don't let Benny scare you, you're a *piano player*, Johnny – and you *swing*.' As a matter of fact, Lionel and Charlie were the only two guys in the band who would talk to me when I joined. All the other guys were 'big shots' and I wasn't.

BENNY GOODMAN: I suppose I do have a hard time remembering names. There wasn't much of that trouble with the first bands I had though – all *those* guys were characters, weren't they? Bunny Berigan, Harry James, Jess Stacy, Harry Goodman, and the rest. But, later on, I suppose it might take me two months to learn a new man's name. You might say that a guy had to prove himself – or *make* a name for himself before I'd know who he was.

POPSIE RANDOLPH: Benny wanted what he wanted, that's all. If a guy worked for him, he had to do the job right. Sure, he was changeable all right, like the weather – a little fickle you might say. But man, he was a perfectionist. A guy would come into the band one day and two days later Benny'd say he was no good – and out he'd go.

But he was real good to the boys, and me, too. I was his band-boy from 1941 to 1947, only in 1945 he made me road manager when he re-formed the last band.

When a guy got in trouble or something, Benny'd take an interest and help out with emergency money. He'd always lend the guys money and things like that. Sure, some of the guys didn't appreciate it – said he was buttin' in, but I don't know of another leader in the business who took as much interest in the men as Benny – except Woody, maybe.

I remember once he sent me over to Mark Cross to buy the guys wallets for Christmas, and he put a fifty-dollar bill in each. And on Christmas Day, I was feelin kinda low 'cause I didn't get one. Benny and I were in Philly and we were ridin' back to the hotel on the trolley car when he says to me, 'You got my wallet, Pops?' I had a couple of blank cheques with me and he wrote me a cheque for five hundred dollars. He told me, 'Now, that's better'n a wallet, isn't it?'

One thing he didn't tolerate and that was drinking – or for that matter, any of the vices. Benny didn't go for that playboy style.

The guys that Benny liked a lot and talked about were Jess Stacy, Mel Powell, Teddy Wilson, Harry James, Ziggy Elman, Manny Klein, Vernon Brown, in fact, all the guys from his early bands. They're his idols for playin'. He also respected people like Basie, Teagarden, Artie Shaw, Tommy Dorsey, for their playin' too.

He thought a lot of Gene Krupa too. I wasn't with Benny when Gene was with him originally, but right after he got out of jail for that dope thing, he came up to the Paramount where we were playin' and was in the dressing-room wearing dark glasses. Benny says to me, 'Popsie, we're gonna have Gene in the band.' We went on a tour of army camps after that. In the band were Teddy Wilson and Red Norvo. There were lots of kicks.

JOHNNY GUARNIERI: I guess I could have been a big name with Benny if I played up to him, but after a while I left him to join Artie Shaw, went back to Benny, and then back to Shaw again. It was with Artie Shaw that I played harpsichord on those Gramercy Five records. All Artie ever wanted was for you to tell him how good he was, or more, how much better he was than Benny. He lived to cut Benny and Benny lived to cut him. But they were both great musicians. Each was great in his own style.

ARTIE SHAW: By the time we got to New York and the Lincoln Hotel, our opening night there was like a madhouse. From then on I couldn't think straight. My life wasn't my own. *Life* magazine, autograph hunters, everything all at once, plus all kinds of disagreeable pressures being put on me.

The bigger our success, the more dissatisfaction there seemed to be in the band. Billie Holiday, who had gotten along fine with Helen Forrest, began to resent her. Georgie Auld came in for a hundred and twenty-five dollars while the rest of the band, getting scale, objected. Buddy Rich joined us and the older guys didn't like it when he got so much applause. Instead of a bunch of guys that were happy to be struggling towards a common objective, we became a bunch of cliques, and I became gradually estranged from the men.

When we went into the Strand Theatre, it was even worse. People jumping up on the stage, cops, riots – things that were almost impossible to live through. I was making more money than I had ever thought existed, and I guess I got carried away by it.

BUD FREEMAN: The big bands *needed* individualists – they *needed* stars. Certainly, leaders might have had trouble with some of us, but we believed what we were doing, we grew up with jazz, felt strongly about our music, and each of us developed in his own way, becoming both distinct individuals and *soloists*. We weren't just another sideman!

Back in the twenties, it was almost unheard of for a musician to sit in, let alone work with just any band. We had to like the music the band was playing. Nowadays, in order to make a living, a musician may have to do anything to keep working.

Take Benny Goodman. He needed stars, didn't he? After all, although he's a great performer, he isn't creative and I don't think he would have been as important without all of those wonderful individual musicians.

Of all the big bands I played with, I suppose I enjoyed being with Tommy Dorsey most. Tommy allowed me more freedom, more opportunity to play. And the same went for Dave Tough. I think he was happier with Dorsey than anywhere else too.

As for Bunny Berigan, who was also with Tommy in those days, well, Bunny was a true musician, but he just hated the music business. Bunny loved music, he loved people, but you have to be tough to get along in the band business. When he had his own band, he didn't want to do what he had to do.

RAY CONNIFF: Yeah, it was quite an experience working with the Berigan band. It was a tight little band, just like a family of bad little boys, with Bunny the worst of all. We were all friends. In fact, Bunny wouldn't hire anybody he didn't like. And all of us would take turns rooming with him. Oh, it was a mad ball. You should've see those hotel rooms! Ribs, booze, and women all over the place.

Bunny didn't take much interest in arrangements and business and things like that. In fact, he wasn't much of a leader type. But as a musician, we all idolized him. Even when he was drunk, he'd blow good. And when he was sober – man! Whenever we'd play the Savoy up in Harlem, if we'd walk along the streets or go into a rib joint they would say, 'Hey, Pops, them's Bunny boys.' They loved him up there. He had that beat.

FERDINAND ARBELO: When you talk about bands that could swing, don't forget the Lunceford band! I was with them for three or four years, and I'm telling you that that was one swinging band! There were times when we played in some places and even the walls would shake.

Willie Smith was playin' on alto; Trummy Young, lead trombone; Sy Oliver as trumpet and (arrangin'); and Jimmy Crawford on drums. As for Jimmie Lunceford, he was out of Memphis and a wonderful musician who knew every corner of music. He knew what the people liked.

GENE SEDRIC: One-nighters were very rough. Many times there were halls with no windows and inside there were thousands of people shouting and fighting. And it was very rough when you had to go over mountains to make another town and you'd skid on ice. Man, there were some long hauls between states.

Many times we'd get into town, check into a hotel, and we'd actually hear them planning how they were going to start the fights and shootings where we were going to play that night.

There were some of those towns that had special prices just for the bands that came through, that were touring. When they knew we were coming, the prices would be higher by twice as much. Many times we'd get in earlier though, before they had a chance to change the signs.

EDMOND HALL: This incident will give you some idea of how terrible things were touring in the South. . . . This happened in 1934 or 1935 in Little Rock, Arkansas. I was in the Claude Hopkins band. We had been touring the country for about four months. On this Saturday night we were supposed to have the night off, but the booking agent had put us in a place ten miles out of town. The next night we were supposed to play a dance in Little Rock itself and we played on this Saturday night until about twelve-fifteen. We stopped because of the 'blue law'. But the man who ran the place said, 'We don't close until three,' and pulled out a gun and made us play until three. Some of the guys had gotten away, so not all of us were stuck there. The way some of us had gotten away was that the Casa Loma band had taken our place at Roseland and also had our radio wire and the guys who didn't have to take time to pack up their instruments had gone out to the cars to hear how the Casa Loma band was making out. Well, the ones that escaped called our road manager and told him what was happening. He called the sheriff and the sheriff said, 'The best way is the easiest way. Tell them to keep on playing.'

The farthest south we played with Claude Hopkins was Birmingham, Alabama. When we played there they had a rope right down the middle of the floor. There was white on one side and coloured on the other.

The Claude Hopkins band had a big drawing power. It drew as well as any band on the road at that time. There were crowds wherever we used to go. One of the big factors in its success was Orlando Robeson. He was a romantic ballad singer. He sang 'Trees' and songs like that.

MILT HINTON: The one-night scene in the South was just simply terrible. I had a better deal with Cab Calloway because we always travelled first-class. Cab would always retain a Pullman. We'd pull into one of those southern towns and we slept in. But we had meals in holes and things. Cab had it easier because of his great popularity, so when you travelled with his band you were as comfortable as a member of a Negro band could be in the South.

I remember Longview, Texas. They had recently struck oil there. Before that they were all poor people, accustomed to nothing. Drought, strikes, and all, and the oil had been seeping through the land, and they had been selling the land cheap because the oil had been making the cattle sick. But when they found out it was oil many of them became rich overnight. They had no education so they were berserk with the money. They had big riotous parties and hired large bands. At those dances the prejudice was terrible. Some of them would say, 'I'd pay a three-hundred-dollar fine just to hit one of those boys.' Invariably they would begin to fight. The promoter would say, 'Come on downstairs,' and he'd put us in a room to keep the people from getting at us. The dance would always end up in a fight. When they didn't see us they'd fight amongst themselves. I can tell you I was scared. Like when we were at a road-house. There was no way for us to get out. Cab eventually stopped going through the South because he had enough work without it.

I remember the dances at Fort Lauderdale, Florida. There were some northern people there on vacation and some northern musicians whom we used to know when we played at the Cotton Club. Both the people who used to know us from the Cotton Club where we were famous and those northern white musicians would talk to us between sets. But the southern people would resent it. Sometimes it would be so bad at intermission we couldn't get off the stand for a drink of water unless we had a police escort. I remember it. There were two police in front and two behind, and we had to walk through the dancehall that way just to get a drink of water. And you know they would poke at us through the police! So you can see we didn't feel like playing much. And Cab was less likely to knock himself out entertaining people like that. After intermission we always had a tough time because the drinking had started and the insults got worse.

Then there was Greenfield, Mississippi. One of the valets in the band was a young kid who had just gotten back from overseas where he'd been decorated. This was the late forties. And among the other things he would do was to sell programmes at intermission. There was a police officer who asked him a question, and Paul answered 'Yes' without putting 'Sir' on it. This was a real muscle-bound cop. He swung at Paul but Paul with all his military training and GI know-how just kept ducking away from him. So this cop couldn't hit him. The cop pulled his gun on Paul and dared him to duck. The crowd was screaming. The dancehall parted, and just Paul and the cop were standing and everybody fell to the floor. This officer became ashamed of himself. The band had stopped playing; the girl singer, Mary Louise Jones, screamed; and that's what alerted the audience to fall to the floor so the cop became aware of everybody looking on and became ashamed of himself and said, 'Go on with the dance.' Our road manager then was Hugh Wright. He had formerly been a lieutenant-colonel in the Army. He was about fifty-five or sixty, straight military bearing, pretty manly. He went over to the officer to try to straighten it out. The guy said to keep out of it and get out of town.

Eventually, Cab had to go back down South again when the band business was real bad. The guys in the other bands who had to go through the South had the same and similar experiences. We discussed them amongst each other sometimes. The same towns, the same officers. I'm telling you, some of those people came and paid their money just to heckle the Negro bands, like some people like to tease an animal, and we had no recourse. Did you know that in Miami, Florida, where we used to play after nine o'clock at night, Negroes had to be off the streets unless they had a note saying something like: 'This boy works for me'? There were white musicians we knew from New York playing there. They had come to the dance and said, 'Let's have a session afterwards.' We could have gone to the Negro section for a session, but elsewhere it would be impossible because if the police saw them they would be in trouble too.

We never had trouble with southern musicians – they didn't fraternize with us much but they would come to listen and to learn. They enjoyed talking music with us and they weren't insulting. Most of them, however, didn't choose our company after the dances, but a few did. Of course, the white northern guys were there just for the session, and they were the same guys we used to hang out with on 52nd Street.

ROY ELDRIDGE: One thing you can be sure of, as long as I'm in America, I'll never in my life work with a white band again! It goes all the way back to when I joined Gene Krupa's band. Until that time no coloured musician had worked with a white band except as a separate attraction, like Teddy and Lionel with Benny Goodman.

That was how I worked with Gene at first; I wasn't treated as a full member of the band. But very soon I started sharing Shorty Sherock's book, and when he left the band, I took over. It killed me to be accepted as a regular member of the band. But I knew I'd have to be awful cool; I knew all eyes were on me to see if I'd make time or do anything wrong.

All the guys in the band were nice, and Gene was especially wonderful. That was at the Pennsylvania Hotel. Then we headed west for some one-nighters, winding up in California. That was when the trouble began.

We arrived in one town and the rest of the band checks in. I can't get into their hotel, so I keep my bags and start riding around looking for another place, where someone's supposed to have made a reservation for me. I get there and move all my bags in. Naturally, since we're going to be out on the Coast several months, I have a heavy load, at least a dozen pieces of baggage.

Then the clerk, when he sees that I'm the Mr Eldridge the reservation was made for, suddenly discovers that one of their regular tenants just arrived and took the last available room. I lug that baggage back into the street and start looking around again.

By the time that kind of thing has happened night after night, it begins to work on my mind; I can't think right, can't play right. When we finally got to the Palladium in Hollywood, I had to watch who I could sit at the tables with. If they were movie stars who wanted me to come over, that was all right; if they were just the jitterbugs, no dice. And all the time the bouncer with his eye on me, just watching for a chance.

On top of that, I had to live way out in Los Angeles, while the rest of the guys stayed in Hollywood. It was a lonely life; I'd never been that far away from home before, and I didn't know anybody. I got to brooding.

Then it happened. One night the tension got so bad I flipped. I could feel it right up to my neck while I was playing 'Rockin' Chair' I started trembling, ran off the stand, and threw up. They carried me to the doctor's. I had a hundred-and-five fever; my nerves were shot.

When I went back a few nights later I heard that people were asking for their money back because they couldn't hear 'Let Me Off Uptown'. This time they let me sit at the bar.

Later on, when I was with Artie Shaw, I went to a place where we were supposed to play a dance and they wouldn't even let me in the place. 'This is a white dance,' they said, and there was my name right outside, Roy 'Little Jazz' Eldridge, and I told them who I was.

When I finally did get in, I played that first set, trying to keep from crying. By the time I got through the set, the tears were rolling down my cheeks. I don't know how I made it. I went up to a dressing-room and stood in a corner crying and saying to myself why the hell did I come out here again when I knew what would happen. Artie came in and he was real great. He made the guy apologize that wouldn't let me in, and got him fired.

Man, when you're on the stage, you're great, but as soon as you come off, you're nothing. It's not worth the glory, not worth the money, not worth anything. Never again!

LENA HORNE: The statement by Roy Eldridge that he will never again work with a white band made me very unhappy. I love Roy. He is a great musician and one of my best friends. I don't want him or anyone else to feel as bitter as he evidently did when he made that statement.

I hope others will not be influenced by his decision, if he really meant what he said, because we can't lick a problem by running away from it.

We've all had to face very difficult situations. Many times when I was singing with Charlie Barnet I wanted to quit for the same reasons Roy mentions. I might have, too, had it not been for the wonderful support I always got in every way from Charlie and the boys in the band. And I'll never forget that it was Charlie who took a chance to give me my first real break.

Thanks to pioneers like Charlie, Benny Goodman, Gene Krupa, Tommy Dorsey, Red Norvo, and others not so well known, all of whom knew they were letting themselves in for some real head-aches, too, the greatest strides have been made in breaking down age-old prejudices.

If we all took Roy's attitude, we would be letting those fellows down. I'm sure Roy will snap out of it when he thinks this over.

JO JONES: Twenty and twenty-five years ago conditions were involved with far more ignorant attitudes, social conditions that is. You can just imagine how many fine musicians the world lost because of these ignorant attitudes and prejudices. In 1940, I remember when I played a date at Harvard telling the guys there that things were changing and were going to change in the South, and they didn't believe it. But then in 1948 I played in Florida with Lena Horne and I remember after the set another guy in the band and I stopped at the bar to have a drink and the guy, while we were being served our drink at the bar, said to me, 'This is Florida?' And yet I remember when I couldn't cross the tracks in Florida.

I remember, years ago, a little white boy sitting in a coloured club, and the police caught him and whipped him. But things change.

BUSTER BAILEY: One thing I'm happy to see is the integration that's been happening among musicians. And I've been watching music a long time. I've been playing since I was eleven. Years ago, if it had been like this when I came up I would be able to play with some symphony orchestra. I would have had more of an incentive to study because there would have been more of a prospect of my making a living the way I wanted to. Sure, we played concerts and overtures and numbers like that in the theatres, but when I started you couldn't even think, if you were a Negro, of making symphony orchestras. So the highest I got was theatres. In later years, I would get a chance to do a few things, like I made some records for Victor with the New Friends of Music – a string group. And they were good records. But as for making a career out of classical music, it was too late then. I have played with NBC and CBS symphony orchestras, and I could have made a career in symphony music like I said. We did have a mixed group going a few years ago, with Everett Lee conducting. It was called the Cosmopolitan Symphony, and we gave quite a few concerts at Town Hall. I guess you could say the only regret I have is that I didn't have a chance to make it in symphony music.

When I was starting up, they used to say the two races couldn't get along playing. They used to say stuff like they were afraid we'd go after their women. All that's been proved false, and everything else on that prejudice kick has been proved false.

Picking up Money

By the time Mom and I had got together and found us a place of our own in Harlem the depression was on. At least, so we heard tell. A depression was nothing new to us, we'd always had it. The only thing new about it was the bread lines. And they were about the only thing we missed.

We moved into an apartment on 139th Street, and not long after, for the first time since I could remember, Mom was too sick to make Mass on Sunday. For her, that was really sick. Give her coffee every morning and Mass every Sunday, and she thought she could go on working forever. But she had to quit working out as a maid. She couldn't even walk, her stomach was so shot. She just had to stay put in bed.

What little money we had saved started running out and she was getting panicky. She had worked for most of her life, and it was beginning to tell on her. For almost half of that time she had been grieving over Pop. This didn't help any.

I had decided I was through turning tricks as a call-girl. But I had also decided I wasn't going to be anybody's damn maid. The rent always seemed to be due, and it took some scuffling to keep from breaking my vows.

About that time Fletcher Henderson's band was working downtown at the Roseland Ballroom. It was the first Negro band to work there, and Pop Holiday was with them on the guitar. Sick as she was, Mom was too proud to turn to Pop and ask his help with the rent money. But not me.

I used to go right down there and haunt him. Pop was in his early thirties then, but he didn't want anyone to guess it – especially the young chicks who used to hang around the entrance waiting for the musicians.

I was around fifteen then, but I looked plenty old enough to vote. I used to wait for him down in the hallway. I'd try to catch his eye and call out to him, 'Hey, Daddy.' I soon found out just waving at him would make him feel like forty-five, and he didn't like that. He used to plead with me.

'Please,' he'd say, 'whatever you do, don't call me Daddy in front of these people.'

'I'm going to call you Daddy all night unless you give me some damn money for rent,' I'd tell him. That would do it.

I'd take the money home to Mom, proud as all get out. But I couldn't hurt her feelings by telling her where it came from. If she kept worrying me about it, I'd finally tell her I stole it. Then we'd have a fight and she'd tell me I was going to end up in jail again.

One day when the rent was overdue, she got a notice that the law was going to put us out on the street. It was in the dead cold of winter and she couldn't even walk.

I didn't know they did things like that up North. Bad as it was down South, they never put you out on the street. When we were due to get set out on the street the next morning, I told Mom I would steal or murder or do anything before I'd let them pull that. It was cold as all hell that night, and I walked out without any kind of coat.

I walked down 7th Avenue from 139th Street to 133rd Street, busting in every joint trying to find a job. In those days 133rd Street was the real swing street, like 52nd Street later tried to be. It was jumping with after-hours spots, regular-hour joints, restaurants, cafés, a dozen to a block.

Finally, when I got to Pod's and Jerry's, I was desperate. I went in and asked for the boss. I think I talked to Jerry. I told him I was a dancer and wanted to try out. I knew exactly two steps, the time step and the crossover. I didn't even know the word 'audition' existed, but that was what I wanted.

So Jerry sent me over to the piano player and told me to dance. I started, and it was pitiful. I did my two steps over and over until he barked at me and told me to quit wasting his time.

They were going to throw me out on my ear, but I kept begging for the job. Finally the piano player took pity on me. He squashed out his cigarette, looked up at me, and said, 'Girl, can you sing?'

I said, 'Sure I can sing, what good is that?' I had been singing all my life, but I enjoyed it too much to think I could make any real money at it. Besides, those were the days of the Cotton Club and all those glamour pusses who didn't do nothing but look pretty, shake a little, and take money off tables.

I thought that was the only way to make money, and I needed forty-five bucks by morning to keep Mom from getting set out in the street. Singers were never heard of then, unless it was Paul Robeson, Julian Bledsoe, or someone legit like that.

So I asked him to play 'Trav'lin' All Alone'. That came closer than anything to the way I felt. And some part of it must have come across. The whole joint quieted down. If someone had dropped a pin, it would have sounded like a bomb. When I finished, everybody in the joint was crying in their beer, and I picked thirty-eight bucks up off the floor. When I left the joint that night I split with the piano player and still took home fifty-seven dollars.

I went out and bought a whole chicken and some baked beans – Mom loved baked beans – and raced up 7th Avenue to the house. When I showed Mom the money for the rent and told her I had a regular job singing for eighteen dollars a week, she could hardly believe it.

As soon as she could get out of bed she came down to see for herself and became my biggest booster. In those days they had five or six singers in the clubs and they called them 'ups'. One girl would be 'up' and she would go from table to table singing. Then the next one would be 'up' and she'd take over. I was an 'up' from midnight every night until the tips started thinning out, maybe around three o'clock the next morning.

In those days, too, all the girls took money off the tables, but I broke that up. With the first loot I got me a pair of fancy drawers with little rhinestones on them. But I didn't like the idea of showing my body. There was nothing wrong with my body, I just didn't like the idea. When the time came to take those bills off the table, I was always messing up.

One night a millionaire came in the joint and put out a twenty-dollar bill on the table. I wanted that twenty-dollar bill so bad. I really tried, but I dropped it so many times he got disgusted and said, 'Why, you're nothing but a punk kid. Get the hell away from here.'

When I finished my 'up' he must have felt sorry for me. Anyway, he asked me to come back and have a drink with him. When I did, he gave me the twenty-dollar bill in my hand. I figured, if a millionaire could give me money that way, everybody could. So from then on I wouldn't take money off tables. When I came to work the other girls used to razz me, call me 'Duchess' and say, 'Look at her, she thinks she's a lady.'

I hadn't got my title Lady Day yet, but that was the beginning of people calling me 'Lady'.

1956

RALPH ELLISON

Remembering Jimmy Rushing

In the old days the voice was high and clear and poignantly lyrical. Steel-bright in its upper range and, at its best, silky smooth, it was possessed of a purity somehow impervious to both the stress of singing above a twelve-piece band and the urgency of Rushing's own blazing fervour. On dance nights, when you stood on the rise of the school grounds two blocks to the east, you could hear it jetting from the dancehall like a blue flame in the dark; now soaring high above the trumpets and trombones, now skimming the froth of reeds and rhythm as it called some woman's anguished name – or demanded in a high, thin, passionately lyrical line, 'Baaaaay-bay, Bay-aaaay-bay! Tell me what's the matter now!' – above the shouting of the swinging band.

Nor was there need for the by now famous signature line: 'If anybody asks you who sang this song/ Tell 'em/ it was little Jimmy Rushing/ he's been here and gone' – for everyone on Oklahoma City's 'East Side' knew that sweet, high-floating sound. 'Deep Second' was our fond nickname for the block in which Rushing worked and lived, and where most Negro business and entertainment were found, and before he went to cheer a wider world his voice evoked the festive spirit of the place. Indeed, he was the natural herald of its blues-romance, his song the singing essence of its joy. For Jimmy Rushing was not simply a local entertainer, he expressed a value, an attitude about the world for which our lives afforded no other definition. We had a Negro church and a segregated school, a few lodges and fraternal organizations, and beyond these there was all the great white world. We were pushed off to what seemed to be the least desirable side of the city (but which some years later was found to contain one of the state's richest pools of oil), and our system of justice was based upon Texas law, yet there was an optimism within the Negro community and a sense of possibility which, despite our awareness of limitation (dramatized so brutally in the Tulsa riot of 1921), transcended all of this; and it was this rock-bottom sense of reality, coupled with our sense of the possibility of rising above it, which sounded in Rushing's voice.

And how it carried! In those days I lived near the Rock Island roundhouse, where, with a steady clanging of bells and a great groaning of wheels along the rails, switch engines made up trains of freight unceasingly. Yet often in the late-spring night I could hear Rushing as I lay four blocks away in bed, carrying to me as clear as a full-bored riff on 'Hot Lips' Page's horn. Heard thus, across the dark blocks lined with locust trees, through the night throbbing with the natural aural imagery of the blues, with high-balling trains, departing bells, lonesome guitar chords simmering up from a shack in the alley – it was easy to imagine the voice as setting the pattern to which the instruments of the Blue Devils Orchestra and all the random sounds of night arose, affirming, as it were, some ideal native to the time and to the land. When we were still too young to attend night dances, but yet old enough to gather beneath the corner street lamp on summer evenings, anyone might halt the conversation to exclaim, 'Listen, they're raising hell down at Slaughter's Hall,' and we'd turn our heads westward to hear Jimmy's voice soar up the hill and down, as pure and as miraculously unhindered by distance and earthbound things as is the body in youthful dreams of flying.

'Now, that's the Right Reverend Jimmy Rushing preaching now, man,' someone would say. And rising to the cue another would answer, 'Yeah, and that's old Elder "Hot Lips" signifying along with him; urging him on, man.' And, keeping it building, 'Huh, but though you can't hear him out this far, Ole Deacon Big-un [the late Walter Page] is up there patting his foot and slapping on his big belly [the bass viol] to keep those fools in line.' And we might go on to name all the members of the band as though they were the Biblical four-and-twenty elders, while laughing at the impious wit of applying church titles to a form of music which all the preachers assured us was the devil's potent tool.

Our wit was true, for Jimmy Rushing, along with the other jazz musicians whom we knew, had made a choice, had dedicated himself to a mode of expression and a way of life no less 'righteously' than others dedicated themselves to the church. Jazz and the blues did not fit into the scheme of things as spelled out by our two main institutions, the church and the school, but they gave expression to attitudes which found no place in these and helped to give our lives some semblance of wholeness. Jazz and the public jazz dance was a third institution in our lives, and a vital one; and though Jimmy was far from being a preacher, he was, as official floor manager or master-of-the-dance at Slaughter's Hall, the leader of a public rite.

He was no Mr Five-by-five in those days, but a compact, debonair young man who dressed with an easy elegance. Much later, during theatre appearances with Basie's famous band, he sometimes cut an old step from slavery days called 'falling off the log' for the sheer humour provided by the rapid, and apparently precarious, shifting of his great bulk, but in the Oklahoma days he was capable of an amazing grace of movement. A nineteenth-century formality still clung to public dances at the time, and there was quite a variety of steps. Jimmy danced them all, gliding before the crowd over the polished floor, sometimes with a girl, sometimes with a huge megaphone held chest-high before him as he swayed. The evenings began with the more formal steps, to popular and semi-classical music, and proceeded to become more expressive as the spirit of jazz and the blues became dominant. It was when Jimmy's voice began to soar with the spirit of the blues that the dancers – and the musicians – achieved that feeling of communion which was the true meaning of the public jazz dance. The blues, the singer, the band and the dancers formed the vital whole of jazz as an institutional form, and even today neither part is quite complete without the rest. The thinness of much of the so-called 'modern jazz' is especially reflective of this loss of wholeness, and it is quite possible that Rushing retains his vitality simply because he has kept close to the small Negro public dance.

The occasion for this shamelessly nostalgic outburst is provided by a series of Rushing recordings issued over the past few years: Vanguard's *Jazz Showcase*; Columbia's *Goin' to Chicago, Listen to the Blues with Jimmy Rushing, If This Ain't the Blues, The Jazz Odyssey of James Rushing, Esq.,* and *Little Jimmy Rushing and the Big Brass.* An older recording, Decca's *Kansas City Jazz,* contains Rushing's best version of his classic 'Good Morning Blues', and offers a vivid idea of the styles and combinations of musicians which made up the milieu in which Rushing found his early development. These discs form a valuable introduction to the art of Jimmy Rushing in all its fervour and variety.

Rushing is known today primarily as a blues singer, but not so in those days. He began as a singer of ballads, bringing to them a sincerity and a feeling for dramatizing the lyrics in the musical phrase which charged the banal lines with the mysterious potentiality of meaning which haunts the blues. And it was, perhaps, Rushing's beginning as a ballad singer which gives his blues interpretations their special quality. For one of the significant aspects of his art is the imposition of a romantic lyricism upon the blues tradition (compare his version of 'See See Rider' with that of Ma Rainey); a lyricism which is not of the Deep South, but of the Southwest: a romanticism native to the frontier, imposed upon the violent rawness of a part of the nation which only thirteen years before Rushing's birth was still Indian territory. Thus there is an optimism in it which echoes the spirit of those Negroes who, like Rushing's father, had come to Oklahoma in search of a more human way of life.

Rushing is one of the first singers to sing the blues before a big band, and even today he seldom comes across as a blues 'shouter', but maintains the lyricism which has always been his way with the blues. Indeed, when we listen to his handling of lyrics we become aware of that quality which makes for the mysteriousness of the blues: their ability to imply far more than they state outright and their capacity to make the details of sex convey meanings which touch upon the metaphysical. For, indeed, they always find poetry in the limits of the Negro vocabulary. Perhaps because he is more educated and came from a family already well on its rise into what is called the 'Negro middle class', Jimmy has always shown a concern for the correctness of language, and out of the tension between the traditional folk pronunciation and his training in school, he has worked out a flexibility of enunciation and a rhythmical agility with words which make us constantly aware of the meanings which shimmer just beyond the limits of the lyrics. The blues is an art of ambiguity, an assertion of the irrepressibly human over all circumstances whether created by others or by one's own human failings.

They are the only consistent art in the United States which constantly reminds us of our limitations while encouraging us to see how far we can actually go. When understood in their more profound implication, they are a corrective, an attempt to draw a line upon man's own limitless assertion.

Significantly, Jimmy Rushing was able to spread the appeal of the blues to a wider American audience after the Depression had made us a bit more circumspect about the human cost of living of our 'American way of life'. It seems especially fitting now, when circumstance and its own position of leadership has forced the nation once more to examine its actions and its intentions, that the blues are once more becoming popular. There is a great demand for Rushing in Europe, from which he has just returned with the Goodman band. And I think we need him more here at home. Certainly this collection of discs will make us aware that there is emotional continuity in American life, and that the abiding moods expressed in our most vital popular art form are not simply a matter of entertainment; they also tell us who and where we are.

1958

ANN PETRY

Solo on the Drums

The orchestra had a week's engagement at the Randlert Theater at Broadway and 42nd Street. His name was picked out in lights on the marquee. The name of the orchestra and then his name underneath by itself.

There had been a time when he would have been excited by it. And stopped to let his mind and his eyes linger over it lovingly. Kid Jones. The name – his name – up there in lights that danced and winked in the brassy sunlight. And at night his name glittered up there on the marquee as though it had been sprinkled with diamonds. The people who pushed their way through the crowded street looked up at it and recognized it and smiled.

He used to eat it up. But not today. Not after what happened this morning. He just looked at the sign with his name on it. There it was. Then he noticed that the sun had come out, and he shrugged, and went on inside the theatre to put on one of the cream-coloured suits and get his music together.

After he finished changing his clothes, he glanced in the long mirror in his dressing-room. He hadn't changed any. Same face. No fatter and no thinner. No grey hair. Nothing. He frowned. Because he felt that the things that were eating him up inside ought to show. But they didn't.

When it was time to go out on the stage, he took his place behind the drums, not talking, just sitting there. The orchestra started playing softly. He made a mental note of the fact that the boys were working together as smoothly as though each one had been oiled.

The long grey curtains parted. One moment they were closed. And then they were open. Silently. Almost like magic. The high-powered spots flooded the stage with light. He could see specks of dust gliding down the wide beams of light. Under the bands of light the great space out front was all shadow. Faces slowly emerged out of it – disembodied heads and shoulders that slanted up and back, almost to the roof.

He hit the drums lightly. Regularly. A soft, barely discernible rhythm. A background. A repeated emphasis for the horns and the piano and the violin. The man with the trumpet stood up, and the first notes came out sweet and clear and high.

Kid Jones kept up the drum accompaniment. Slow. Careful. Soft. And he felt his left eyebrow lift itself and start to twitch as the man played the trumpet. It happened whenever he heard the trumpet. The notes crept up, higher, higher, higher. So high that his stomach sucked in against itself. Then a little lower and stronger. A sound sustained. The rhythm of it beating against his ears until he was filled with it and sighing with it.

He wanted to cover his ears with his hands because he kept hearing a voice that whispered the same thing over and over again. The voice was trapped somewhere under the roof – caught and held there by the trumpet. 'I'm leaving I'm leaving I'm leaving.'

The sound took him straight back to the rain, the rain that had come with the morning. He could see the beginning of the day – raw and cold. He was at home. But he was warm because he was close to her, holding her in his arms. The rain and the wind cried softly outside the window.

And now – well, he felt as though he were floating up and up and up on that long blue note of the trumpet. He half closed his eyes and rode on it. It had stopped being music. It was that whispering voice, making him shiver. Hating it and not being able to do anything about it. 'I'm leaving it's the guy who plays the piano I'm in love with him and I'm leaving now today.' Rain in the streets. Heat gone. Food gone. Everything gone because a woman's gone. It's everything you ever wanted, he thought. It's everything you never got. Everything you ever had, everything you ever lost. It's all there in the trumpet – pain and hate and trouble and peace and quiet and love.

The last note stayed up in the ceiling. Hanging on and on. The man with the trumpet had stopped playing but Kid Jones could still hear that last note. In his ears. In his mind.

The spotlight shifted and landed on Kid Jones – the man behind the drums. The long beam of white light struck the top of his head and turned him into a pattern of light and shadow. Because of the cream-coloured suit and shirt, his body seemed to be encased in the light. But there was a shadow over his face, so that his features blended and disappeared. His hairline receding so far back that he looked like a man with a face that never ended. A man with a high, long face and dark, dark skin.

He caressed the drums with the brushes in his hands. They responded with a whisper of sound. The rhythm came over but it had to be listened for. It stayed that way for a long time. Low, insidious, repeated. Then he made the big bass drum growl and pick up the same rhythm.

The Marquis of Brund, pianist with the band, turned to the piano. The drums and the piano talked the same rhythm. The piano high. A little more insistent than the drums. The Marquis was turned sideways on the piano bench. His left foot tapped out the rhythm. His cream-coloured suit sharply outlined the bulkiness of his body against the dark gleam of the piano. The drummer and the pianist were silhouetted in two separate brilliant shafts of light. The drums slowly dominated the piano.

The rhythm changed. It was faster. Kid Jones looked out over the crowded theatre as he hit the drums. He began to feel as though he were the drums and the drums were he.

The theatre throbbed with the excitement of the drums. A man sitting near the front shivered, and his head jerked to the rhythm. A sailor put his arm around the girl sitting beside him, took his hand and held her face still and pressed his mouth close over hers. Close. Close. Close. Until their faces seemed to melt together. Her hat fell off and neither of them moved. His hand dug deep into her shoulder and still they didn't move.

A kid sneaked in through a side door and slid into an aisle seat. His mouth was wide open, and he clutched his cap with both hands, tight and hard against his chest as he listened.

The drummer forgot he was in the theatre. There was only he and the drums and they were far away. Long gone. He was holding Lulu, Helen, Susie, Mamie close in his arms. And all of them – all those girls blended into that one girl who was his wife. The one who said, 'I'm leaving.' She had said it over and over again, this morning, while rain dripped down the window panes.

When he hit the drums again it was with the thought that he was fighting with the piano player. He was choking the Marquis of Brund. He was putting a knife in clean between his ribs. He was slitting his throat with a long straight blade. Take my woman. Take your life.

The drums leaped with the fury that was in him. The men in the band turned their heads toward him – a faint astonishment showed in their faces.

He ignored them. The drums took him away from them, took him back, and back, and back, in time and space. He built up an illusion. He was sending out the news. Grandma died. The foreigner in the litter has an old disease and will not recover. The man from across the big water is sleeping with the chief's daughter. Kill. Kill. Kill. The war goes well with the men with the bad smell and the loud laugh. It goes badly with the chiefs with the round heads and the peacock's walk.

It is cool in the deep track in the forest. Cool and quiet. The trees talk softly. They speak of the dance tonight. The young girl from across the lake will be there. Her waist is slender and her thighs are rounded. Then the words he wanted to forget were all around Kid Jones again. 'I'm leaving I'm leaving I'm leaving.'

He couldn't help himself. He stopped hitting the drums and stared at the Marquis of Brund – a long, malevolent look, filled with hate.

There was a restless, uneasy movement in the theatre. He remembered where he was. He started playing again. The horn played a phrase. Soft and short. The drums answered. The horn said the same thing all over again. The drums repeated it. The next time it was more intricate. The phrase was turned around, it went back and forth and up and down. And the drums said it over, exactly the same.

He knew a moment of panic. This was where he had to solo again and he wasn't sure he could do it. He touched the drums lightly. They quivered and answered him.

And then it was almost as though the drums were talking about his own life. The woman in Chicago who hated him. The girl with the round soft body who had been his wife and who had walked out on him, this morning, in the rain. The old woman who was his mother, the same woman who lived in Chicago, and who hated him because he looked like his father, his father who had seduced her and left her, years ago.

He forgot the theatre, forgot everything but the drums. He was welded to the drums, sucked inside them. All of him. His pulse beat. His heart beat. He had become part of the drums. They had become part of him.

He made the big bass rumble and reverberate. He went a little mad on the big bass. Again and again he filled the theatre with a sound like thunder. The sound seemed to come not from the drums but from deep inside himself; it was a sound that was being wrenched out of him – a violent, raging, roaring sound. As it issued from him he thought, this is the story of my love, this is the story of my hate, this is all there is left of me. And the sound echoed and re-echoed far up under the roof of the theatre.

When he finally stopped playing, he was trembling; his body was wet with sweat. He was surprised to see that the drums were sitting there in front of him. He hadn't become part of them. He was still himself. Kid Jones. Master of the drums. Greatest drummer in the world. Selling himself a little piece at a time. Every afternoon. Twice every evening. Only this time he had topped all his other performances. This time, playing like this after what had happened in the morning, he had sold all of himself – not just a little piece.

Someone kicked his foot. 'Bow, you ape. Whassamatter with you?'

He bowed from the waist, and the spotlight slid away from him, down his pants legs. The light landed on the Marquis of Brund, the piano player. The Marquis's skin glistened like a piece of black seaweed. Then the light was back on Kid Jones.

He felt hot and he thought, I stink of sweat. The talcum he had dabbed on his face after he shaved felt like a constricting layer of cement. A thin layer but definitely cement. No air could get through to his skin. He reached for his handkerchief and felt the powder and the sweat mix as he mopped his face.

Then he bowed again. And again. Like a – like one of those things you pull the string and it jerks, goes through the motion of dancing. Pull it again and it kicks. Yeah, he thought, you were hot all right. The jitterbugs ate you up and you haven't any place to go. Since this morning you haven't had any place to go. 'I'm leaving it's the guy who plays the piano I'm in love with the Marquis of Brund he plays such sweet piano I'm leaving leaving leaving—'

He stared at the Marquis of Brund for a long moment.

Then he stood up and bowed again. And again.

PHILIP LARKIN

For Sidney Bechet

That note you hold, narrowing and rising, shakes
Like New Orleans reflected on the water,
And in all ears appropriate falsehood wakes,

Building for some a legendary Quarter
Of balconies, flower-baskets and quadrilles,
Everyone making love and going shares –

Oh, play that thing! Mute glorious Storyvilles
Others may license, grouping round their chairs
Sporting-house girls like circus tigers (priced

Far above rubies) to pretend their fads,
While scholars *manqués* nod around unnoticed
Wrapped up in personnels like old plaids.

On me your voice falls as they say love should,
Like an enormous yes. My Crescent City
Is where your speech alone is understood,

And greeted as the natural noise of good,
Scattering long-haired grief and scored pity.

Guitar

Ma six string guitar with the lonesome sound
Can't hold its own against a Georgia hound.

O mamma when the sun goes the downstairs way
And the night spreads out an the moon make day,

I sits with ma feet raised to the rail
And sings the song bout ma buddy in jail:

> *In the red-dirt land,*
> *And the pine tree high,*
> *Gonna find me peace*
> *By-an-by.*
>
> *Gonna find me a baby*
> *Some pretty-eye gal*
> *To be ma mother*
> *Ma wife and pal.*
>
> *Ain't had nobody*
> *To call me home*
> *From the electric cities*
> *Where I roam.*
>
> *Yes, I been travelin*
> *Over all*
> *To find a place*
> *What I could call*
> *Home, baby,*
> *Sweet cotton-field home. . . .*

When I gets to the place where a cracker got mad,
Struck ma fine buddy, struck all I had,

The hound start howlin till the stars break down
An make ma song like a boat what's drown.

Ma six string guitar with the lonesome sound
Can't hold its own against that Georgia hound.

LANGSTON HUGHES

Dream Boogie

Good morning, daddy!
Ain't you heard
The boogie-woogie rumble
Of a dream deferred?

Listen closely:
You'll hear their feet
Beating out and beating out a—

> *You think*
> *It's a happy beat?*

Listen to it closely:
Ain't you heard
something underneath
like a—

> *What did I say?*

Sure,
I'm happy!
Take it away!

> *Hey, pop!*
> *Re-bop!*
> *Mop!*

> *Y-e-a-h!*

JOSEPH LEVEY

'Tammy' . . . 'Ida' . . . 'Dinah' . . . 'Margie' . . .

What is the American popular music idiom? When jazz first came into existence as a form of musical expression, the musicians used the American popular idiom of the day – marches, polkas, waltzes, work-songs, theatre songs, barroom ballads, bordello songs, spirituals, sentimental parlour ballads, revival songs, etc. – as a basis for jazz expression. The use of the popular song continued in each decade, and it is still a valid practice today.

From the 1920s to the early 1950s, the American popular song was a thriving business, supplying dance bands and their singers, radio and recording orchestras and their singers, Broadway musicals, and movie studios with a continuous stream of new songs. Nearly the entire pop song business was at one time centred in a few office buildings in Manhattan, known as 'Tin Pan Alley'.

Conversely, the quality of many of both yesterday's and today's songs is often poor, and many hacks survive and make a living with second-rate material. But talented song composers have always been able to produce artistic gems. These often become evergreens, and they continue to be used long after their initial publication. Jazz musicians contribute to the evergreen status by continuing to perform, arrange, and record certain songs which, because of their melody and harmony, are interesting to play. Some evergreens are still attractive to jazz musicians forty or fifty years after their first publication.

The broad spectrum of the American pop idiom encompasses music with Cuban, Brazilian, Caribbean, and Mexican flavours as well as gospel, rock, country and western, bluegrass, urban blues, country blues, and many more regional influences. There are differences, of course, but there are also many common elements. A look at the title groupings that follow might aid in discovering common properties:

US Cities or States in Titles

'Goin' Back to Houston'
'St Louis Blues'
'Autumn in New York'
'Moonlight in Vermont'
'Old Cape Cod'
'Jersey Bounce'
'On the Boardwalk in Atlantic City'
'Oklahoma'
'Do You Know the Way to San Jose?'
'California Here I Come'
'I Left My Heart in San Francisco'
'Wichita Lineman'
'By the Time I Get to Phoenix'
'Moon over Miami'
'Back Home Again in Indiana'
'I Got a Gal in Kalamazoo'
'Pennsylvania Polka'
'Rainy Night in Georgia'
'Georgia on My Mind'
'Hooray for Hollywood'
'Chicago'
'Yellow Rose of Texas'
'Stars Fell on Alabama'
'Kansas City'
'Carolina in the Morning'
'Do You Know What It Means to Miss New Orleans?'
'Nevada'
'Big D'
'Mississippi Mud'
'Down by the O-hi-o'
'Poor Little Rhode Island'
'Manhattan'
'Just a Little Bit South of North Carolina'

'Louisiana Hayride'
'Deep in the Heart of Texas'
'New York State of Mind'

Weather Titles

'Rainy Days and Mondays'
'Soon It's Gonna Rain'
'Into Each Life Some Rain Must Fall'
'Stormy Weather'
'September in the Rain'
'April Showers'
'With the Wind and the Rain in Your Hair'
'Singin' in the Rain'
'Come Rain or Come Shine'
'Raindrops Keep Fallin' on My Head'
'Here's That Rainy Day'
'Don't Rain on My Parade'
'Rainy Night in Rio'
'Till the Clouds Roll By'
'Let the Sun Shine In'
'On a Clear Day'
'Sunny Side of the Street'
'Having a Heat Wave'
'Too Darned Hot'
'High on a Windy Hill'
'Gone with the Wind'
'Foggy Day in London Town'
'Winter Wonderland'
'Let It Snow'
'Baby, It's Cold Outside'
'When the Sun Comes Out'

Month or Season Titles

'Autumn in New York'
'Autumn Leaves'
'Early Autumn'

''Tis Autumn'
'Indian Summer'
'September Song'
'September in the Rain'
'Lost April'
'April in Paris'
'April Showers'
'I'll Remember April'
'Spring Is Here'
'Love Turns Winter into Spring'
'It Might as Well Be Spring'
'Spring Will Be a Little Late This Year'
'The Isle of May'
'June in January'
'June Is Bustin' Out All Over'
'Summertime'
'The Summer Knows'

'Blue' in Titles

'Blue Skies'
'Serenade in Blue'
'Blue Moon'
'My Blue Heaven'
'Birth of the Blues'
'I've Got a Right to Sing the Blues'
'St Louis Blues'
'Little Girl Blue'
'Blues in the Night'
'Am I Blue?'
'When the Blue of the Night'
'Blue Room'
'Basin Street Blues'
'Beyond the Blue Horizon'
'Blue Hawaii'
'Blue Tango'
'Blue Champagne'
'Under a Blanket of Blue'

'When Sunny Gets Blue'
'Love Is Blue'
'Alice Blue Gown'
'In the Blue of Evening'

Other Colours in Titles

'Red Sails in the Sunset'
'Deep Purple'
'Green Eyes'
'Yellow Rose of Texas'
'Tie a Yellow Ribbon'
'Yellow Days'
'Pink Champagne'
'Rose Room'
'Red Roses for a Blue Lady'
'Look for the Silver Lining'
'Scarlet Ribbons'
'My Little Brown Book'
'Blue, Green, Grey and Gone'
'That Old Black Magic'
'Green Dolphin Street'
'Evergreen'
'Bye, Bye, Blackbird'

'Moon' in Titles

'Racing with the Moon'
'Blue Moon'
'Moonlight in Vermont'
'Moon over Miami'
'Carolina Moon'
'Moonglow'
'How High the Moon'
'Moonlight Cocktail'
'Moon River'
'Chapel in the Moonlight'
'Moonlight Becomes You'

'Moonlight and Shadows'
'When the Moon Comes over the Mountain'
'Orchids in the Moonlight'
'Full Moon and Empty Arms'
'Harvest Moon'
'That Old Devil Moon'
'Moon Love'
'By the Light of the Silvery Moon'
'On Moonlight Bay'
'Polka Dots and Moonbeams'
'Paper Moon'

Female Name in Titles

'Marie'
'Maria'
'Charmaine'
'Louise'
'Louisa'
'Sweet Sue'
'Laura'
'Hello Dolly'
'Mame'
'Sweet Georgia Brown'
'Liza'
'I'm Coming Virginia'
'Sweet Lorraine'
'Mandy'
'Stella by Starlight'
'Josephine'
'Peg o' My Heart'
'Jean'
'Jeannine'
'Ramona'
'Dolores'
'Tangerine'
'Chloe'
'Nola'

'Once in Love with Amy'
'Portrait of Jenny'
'Michelle'
'Tammy'
'Ida'
'Dinah'
'Margie'
'Nancy with the Laughing Face'
'Rosalie'
'Gigi'
'Georgie Girl'
'Proud Mary'
'Sunny'
'Second-Hand Rose'

Male Name in Titles

'Happiness Is Just a Thing Called Joe'
'Joey'
'I'm Just Wild about Harry'
'Just My Bill'
'Alexander's Ragtime Band'
'Oh, Johnny'
'Bill Bailey'
'Roger Young'
'Sam, You Made the Pants Too Long'
'Mack the Knife'
'Leroy Brown'
'Open the Door, Richard'
'Rudolph the Red-Nosed Reindeer'
'Alfie'
'Charlie My Boy'
'Johnny-One-Note'
'Danny Boy'

Time of Day Titles

'Night and Day'
'All through the Night'

'Tonight'
'In the Still of the Night'
'The Night Has a Thousand Eyes'
'The Night is Young'
'Night Train'
'Saturday Night'
'The Way You Look Tonight'
'If I Could Be with You One Hour Tonight'
'You and the Night and the Music'
''Round Midnight'
'The Night Was Made for Love'
'Just the Way You Look Tonight'
'I Could Have Danced All Night'
'The Night We Called It a Day'
'Dancing in the Dark'
'In the Cool of the Evening'
'Some Enchanted Evening'
'At Sundown'
'Suppertime'
'When Day is Done'
'Daybreak'
'Come Saturday Morning'
'Sunrise Serenade'
'Carolina in the Morning'
'Softly, as in a Morning Sunrise'
'A Lazy Afternoon'
'High Noon'

Travel Titles

'Route 66'
'Chattanooga Choo Choo'
'Atcheson, Topeka and the Santa Fe'
'Leavin' on a Jet Plane'
'By the Time I Get to Phoenix'
'Country Roads'
'Sentimental Journey'

'Lonesome Road'
'The Happy Wanderer'
'Take the "A" Train'
'Trolley Song'
'Wagon Wheels'
'Around the World'
'Two for the Road'
'Slow Boat to China'
'My Ship'
'Let's Get away from It All'
'Flying down to Rio'
'Up, Up, and Away'
'Beyond the Blue Horizon'
'Homeward Bound'
'Get out of Town'
'Cruising down the River'

'Street' in Titles

'Street of Dreams'
'Sunny Side of the Street'
'Easy Street'
'On the Street where You Live'
'Green Dolphin Street'
'Boulevard of Broken Dreams'
'Basin Street Blues'
'Forty-Second Street'
'Just a Little Street where Old Friends Meet'

Occult Titles

'Ghost of a Chance'
'That Old Black Magic'
'It's Witchcraft'
'That Old Devil Moon'
'Voodoo Woman'
'Ghost Riders in the Sky'

'Love Your Magic Spell Is Everywhere'
'It's Magic'
'The Witch Doctor'
'Out of This World'
'You Stepped out of a Dream'

MARIAN McPARTLAND

The International Sweethearts
of Rhythm

The theatre was ablaze with lights that proclaimed – THE INTER-
NATIONAL SWEETHEARTS OF RHYTHM. The Sweethearts, an
all-woman sixteen-piece band, were familiar to the tough, show-
wise audience, and a long line of eagerly expectant people stretched
down the street and around the corner, waiting for the doors to
open. Known to the audience as the finest all-girl jazz band in the
country, the Sweethearts had in seven years attained a reputation
equal to that of the great male bands of the period, those led by
Jimmie Lunceford, Count Basie, and Fletcher Henderson. The year
was 1945; the place, the Apollo Theater in Harlem.

A hot attraction, the Sweethearts were then at the height of their
fame, although to some they were merely a novelty – sixteen pretty
girl musicians led by an extravagantly beautiful young woman,
Anna Mae Winburn. They played with assurance, discipline and
excitement, reflecting the expert teaching of their director, Maurice
King. There were some fine soloists, including Violet (Vi) Burnside,
a driving, gutty tenor sax player with more than a suggestion of
Coleman Hawkins in her style. The star soloist of the trumpet
section was Ray Carter, whose muted sound was colourful and
technically brilliant. The hard-swinging drummer, Pauline Braddy,
inspired by her idol and mentor Big Sid Catlett, whipped the band
along with a strong rhythm. Her foot beating on the bass drum
pedal matched exactly the time-keeping of the bassist, Margaret
(Trump) Gibson, and together they gave solid, dependable backing
to the soloists.

The main attraction was roly-poly Ernestine (Tiny) Davis, billed
as '245 Lbs. of Solid Jive and Rhythm'. A compelling personality,
she had a distinct flair for comedy and a humorous way with a song.
Her comic dancing, rolling eyes, and funny rendition of 'Stompin'

the Blues' broke up the audience; and she played a strong, forceful trumpet on 'I Can't Get Started', another crowd-pleaser.

The band played at the beginning of each show (four a day), and again later in the show. There were other name acts on the bill, but the Sweethearts opened and closed the programme.

This band was truly unique in that it was a racially mixed group, a phenomenon unheard of even in blasé New York City. They were known to have travelled widely in the South and Midwest, many miles from their starting-point, the Piney Woods Country Life School near Jackson, Mississippi, where the original band was formed in 1938. The members of that first band were all approximately fourteen or fifteen years old, high-spirited, naive youngsters who enjoyed playing for dances in small towns within driving distance of the school.

Between 1938 and the present date at the Apollo, the band's personnel had changed many times. Ione and Irene Gresham, who both played sax with the original band, had decided to stay at Piney Woods when the band turned professional; this was a decision reached by several of the girls. Others had concluded that life on the road was not for them; still others had left the band to get married. However, some of the members of the original group remained – Helen Jones and Ina Belle Byrd, trombone; Willie Mae Lee Wong, baritone sax; Edna Williams, trumpet and vocals; Johnnie Mae Rice, piano; and Pauline Braddy, drums. Inside the theatre the girls were dressing and warming up on their instruments. Tiny Davis practised high notes on the trumpet, getting ready for her feature numbers. Anna Mae Winburn gave final touches to her sleek, upswept hairdo. She wore an exquisite, tightly-fitted sequin gown, while the band members were dressed in decorous black skirts and jackets, with white blouses. Each girl wore a flower in her hair, which added a feminine touch to their rather severe attire. Mrs Rae Lee Jones was the manager of the band, a tall, imposing woman and a disciplinarian reminiscent of a boarding school matron. She walked among the girls, adjusting a neckline here, tucking in a stray hair there, checking the girls' lipstick and eye make-up. 'That'll do; off you go,' she ordered. With a last minute flurry of practice notes, the girls filed out of the dressing-room to take their places on stage.

The huge curtain parted as strains of the Sweethearts' theme song, featuring Rosalind (Roz) Cron on alto sax, filled the theatre. Next, a solid, swinging arrangement of 'Tuxedo Junction' kept the audience snapping their fingers. Among the several outstanding soloists featured on the programme was diminutive Evelyn McGee, who drew whistles of appreciation for her singing of 'Candy' and 'Rum and Coca Cola'. Anna Mae Winburn put aside her baton to sing 'Do You Want To Jump, Children?'. 'Yeah, yeah,' shrilled the band, answering her musical question in childlike voices. Following this was a wild, frantic version of 'Sweet Georgia Brown' taken at an impossible tempo, with Vi Burnside free-wheeling in and around the melody, playing a shower of notes on her tenor sax that took one's breath away. When the show was over, and with the echoes of the cheers and applause still ringing in their ears, the girls could now look forward to a quick snack between shows, visits from friends, and the heady excitement of being back in New York City.

Few white people ever saw the Sweethearts. At that time the Apollo and other theatres like it – the Howard in Washington, the Regal in Chicago, the Paradise in Detroit – catered to black audiences, and the small number of whites who ventured there were the real jazz aficionados. Among them was record producer John Hammond, who thought the band was 'just marvellous; a great band'. It might even have been, as one of the fans remarked, 'the world's greatest girl dance band'. Pianist Earl 'Fatha' Hines had high praise for the group – 'a wonderful swinging bunch of gals' – but there were negative comments, too. Huffed one well-known woman player when asked if she had ever worked with the Sweethearts, 'You wouldn't catch me anywhere near *that* band.' And the typical remark from male musicians was, 'You certainly couldn't consider them in the same league as any good *male* band.' Yet musical director Maurice King was enthusiastic. 'You could put those girls behind a curtain and people would be convinced it was men playing.' The group was often likened to the Lunceford band, and Jimmie Lunceford himself had high praise for the girls.

It had taken stamina, long hours of practice, dedication, and experiences both rewarding and frustrating to bring the International Sweethearts of Rhythm all the way from Piney Woods, Mississippi, to the Apollo Theater in New York. The newer band members were all aware of the pioneering spirit that had helped the first schoolgirl band to pave the way for the present group's highly acclaimed reputation.

Research indicates that the principal of Piney Woods Country Life School, Laurence C. Jones, was a most unusual man – well-educated (University of Iowa), charming, knowledgeable in the ways of the world, and totally committed to raising money for the betterment of his school. Money was constantly needed to take care of the thousand boys and girls, many of them orphans, who lived at the school.

Mr Jones believed in keeping everybody working. The bell rang at 5 a.m.; at six the children had breakfast; and by seven they were all busy with school work or some other activity. There was a farm – boys were taught farming and furniture-making among other things – and the girls learned domestic skills such as cooking and dressmaking. The football team bested everyone in the area, and there were two marching bands, one of boys, one of girls. The school had everything – there never had been a place like it for blacks in the South. At that time they were held back, yet Mr Jones's powers of persuasion were so strong that he was able to convince the white businessmen that he met that his idea of teaching every child a trade was of prime importance. He knew the right people to approach, and money flowed into the school from many sources.

There was a great deal of musical activity before the formation of the Sweethearts. In addition to the forty-five-piece marching bands, there was a group called 'The Cotton Blossom Singers', who were at that time the main fund-raisers for the school. Mr Jones personally supervised all these activities.

This was the burgeoning swing era – the great bands of Ellington, Hines, Basie, and Lunceford were developing unique stylings from their jazz heritage. A new kind of jazz, jazz people could dance to, began to flourish, and it burst forth all over the country, inspiring white musicians – the Dorsey Brothers, Benny Goodman, Artie Shaw, Glenn Miller – to form their own bands. It was inevitable that someone would think of putting together a different type of show business package, one that was bound to succeed – an all-girl (white) swing band, Ina Ray Hutton and Her Melodears. Irving Mills, mentor of the Ellington band, did just that.

According to Helen Jones, who had been adopted at the age of three months by Laurence Jones and his wife and brought up at Piney Woods, Mr Jones heard Ina Ray and her band in Chicago, and his fertile mind instantly grasped the possibilities and advantages of establishing such a group to raise funds for Piney Woods. As soon as he returned, he set about selecting girls for the band. There were many who had musical talent and who, with training, would develop into competent musicians. Helen Jones recalls that Mr Jones wanted her to play the violin, but she begged for a chance to learn the trombone, because she 'loved to watch that slide going in and out'. This was a fortunate decision, because Helen's strong, full tone enhanced the Sweethearts' trombone section from the formation of the group until they disbanded.

No one remembers who was the first director of the band. After Laurence Jones had assembled the group, they were rehearsed for a short time by a teacher named Lawrence Jefferson. Then Edna Williams, a talented young pianist and trumpet player not much older than the band members themselves, took over. It seems that Edna Williams, or someone like her, taught the girls their first tunes, which were, according to drummer Pauline Braddy, 'Baby, Don't Tell On Me', 'How Long, Baby', '720 in the Books', and 'Stardust'. Some of the girls were given half notes or whole notes to play, while others played the melody. A few learned the tunes by reading the music, while the others would imitate notes and phrases sung or played by the teacher. She also taught them breath control and how to produce a tone. Gradually they became proficient enough to move on to 'stocks' – sheet music copies of popular tunes of that day. Finally, they were ready to set forth on a fund-raising trip in the area, as Mr Jones had envisioned. Sixteen in all, the girls rode in a special bus to play dates in armouries, halls, and high school gymnasiums. Mr Jones thought of everything. He even hired a chaperone, Mrs Ella P. Gant, who travelled along with the girls.

As the girls gained in experience and proficiency, the band blossomed. The plain blouses and dark skirts the girls wore gave them a fresh appearance. Their neatly combed hair and well-scrubbed faces emphasized how young they were (14–15) to be on the road. Soon the trips became longer, and Mr Jones hired Vivian Crawford as tutor for the girls, and Mrs Rae Lee Jones (no relation) to replace Mrs Gant. Mrs Jones was a social worker from Omaha, whom Laurence Jones had met on one of his fund-raising trips. She kept order among the girls and brooked no disobedience, but was concerned enough about their health to see that they all ate well and drank plenty of milk.

By now the band was beginning to sound more professional. Some of the original group had dropped out, and others took their places. Evelyn McGee, a talented youngster from Anderson, South Carolina, joined the band as vocalist. Mr Jones had an uncanny way of spotting talent. On a trip with the band to Bolivar, Mississippi, he espied a very beautiful girl, Helen Saine, playing basketball, and invited her to come to Piney Woods and join the band. 'But I can't play an instrument,' said Helen. 'We'll teach you,' Mr Jones replied. Something in his approach must have made the invitation seem worthwhile to her parents, because Helen Saine was allowed to leave immediately for Piney Woods and was soon learning to play tenor and alto sax.

Then came Grace Bayron and her sister, Judy. While on a trip to New York the year before, Laurence Jones had noticed Gracie carrying her saxophone case on an East Harlem street. He followed her home and asked her parents if they would relocate their family to Piney Woods – Mr Bayron to teach Spanish, Gracie and Judy to play in the band. The parents declined the offer, but by some strange quirk of fate both died within the same year. Remembering Laurence Jones's invitation, Gracie Bayron telephoned him soon after her parents' death. Arrangements were made, and a few days later a chaperone arrived to escort the girls to Piney Woods. 'Gracie started playing in the band right away,' Judy Bayron recalls. 'I was just given a guitar to hold so I could sit in the rhythm section. But eventually I learned to play trombone.'

The band began to take on an air of professionalism that Rae Lee Jones helped to bring about with her constant supervision and strict rules. She had insisted that each girl wear a flower in her hair on stage. Now she started buying costumes for them that gave them a more sophisticated appearance.

Hotel accommodations for a racially mixed group were impossible to find, so trips were made in a bus fitted with bunk beds so that the group could travel all night and wake up refreshed. They ate on the bus, practised, prepared their lessons, got dressed, and, as the bus pulled into town, were ready in their costumes for their performance. It would seem as if the Sweethearts led an exciting life, travelling from town to town, playing to packed houses and appreciative audiences, but in fact it was a hard, rugged existence, with no chance for social life. The girls looked glamorous on stage, but, says Helen Jones, 'We were the biggest bunch of virgins in America.'

The band's fund-raising endeavours took them farther and farther afield, and in October 1939 they played Chicago, Des Moines, Omaha, and Kansas City in the space of a week. Their Chicago appearance was sponsored by the Chicago-Piney Woods Club, and a review of their performance at the Romping Earl's Club House read in part:

'Sixteen girls, best known in music circles as the "International Sweethearts of Rhythm", who hail from Piney Woods, Mississippi, right in the heart of the Delta, invaded Chicago Saturday night and gave jitterbugs, swing fans and hep-cats something to talk about.

'They beat out a bit of mellow jive, sang the latest song hits, then started a swing session that caused the dance lovers to stop in their tracks and listen to the hot sounds that blared out from the instruments played by these Mississippi girls.

'Together for two years, these girls handle their instruments like veterans and can rightfully take a place among the leading male aggregations.'

Perhaps reviews such as this helped to pique the interest of a talent promoter from Washington, D.C., for Daniel M. Gary suddenly appeared on the scene, approaching Mrs Jones with the suggestion that he take over the bookings for the band. It seems that after consulting with Laurence Jones, Mr Gary did indeed start booking the band, and they embarked on their most successful tour thus far, playing major cities in the South and Midwest.

However, as their musicianship improved and their successes increased, so in direct proportion did their problems – problems that would soon lead to a decision that would drastically affect the future of the band and its members.

It appears that Laurence Jones thought he was losing control of the band, primarily because Rae Lee Jones was encouraging the girls to question his judgment in financial and other matters. He therefore confronted her with the threat of dismissal. When the girls decided to stand by her, he informed them that they would not receive their high school diplomas unless they returned to Piney Woods immediately. To his dismay, the girls refused to change their minds; even his adopted daughter, Helen, defied him. Perhaps they had already been influenced in their decision by thoughts of the bright future Dan Gary had promised them.

It was a momentous decision, especially since everyone knew they were virtually running away from Piney Woods, taking with them the uniforms and instruments belonging to the school, as well as the bus. Perhaps the consequences of such a decision had not yet dawned on them – that Mr Jones, hurt and furious at what he thought was a betrayal, would later have Rae Lee Jones arrested for theft. Even this did not stop the forward movement of the band, because Dan Gary, through his various political connections, managed to secure her release, on the condition that the bus, uniforms, and instruments be returned to Piney Woods.

At this point, having lost Piney Woods as home base, the band needed a new headquarters. Property records show that Rae Lee Jones, as Trustee of the International Sweethearts of Rhythm, Inc., purchased a ten-room house at 908 South Quinn Street, Arlington, Virginia. The girls believed they were members of the corporation and that they owned shares in the house, as they had been told that a portion of their salaries would be used to help pay the mortgage. It was a beautiful idea – their very own house where they could rest and relax. To girls who had started in the band with nothing, the prospect of having their own house was thrilling indeed.

Once settled in Arlington, the girls rehearsed every day, sometimes for as long as six hours at a stretch, and consequently their playing became more polished. They began to believe that their dreams of hitting the big time would come true when they were plunged into the exciting, fast-moving, sometimes sinister web of black night-clubs, while continuing to play at well-known ballrooms and theatres. There were more changes in the band personnel – stronger, more experienced musicians were brought in. Anna Mae

Winburn, who had once led a group of her own, was hired to front the band; her beauty and stage presence were a definite asset. She brought down the house with her rendition of 'Blowtop Blues', a song written for her by jazz critic Leonard Feather.

It was becoming quite evident that despite the many changes and improvements in the band, their repertoire was too limited for the bookings Dan Gary had scheduled for them at theatres such as the Apollo, the Howard Theater in Washington, DC, the Regal in Chicago, and other top-rated theatres across the country. It was time to bring in an arranger, and Mrs Jones was advised to hire Eddie Durham, who had been prominent in the Count Basie Band and who was also well-known as a songwriter, guitarist, and trombone player. He had to his credit a hit song, 'I Don't Want To Set the World on Fire', and other original tunes. His arrangements of 'St Louis Blues' and 'At Sundown' were simple, but effective. He also arranged a beautiful Harold Arlen song, 'When the Sun Comes Out', as well as some of his own compositions, 'Moten Swing' and 'Topsy', for the Sweethearts. Durham had had his own all-woman band, so he knew the best approach to take in teaching the Sweethearts. Knowing that there were few improvisers in the band, he wrote out solos for them that sounded as if they were improvised on the spot when played.

Durham had high regard for the Sweethearts, and he enjoyed working with them. 'People couldn't believe it was women playing,' he commented, 'so sometimes when the curtain opened I'd make off that I was playing and the girls were just pantomiming. Then I'd stop, and people could see they really were playing. I simplified things for them as much as possible. You structure arrangements for people ... you write for what you've got. I had to train the Sweethearts, but at the Apollo nobody believed girls could play that way.'

Durham showed considerable sensitivity in allowing for the girls' technical limitations while stressing their strong points. He played an important role, as a teacher as well as an arranger, in the development of the band. Through his efforts they were beginning to know where they were going musically.

None of the surviving members of the band's early days recalls exactly when their romantic fantasies of success ran headlong into reality. They were becoming aware that real life was turning out to be not only places like the Apollo, but also endless and gruelling one-nighters, tedious rehearsals, and long nights on the bus. They sometimes had to eat in dirty restaurants, where often they were handed their food through a back window, typical treatment for blacks in the South at that time. (Anna Mae Winburn recalls screaming angrily at one restaurant owner, 'My brother is overseas fighting for people like you, and you're treating me this way?')

Most of the time the girls slept on the bus because it was too risky for mixed groups to stay in black hotels. On the rare occasion that they did, there was always the danger that the police would question the hotel owner, trying to find out if some of the girls were white. Ironically, the white girls, and those who looked white, suffered as much from southern racism as the black band members.

The girls were harassed in hotels and restaurants, and even while on stage. Policemen would roam the clubs, trying to spot the white band members. Often they succeeded, despite the heavy, dark make-up the lighter-skinned girls used in an attempt to disguise their pale complexions, and the wigs they wore to hide their light hair. When this happened, Mrs Jones was ready with false credentials to prove the girls were Negro. It was a constant worry in the minds of the girls that, despite all their precautions, one of their number might be taken away at any time, not for any wrongdoing but simply because of her colour.

Harassment of another sort was experienced by some of the black band members. During a performance in a night-club, Anna Mae Winburn tripped while stepping onto the stage. When a white man rose to help her, he was immediately forced back into his seat by a nearby policeman who ordered, 'You sit down and let that nigger woman help herself.'

(A few years later Anna Mae and her husband, Duke Pilgrim, fared better in a confrontation with southern police. While driving through town with two white members of the band they had formed, their car was stopped by a policeman. 'You know you're not supposed to have them white women in the car,' rasped the officer. Pilgrim, with a look of innocence, replied, 'I know that, officer, that's why I've got them sitting in the *back* seat.' He drove away, leaving the befuddled policeman standing there.)

The band kept improving, kept moving ahead. They had seen their names on theatre marquees and billboards, and they had heard the warm applause of audiences all over the country.

Their next big milestone musically was the hiring of Jesse Stone as the band's coach-arranger. Like Eddie Durham, Stone was a highly respected and successful figure in the world of topflight Negro swing bands. He had written several well-known songs, 'Idaho' and 'Smack Dab in the Middle' being the most familiar.

Jesse Stone made many changes and improvements in the band. He brought in several new musicians, among them Lucille Dixon, bass; Marjorie Pettiford (Oscar's sister), alto sax; Johnnie Mae (Tex) Stansbury, trumpet; Amy Garrison, sax; and Roxanna Lucas, guitar. The addition of these talented women, whose reading and playing skill was at an advanced level, raised the calibre of the entire group. He made a special point of teaching the girls how to improve their intonation, how to listen to each other in order to achieve a smooth blend and a sharp attack. Some of his new arrangements were more challenging than anything the girls had attempted thus far, and therefore special coaching was necessary.

The major innovation that Stone made was the formation of a singing group drawn from the band. Helen Jones recalls, 'We had some numbers where a group of us went down front and sang. Evelyn, Ella Ritz Lucas, somebody else and myself had a quartet. We went down front after we played part of the show and we sang and everybody liked it. Jesse is really the one who did that. In fact, we sang some of his numbers.'

During Jesse Stone's first year with the band the Sweethearts made considerable musical progress. The overall sound was smoother, the musicianship improving. It was a rough life, but a free one to the extent that the girls had broken loose from familial ties, from school and similar restraints. Also, the earlier camaraderie had grown into a bond of friendship that had been strengthened by the many experiences, good and bad, that the girls had shared.

But not only did the band members learn more about music from Jesse Stone, they also became fully aware through him that they were performing for less than adequate wages.

Evelyn McGee recalls, 'Jesse would fight with Mrs Jones about how she was taking advantage of the girls. For example, we played five shows a day in Baltimore during Christmas week. The lines were unbelievable, the audiences fantastic – but at the end of the week Mrs Jones gave each girl less than $100.

'Jesse hit the ceiling, and gave his notice. But Mrs Jones held him to his two-year contract, so he stayed on another year. When he finally left, it wasn't because he was dissatisfied with the band. It was because of the treatment we were getting from Rae Lee Jones.'

The girls were becoming disenchanted, and some of them left. Those who stayed on seemed to have a more philosophical attitude about things. 'It's funny, when you're young and don't know anything, you do a lot of things without thinking,' Helen Jones reflected recently. 'You believe a lot of things people tell you when you're "country" and don't know much about the world. I can see how certain people kept control of our destiny then. Deep down, we knew we weren't making much money, and we knew the hotels were dirty and the food was bad. But we didn't think about that so much – we were enjoying ourselves.'

The year was 1944; the Americans had been involved in the Second World War for three years. Perhaps because many male musicians had been drafted, all-girl orchestras proliferated and flourished. Among them the groups directed by Phil Spitalny, Ina Ray Hutton, and Ada Leonard were best known, but all the girl bands were more in demand than they had ever been before.

Not only were the Sweethearts busy, they were perhaps more stable, since there were fewer changes of personnel that year. One notable change was replacement of Marge Pettiford as lead alto by Rosalind (Roz) Cron, a Jewish girl from Boston, Massachusetts. Roz had been with Ada Leonard's band for some time. There were violins in that band, and the music was more sedate. Consequently Roz, a high-spirited girl who was an extremely good player, relished the freer, more swinging style of the Sweethearts.

'I remember something about the difference between working for Ada Leonard and being with the Sweethearts,' Roz says. 'In all the theatres, when the Sweethearts started playing the audience would come in, dancing down the aisles to their seats. Black audiences were always like that. But if you'd go to hear Tommy or Jimmy Dorsey, or Ada Leonard, people just *walked* to their seats and sat down.'

Shortly after Roz Cron joined the band, Maurice King arrived from Detroit to replace Jesse Stone as musical director. He had a cataclysmic effect on the band. Roz Cron in particular was impressed. 'Maurice immediately put us through the most gruelling rehearsals. It was a tough struggle, but we made it. "Tuxedo Junction" turned into a really polished thing.'

Maurice King recalls, 'When I worked with the girls I would show them a passage in an arrangement and how to phrase it, four bars at a time. We'd keep on going over it, and finally, when it jelled, you could see their little eyes beam. It was like putting an erector set together.'

King obviously enjoyed teaching and working with the girls. He began writing speciality numbers for the band, and his 'Vi Vigor', 'Slightly Frantic', 'Don't Get It Twisted', and 'Diggin' Dirt' became part of the Sweethearts' book. ' "Diggin' Dirt" was what we called a dance stopper,' said King. 'We'd end the tune, pause, and then start it all over again. We'd do this several times. It was a big number.'

En route to California, where they were scheduled to record for the Armed Forces Radio Network, the girls spent their days playing, rehearsing, and sleeping on the bus. Finally, they reached Texas, where they were booked on a series of night-club dates. One afternoon in Austin a policeman who was watching them rehearse asked King, 'Isn't that a white girl over there?' 'What makes you think she's white?' King replied. Looking right at Roz Cron, the policeman said, 'Well, she looks white to me.' At this point King answered piously, rolling his eyes heavenward, 'Well, our girls are not responsible for what one of their parents may have been forced to do.' He then turned back to the band and continued the rehearsal, while Roz, red as a beet, had a difficult time keeping quiet.

Attired in their brand new USO uniforms, the Sweethearts sailed for Europe on 15 July 1945, reaching Le Havre on 22 July. They were chaperoned by Maurice King, as Rae Lee Jones had become ill and couldn't make the trip. In the European Theatre the war was already over, but there were still thousands of GIs in the Occupational Forces to be entertained. When the girls arrived, they were ecstatically received, and, every time the band performed, the audiences went wild. The programme varied somewhat from the routine they used in night-clubs. Tunes were added that the GIs knew and liked, but basically it was the same show that had excited the Apollo audiences earlier that year.

They were all living together in a hotel, and Maurice King was required to conduct a room check at 10.30 p.m. every night, because of the curfew. He would make the room check and leave, knowing full well that some of the girls would sneak out afterwards. 'I should have received a medal for bringing back that band intact,' King has said with a mysterious smile. Piney Woods seemed a million light-years away.

When the band returned to the States after Christmas 1945, the girls had money in the bank for the first time in their lives. As financial guardian of the band, Maurice King had seen to it that most of the money the girls earned was deposited in US banks to await their return from Europe. Only Helen Jones had elected to have Rae Lee Jones hold her money for safekeeping, instead of depositing it in the bank.

The controlling factors of the band were still the Washingtonians, Dan Gary and his partner, Al Dade. Gary was still the president of the corporation, and Rae Lee Jones was still the trustee, although she had left Arlington to return to her home town of Omaha, seriously ill.

The band went on. More and different projects were being undertaken. Leonard Feather, who has always admired women musicians and done his best to further their careers, now prepared to record for RCA Victor, using different women's groups. The Sweethearts recorded two numbers for Leonard Feather – 'Don't Get It Twisted' and 'Vi Vigor', both written by Maurice King. They also made two sides for Guild Records, with one side featuring Tiny Davis singing and playing 'Stompin' the Blues'. The reverse side spotlighted Anna Mae Winburn singing 'Do You Want To Jump, Children?'. The culmination of all this activity was a short film, *That Man Of Mine*, which starred Ruby Dee and featured the Sweethearts. Maurice King wrote the theme song, and the Sweethearts played it.

At last the Sweethearts had realized some of their earlier dreams. They had played to audiences of thousands in the United States and abroad, recorded overseas broadcasts with big-name Hollywood stars, had made records and films. What was left for them?

For some it seemed a good time to leave the band and go back to school. Others had already met their future husbands, and they left to get married. A few stayed on, but there were many new girls coming in. Some remained for a while, but others left after only a week or two, so it is impossible to document all the band members during the last years the group was together. Nevertheless the band continued to grow in stature. Some of the musicians were the best the band had ever had, and this is confirmed by the following enthusiastic review carried in the 27 July 1946 issue of *Billboard*. Noting the band's appearance at the Million Dollar in Los Angeles, the review read in part:

> The joint is jumpin' again this week with a solid bill headlined by the International Sweethearts of Rhythm ... Anna Mae Winburn fronts the Sweethearts (all-gal ork) in smooth and easy style. Fem musikers are top instrumentalists and dish out a polished brand of music, offering such widely titled concoctions as 'Don't Get It Twisted' and 'Just the Thing'. Instrumental breaks fall to Pauline Braddy on the skins and a sensational sax tooter, Vi Burnside. Latter socked 'em between the eyes with 'After You've Gone' and 'I Cover the Waterfront'.
>
> In the vocal bracket, featured thrush Mildred McIver does 'Day by Day' and 'Mr Postman Blues' well ... Surprise vocal shot was guitarist Carline Ray doing 'Temptation'. Gal has a deep voice and knows how to peddle a tune.

The band was to continue until the end of 1948, playing brilliantly and getting excellent reviews. And yet, something was missing now that virtually all the original Sweethearts had left.

Helen Jones was on her way back to Omaha to visit Rae Lee Jones, now desperately ill. It was a shock to Helen to see her so obviously near death, but just as shocking was the admission Mrs Jones made – that she had spent all the money Helen had entrusted to her. She begged Helen's forgiveness. 'I didn't realize the magnitude of it until years later,' Helen reflected recently. 'I felt so sorry for her. There she was, down and out, in this little old house that she had bought for her parents. And when she died she left it to me, but I didn't take it. Her parents were still there, and I didn't want to put them out. So there was nothing I could do. At that time I was young, and I didn't know anything, so whatever came up, I just accepted it. That's life – everyone learns one way or another.'

Somehow, in spite of the mystery surrounding the management of the band, Rae Lee Jones had been the life force that held it together. When she died, the band also died.

But memories and dreams do not die easily. They still flourish in the hearts and minds of these women, who open their scrapbooks and point with pride to the fresh-faced group of girls with whom they once had shared so much. No matter that their moment in the spotlight was brief. Their spirit and courage has been passed on to a new generation of talented young women, who are seeking their own dreams.

ERIC VOGEL

Jazz in a Nazi Concentration Camp

Eric Vogel was an amateur musician in Czechoslovakia, when he was arrested and sent to a concentration camp by the Nazis. When this memoir was first published in Down Beat, *Vogel graced it with a brief note:*

> *I am writing this story without hate or feelings of revenge. It is my desire that the memory of this short-lived band, the Kille Dillers, should not die. . . .*

This is a story of horror, terror, and death but also of joy and pleasure, the history of a jazz band whose members were doomed to die.

It began in 1938 in Brno, the second largest city in Czechoslovakia. We were immensely interested in jazz, and we had our little combo consisting of the talented Paszkus brothers, guitar and drums; Bramer, piano; Kolck, clarinet; myself, trumpet.

We were playing semi-professionally but mostly for fun. I was a jazz fan of long standing and had one of the largest collections of American jazz records in my country. I also had a few issues of *Down Beat*, and despite my poor knowledge of the English language, I understood almost everything that was written about jazz in the United States.

Things were calm and peaceful – except the political situation. But we were living in another world, in the world of jazz sounds, and did not pay any attention to the dark political clouds, which grew bigger and bigger every day. We did know about the fate of Jews in Germany, but we were sure Hitler would never come to Czechoslovakia. But on 15 March 1939, it happened, and we were taken by surprise.

The same day the bell rang at many apartments occupied by Jews, and a voice commanded, 'Open the door, Gestapo!' This meant in many cases the end of countless Jews, who were taken away, beaten to death, or sent to concentration camps and never seen again.

At 5 p.m. the bell rang at our apartment.

'*Aufmachen. Gestapo!*'

My parents were struck by horror. I opened the door, and outside in the SS uniform, with a big swastika on his arm, a man stood who a few weeks before had been in the apartment of one of my friends to listen to one of our jam sessions.

'Oh, that's you!' he said, more surprised than I was. He assured me that nothing would happen to me. This was the first time that jazz was deeply involved in shaping my life. It was not to be the last.

After the first wave of arrests, the horror subsided, only to make way for a well-organized persecution. After a few weeks, I lost my job as a design engineer, and to make my living I began to write and sell arrangements for Bobek Bryen's big band. I also transcribed some American records. I remember some titles – 'Squeeze Me' by Chick Webb, 'Livery Stable Blues' by Bunny Berigan, and 'Gin Mill Blues' by Bob Crosby.

One of the first anti-Semitic laws was the order for all Jews to wear the yellow Star of David and not to mingle or speak with non-Jews. Later, Jews were forbidden to be on the street after 8 p.m. and were not permitted to frequent public places, such as movies, theatres, coffee-houses, or night-clubs, where all the bands were playing. If you were caught without the star, you were sent immediately to a concentration camp.

A few weeks later, Jews had to abandon their apartments and were confined to a relatively small area of Brno. The evacuated families were forced to live with other Jewish families in the 'permitted' zone and share apartments. We were very happy not to be evacuated, even though we had to share our two-bedroom apartment with two other Jewish families. I still managed to play somewhat muted jazz in my apartment and was in demand by band leaders to write more arrangements. I had composed and arranged 'Boogie Woogie Blues' and one night was rehearsing the Bryen band when I suddenly discovered that it was already 9 p.m. Three Gestapo men entered the rehearsal room on a routine inspection and discovered me. I was arrested. On the way to the Gestapo head-quarters we met my SS friend, and he said, 'With this pig Jew I have to settle a personal account – leave him to me.' I was promptly handed over to him. He saved my life again – he took me home. He came into my apartment, and I gave him some of my jazz records and books about jazz music.

Other jazz fans and I listened regularly to American short-wave radio, and it was a holiday when we could get some of the better bands on our loudspeaker. It was our only connection with the outside world. I mention this because the order of the Gestapo to hand over all radio receivers within twenty-four hours was the hardest blow of all for us.

A few weeks later another terrible blow came. We had to deliver all our musical instruments to the Gestapo, and this was the end of our beloved jam sessions. I remember the dark day when I had to hand over my horn. It had given me so many hours of joy and pleasure it was like losing a beloved friend. I soaked the valves in sulphuric acid to prevent anyone from playing military marches on the horn used to playing jazz. I was also deprived of my piano, and I found it very difficult to arrange without it. This was the end of the period when I made my living with jazz.

I took a job with the Jewish community in Brno and was employed in the so-called technical bureau. We worked under direct supervision of the Gestapo and had to fulfil their orders. All the Jews had to register for emigration and hand over a list of their property, what was left. But there was no hope of emigration – it was only a trick of the Gestapo to get the list of *all* Jews in Czechoslovakia.

Suddenly we got the order to organize the *Umschulungskurse* (course for vocational retraining). In most cases these were for manual labour, but to my great surprise, I was asked to take over a course on jazz.

I was fascinated by the idea of playing again and getting some instruments. I recruited a teaching staff among some fellow jazz musicians, and within a few hours we had applications from about forty pupils. Some of them were elderly men who were hoping to play some music again. Naturally, we also had some youngsters who were already interested in or playing jazz. It took a few weeks before we got back our instruments. Until we did, we gave a few lectures about theory, history, and the aspects of jazz, and I will never forget the lecture I gave in the first session.

Most of my pupils were longhairs and never before had been interested in jazz. I managed to get hold of twelve jazz records of 'St Louis Blues', played by different artists. With them I set about to prove that in jazz the interpretation and spontaneous improvisation counts for more than the composition. Every jazz musician is a composer when he plays, and to make it clear for the longhairs, I compared the jazz musician to a painter who has freedom to paint as he likes. Then I compared the musician playing a classical composition to a photographer who is trying to get a sharp picture and can't do too much about it. This came as a shock to most of the 'classics', but after a few lessons and many more recordings, all the longhair musicians were excited about jazz and completely taken with its qualities.

After two or three weeks of theoretical lessons, we got instruments, and the real work of re-education began. Most of the pupils were string musicians, some of high level, and they had to switch now to trumpet, trombone, clarinet, sax, drums, etc., and after several weeks of giving individual lessons, we finally came together for ensemble playing. To our surprise, the band sounded better than we ever dreamed. We called the band the Kille Dillers. I had found in one *Down Beat* an expression, 'killer diller', that I liked very much, thought I didn't know the exact meaning of the words. I changed the first word to Kille. This was the name of the Jewish community (from the Hebrew word *kehilah*), so what was more natural than Kille Dillers?

But the glory of this band was not lasting. The 'transports to the east', until then only a rumour, suddenly became reality. Every two weeks, 1,000 Jews from Brno and Moravia were assembled in a camp and sent to an unknown destination. On 25 March 1942, the fateful order was delivered to me: 'You are included in the AF transport. Your transport number is AF 714. You have to be in the collection camp on 26 March and you may take with you not more than thirty pounds of baggage. . . .'

Late in the night, we were transported in closed trucks to the railway station, and under threatening machine-guns pointed at us by hundreds of SS men, we were forced into a waiting train that soon moved out of Brno, my home town. Nobody knew our destination, but in the first glimpse of the morning sun we discovered to our surprise that we were going west instead of east.

After a twenty-four-hour trip in an overcrowded train, we arrived at our destination: Ghetto Theresienstadt. We were greeted by the all-too-familiar commanding voices of the SS troopers: 'Everybody out!' We had to leave the train at once, leaving our luggage behind. We then marched to the city under heavy escort.

Theresienstadt was an old fortress surrounded by deep ditches. It was a city with a population of about 3,000 and a garrison of a few thousand soldiers. There were barracks all over the city, and we had to spend our first few days in the stables of the so-called Kavalier Kaserne, an old, rotten building. No beds, only straw on the floor, 100 persons in a room, no heat, no water, no food. Because I had brought pictures of jazz musicians with me, I soon was contacted by jazz men from Prague, Czechoslovakia, already in the ghetto. There were no instruments this time in the ghetto, and the only music was vocal.

Soon the ghetto was overcrowded, and transports from all Europe arrived daily. The Aryan population of Theresienstadt was evacuated, and the ghetto was sealed by heavy guards. Hunger grew with the population. In a room of normal living-room size thirty to forty persons were billeted – and they could be glad to be in a 'living' room and not in the attic or basement. The ghetto had the so-called *Juedische Selbstverwaltung* (Jewish Self-Government), a body of men which got daily orders from the German *Kommandantur* and had almost nothing to decide or to say. There was a steady coming and going of transports (usually 1,000 Jews) and a steady excitement and fear of being sent away to the 'east' with one of the outgoing transports.

One day we found a very old piano in one of the attics, and some instruments were smuggled into the ghetto by incoming transports. We made music again. Muted music, naturally, because every form of entertainment was strictly forbidden. So we stood guard around the house, just in case. Suddenly, the situation changed and the Germans not only permitted 'entertainment' but ordered it. We didn't know why exactly, but at the same time there was also the so-called *Stadtverschoenerung* (Improvement of the City) programme being carried out. Soon a new department of the Jewish Self-Government body was established, the *Freizeitgestaltung* (this word, loosely translated, means entertainment in your free time).

The change in policy was, for many of us, a mystery. But soon we discovered the reason: Theresienstadt was destined to be the model ghetto, to be shown to a commission of the International Red Cross as proof that everything written in the enemy press about concentration camps, with gas chambers, forced labour, and killing, was a lie. So the façades of all buildings were painted in shining colours, and everything not fit for the eyes of the expected commission – all the misery, the hunger, the filth, and the diseases – was hidden behind the fresh paint. A few days before, music had been forbidden and dangerous, but now. . . .

Instruments came into the ghetto, and soon some classical groups were organized. There were hundreds of wonderful musicians in the ghetto, the cream of Jewish musicians from all Europe, and despite the fact that the instruments were poor, the music was good. I had long ago thought to organize a jazz band, and on 8 January 1943, I wrote a letter to the *Freizeitgestaltung* about my intention to establish a jazz orchestra with the name Ghetto Swingers. After a few days, I got permission to do so. This was the birth of the band. We intended to play for our pleasure and the pleasure of listeners, but soon our role became official. To our surprise, a coffee-house was opened and a band shell erected on the main square of the ghetto. We had to play there every day for many hours.

Do not think the coffee-house was freely accessible to all ghetto inmates. No. There were tickets distributed that gave the receiver the right to be there for two hours. Elderly people, often without any understanding of our music, had to listen to the band, but they accepted our performance with great gratitude as a welcome change from the daily chores, the misery and hunger. No food was served here, but the guest got a cup of imitation coffee.

Not having written music, it was necessary at first to play some kind of improvised jazz, with sketchy head arrangements. The star of our band was a clarinet player, Fritz Weiss, who was, without any doubt, one of the best jazz musicians of the prewar era in Europe. He was also a terrific arranger, and soon we had a library of twenty or thirty pieces. There was no manuscript paper in the ghetto, so all the five lines had to be drawn singly and laboriously by hand. That is until I, being a mechanical engineer, had the idea to tape five pencils together to save time. I also arranged the theme song of the Ghetto Swingers, 'I Got Rhythm', but the bulk of our music was written by Weiss. Playing mostly written music now, I found it very difficult, being an amateur musician with limited reading ability, to follow the score. The band was augmented by three trumpets and one trombone, and I was politely asked by the other members of the band to take the third chair and not play too loudly.

One day a transport from Holland came, and screening the refugees for jazz musicians, I found Martin Roman, a piano player originally from Germany, where he had played with the famous Marek Weber Band. With the first few bars he played, he convinced me of his ability. He soon took over and became the leader of the band. We now had plenty to rehearse and because all of us were also members of the fifty-piece symphonic orchestra, under the direction of the Danish conductor Peter Deutsch, we had to play ten or twelve hours a day.

The Ghetto Swingers was quite a good band. We were playing with swing and feeling, mostly in the style of Benny Goodman. Closing my eyes now, I can almost hear Benny Goodman emanating from Fritz Weiss's clarinet. I think he came close to the quality of his idol. He also wrote some wonderful arrangements, some overnight, and excelled in a trio with Martin Roman on piano and Koko Schuman on drums. In the final weeks of the existence of the Ghetto Swingers, we were playing with a complete rhythm section, Nettl, piano; Schuman, drums; Goldschmidt, guitar; Lubensky, bass. In the reed section we had Weiss, clarinet; Vodnansky, alto saxophone; Donde, tenor saxophone; and in the brass section, Kohn, Chokkes, and myself on trumpets, and Taussig on trombone.

The rumours about the visit by the Red Cross commission came true, and on 23 June 1944, the commission (two Danes and one Swiss) came to the ghetto. They must have got the impression that everything was fine in Theresienstadt, so skilfully was the truth hidden. We had to play on the main square and in the coffee-house to strengthen the picture of a happy community. None of the ghetto inmates was permitted to speak to the commission, and typical was the scene in which *Lagerkommandant* Rahm gave sardine sandwiches to some children (undernourished on a 900-calorie hunger diet), and the children had to say, in an expression of gratitude, '*Onkel Rahm, schon wieder Sardinen!*' ('My, sardines again!')

A few days later there was much excitement in the ghetto. The Nazis had decided to a make a film of the ghetto to show the outside world how wonderful the life was in Theresienstadt. Naturally, the Ghetto Swingers had to participate. We had to augment the band, to our sorrow, with three violin players not of the swinging type. We appeared several times in the movie.

The cameramen and other movie experts who came from Prague to film the ghetto were amazed by the quality of our band, and we were happy. The movie people stayed several weeks in the ghetto, and everything was filmed that would please the eye and ear – sporting events, symphonic concerts, theatre and vaudeville and all the shining façades of the buildings hiding the terrible truth about the misery, the hunger, the suicides, the diseases, the cramped 'living' conditions, the daily beatings, the horror. We, the musicians, did not feel that we were but a tool in the hands of our oppressors. We were so concerned and so happy to play our beloved jazz that we had tranquillized ourselves into the dream world produced by the Germans for reasons of propaganda. We felt safe and were prepared to stay in the ghetto until the end of the war and even made plans to keep the band together after the war.

But one day the party was over. Our mission as propaganda musicians had been fulfilled. The day the last movie man left the ghetto, bad news struck like lightning from a blue sky: new transports were going to the east, and almost everybody had to go. On 28 September 1944, the first transport, with 2,500 men, left Theresienstadt, ostensibly for a new labour camp in Germany. In this transport were all the members of the Ghetto Swingers except me. But this transport went directly to the liquidation camp, Auschwitz, where during the war, more than 4,000,000 people were killed in the gas chambers.

When I left a few days later with the second transport, I did not know that some members of the Ghetto Swingers went directly from the train into the gas chambers, marked innocently as 'showers', and there, within a few painful minutes, lost their lives. Among them was our beloved and wonderfully gifted Fritz Weiss, one of the best jazz musicians Europe ever had.

There were twenty of us in a compartment built for six persons as our train went to the east. We passed ruins of railway stations and locomotives bearing big posters '*Deutsche Raeder rollen zum Sieg*' (German wheels are rolling to victory), and we made jokes about it, not knowing that for most of us our last hours were passing.

Finally our train pulled into a station surrounded by barbed wire and watchtowers. And soon we heard the all too familiar command, '*Alles heraus!*' ('Everybody out!') We had no time to grab our few pieces of luggage. Soon we stood in front of the train not far from a building that looked like an old factory with a smoking chimney. We were driven to a little hill, where an SS officer pointed with his thumb to a right side or the left. An elderly SS man liked my watch and asked me to sell him the watch for ten cigarettes. How could I say no?

The SS man asked me what I had done in Theresienstadt. I told him that I was a musician and played in a jazz band. He said, 'That's what we need here. When you come to the hill and the officer asks you your age and your health, tell him that you are in perfect health and make yourself ten years younger.'

I had no idea how important this advice was, but when the man on the hill asked me these questions, I answered with a loud voice, almost in military fashion, that I was fine and twenty years old. He smiled and pointed to the left. Not knowing that this little movement with his thumb meant life or death, many of my friends reported ill, because they thought to get lighter work. In many cases this SS man never asked a question. He just sent most of our transport to the right side – and to the gas chambers.

There have been many books written about Auschwitz. Four million people were driven into the gas chambers, labelled from the outside as *'Brausebad'* (showers). But instead of water a deadly gas came from the nozzles, and in ten to twelve minutes everybody was dead. The bodies were burned in ovens, but not before all gold was removed from teeth and hair cut off. The ashes were used as fertilizer and the fat for fabrication of soap. One hour after our arrival, I got the truth about the factory-like building: the dense smoke coming from the chimney was the last of my friends. A few hours before, we were joking about the bombed-out railway stations.

I had no time to think about the terrible fate of my friends. I was chased by men in striped pyjamas to a big hall where we had to take off our clothes. Then we were shaved all over and driven into an actual shower but not before our heads were immersed in a biting liquid for what was called disinfection purposes. Half-blind, we left the shower room in the nude and had to stand for many hours in front of the building, trembling and shaking because of freezing winds and mounting hunger. Finally we got some dirty rags and sheets to serve as clothes. We looked so bizarre that some of us were laughing again. Hours later we were driven into a barracks, formerly stables. Before I fell asleep, I witnessed a terrible thing. A Dutch Jew who had collaborated with the Germans and was the cause of the death of many Jewish families was killed by other Dutch Jews, killed slowly and painfully. When I protested, I was beaten. I was so tired from the ordeal that I fell asleep on a wooden board six feet square, which I had to share with about a dozen other prisoners.

A few hours later: *'Zaehlapell!'* Everybody had to get out and had to remain, hungry and tired, in a snowstorm until SS men came and counted to see if the number of prisoners was correct. Some weak-looking prisoners were taken away. This was the so-called selection, and these prisoners went right to death. Two horrible days passed, two days without food, and in those two days I was beaten by young fellow prisoners in striped pyjamas, who were in charge of the barracks.

After two days of *Zaehlapell*, an SS man commanded, *'Musiker, vortreten!'* ('Musicians, step forward'). I did so, and the first thing that happened was that an SS man punched me in the stomach with all his strength. I was not prepared for this attack, but I did not fall to the floor. He told me to come with him. We went into barracks No. 2, and suddenly I was surrounded by members of the Ghetto Swingers, embracing me and kissing me. 'We were looking for you,' said band leader Martin Roman, 'and we were sure to find you!'

In a few hours I was no longer dressed in rags but in a blue and very sharp-looking band uniform. I got shoes and food, cigarettes, and I felt like a human being again. I was introduced to the two German mass-murderers who were in charge of the camp. One of them, Willy, asked what instrument I played. 'Trumpet,' I said.

'We have only two trumpets and already two trumpet players here,' said the music-loving Willy. 'But I'll get you a trumpet even if I have to pay for it with a bottle of whisky or a three-carat diamond.' I was glad of this, but soon I was plunged into deep sorrow upon hearing of the death of some band members, among them Fritz Weiss.

There were about thirty of us musicians. We had to play from early in the morning until late in the evening for the German SS, who came in flocks to our barracks. We had no music; everything was played ad lib. We had to play classical compositions, opera, operettas, dance music, and jazz. We had some good singers among us, and we made good music despite the fact that some SS man told us, 'Before you we had a wonderful gypsy band here which lasted six weeks – then they went up the chimney. You'll go up in four weeks.'

Not having a trumpet yet, I played drums on an empty accordion case, keeping time with a wooden ladle. Sometimes I played one of the two trumpets, and for a command performance for an SS officer, I played a tune he loved – 'Tiger Rag'. He liked it, and I received a pair of almost-new shoes and a hundred cigarettes.

After four weeks, the end came abruptly. It was in November 1944, and to our surprise, we were not sent to the chimney. But we were stripped of our band uniforms, given rags again, and were marched to a freight train on which we left the camp. Some members of the band managed to stay together, and at the beginning of the trip we had the strength to joke and to vocalize our arrangements in the manner which is now done by Lambert–Hendricks–Ross. We had no food and were packed like sardines in the freight car. There were no toilet facilities. People were lying one on the other. Some were crying, and a few were dying.

After two days, we arrived in Berlin. The SS permitted us to open the door, and we witnessed one of the fiercest bombardments on Berlin. After the terrible noise of the bombs and the anti-aircraft guns subsided, our train began to roll again, and a few hours later we were driven from the train and assembled in a big hall of the Heinkel aircraft factory in Oranienburg. There was naturally the *Zaehlapell* again, and somebody said to the SS officer, hoping to better our fate, 'We are the *Lagerkapelle* (camp choir) from Auschwitz.' But he was beaten so badly nobody ever mentioned our musical profession. We spent two very bad weeks in Oranienburg, mostly standing hungry in the rain. We were desperate and grew weaker every day. We could not sleep because of nightly bombing raids. Finally we were marched to the nearby concentration camp of Sachsenhausen, where, after two weeks of hunger, we got our first hot meal. We spent only two days here. Then it was one concentration camp after another ... Kaufering in Bavaria, where Roman chanced upon a camp inspector who remembered his piano playing with the Marek Weber Band and who saved us from death-dealing labour ... Augsburg-Pfersee, where I worked in a Messerschmitt airplane plant, marching ten miles to and from the factory ... long hours, hard labour ... growing weaker ... little food ... stomach so caved in I could feel my spine ... vision blurred ... hearing distorted.

Fortunately, the war was nearly over. Each day the sound of battle came closer. It sounded better to me than the hottest jazz.

But still no liberation. We were loaded on open freight cars and sent on the way to Dachau for final liquidation in the gas chambers. At a slow curve I jumped off the train and ran for my life through machine-gun fire. I hid in the deep forest, in the rain, without food. Finally, a car came, and I crawled out of my hiding place only to discover that in the car were German air force officers. They did not kill me but gave me some bread and directed me to the nearest village. A few hours later I arrived at a village, Petzenhausen, where I was given hot black coffee and potatoes and hidden by the villagers in a barn.

On 30 April 1945, the first US jeep came into the village, and on the jeep was written BOOGIE-WOOGIE. I ran to a GI, a six-footer, knelt in front of him, and began to kiss his feet. He gave me chocolate and cigarettes. I asked him about the inscription on his jeep and about a dozen or so American piano players, Count Basie, Duke Ellington, Meade Lux Lewis, Teddy Wilson . . . I think I was the biggest surprise of his life. I looked more dead than alive, my weight was seventy pounds. I had lost about a hundred and forty pounds. The next thing – I was surrounded by GIs and brought in triumph to the officers' club in a nearby German town, Landsberg.

Here, I underwent a record blindfold test, and despite the fact that I had been cut off from American jazz for more than four years, I recognized most recordings of bands and soloists that were played for me. I was the sensation of the club. I was fed and clothed. The reign of terror was over. I again became a human being. I truly and literally had made my living with jazz.

JOSEF ŠKVORECKÝ

Red Music

Škvorecký wrote this essay about the fate of jazz and jazz musicians under two totalitarian regimes – first the Nazis, then the Communists – as an introduction to his novella, The Bass Saxophone *(1967).*

In the days when everything in life was fresh – because we were sixteen, seventeen – I used to blow tenor sax. Very poorly. Our band was called Red Music which in fact was a misnomer, since the name had no political connotations: there was a band in Prague that called itself Blue Music and we, living in the Nazi Protectorate of Bohemia and Moravia, had no idea that in jazz blue is not a colour, so we called ours Red. But if the name itself had no political connotations, our sweet, wild music did; for jazz was a sharp thorn in the sides of the power-hungry men, from Hitler to Brezhnev, who successively ruled in my native land.

What sort of political connotations? Leftist? Rightist? Racialist? Classist? Nationalist? The vocabulary of ideologists and mountebanks doesn't have a word for it. At the outset, shortly before the Second World War, when my generation experienced its musical revelation, jazz didn't convey even a note of protest. (Whatever shortcomings the liberal republic of T. G. Masaryk may have had, it was a veritable paradise of cultural tolerance.) And no matter what LeRoi Jones says to the contrary, the essence of this music, this 'way of making music', is not simply protest. Its essence is something far more elemental: an *élan vital*, a forceful vitality, an explosive creative energy as breathtaking as that of any true art, that may be felt even in the saddest of blues. Its effect is cathartic.

But of course when the lives of individuals and communities are controlled by powers that themselves remain uncontrolled – slavers, czars, führers, first secretaries, marshals, generals and generalissimos, ideologists of dictatorships at either end of the spectrum – then creative energy becomes a protest. The consumptive clerk of a working man's insurance company (whose heart had reportedly been moved by the plight of his employer's beleaguered clients) undergoes a sudden metamorphosis to become a threat to closely guarded socialism. Why? Because the visions in his *Castle*, his *Trial*, his *Amerika* are made up of too little paper and too much real life, albeit in the guise of non-realist literature. That is the way it is. How else explain the fact that so many titles on Senator Joe McCarthy's index of books to be removed from the shelves of US Information Libraries abroad are identical to many on the one issued in Prague by the Communist party early in the seventies? Totalitarian ideologists don't like real life (other people's), because it cannot be totally controlled; they loathe art, the product of a yearning for life, because that too evades control – if controlled and legislated, it perishes. But before it perishes – or when it finds refuge in some kind of *samizdat* underground – art, willy-nilly, becomes protest. Popular mass art, like jazz, becomes mass protest. That's why the ideological guns and sometimes even the police guns of all dictatorships are aimed at the men with the horns.

Red Music used to play (badly, but with the enthusiasm of sixteen-year-olds) during the reign of the most Aryan Aryan of them all and his cultural handyman, Dr Goebbels. It was Goebbels who declared, 'Now I shall speak quite openly on the question of whether German radio should broadcast so-called jazz music. If by jazz we mean music that is based on rhythm and entirely ignores or even shows contempt for melody, music in which rhythm is indicated primarily by the ugly sounds of whining instruments so insulting to the soul, why then we can only reply to the question entirely in the negative.' Which was one reason we whined and wailed, rasped and roared, using all kinds of wa-wa and hat mutes, some of them manufactured by ourselves. But even then, protest was one of the lesser reasons. Primarily, we loved that music that we called jazz, and that in fact was swing, the half-white progeny of Chicago and New Orleans, what our non-blowing contemporaries danced to in mountain villages, out of reach of the *Schutzpolizei*, the uniformed security service. For even dancing was forbidden then in the Third Reich, which was in mourning for the dead of the Battle of Stalingrad.

The revelation we experienced was one of those that can only come in one's youth before the soul has acquired a shell from being touched by too many sensations. In my mind I can still hear, very clearly, the sound of the saxes on that old, terribly scratchy Brunswick seventy-eight spinning on a wind-up phonograph, with the almost illegible label, ' "I've Got a Guy", Chick Webb and His Orchestra with Vocal Chorus'. Wildly sweet, soaring swinging saxophones, the lazy and unknown voice of the unknown vocalist who left us spellbound even though we had no way of knowing that this was the great, then seventeen-year-old, Ella Fitzgerald. But the message of her voice, the call of the saxes, the short wailing and weeping saxophone solo between the two vocal choruses, they all came across. Nothing could ever silence them in our hearts.

And despite Hitler and Goebbels the sweet poison of the Judeo-Negroid music (that was the Nazi epithet for jazz) not only endured, it prevailed – even, for a short time, in the very heart of hell, the ghetto at Terezín. The Ghetto Swingers . . . there is a photograph of them, an amateur snapshot, taken behind the walls of the Nazi-established ghetto during the brief week that they were permitted to perform – for the benefit of the Swedish Red Cross officials who were visiting that Potemkin village of Nazism. They are all there, all but one of them already condemned to die, in white shirts and black ties, the slide of the trombone pointing diagonally up to the sky, pretending or maybe really experiencing the joy of rhythm, of music, perhaps a fragment of hopeless escapism.

There was even a swing band in the notorious Buchenwald, made up for the most part of Czech and French prisoners. And since those were not only cruel but also absurd times, people were put behind barbed wire because of the very music that was played inside. In the concentration camp near Wiener Neustadt sat Vicherek, a guitar player who had sung Louis Armstrong's scat chorus in 'Tiger Rag' and thus, according to the Nazi judge, 'defiled musical culture'. Elsewhere in Germany several swingmen met a similar fate and one local *Gauleiter* issued an extraordinary (really extraordinary? in this world of ours?) set of regulations which were binding for all dance orchestras. I read them, gnashing my teeth, in Czech translation in the film weekly *Filmový kurýr*, and fifteen years later I paraphrased them – faithfully, I am sure, since they had engraved themselves deeply on my mind – in a short story entitled 'I Won't Take Back One Word':

1) Pieces in foxtrot rhythm (so-called swing) are not to exceed 20 per cent of the repertoires of light orchestras and dance bands;

2) in this so-called jazz type repertoire, preference is to be given to compositions in a major key and to lyrics expressing joy in life rather than Jewishly gloomy lyrics;

3) as to tempo, preference is also to be given to brisk compositions over slow ones (so-called blues); however, the pace must not exceed a certain degree of allegro, commensurate with the Aryan sense of discipline and moderation. On no account will Negroid excesses in tempo (so-called hot jazz) or in solo performances (so-called breaks) be tolerated;

4) so-called jazz compositions may contain at most 10 per cent syncopation; the remainder must consist of a natural legato movement devoid of the hysterical rhythmic reverses characteristic of the music of the barbarian races and conducive to dark instincts alien to the German people (so-called riffs);

5) strictly prohibited is the use of instruments alien to the German spirit (so-called cowbells, flexatone, brushes, etc.) as well as all mutes which turn the noble sound of wind and brass instruments into a Jewish-Freemasonic yowl (so-called wa-wa, hat, etc.);

6) also prohibited are so-called drum breaks longer than half a bar in four-quarter beat (except in stylized military marches);

7) the double bass must be played solely with the bow in so-called jazz compositions;

8) plucking of the strings is prohibited, since it is damaging to the instrument and detrimental to Aryan musicality; if a so-called pizzicato effect is absolutely desirable for the character of the composition, strict care must be taken lest the string be allowed to patter on the sordine, which is henceforth forbidden;

9) musicians are likewise forbidden to make vocal improvisations (so-called scat);

10) all light orchestras and dance bands are advised to restrict the use of saxophones of all keys and to substitute for them the violoncello, the viola, or possibly a suitable folk instrument.

When this unseemly decalogue appeared in that story of mine in Czechoslovakia's first jazz almanac (it was in 1958), the censors of an entirely different dictatorship confiscated the entire edition. The workers in the print shop salvaged only a few copies, one of which got into the hands of Miloš Forman, then a young graduate of the Film Academy in search of material for his first film. After several years of writing and arguing with the censors, we finally got official approval for our script, whereupon it was personally banned by the man who was at the time the power in the country, President Antonín Novotný. That was the end of our film. Why? Because the decrees of the old *Gauleiter* were once again in force, this time in the land of the victorious proletariat.

But back in the days of the swastika it was not just that one isolated German in the swing band at Buchenwald, not just the few imprisoned pure-Aryan swingmen – many far more reliable members of the master race were tainted with the sweet poison. How vividly I recall them, in their blue-grey Nazi uniforms, recently arrived from Holland with Jack Bulterman's arrangements of 'Liza Likes Nobody', in exchange for copies of which we gave them the sheet music for 'Deep Purple' and the next day they were off to Athens, where there were other saxophones swinging, underlined with Kansas riffs. I can see those German soldiers now, sitting in a dim corner of the Port Arthur Tavern, listening hungrily to the glowing sounds of Miloslav Zachoval's Big Band, which was the other, far better swing band in my native town of Náchod. Vainly did I dream of becoming one of Zachoval's swingers. Alas, I was found lacking in skill, and doomed to play with the abominable Red Music.

How naive we were, how full of love and reverence. Because Dr Goebbels had decided that the whining Judeo-Negroid music invented by American capitalists was not to be played in the territory of the Third Reich, we had a ball inventing aliases for legendary tunes so that they might be heard in the territory of the Third Reich after all. We played a fast piece – one of those forbidden 'brisk compositions' – called 'The Wild Bull', indistinguishable to the naked ear from 'Tiger Rag'; we played a low tune, 'Abendlied' or 'Evening Song', and fortunately the Nazi censors had never heard the black voice singing, 'When the deep purple falls over sleepy garden walls ...' And the height of our effrontery, 'The Song of Řešetová Lhota', in fact 'St Louis Blues', rang out one misty day in 1943 in eastern Bohemia, sung in Czech by a country girl, the lyrics composed so that they might elaborate on our new title for W. C. Handy's theme song: 'Řešetová Lhota ... is where I go ... I'm on my way ... to see my Aryan folk. . . .' In fact, we were fortunate that the local Nazis had never seen Chaplin's *The Great Dictator*, never heard the bullies sing about the 'Ary-ary-ary-ary-aryans'. Neither had we, of course – 'The Song of Řešetová Lhota' was simply an indigenous response to Nazism.

It was, like most of our songs, ostensibly the composition of a certain Mr Jiří Patočka. You would search for his name in vain in the lists of popular composers of the time since he too was a figment of our imagination. That mythical gentleman's large repertoire also included a tune indistinguishable from 'The Casa Loma Stomp'. In our ignorance we hadn't the faintest idea that there was a castle of that name in distant Toronto. We believed that Casa Loma was an American band leader, one of the splendid group that included Jimmy Lunceford, Chick Webb, Andy Kirk, the Duke of Ellington (Ellington had been placed among the nobility by a Czech translator who encountered his name in an American novel and decided that this must be a member of the impoverished British aristocracy, eking out a living as a band leader at the Cotton Club), Count Basie, Louis Armstrong, Tommy Dorsey, Benny Goodman, Glenn Miller – you name them, we knew them all. And yet we knew nothing. The hours we spent racking our brains over song titles we couldn't understand ... 'Struttin' with Some Barbecue' – the definition of the word 'barbecue' in our pocket Webster didn't help at all. What on earth could it mean: 'walking pompously with a piece of animal carcass roasted whole'? We knew nothing – but we knew the music. It came to us on the waves of Radio Stockholm mostly, since that was the only station that played jazz that the Nazis didn't jam. Swedish style: four saxes, a trumpet plus rhythm – perhaps the first distinct jazz style we knew, except for big band swing. Curiously there was one film, also of Swedish provenance, that among all the Nazi war-propaganda films, the *Pandur Trencks* and *Ohm Kruegers*, escaped the eyes of the watchmen over the purity of Aryan culture. In translation it was entitled *The Whole School Is Dancing*. The original title appealed to us more, even though we understood no Swedish: *Swing It, Magistern!*. In the territory of the Third Reich, that was the movie of the war. We all fell in love with the swinging, singing Swedish girl called Alice Babs Nielsson, another reassuring indication that though we lacked knowledge we at least had an ear for jazz: much, much later she recorded with Ellington. But that film – I must have seen it at least ten times. I spent one entire Sunday in the movie theatre, through the matinée, through the late afternoon show and the evening show, inconsolably sad that there was no midnight mass of *Swing It, Magistern!*.

'Swing It, Magistern, Swing It!' became one of the standard pieces played at public concerts in obscure little towns in eastern Bohemia, much to the joy of fans of swing. But of course, enemies of jazz and swing were also to be found among our Czech contemporaries. The milder ones were the jazz conservatives to whom swing was an outlandish modern distortion. They would just boo loudly at our concerts. The radicals, the polka buffs, did more than that. They threw apple cores at us, rotten eggs, all kinds of filth, and the legendary concerts in the legendary hick towns often ended in a brawl between the polka buffs and the fans of swing. Then the band would have to flee by the back door to save their precious instruments, irreplaceable in wartime, from the wrath of the protectors of the one and only true Czech music: the polka – played, horror of horrors, on an accordion.

The polka buffs never dared throw eggs at our Ella, though. Yes, we even had our own Goddess, our Queen of Swing, Girl Born of Rhythm, Slender Girl with Rhythm at Her Heels, our own Ella. She was white, of course, and her name was Inka Zemánková. She distinguished herself by singing Czech lyrics with an American accent, complete with the nasal twang so alien to the Czech language. My God, how we adored this buggering up of our lovely language, for we felt that all languages were lifeless if not buggered up a little. Inka's theme song was something entitled 'I Like to Sing

Hot', not one of Jiří Patočka's ostensible compositions but a genuine Czech effort. The lyrics described a swinging girl strolling down Broadway with 'Harlem syncopating in the distance'. It contained several bars of scat and concluded with the singer's assertion, 'I like to sing Hot!' This final word, sung in English, alerted the Nazi censors, and on their instructions Inka had to replace it with the equally monosyllabic expression '*z not*' – a charmingly absurd revision, for although it rhymes with 'hot' the expression means exactly the opposite of singing hot music: it means singing from sheet music, from the notes.

Far from Harlem, from Chicago, from New Orleans, uninformed and naive, we served the sacrament that verily knows no frontiers. A nucleus existed in Prague that published an underground magazine entitled *O.K.* (an abbreviation not of *Ol Korekt* but of *Okružní Korespondence*, i.e. Circulating Correspondence). Pounded out on a typewriter with about twenty almost illegible carbon copies, this underground publication (really underground, its very possession punishable by a stint in a concentration camp) was our sole source of reliable information. It was distributed through the Protectorate by lovely *krystýnky* on bicycles, the bobbysoxers of those perished times. I can see them in their longish skirts, dancing and 'dipping' in the taverns of remote villages, with one fan always standing guard at the door, on the lookout for the German police. When a *Schupo* appeared over the horizon, a signal was given, and all the *krystýnky* and their boyfriends, the 'dippers', would scurry to sit down to glasses of green soda-pop, listening piously to the Viennese waltz that the band had smoothly swung into. When the danger had passed, everyone jumped up again, the Kansas riffs exploded, and it was swing time once again.

Then the Great War ended. In the same movie theatre where I had once sat through three consecutive showings of *Swing It, Magistern!* I sat through three screenings of the lousy print of *Sun Valley Serenade*, with Russian subtitles. I was impervious to the Hollywood plot, but hypnotized by Glenn Miller. The print had found its way to our town with the Red Army, the film badly mangled by frequent screenings at the battlefront, the damaged sound track adding Goebbelsian horrors to 'In the Mood' and 'Chattanooga Choo Choo'. None the less, I had the splendid feeling that, finally, the beautiful age of jazz had arrived.

My mistake. It took only a lean three years before it was back underground again. New little Goebbelses started working diligently in fields that had been cleared by the old demon. They had their own little Soviet bibles, primarily the fascistoid *Music of Spiritual Poverty* by a V. Gorodinsky, and I. Nestyev's *Dollar Cacophony*. Their vocabulary was not very different from that of the Little Doctor, except that they were, if possible, even prouder of their ignorance. They characterized jazz and jazz-inspired music by a rich assortment of derogatory adjectives: 'perverted', 'decadent', 'base', 'lying', 'degenerate', etc. They compared the music to 'the moaning in the throat of a camel' and 'the hiccuping of a drunk', and although it was 'the music of cannibals', it was at the same time invented by the capitalists 'to deafen the ears of the Marshallized world by means of epileptic, loud-mouthed compositions'. Unfortunately, these Orwellian masters soon found their disciples among Czechs, who in turn – after the fashion of disciples – went even further than their preceptors, declaring wildly that jazz was aimed at 'annihilating the people's own music in their souls'. Finally the aggressive theoreticians even organized a concert of 'model' jazz pieces composed to order for the Party's cultural division. It was an incredible nightmare. Band leader Karel Vlach, the greatest among Czech pioneers of swing, sat in the front row, going from crimson to ashen and from ashen to crimson again, probably saying a prayer in his soul to Stan Kenton. Beside him sat an unholy trinity of Soviet advisers on jazz (led by, of all men, Aram Khachaturian, colleague of Prokofiev and Shostakovitch), gloomy, silent, and next to them a senile choirmaster using a hearing aid. And yet not even the emasculated musical monster presented to them satisfied the Soviet advisers. They criticized its 'instrumental make-up' and described it as 'the music of a vanishing class'. Finally, the old choirmaster rose, and we heard him add the final chord: 'Now, take the trumpet. Such an optimistic-sounding instrument! And what do those jazz people do? They stuff something down its throat and right away it sounds despicable, whining, like a jungle cry!'

After that Vlach was unable to refrain from a few heretical

remarks: if they didn't give him something better than Stan Kenton, said he, he would keep on playing Stan Kenton. Which is perhaps what he did in the travelling circus to which he was shortly thereafter relegated along with his entire band. The Party also proclaimed the creation of an 'official' model jazz band, and in the Youth Musical Ensembles the most avid ideologists even tried to replace the hybrid-sounding (therefore supposedly bourgeois) saxophones with the non-hybrid (therefore more proletarian) violoncello – but it takes at least five years to learn to play the cello passably, while a talented youth can master the saxophone in a month, and what he wants to do is play, play, play. But ideological thinking follows paths free from the taint of reality. In place of Kenton, they pushed Paul Robeson at us, and how we hated that black apostle who sang, of his own free will, at open-air concerts in Prague at a time when they were raising the socialist leader Milada Horáková to the gallows, the only woman ever to be executed for political reasons in Czechoslovakia by Czechs, and at a time when great Czech poets (some ten years later to be 'rehabilitated' without exception) were pining away in jails. Well, maybe it was wrong to hold it against Paul Robeson. No doubt he was acting in good faith, convinced that he was fighting for a good cause. But they kept holding him up to us as an exemplary 'progressive jazz man', and we hated him. May God rest his – hopefully – innocent soul.

But in the early fifties, although the bishops of Stalinist obscurantism damned the 'music of the cannibals', they had one problem. Its name was Dixieland. A type of the cannibal music with roots so patently folkloristic and often (the blues) so downright proletarian that even the most Orwellian falsifier of facts would be hard put to deny them. Initiates had already encountered isolated recordings of Dixieland during the war, and after it ended a group of youths heard the Graeme Bell Dixieland Band performing at a Youth Festival in Prague. They created the first Czechoslovak Dixieland Band, and soon there was a proliferation of Louisiana-sounding names: Czechoslovak Washboard Beaters, Prague City Stompers, Memphis Dixie, and dozens of others. Uncle Tom music was really the only form of jazz suffered at the depressing congregations called youth entertainments, where urban girls in pseudo-national costumes got up and sang bombastic odes to Stalin in the style of rural yodelling.

An apostle of Dixieland, Emmanuel Uggé, took the Czechoslovak Dixieland on the road. Once again, obscure little towns in the northeast of Bohemia resounded with loud syncopations, wound around with the boring, hyperscholarly commentaries of this devoted *Doctor Angelicus* of Dixieland who, for the ears of the informers attending the concert, succeeded in interpreting the most obscene tune from the lowest speakeasy in Chicago as an expression of the Suffering Soul of the Black People, waiting only for Stalin and his camps where re-education was carried out directly for the other world. But it turned out that going on the road with Dixieland was a double-edged move. On the one hand it kept the knowledge of jazz alive, but on the other hand what the more enlightened and therefore less brazenly orthodox supervisors in Prague had passed off as a 'form of Negro folklore', the true-believing provincial small fry recognized for what it was: an effort to 'smuggle western decadence into the minds of our workers. . . . Such orchestras conceal their vile intentions in music that has no educational merit,' says a letter from the town council of Hranice to the management of the Hranice Cement Workers. 'Eighty per cent of what the ensemble played was westernist, cosmopolite music which had an eccentric effect, going so far as to cause one of the soldiers to come up on the stage and do a tap dance.' Horrors! A soldier in the Czech Red Army, tap-dancing to some Nick La Rocca tune! Years later I recalled this Harlemized soldier when I read in an article by Vassily Aksyonov (author of the epochal *A Ticket to the Stars* – but who in the West has heard of him? Who knows that the liberating effect of this novel, written in Moscow slang, had perhaps a more profound influence on contemporary Russian prose than *Doctor Zhivago*?) about a big band that existed somewhere in Siberia during Stalin's last days, and played 'St Louis Blues', 'When the Saints', 'Riverside Blues'. . . . Another chapter in the legends of apostles who were often martyrs.

Even Inka, our idolized Queen of Swing, became one. After the war she had put aside her career in order to study singing professionally. Five years later, she decided it was time to make her comeback. The concert agency booked her for a Sunday matinée at the Lucerna Hall in Prague. She sang one song just before the intermission and was to sing another one after. It was an old swing tune, but while Inka's sense of rhythm had remained, her vocal range had doubled. She was rewarded by thunderous applause, gave them an encore, and this time sang one whole chorus in scat. The applause was endless. 'When I stumbled offstage,' she told me years later, 'I thought to myself – there, I've made it again! But there was a guy there, in one of those blue shirts, you know, I think they called them the Young Guard, all scowling and furious, and he yelled at me, "That's it! Out! I can assure you you'll never sing another note in public." And in fact, that's what happened, they didn't even let me sing my second number after the intermission.' At that moment I couldn't help thinking about Vicherek and his scat chorus in 'Tiger Rag' during the Nazi occupation.

However, with the passage of years political events threatened the unlimited rule of the provincial small fry (and the blue-shirted Communist Youth storm trooper) and also the validity of their musicological opinions. We began to consider how we might get permission for the Czechoslovak Dixieland Band (now metamorphosed into the Prague Dixieland Band) to perform in public again – and found unexpected and unintended help from the US. An American bass player named Herbert Ward had asked for political asylum in Czechoslovakia, 'delivering another serious blow to American imperialism', the Party press announced. It also said that Ward used to play with Armstrong. We immediately looked him up in his hotel in Prague and talked him into playing a role of which he was totally unaware and which is referred to in Stalinist slang as 'shielding off'. In fact, we used him ruthlessly. We quickly put together a jazz revue entitled *Really the Blues* (title stolen from Mezz Mezzrow), printed Herb's super-anti-American statement in the programme, provided the Prague Dixieland to accompany Herb's homemade blues about how it feels to be followed by American secret-police agents (a particularly piquant blues in a police state where everybody knew the feeling only too well), dressed his sexy dancer-wife Jacqueline in original sack dresses borrowed from a Prague matron who had lived it up in Paris in the twenties, then settled down to enjoy her dancing of the eccentric, decadent Charleston. Since Herb's terribly shouted blues had anti-American lyrics and because Jackie's skin was not entirely white the authorities didn't dare protest, and left us alone with our towering success. The show finally folded as a result of difficulties of a more American nature. Herb and Jacqueline wanted more money. The producer, bound by state norms, was unable to give them more, and *Really the Blues* died a premature death. Later on, Herb and Jacqueline went the way of many American exiles: back home to the States, the land where the words 'you can't go home again' generally seem not to apply. Apply they do, though, for other countries, the ones that send their own writers into exile, to prison, or to their death.

Really the Blues was the end of a beginning. Jazz had grown to resemble the Mississippi, with countless rivulets fanning out from its delta. The Party found other targets: Elvis Presley, little rock'n'roll groups with guitars electrified and amplified on home workbenches, with a new crop of names recalling faraway places – Hell's Devils, Backside Slappers, Rocking Horses – new outcries from the underground. By the end of the fifties, a group of young people had been arrested and some of them sentenced to prison for playing tapes of 'decadent American music' and devoting themselves to the 'eccentric dancing' of rock 'n' roll. (Again, the spirit of Vicherek was present at their trial.) And because the mass of young people had turned to follow other stars, jazz proper, be it mainstream or experimental, was no longer considered dangerous, and so the sixties were a time of government-sponsored International Jazz Festivals. The stage at Lucerna Hall in Prague echoed with the sounds of Don Cherry, The Modern Jazz Quartet, Ted Curson. . . . We applauded them, although, for the most part, this was no longer the music we had known and loved. We were the old faithfuls. The broad appeal of the saxes was gone, either this was esoteric music or we had simply grown old. . . . Jazz is not just music. It is the love of youth which stays firmly anchored in one's soul, forever unalterable while real live music changes, for everthe calling of Lunceford's saxophones. . . .

That was when I wrote *The Bass Saxophone*, and I was writing about fidelity, about the sole real art there is, about what one must be true to, come hell or high water; what must be done to the point of collapse, even if it be a very minor art, the object of condescending sneers. To me literature is forever blowing a horn, singing about youth when youth is irretrievably gone, singing about your homeland when in the schizophrenia of the times you find yourself in a land that lies over the ocean, a land – no matter how hospitable or friendly – where your heart is not, because you landed on these shores too late.

For the steel chariots of the Soviets swung low, and I left. Jazz still leads a precarious existence in the heart of European political insanity, although the battlefield has shifted elsewhere. But it is the same old familiar story: a spectre is again haunting Eastern Europe, the spectre of rock, and all the reactionary powers have entered into a holy alliance to exorcize it – Brezhnev and Husák, Suslov and Honecker, East German obscurantists and Czech police-spies. Lovely new words have emerged from the underground, like the *krystýnky* and the 'dippers' of the Nazi era: now there are *Manichky*, 'little Marys', for long-haired boys, *undrooshy*, from the Czechified pronunciation of the word 'underground', for rock fans of both sexes. Anonymous people hold underground Woodstocks in the same old obscure hick towns, gatherings often ruthlessly broken up by police, followed by the arrest of participants, their interrogation, their harassment, all the joys of living in a police state.

And so the legend continues . . . and the chain of names. The Ghetto Swingers, the nameless bands of Buchenwald, the big band in Stalin's Siberia, the anonymous jazz messengers in Nazi uniforms criss-crossing Europe with their sheet music, the Leningrad Seven – nameless aficionados who in the Moscow of the sixties translated, from the Czech translation of original American material into Russian *samizdat*, the theoretical anthology *The Face of Jazz* – and other buffs and bands, even more obscure, blowing away for all I know even in Mao's China. To their names new ones must be added, the Plastic People of the Universe, and DG307, two underground groups of rock musicians and avant-garde poets whose members have just been condemned (at the time I am writing this) to prison in Prague for 'arousing disturbance and nuisance in an organized manner'. That loathsome vocabulary of hell, the vocabulary of Goebbels, the vocabulary of murderers. . . .

My story is drawing to a close. *'Das Spiel ist ganz und gar verloren. Und dennoch wird es weitergehen. . . .'* The game is totally lost. And yet it will go on. The old music is dying, although it has so many offspring, vigorous and vital, that will, naturally, be hated. Still, for me, Duke is gone, Satchmo is gone, Count Basie has just barely survived a heart attack, Little Jimmy Rushing has gone the way of all flesh. . . .

> . . . anybody asks you
> who it was sang this song,
> tell them it was . . .
> he's been here, and's gone.

Such is the epitaph of the little Five-by-Five. Such is the epitaph I would wish for my books.

Translated by Káča Poláčková-Henley

BORIS VIAN

Jazz Chronicle

Boris Vian was a novelist, poet, playwright, translator and an inventor. Not content with doing all that, he was also a trumpeter, a songwriter and a jazz critic. In 1950, he started up his own magazine in Paris, Jazz News, in which he wrote sometimes whimsical but always witty and perceptive editorials.

HE WHO WANTS TO CAN

Antonin, one of my beloved readers, wrote a kind letter wishing me a happy new year (why didn't you think of that?), and took advantage of the occasion to ask my advice. 'I'm young,' he said, 'and I would like to learn to play a jazz instrument. Can you help me choose?'

Seeing as how I want to, and remembering the immortal words of Busch – 'he who wants to can' – I am going to give him some advice, what's more in public.

Generally speaking, the choice is as follows: the trumpet (or cornet); alto, tenor and baritone sax (plus, more rarely, soprano and bass); the clarinet; trombone; the rhythm instruments piano, bass, guitar and drums. Actually, certain freaks use other pieces of plumbing like the French horn, the finger piano, the electric violin and the jawbone of an ass. But we will limit our study to the first group, leaving the second for the weirdos.

The trumpet can be recommended only in that it involves having three dexterous fingers of one hand, the easiest part, and a certain labial muscular ability which can be developed painlessly during adolescence through practice with the little girl next door. Other than that, it's a nasty business, physically very tiring and full of unexpected quacks (called clinkers in the King's English).

Combat: 14 January 1949

SENSATIONAL COCKTAILS

I've been editor for two months already! How times flies when you're having fun. During that period, I discovered a recipe for a really sensational cocktail – pour a glass of Cointreau, a glass of lemon-juice liqueur, a glass of kirsch, add sugar and ice in a beaker and shake well. Pour into a beer mug and then add dry, chilled champagne to the brim. You can drink this like lemonade; it helps pass the time. But let's get to the point. Our previous issue has earned nothing but reproaches. That being said, everybody agrees about one thing. There were no girlie photos. Well, it was conscious – we were saving them for this issue.

As you might imagine, finding enough women to fill this issue was something of a tour-de-force. Which accounts for its late publication. (This is supposed to be funny, but we need some justification for the scandalous inertia of those responsible for the delay.) In return for your patience, I recommend the following – take a bottle of vodka, crème de cacao and Cointreau and mix ¾ths of the first with ⅛th of each of the two others in an ice-filled beaker. If you have taken the trouble to choose a fifty-seven-degree vodka, the effect will be immediate – and will not harm your liver. For added body, place on your turntable an MGM platter written by Sy Oliver titled 'Slow Burn'. Which is, by the way, the name of this swinging cocktail.

Perhaps, you may be saying to yourself, perhaps he is handing out these chemical formulas to dull our perceptions, because he is depressed, just to fill the page, or because he's drunk. Well, no, my cherished readers, it is not by chance that this editorial already includes two practical recipes. Because it is our intention to make this classy review a didactic magazine to help raise the intellectual level of jazz fans, who may never be smart enough to understand the depth and beauty of the twelve pages of intelligent analytical articles which we dump on the market every month, and who will continue to run not walk to throw it into the nearest rubbish bin.

Yes, *Jazz News* has chosen the most difficult road (if nothing else, we have guts – *Jazz News* is owned, among other things, by Eddie Barclay, the biggest crook since the beginning of time), the apostolate road. We persist, and will continue to persist, as long as this review, burdened with idiotic writers, manages to avoid bankruptcy, to try and make you, valued readers, the most elite of all jazz fans and even, putting it mildly, the most elite of all Frenchmen. Do you realize the importance of your mission? Think of your future role if, God willing, we succeed. Frenchmen, the moment has arrived. Take a shaker, fill it with ⅓rd cognac, ⅓rd crème-de-fraise Héritier-Guyot, ⅓rd whipped cream, shake well and serve in a cocktail glass. It's called 'Rosemilk', and is good for your health.

Jazz News: March 1950

THE ART OF DIMINISHED FIFTHS

Now that everybody is talking about it, we thought it would be a good idea to bring our readers up to date about a new art people are bad-mouthing a lot lately: bebop. After studying textbooks by the only reliable source, M. Hugues Panassié, we have come to the conclusion that bebop is essentially the art of diminished fifths. Our collaborator Eddy Barnard, known as Eddy-the-Barbarian, insisted on writing down his thoughts on the subject and we undertook to translate them because he mutilates the French language with outrageous disrespect.

1) A primitive method consists of amputating one end of the fifth. This practice can be traced back to the emperor Charles the Fifth, whom we salute as the precursor of bop.

2) A more brutal amputation was practised by the Stammerers in northern France – the Fi-fil-filth-fifth method.

3) The classic diminishing method of our grandmothers – drop a stitch every two or three rows. This is called 'Knitty-gritty'.

4) Issue confidential buy-orders for a large block of fifths and then dump them all on the market without warning. The fifth will diminish automatically by the law of supply and demand. The diminished stockbroker method.

5) Large doses of detergent poured into a family-size washing-machine will result in massive quantities of diminished fifths. The housewife method, also known as 'The Clean Shrink'.

6) Take an acclaimed musician and hire him, under the pretext of demonstrating correct French pronunciation, to repeat the following phrase out loud: 'The fifth is an anti-jazz interval which Buddy Bolden disapproved of.' Record it on tape and publish the text in your official organ. Great orchestrators call this method 'Diminishing by Prestige'.

7) Play your records on a turntable using an expensive diamond stylus. Already diminished fifths will eventually evaporate, and everything else will diminish considerably in thickness and intensity. The oldest rag will sound boppish – 'Diminishing by Perfection'.

8) Buy codeine syrup in your neighbourhood pharmacy.

9) We sound a warning note for those who have the idea to play howel, mortice knife or woodworking plane – instruments which demand precision and fast fingering which will always remain the exclusive property of superior soloists. Superior bop soloists (names furnished upon request) have spoken to us of their aversion to those who use the plane without proper preparation and consequently do considerable damage to real jazz music.

10) Above all, never confuse a diminished fifth with an augmented fourth became Mme Nadia Boulanger has a weak heart.

11–12) Nothing to do with anything . . . we had to fill out the page.

Jazz News: March 1950

WHY WE DETEST JAZZ (I)

. . . Investigative reporting for Jazz News *by Freddy Flabby*
(Saturday painter, winner of the Agricultural Grand-Croix du
Mérite, colonial doctor and ex-male nurse)

The article 'Jazz is Dangerous' in our last issue warned you about the serious physical problems which can come from jazz-abuse. Hoping to enlarge the debate, we have decided to reserve one page for the enemies of jazz, who heretofore have not had any journalistic platform. This injustice will now be corrected, and we hope that everybody who is, as we are, profoundly disgusted by jazz will make it their duty to send our editors material for the new page. We particularly welcome articles that investigate the hypocritical lie at the root of this rotten corpse, because objective reasoning leads inevitably to rejection of that jungle music called jazz, which is obviously unworthy of any white man who drinks Pernod, drives a limousine and feels up his best friend's wife while dancing the samba. We welcome, with particular enthusiasm, calumnies, gossip and slander calculated to ruin the reputations of big-name jazz musicians, as well as elegiac prose about individuals who heap dishonour upon what our enemies call 'real jazz'.

There will be no censorship – if we read in *Paris-Match* that Louis Armstrong wears flowered underwear and that he loves brightly coloured handkerchiefs, we will reproduce the information in integral form, and so much the better if it isn't true. Down with jazz, that degenerate music – long live our very own military marches, the bourgeoisie and so on.

Among the material already received, we cite in particular an anonymous envelope containing a remarkable study entitled 'Jazz and Epiphany'. This document is an admirable indictment of jazz, written in clear and simple language, and the harm such articles can do to that banal music cannot be overestimated.

Our most sincere compliments to the fine Parisian weekly magazine, *La Presse*, several lines from which we cannot resist the pleasure of citing. After correctly deploring the loss of the first 'racktimes' (*sic*) which inspired the pioneers of jazz, *La Presse* deals with recent declarations by Armstrong concerning bebop. The thrust is something like this . . .

The playing of Armstrong and his celebrated pianist Earl Hines, exponents of the New Orleans style, were not enough to overcome the 'bellowing bebop of Russell Moore' (known as Big Chief).

Upon arriving in Paris, Louis Armstrong had not hesitated to call bebop 'wrestling music'. Maybe that's why *La Presse* mentioned Big Chief, who is *big*. Well, I certainly hope their fine critique will make the poorly informed very, very angry. Bravo, *La Presse*! We support you all the way.

We are trying to procure sexy photos of bad female singers who lure into their insidiously charming traps those imbeciles who still prefer the vulgarity of someone like Bessie Smith to the sweet, captivating voices of Martha Tilton or Anita O'Day.

Dr F. Flabby

Jazz News: March 1950

Translated by Mike Zwerin

JOHN McDONOUGH

The Court-Martial of Lester Young

Drafted off a night-club bandstand, busted in basic training, imprisoned for ten months in a Georgia stockade, Lester Young
had a sensational and almost non-existent military career. A few
years earlier, Bessie Smith's death had come to represent racial
bigotry after John Hammond reported the story in the November
1937 *Down Beat*. Young's story, too, became a *cause célèbre*, a
certain demonstration of the Army's racism in the wartime years.
At the time, the music press offered little news about the imprison-
ment of the great tenor saxophonist. But in the years to come,
fragmented details began to appear – and to be fantastically
distorted.

Were the original charges trumped up? Was Lester Young running an illegal still on the Army base? Did a perverted southern
white officer instigate the whole sickening affair out of fury at seeing
Young's billfold photo of his white wife? There were other stories –
that Young was psychologically tortured at Fort Gordon, Georgia,
even a completely preposterous yarn that he'd been involved in a
murder – and indeed, some writers who hear deterioration and
decline in his postwar performances find a cause in his Army prison
experience.

In the decades since the event, the story of Lester Young's Army
period has been a matter of rumour, speculation and educated
guesswork. Until now, the distinguishing feature of the case has
been its lack of documented facts.

Early in 1980, while Richard M. Sudhalter and I were preparing
the booklet for Time-Life's *Lester Young Giants of Jazz* album box, I
began looking beneath the rumours. Even the chronology of Lester's
induction and service was hazy, so I suggested that Ann Holler of
the Time-Life research department request from the Pentagon, under
the Freedom of Information Act, documents relating to Young's
Army experience. Holler came back with a complete transcript of

Lester Young's general court-martial plus a number of related documents. . . .

In late September, 1944, only days after Young completed filming the famous short film *Jammin' The Blues* at Warner Bros, the Army finally caught up with Lester, who had been ignoring draft notices for over a year, at Los Angeles' Plantation Club with Count Basie's band. An FBI agent, posing as a jazz fan, personally served papers to Young and drummer Jo Jones there in the club.

Few who knew him expected Young to pass the physical, medical and psychological tests. To no avail, Milt Ebbens, Basie's manager, and Norman Granz, then a Los Angeles area concert promoter, appealed the draft notice. Young may have believed that his reliance on alcohol and soft drugs would keep him out of the service. A medical exam revealed that Young was syphilitic at the time of his induction, and Young told authorities at his induction interview that he had used marijuana continuously for eleven years. But the Army was accustomed to hearing tall tales from draft-shy inductees. On 30 September 1944 (not '43, as the Time-Life booklet's first printing claims in a typographical error), the thirty-three-year-old Lester became Private Young, serial number 39729502.

Private Young was sent to Ft. MacArthur in northern California for five weeks of basic training, and passed through two other bases before finally reaching Ft. McClellan in Alabama on 1 December. There, his troubles began. Young was assigned to Company E of the second training battalion of the first training regiment, commanded by Captain William Stevenson. On 1 January 1945, Young was injured while running an obstacle course and was sent to the base hospital, where he underwent minor rectal surgery and received regular doses of pain-killing drugs while recovering. On 24 January he was released from the hospital and put back on active duty. While Young was in the hospital, Dr Luis Perelman, Ft. McClellan chief of neuropsychology, diagnosed him as being in a 'constitutional psychopathic state manifested by drug addiction (marijuana, barbiturates), chronic alcoholism, and nomadism.' Yet Dr Perelman felt Lester Young had 'a purely disciplinary problem and that disposition should be effected through administrative channels'.

On 1 February, Young was arrested for wrongful 'possession of habit-forming drugs, to wit, about one ounce of marijuana and about one ounce of barbiturates'. A military court convened on 16 February. Meanwhile, Lester had been examined by Army psychiatrist Lawrence J. Radice, who diagnosed Young as a 'constitutional psychopath' who drank 'excessively' and used marijuana and barbiturates. Also mentioning Young's common law wife, Dr Radice wrote, 'In view of his undesirable traits and inadequate personality, he is unlikely to become a satisfactory soldier.'

Lester's appointed counsel, Major Glen Grimke, entered a plea of not guilty. Waiving its opening statement, the prosecution called Young's commanding officer, Capt. Stevenson.

Q Was [Lester Young] a member of your command on the 30th of January 1945?

A He was, sir.

Q Did you have a conversation . . . with him on that date?

A I did, sir.

Q Will you relate the circumstances to the court?

A He was detailed on assignment to battalion headquarters, and looking over the detail I noticed a man who didn't seem to be in very good condition. I questioned him as to what was wrong . . . and he said that he was 'high' and [I] asked him to elaborate on that and asked him if he had any drugs and he said that he had and I asked him if he had any on him – any more of what he had taken – and he handed me a few pills. Then I had the company executive officer, Lt. Hutton, go with me. We searched Private Young's clothing and his possessions . . . I found several small white pills, smaller than an aspirin and a little harder formed than an aspirin, and three red capsules and some marijuana cigarettes, homemade marijuana cigarettes. Two of them had been smoked, had been burned and butted. . . . There were [also] two bottles of pink liquid . . . One with a very raw smell – well, like a sensation . . . like smelling alcohol – irritating to your nostrils. . . . They were number three prescription bottles and they were full.

Stevenson said he had turned all the material over to investigating officer Lt. Joe Humphreys. Grimke then cross-examined.

Q And when did you first become aware . . . that [Lester Young] was under the influence of something like narcotics?

A I had suspicioned it when he first came in the company.

Q Did you ever say anything to him about it?

A No, sir. The man had good control of himself . . .

Q What made you suspect?

A Well, his colour, sir, and the fact that his eyes seemed bloodshot and he didn't react to training as he should.

After Stevenson left the witness stand, Lt. Humphreys was called. He testified that Stevenson had given him the cigarettes, pills and pink liquid taken from Young's quarters, and that he, in turn, had delivered them to Scott Holman, a chemist for the US Government Narcotics Division. Holman later returned the evidence with a written analysis of the materials, Humphreys said. The prosecutor then asked the investigator about his interrogation of Lester Young.

A . . . He started off by telling me that he had been using – I believe he used the word dope – for eleven years and smoking marijuana for ten and he was a tenor saxophone player in Count Basie's band for the past ten years and as a musician he resorted to the use of marijuana smoking and called them 'sticks' and on that occasion that he had gotten these barbiturates. I know that he referred to the marijuana, and that he intended to hide it, and I guess he got to feeling too good and he forgot to hide it before Capt. Stevenson got it. . . . He stated further that although some doctors had given him drugs, that he had no prescription from any Army doctor to get it and stated that at Ft. McClellan, Alabama, you could get it if you had the money to buy it. . . . He stated that he had never harmed anyone. He told the authorities before coming in [the Army] about [his use of drugs]. He never harmed anyone.

Grimke, in his cross-examination, asked Humphreys what Young meant by telling the authorities.

A Well . . . that he never made any denial of having used drugs or smoking marijuana. . . . He related [his drug use] to the induction authorities before they ever took him into the Army. . . .

At this point in the court-martial, prosecution and defence agreed that investigator Holman's report described the evidence as one and a half marijuana cigarettes and three capsules and eleven tablets which contained barbiturates. It was also stipulated that barbiturates were habit-forming drugs. The prosecution's case was closed.

The only witness for the defence was Pvt. Lester Young himself, who admitted virtually everything. He was a cooperative, if bewildered, witness on his own behalf. He was a man of music now caught in a rigid system of discipline he could not begin to understand – and the Army was no less puzzled by him. Whether they were trying, the representatives of two cultures showed no mutual understanding. Defence counsel Grimke asked the questions:

Q How old are you, Young?
A I am thirty-five, sir.
Q You are a musician by profession?
A Yes, sir.
Q Had you played in a band or orchestra in California?
A Count Basie. I played with him for ten years.
Q Had you been taking narcotics for some time?
A For ten years. This is my eleventh year.
Q Why did you start taking them?
A Well, sir, playing in the band we would play a lot of one-nighters. I would stay up and play another dance and leave and that is the only way I could keep up.
Q Any other . . . musicians take them.
A Yes, all that I know.
    . . .
Q Did [the draft board] know you had this habit . . .?
A Well, I'm pretty sure they did, sir, because before I went to join the Army I had to take a spinal and I didn't want to take it. When I went down I was very high and they put me in jail and I was so high they took the whiskey away from me and put me in a padded cell, and they searched my clothes while I was in the cell. . . .
Q You say you were pretty high. What do you mean by that? Do you mean because of the whiskey?
A The whiskey and the marijuana and the barbiturates.
Q What I want to know is, did the board that inducted you have any reason to believe that they knew you took habit-forming drugs? . . . Did you tell them you took it?
A Yes, sir.
Q Now, since you have been at Ft. McClellan, Alabama, have you been in the hospital?
A Well, in training on the obstacle course I hurt myself and I went to the dispensary, and they ordered me to go to the hospital. While there, they found out about it . . . The doctor was giving me the same pills you have there. He gave me one at nine o'clock

in the morning and one in the afternoon and five and nine at night.

Q How long were you in the hospital here?

A From the first of January to about the 22nd or 23rd.

. . .

Q What did you do when you came out of the hospital – go to bed?

A Sent me out on the field.

Q Carry a full pack?

A I don't know. . . . It was a pack and a rifle.

Q And that is when you immediately returned from the hospital?

A Yes, sir.

. . .

Q Did you ever have any conversation with [Capt. Stevenson] about drugs?

A Yes, sir. One morning when I was sitting in the day-room . . . he asked me about it and said that he knew I was very high.

Q When you refer to being high, would you explain that?

A Well, that is the only way I know how to explain myself.

. . .

Q It is not whiskey alone that makes you high when you refer to being high?

A No, sir.

Q Now if you do not take these drugs, smoke these things, does it affect you in any way physically?

A Yes, sir, it does. I don't want to do anything. I don't care to blow my horn and I don't care to be around anybody.

Q Affects you badly?

A Just nervous.

Q Could you do this training here if you left them alone?

A No, sir. Because I tried, sir. I tried it truthfully.

Q Have you had any of these drugs . . . in the last few days?

A Haven't . . . not since I have been in the stockade now.

Q Feel pretty nervous now?

A I think about it all the time.

That ended the defence case. In a brief cross-examination, Young testified that he had obtained the barbiturates without a doctor's prescription. Final arguments followed, and the court-martial of Lester Young was over; the whole proceeding lasted an hour and thirty-five minutes. The five-judge panel promptly found Young guilty and sentenced him immediately: dishonourable discharge from the service, forfeit of all his $50 a month pay (except a $7.60 deduction for government insurance and $22 a month for dependants). Worst, before his discharge, Lester Young was sentenced to a year in the US disciplinary barracks at Ft. Leavenworth, Kansas.

First Lt. William Moffet, of the judge advocate's staff, reviewed the case, but found no irregularities to upset the verdict. A few comments by Moffet are worth noting: 'Testimony of the accused indicates he used drugs during the past ten years, that the draft board knew it at the time of his induction, and further that he cannot get along without them. . . . The record of accused both civilian and military shows that he is not a good soldier. His age as well as the nature and duration of his undesirable traits indicate he can be of no value to the service without proper treatment and severe disciplinary training . . . The sentence . . . is both legal and appropriate.'

Young served his sentence – actually ten months – at Ft. Gordon, Georgia instead of Leavenworth. After his release in the first week of December 1945, he resumed his real career.

The court martial record says nothing about Young's ten months at Ft. Gordon. It is known, however, that he played music regularly while confined. Every Sunday, there was a dance for the noncoms on the base, and Lester would be let out to play. Fred Lacy, who became Young's regular guitarist in the postwar years, was also a prisoner there, and played in the little group. Sitting in most of the time on piano was Sergeant Gil Evans, who was assigned to Oliver General Hospital ten miles away in Augusta. On his way to Ft. Gordon every Sunday, Evans would pick up a few bottles of whiskey and perhaps some other gifts, which he made sure found their way discreetly to Lester.

Lester Young was unfit for military service and the Army knew it when it inducted him. If Young is to be held accountable for his behaviour, then the Army is no less responsible for inducting a man who was medically and emotionally unsuited to be a soldier. That act of bureaucratic ineptitude served neither the Army nor the public interest. The Army's system of screening and classification clearly and tragically failed. Once the military procedures were begun, there was no way to set the error right. Defence counsel Grimke's efforts to make Young's original induction an issue in the court-martial were disallowed; the tribunal would only consider Young's case on the evidence of the charge itself.

He had coped with prejudice all his life, but wartime military discipline was probably the worst thing that could have happened to a sensitive individual like Lester Young.

Wing

He fled down the immemorial Big River of his music, wanting to follow moving water because it went somewhere, and all complexities and attitudes and wraths were swept away before it. And so he fled down the Great Brown Snake that made the entire continent one vast watershed to it, and that from deepest, woodsy north at its trickling beginnings over smooth Canadian pebbles, to its final, timeless spending in the Gulf, drained out of the heart of America, smelling Pittsburgh slag from the Monongahela with dust that blew across the faceless Badlands to the Milk, gathering as the rivers, tributary to it, met (the Platte, the Kansas, the Missouri; the Minnesota, the Chippewa, the Illinois; the Little Sandy, the Cumberland, and the Ohio) to flow, terrific, widening and assuageless, ever south, where still others emptied into it (the White, the Big Black, and the Red), until in huge, instinctive death beyond the last bayous, it joined the other waters of the world. Wing went down the river as jazz, just forty years before, had beaten its way back up after the Great Dispersal, going down it as if to listen to the source again, to hear the secrets of the river's mouth that in cane field, board church, sod levee or cheap crib had aroused some inexpungeable longing once that only jazz could ease.

He never got to New Orleans (perhaps it was fortunate), because one night in Louisiana, drifting down a shanty street on the edge of Algiers, he heard the crude guttural of a cornet, poked his head through a paintless door, and found a Saturdaynightfull of dockworkers, drinking sour mash and whooping as they danced. Through the wild candour of all those hot faces, the faded print dresses snatched above the pumping knees of the girls, and the outlandish gusto that rocked the worn floorboards, his eye fell on one girl across the room.

Her dark face shone with that lip-parted, calm-eyed expression of anticipated tenderness, that tensionless acceptance of the world and its dealings which is a rebuke to all who look upon it. Her dewy gaze, eager for an object on which to lavish itself, was so utterly simple, so without sin, that had she suddenly impelled herself forward right into the throng of bent-kneed, flung-footed dancers, into the thresh of peg pants and French stockings, shaking her wide shoulders until her small hard breasts lifted, and raising her skirt, the action would have seemed too natural to the onlooker to be unchaste. For the whole reality of that night (so wild and rich and powerful-with-life after what he had just left) – the dusty pavements, the sweet odour of parched oleanders, the proximity of giddy flesh – seemed poised around her seventeen-year-old face, to which time had yet to add that something that denoted she must perish. She had more life ahead than death beyond, and she was as slender, fresh and inwardly shy as young girls have always been who made aging men stop dead and gasp with loss.

Her name was Fay Lee, and Wing never got to New Orleans, but found himself a room in a crumbling house by the river, and saw her whenever he could. He had no reason, and that was why.

He never even unpacked his horn, and the afternoon she first came there, noting the dirty shirts and trays of butts with a grave eye of respect for such masculine disorder, and let him touch her young untouched body, she stood, after it was over, looking at his sax (which he got out to show her) that was the colour of new pennies in the shaft of blind sunlight falling through the arras, and suddenly exclaimed, 'Oh, isn't it blessed! Isn't it just holy golden!' But he only seized her hand and drew her down again and lay, shifting and perplexed, through the heavy afternoon, robbed (as grown men sometimes feel robbed) of those furious male obsessions that always prove too brittle and unreal for mating with the simple nakedness of a girl. He wanted to lie upon the rugless floor with her and catch her moan in his mouth, and afterward feel the coolness of her fingers, fond, dear, and comforting. But she only blushed with an incomprehensible joy that somehow infuriated him.

He was near the river, and they loitered there in the long, opaque shadows of the motionless evenings, when silence seemed to swim out of the bayous upriver, huge, ominous and profound. And then night, which wakes a half-savage possibility in the American heart, brought the tart slice of whiskey, the shuttered laments of conflicting radios, and the lights swinging in the river like submerged lanterns. He sweated in his shirts till the backs were rotted through, and drank his whiskey neat, and the uncrushed, calm oval of her face always aroused him, as if it was a strange face, fleetingly glimpsed in a crowd, on which such inner recognition glowed that the intimacy of that one glimpse choked him with an unsuspected loneliness. She was simple, pellucid, and she learned his complex city ways with quiet joy in the learning itself; but still she undressed as if he were not there, folding her slip carefully in a square and placing her shoes side by side. Afterward, bathing his face from the chipped crockery bowl on the washstand, not daring to look back to the bed lest the very languor he had sought to create in her fine, agile limbs should infuriate him with a last desire now that it was achieved, he took to talking aloud, speaking as if he were alone, unconnected, unfinished sentences, a jumble of images from a hip, disordered world that she had never known. He ranted, he mused, he boasted and complained, he talked of Edgar almost obsessively. She listened with a steady, patient gaze, and did not hear or care about the words, and could not be impressed by fame or art; and then he watched her dress again, always with the same annoyed pinch of regret, and they went out and had a drink; and then he took her home to the kitchen that maddened him because, even with the new refrigerator set proudly so that it could be seen from the front room, there was an air of earnest humility about it; home to her waddling, bandannaed mother who treated him like a white man because he had come downriver, and her brothers who lounged around, splay-legged, listening to the radio.

His money started to run out, and he thought furiously, destructively, of marrying her, and forcing that simple, living look out of her eyes with awareness of him, *him*. He bought her fancy underwear, all white girl-silk, all scalloped edges, all hip and jaded and indecent; and talked aloud while she tried it on in the heat of his room, cursing, mocking her, wheedling. But she only giggled to catch sight of herself in his shard of mirror, and said, 'Ain't I cute though! Look at that!' He stopped seeing her for a week and got out his horn for the first time and sat in his drawers on the bed edge and played absently, hoping for accident to seize him, but playing nothing that he had not played before. He slept in long, sweating binges in which he did not even dream. He wanted her blackly, and prolonged the wanting of her, until he realized that it was not her he wanted, but something else, that something else: the calm of her eyes at which he imagined Edgar drawling sarcastically, 'She just a little Topsy, now isn't she? She's a rag doll!'

Then one twilight he wandered down to the river and saw her sitting on the pier, dangling her legs, a small, rapt silhouette watching the lights come on in perfect solitude. He drew nearer, thinking to reach around her unawares, cup her breasts, and frighten her into his life. But then, as he crept closer, he heard her singing an absent line of blues without words, a line too simple, too isolated from all other music by its spontaneity to be remembered, so that the moment it dried on her moist lips he could not recall it. He stood not four feet behind her, paralysed by the perishability and the keenness of that moment, as by an immense truth. And everything there became real to him, at last.

The dusk, the small outline of the girl, beyond which the river swept wide and murky moving heedlessly, deeply, gathering speed before it gave itself up in broad, doomed immolation in the Gulf: its tragic swiftness in the huge hush, and the small awkward silhouette against all that impermanence, and the heavy delta smells, and, at the last, the inconsolable reality of that reality came up into his heart like a sob; and his illusions and his rages left him in an instant, and he was alone there in the way of human beings one with the other, with only a song between. He sat down, and held her hand and used her no more. . . .

Now, in the studio, he stared at the crooner who was reading his ad libs from a cue sheet – that hard, unblinking stare that is so unnerving because there is no attention behind it – and he was wondering distractedly where she had gotten to. Moved to another street, married someone's brother, had gleeful children, given in to fat. Loss! He could not even remember her face, just the huddled outline against the evening river. And for a moment life amazed him again, because human routine, the flawless achievement of ambitions, and even the neatest of men were all part of its great, disordered confluence with time; and the truths and certainties a man shored against that fact changed it not at all. Loss – he had lost it all! He had squandered the calm he might have had with her; he had thrown away the simplicities of contact in his discovery of that song; he *would* have his music at any cost. Yes, yes.

He had used her no more after that, and felt the hungry, Edgar-like ironies in him die, and had known then that everything was simpler than irony, and even thought for a minute that he might show her that he knew, but then had seen in her eyes that utter innocence to which no river could ever be tragic, no dead irony real. So he had taken a bus for New York three days later, with his meagre truth, while she wept on a bench in the bus station, weeping easily as women do, and then walked away, her sources of renewal undamaged. He had been unaccountably separated from the men he worked with ever since, playing a pure line; and finally he had separated himself from them by taking the studio job. And just then he realized in a flash that men have only this sad knowledge with which to heal themselves: when you lose life, you grow wise. But that is better than maiming life to hold it.

'"Blue moon,"' the crooner was warbling, '"you saw me standing alone"' – rubbing his neck – '"without a dream in my heart."' Wing stared at him fixedly over the curve of his horn – the high-waisted trousers, the $25 shoes, the handsome empty face: a nice enough fellow, quick, sharp, friendly, in his own broil. But everything that Wing knew counted for nothing to that boy, the years, the losses, what he had *seen* with his eyes. So what was it worth? he thought, just as they came to the release where sixteen bars had been left open for him.

JACK KEROUAC

'There You Go-Orooni'

But one night we suddenly went mad together again; we went to
see Slim Gaillard in a little Frisco night-club. Slim Gaillard is a tall,
thin Negro with big sad eyes who's always saying, 'Right-orooni'
and 'How 'bout a little bourbon-orooni.' In Frisco great eager crowds
of young semi-intellectuals sat at his feet and listened to him on the
piano, guitar, and bongo drums. When he gets warmed up he takes
off his shirt and undershirt and really goes. He does and says
anything that comes into his head. He'll sing 'Cement Mixer, Put-ti
Put-ti' and suddenly slow down the beat and brood over his bongos
with fingertips barely tapping the skin as everybody leans forward
breathlessly to hear; you think he'll do this for a minute or so, but
he goes right on, for as long as an hour, making an imperceptible
little noise with the tips of his fingernails, smaller and smaller all the
time till you can't hear it any more and sounds of traffic come in the
open door. Then he slowly gets up and takes the mike and says, very
slowly, 'Great-orooni . . . fine-ovauti . . . hello-orooni . . . bourbon-
orooni . . . all-orooni . . . how are the boys in the front row making
out with their girls-orooni . . . orooni . . . vauti . . . oroonirooni . . .'
He keeps this up for fifteen minutes, his voice getting softer and
softer till you can't hear. His great sad eyes scan the audience.

Dean stands in the back, saying, 'God! Yes!' – and clasping his
hands in prayer and sweating. 'Sal, Slim knows time, he knows
time.' Slim sits down at the piano and hits two notes, two Cs, then
two more, then one, then two, and suddenly the big burly bass-
player wakes up from a reverie and realizes Slim is playing 'C-Jam
Blues' and he slugs in his big forefinger on the string and the big
booming beat begins and everybody starts rocking and Slim looks
just as sad as ever, and they blow jazz for half an hour, and then
Slim goes mad and grabs the bongos and plays tremendous rapid
Cubana beats and yells crazy things in Spanish, in Arabic, in
Peruvian dialect, in Egyptian, in every language he knows, and he

knows innumerable languages. Finally the set is over; each set takes two hours. Slim Gaillard goes and stands against a post, looking sadly over everybody's head as people come to talk to him. A bourbon is slipped into his hand. 'Bourbon-orooni – thank-you-ovauti . . .' Nobody knows where Slim Gaillard is. Dean once had a dream that he was having a baby and his belly was all bloated up blue as he lay on the grass of a California hospital. Under a tree, with a group of coloured men, sat Slim Gaillard. Dean turned despairing eyes of a mother to him. Slim said, 'There you go-orooni.' Now Dean approached him, he approached his God; he thought Slim was God; he shuffled and bowed in front of him and asked him to join us. 'Right-orooni,' says Slim; he'll join anybody but he won't guarantee to be there with you in spirit. Dean got a table, bought drinks, and sat stiffly in front of Slim. Slim dreamed over his head. Every time Slim said, 'Orooni,' Dean said, 'Yes!' I sat there with these two madmen. Nothing happened. To Slim Gaillard the whole world was just one big orooni.

LEONARD FEATHER

Monk, Blindfold

*Since the 1940s, Leonard Feather had been carrying out his 'blindfold tests'
for* Down Beat. *The idea was that a musician, or someone associated with
jazz, would be played a new record without knowing who the artists were,
and make comments. Thelonious Monk proved an awkward customer. In
the second part, other musicians, blindfolded, are played Monk's own music.*

Not until the Blindfold Test had been appearing for almost twenty
years did Thelonious Monk participate as a subject. The reason was
clear: Monk is not the most voluble of personalities, and it seemed
improbable that an interview could be obtained.

One day in 1966 Monk broke his long silence. Accompanied by his
wife Nellie, he sat, stood or paced his way through eight records. When
moments of silence engulfed him, Nellie succeeded in prodding him.

After the first minute of the first record, it became obvious that the
only way to complete an interview and retain Monk's interest would
be by concentrating mainly on other artists' versions of his own
compositions. Accordingly, Records 2–6 were all Monk tunes. At this
point, he seemed interested enough to listen to a couple of non-Monk
works. He was given no information about any of the records played.

Monk's reaction to Record No. 7 may have a more than coinci-
dental relationship to the opinions expressed openly by Oscar
Peterson concerning Monk's own value as a pianist.

1. Andrew Hill. 'Flight 19' (from *Point of Departure*, Blue Note).

(*After about two minutes, Monk rises from his seat, starts wandering
around the room and looking out the window. When it becomes clear he is
not listening, the record is taken off.*)

TM The view here is great, and you have a crazy stereo system.
LF Is that all you have to say about that record?

TM About *any* record.

LF I'll find a few things you'll want to say something about.

2. Art Pepper. 'Rhythm-a-ning' (from *Gettin' Together*, Contemporary). Conte Candoli, trumpet; Pepper, alto saxophone; Wynton Kelly, piano; Paul Chambers, bass; Jimmie Cobb, drums.

TM He added another note to the song. A note that's not supposed to be there. (*Sings.*) See what I mean?

LF Did I hear you say the tempo was wrong?

TM No, all tempos is right.

LF How about the solos? Which of them did you like?

TM It sounded like some slow solos speeded up, to me.

LF How about the rhythm section?

TM Well, I mean, the piece swings by itself. To keep up with the song, you have to swing.

LF How many stars would you rate it?

TM (*Indicating Mrs Monk*) Ask her.

LF It's your opinion I'm asking.

TM You asked me for my opinion, I gave you my opinion.

LF Okay, let's forget ratings.

3. Dizzy Gillespie. Medley: 'I Can't Get Started', ''Round Midnight' (from *Something Old – Something New*, Philips). James Moody, alto saxophone.

TM Dizzy. He had a crazy sound, but he got into that upper register, and the upper register took the tone away from him. That was the Freddy Webster sound too, you know, that sound of Dizzy's. (*Later*) That's my song! Well, if that's not Diz, it's someone who plays just like him. Miles did at one time too.

LF You like the way they put the two tunes together?

TM I didn't notice that. Play it again. (*Later*) Yes, that's the Freddy Webster sound. Maybe you don't remember Freddy Webster; you weren't on the scene at the time.

LF I remember Freddy Webster. And the records he made with Sarah.

TM Remember 'I Could Make You Love Me?' The introduction? Play that for me.

LF I don't think I can find it. You think Freddy influenced Diz?

TM Every sound influenced Diz. He had that kind of mind, you know? And he influenced everything too.

LF You like the alto player on here too?

TM Everybody sounded good on there; I mean, the harmony and everything was crazy . . . play it again!

4. Bob Florence. 'Straight, No Chaser' (from *Here and Now*, Liberty).
John Audino, lead trumpet; Herbie Harper, trombone; Florence,
arranger.

LF You liked the arrangement?

TM Did you make the arrangement? It was crazy.

LF No.

TM It was a bunch of musicians who were together, playing an arrangement. It sounded so good, it made me like the song better! Solos . . . the trombone player sounded good . . . that was a good lead trumpet player too . . . I've never heard that before. I don't know how to rate it, but I'd say it was top-notch.

5. Phineas Newborn. 'Well, You Needn't' (from *The Great Jazz Piano of Phineas Newborn*, Contemporary). Newborn, piano.

TM He hit the inside wrong – didn't have the right changes. It's supposed to be major ninths, and he's playing ninths (*walks to piano, demonstrates*). It starts with a D-Flat Major 9. . . . See what I mean? What throws me off, too, is the cat sounds like Bud Powell. Makes it hard for me to say anything about it. It's not Bud; it's somebody sounding like him.

LF Outside of that, did you like the general feeling?

TM I enjoy *all* piano players. All pianists have got five stars for me . . . but I was thinking about the wrong changes, so I didn't pay too much attention to the rest of it. Maybe you better play it again.

   (*Later*) It's crazy to sound like Bud Powell, but seems like the piano player should be able to think of something else too. Why get stuck with that Bud Powell sound?

6. Bud Powell. 'Ruby, My Dear' (from *Giants of Jazz*, Columbia).

TM That's Bud Powell! . . . All I can say is, he has a remarkable memory. I don't know what to say about him – he is a remarkable person, musically.

LF You think Bud is in his best form there?

TM (*Laughs*) No comment about him, or the piano. . . . He's just tired, stopped playing, doesn't want to play no more. I don't know what's going through his mind. But you know how he's influenced all of the piano players.

LF Of course. I was just questioning whether this is his best work.

Mrs Monk (*To Monk*) You don't think so.

TM Of course not.

7. Oscar Peterson. 'Easy Listenin' Blues' (from *With Respect to Nat*, Limelight). Peterson, piano; Herb Ellis, guitar; Ray Brown, bass.

TM Which is the way to the toilet? (*Waits to end of record, leaves room, returns . . . laughs.*) Well, you see where I went. (*To Mrs Monk*) Could you detect the piano player?

LF How about the guitar player?

TM Charlie Christian spoiled me for everybody else.

8. Denny Zeitlin. 'Carole's Garden' (from *Carnival*, Columbia). Zeitlin, piano, composer; Jerry Granelli, drums.

LF You liked that one?

TM I like all music.

LF Except the kind that makes you go to the toilet.

TM No, but you need that kind too. . . . It reminded me of Bobby Timmons, and that's *got* to be good. Rhythm section has the right groove too. Drummer made me think of Art Blakey. Hey, play that again.

(*Later.*) Yeah! He sounds like a *piano* player! (*Hums theme.*) You can keep changing keys all the time doing that. Sounds like something that was studied and figured out. And he can play it; you know what's happening with this one. Yeah, he was on a Bobby Timmons kick. *He* knows what's happening.

MONK AT THE PIANO

Though only once involved in the Blindfold Test as a reactor, Monk has often been discussed by others whose comments about his records have provided an equally mixed range of opinions. Following are a few examples.

'Remember' (Riverside). Monk, solo piano.

Gerry Mulligan (1960): Well, that record made me laugh all over the place – five chuckles, no stars! Well, I don't know if that was Monk. . . . It sounded like something he was working on, and I think he picked a very unfortunate choice of songs to do it on, because when he got into the composition, it kept reminding me of Mac-Dowell pieces. The things he did with the accents in the first chorus were the important parts for him. . . . He wanted to do something with the first part of that tune . . . the changing durations and the shifting accents and making lines out of them.

If you know it is Monk, there is a tremendously humorous approach to it. . . . I think that's one of Irving Berlin's duller songs, is all. Monk did an orchestration on the first part – it's really funny.

'Crepuscule With Nellie' (Riverside). Monk, piano, composer.

Benny Golson (1961): Count Basie at Town Hall. . . . No, I'm only kidding; of course it was Thelonious Monk. There's been a lot of pro and con talk about Thelonious through the years, but from the beginning I was pro. I was fascinated, and I wondered how he arrived at these things. Eventually I found out, by studying and analysing them.

Now, he is not a virtuoso pianist, but there is real thought behind what he is composing. It's all very well laid out.

'Darkness on the Delta' (Columbia). Monk, solo piano.

Bill Evans (1964): Sounded like *Concert by the Sea* there for a minute at the end! That is completely entertaining but it doesn't show Monk the composer. It does show a lot of humour and . . . there he is!

There's nobody like that. . . . Pianistically, I don't think Van Cliburn has anything to worry about, but if he (Monk) gets that stride going a little faster, I don't know . . . maybe Art Tatum will have to come back.

Pianistically, he's beautiful. (A promoter I know uses that phrase; I guess he likes the way it rolls off his tongue.) But Thelonious *is* pianistically beautiful. He approaches the piano somehow from an angle, and it's the right angle. He does the thing completely and thoroughly. . . . He hasn't been influenced through the traditional keyboard techniques because he hasn't worked through the keyboard composers and, therefore, has his own complete approach of musical thinking.

He is such a thinking musician, and I think this is something a lot of people forget about Monk. They somehow feel he's eccentric, but Monk knows exactly what he's doing. Precisely. Structurally, and musically, he's very aware of every note he plays. . . .

'Rhythm-a-ning' (Riverside).

Buddy De Franco (1963): I would venture to say it might be Monk, although I don't remember Monk doing that much playing – consistent playing – as far as the pattern.

Tommy Gumina (1963): All I can say is, Monk writes some beautiful tunes. When it comes to being a piano player, I'll see you later. . . .

'Oska T' (Columbia).

Jack Wilson (1964): Unlike many piano players, I love Monk's playing very much. He was brought to my attention by Richard Abrams, a pianist in Chicago, and we used to analyse Monk's playing.

We found that Monk's penchant for playing the piano is not in velocity, and not in dynamics, but in sound and overtones. He has a lot of other devices for producing the 'sound' – I've noticed a lot of times, playing in clubs, where the audience is inattentive, you play something of a Monk nature and use that sonority, automatically their ears respond to it. No other piano player has done more to find out the notes that really produce sound than Monk. To completely toss him aside as a pianistic influence is an asinine view.

'Sweet and Lovely' (Columbia). Monk, solo piano.

Hampton Hawes (1965): That piano player sounded honest as a little child. I think the left hand during the first part was a little hard. It could be Monk. Also it could be Mingus playing piano – sometimes he plays piano like that.

I liked the record, the honesty of it and the good feeling it had. However, I think it could have been a little better; so I'll give it three. I'd rather hear wrong notes being played by a person with good feeling than another person playing perfect, like a typewriter, and sound cold.

'Light Blue' (Columbia).

Charles Lloyd (1966): I thought Monk sounded particularly good on his solo. . . . His is the sort of music that spans time . . . it's something that's happening, and it always feels good to me. I can always readily identify with it, and it always has a freshness about it because of the way he constructs his phrases and the kind of twists it has.

I sometimes would like to hear him in a context with some more adventuresome musician. . . .

Mingus and His Psychiatrist

'In other words I am three. One man stands forever in the middle, unconcerned, unmoved, watching, waiting to be allowed to express what he sees to the other two. The second man is like a frightened animal that attacks for fear of being attacked. Then there's an over-loving gentle person who lets people into the uttermost sacred temple of his being and he'll take insults and be trusting and sign contracts without reading them and get talked down to working cheap or for nothing, and when he realizes what's been done to him he feels like killing and destroying everything around him including himself for being so stupid. But he can't – he goes back inside himself.'

'Which one is real?'

'They're *all* real.'

'The man who watches and waits, the man who attacks because he's afraid, and the man who wants to trust and love but retreats each time he finds himself betrayed. Mingus One, Two and Three. Which is the image you want the world to see?'

'What do I care what the world sees, I'm only trying to find out how I should feel about myself. I can't change the fact that they're all against me – that they don't want me to be a success.'

'Who doesn't?'

'Agents and businessmen with big offices who tell me, a black man, that I'm abnormal for thinking we should have our share of the crop we produce. Musicians are as Jim-Crowed as any black motherfucker on the street and the . . . the . . . well, *they* want to keep it that way.'

'Charles, I know who you mean by *they*, and that's ironic. Because don't you remember saying you came to me not only because I'm a psychologist but also because I'm a Jew? And therefore could relate to your problems?'

'Haw haw! You're funny, doctor.'

'Ah, you're crying again. Here, dry your eyes, Mingus, and don't bullschitt me.'

'Haw! Now I got *you* cursing!'

'You've got no exclusive on cursing. Don't bullschitt me. You're a good man, Charles, but there's a lot of fabrication and fantasy in what you say. For instance, no man could have as much intercourse in one night as you claim to have had.'

'The hell he couldn't! Maybe I did exaggerate some things like the weight-lifting and all that 'cause I really don't know how much those barbells weighed but only two other guys could pick 'em up and their feet sank into the ground!'

'You're changing the subject, my friend. I was asking about the Mexican girls. Why are you obsessed with proving you're a man? Is it because you cry?'

'I am more of a man than any dirty white cocksucker! I *did* fuck twenty-three girls in one night, including the boss's wife! I didn't dig it – I did it because I wanted to die and I hoped it would kill me. But on the way back from Mexico I still felt unsatisfied so I stopped and. . . .'

'Go on. . . . Are you ashamed?'

'Yes because it felt better when I did it to myself than with all those twenty-three dirty-ass whores. They don't love men, they love money.'

'How can you know what they love, Charles? Here. Dry your eyes.'

'Schitt. Fuck it. Even you just dig money!'

'Then don't pay me.'

'Oh, I dig your psychology! You know saying that makes me want to pay you double.'

'Nope, I don't want your money. You're a sick man. When the time comes that you feel I've helped you, buy me a tie or something. And I won't call you a prevaricator again. What matters is that you stop lying to yourself. Now, earlier you said you were a procurer. Tell me about it. How did you get into that?'

'Why don't you ever let me lie on the couch, doctor?'

'You always choose the chair.'

'I feel you don't want me on the couch 'cause I'm coloured and your white patients might be bugged.'

'Oh, Charles Mingus! You can lie on it, kick it, jump on it, get on it, get under it, turn it over, break it – and pay for it.'

'Man, you're crazy! I'm gonna save you.'

'You're not trained to save. I am.'

'I *can* save you. Do you believe in God?'

'Yes.'

'As a boogie man?'

'We'll get around to that later. Back to the subject, your one – time ill-famed profession.'

'Well, it's true I tried to be a pimp, doctor, but I wasn't really making it 'cause I didn't enjoy the money the girls got me. I remember the first one I knew – Cindy. She had all this bread under her mattress. Bobo laughed at me 'cause I didn't take it – he said I didn't know how to keep a whore.'

'If you didn't want the money, what was it you wanted?'

'Maybe just to see if I could do what the other pimps did.'

'Why?'

'That's almost impossible to explain – how you feel when you're a kid and the king pimps come back to the neighbourhood. They pose and twirl their watchchains and sport their new Cadillacs and Rollses and expensive tailored clothes. It was like the closest thing to one of our kind becoming president of the USA. When a young up-and-coming man reaches out to prove himself boss pimp, it's making it. That's what it meant where I come from – proving you're a man.'

'And when you proved it, what did you want?'

'Just play music, that's all.'

'I've been reading about you in a magazine. You didn't tell me you were such a famous musician.'

'That don't mean schitt. That's a system those that own us use. They make us famous and give us names – the King of this, the Count of that, the Duke of *what*! We die broke anyhow – and sometimes I think I dig death more than I dig facing this white world.'

'We're making progress, Charles, but perhaps we've done enough for today.'

Mingus at Peace

Charles Mingus, the incomparable forty-nine-year-old bassist, composer, band leader, autobiographer, and iconoclast, has spent much
of his life attempting to rearrange the world according to an almost
Johnsonian set of principles that abhor, among other things, cant,
racism, inhibition, managerial greed, sloppy music, Uncle Tomism,
and conformity. His methods have ranged from penny-dreadful
broadsides to punches on the nose. The results have been mixed.
They have also been costly, and have landed Mingus on the
psychiatric couch and in Bellevue (self-committed), lost him jobs,
and made him periodically fat. ('I eat out of nerves.') At the same
time, Mingus's experiences have been steadily distilled into a body
of compositions that for sheer melodic and rhythmic and structural
originality may equal Monk and Ellington. (Their content has been
equally fresh, for they have included, in the Ellington manner,
everything from love songs to social satire.) These experiences have,
as well, been reflected in his playing, which long ago elevated him
to virtuosic rank. But now Mingus has taken another step. He has
written a book about himself – *Beneath the Underdog: His world as
composed by Mingus*.

The book is impressionistic and disembodied (it has almost no
dates), and has a taste of all the Minguses. It is brutal and dirty and
bitter. It is sentimental and self-pitying. It is rude and, in places,
unfair (the curt handling of the great Red Norvo). It is facetious and
funny. It is awkward and unerringly right, and it is the latter when
Mingus's fine ear is receiving full tilt. Duke Ellington's verbal
arabesques have never been captured better:

[Juan] Tizol [an Ellington trombonist] wants you to play a solo
he's written where bowing is required. You raise the solo an
octave, where the bass isn't too muddy. He doesn't like that and
he comes to the room under the stage where you're practising at

intermission and comments that you're like the rest of the niggers in the band, you can't read. You ask Juan how he's different from the other niggers and he states that one of the ways he's different is that HE IS WHITE. So you run his ass upstairs. You leave the rehearsal room, proceed toward the stage with your bass and take your place and at the moment Duke brings down the baton for 'A-Train' and the curtain of the Apollo Theatre goes up, a yelling, whooping Tizol rushes out and lunges at you with a bolo knife. The rest you remember mostly from Duke's own words in his dressing room as he changes after the show.

"Now, Charles," he says, looking amused, putting Cartier links into the cuffs of his beautiful handmade shirt, "you could have forewarned me—you left me out of the act entirely! At least you could have let me cue in a few chords as you ran through that Nijinsky routine. I congratulate you on your performance, but why didn't you and Juan inform me about the adagio you planned so that we could score it? I must say I never saw a large man so agile—I never saw *anybody* make such tremendous leaps! The gambado over the piano carrying your bass was colossal. When you exited after that I thought, 'That man's really afraid of Juan's knife and at the speed he's going he's probably home in bed by now.' But no, back you came through the same door with your bass still intact. For a moment I was hopeful you'd decided to sit down and play but instead you slashed Juan's chair in two with a fire axe! Really, Charles, that's destructive. Everybody knows Juan has a knife but nobody ever took it seriously—he likes to pull it out and show it to people, you understand. So I'm afraid, Charles—I've never fired anybody—you'll have to quit my band. I don't need any new problems. Juan's an old problem, I can cope with that, but you seem to have a whole bag of new tricks. I must ask you to be kind enough to give me your notice, Charles."

The charming way he says it, it's like he's paying you a compliment. Feeling honored, you shake hands and resign.

Mingus's relationship with jazz critics has been generally amiable, and the lumps landed on them in the book are pretty funny. A party is given for Mingus when he first arrives in New York from the West Coast around 1950. No matter that the critics named were never in the same room at the same time in their lives, or that at least two of them were still in college and unpublished. Mingus is talking to Dizzy Gillespie:

"Man, that's a lot of talent, don't you dig it? I see Leonard Feather, he's a piano player. There's Bill Coss and Gene Lees—they sing, I heard. Barry Ulanov must play drums or something, dig, with that *Metronome* beat. Martin Williams can play everything. I can tell by the way he writes. Put Marshall Stearns on bass and let Whitney Balliett score and John Wilson conduct. Let all them other young up-and-coming critics dance. How would you like to review that schitt for the *Amsterdam News*?"

... On a Sunday night a week or so before his book was published, Mingus was sitting at the bar of a restaurant on West Tenth Street. He was dressed in a conservative dark suit and tie, and he was in his middle state. That is, he was neither thin nor huge. A Charlie Chan beard was arranged carefully around his mouth, and he looked wonderful. A year before, his face had been grey and puffy; he had not played a note for two years, and he was very fat and had a listless, buried air. Now he was sitting at the bar sampling a tall white drink. 'Ramos gin fizz,' he blurted out. 'Milk or cream, white of an egg, orange flower water, lemon juice, gin, and soda water. I used to drink ten at a sitting in San Francisco.' Mingus talks in leaping slurs. The words come out crouched and running, and sometimes they move so fast whole sentences are unintelligible. He finished his Ramos fizz and ordered a half bottle of Pouilly-Fuissé and some cheese. He prounced the name of the wine at a run, and it came out 'Poolly-Foos'. 'We went down to the peace demonstration in Washington this weekend to play, and it was a drag,' he said. 'They've never had any jazz at these things, and it seemed like a good idea, but we never did play. My piano player didn't show, and my alto sax couldn't make it, so we only had four pieces, and it wouldn't have made any sense going on like that. I went to bed right after I got back this morning. I hadn't been to bed in two nights. I can't sleep at night anyway, but I do all right with a sleeping pill in the day. I even had a wonderful dream just before I got up. I had everything under control. I was on a diet and losing weight all over the place, and I felt *so* good. But a dream like that is worse than a nightmare. You wake up and the real nightmare starts.'

Mingus asked the bartender if he could get some lobster and was told that the kitchen had closed. 'Maybe they got some across the street in that steak house,' Mingus said. He told the bartender to keep the rest of the wine – that he'd be back right after he'd eaten. He crossed the street and went down some steps into a dark, low, empty room. Mingus moved lightly but gingerly and, squeezing himself into a booth, ordered lobster tails, hearts of lettuce, and another half bottle of Poolly-Foos.

'My book was written for black people to tell them how to get through life,' he said. 'I was trying to upset the white man in it – the right kind or the wrong kind, depending on what colour and persuasion you are. I started it twenty-five years ago, and at first I was doing it for myself, to help understand certain situations. I talked some of it into tape recorders, and that girl in the white Cadillac in the book, she helped me type it up. But I wrote most of it in longhand in the dark backstage or on buses on huge sheets of score paper. The original manuscript was between eight hundred and a thousand pages. It went up and down, what with parts of it getting lost. I started looking for a publisher more than ten years ago. Things hadn't loosened up yet, and a lot of them looked at it and it scared them. It was too dirty, it was too hard on whitey, they said. McGraw-Hill finally bought it, but they put it on the shelf for a long time. Then Knopf got interested and bought it from McGraw-Hill.'

Mingus asked the waitress for a glass of water. She was young and blonde. 'Say, you my same waitress? It's so dark in here you look like you keep changing.' Mingus leaned back and smiled his beautiful smile.

'I'm your waitress,' she said, putting a hand lightly on his arm. 'Are you Jaki Byard?'

'Jaki Byard? Jaki Byard? He's my piano player. He's a super-star now. I'm glad you my same waitress. Now, bring me that glass of water, please. Then I got hold of Nel King, who wrote a movie I was in, and she put the book in shape. It took her a year and a half. A whole lot of stuff has been left out – stuff about blacks wearing Afros because they're afraid not to, and skin-lighteners, and my wife, Celia. There was a lot about her in there, but she didn't want to be in the book, so I left her out. I wrote in a b c d e f g h at first, but then I mixed up the chronology and some of the locations. Like that party when I first came to New York in the late 1940s. It didn't take place at any apartment in the East 70s but over at the old Bandbox, next to Birdland. The critics were there, and they didn't stop talking once. They kept right on even when Art Tatum and Charlie Parker sat in together for maybe the only time in their lives. It was the most fantastic music I ever heard. Tatum didn't let up in either hand for a second – *whoosh-hum, whoosh-hum* in the left, and *aaaaaaaaarrrrrrrrr – hhhhhhheeeee* in the right – and neither did Parker, and to this day I don't know what they were doing. The passages on Fats Navarro are the best part of the book. I loved Fats and I could hear his voice in my head the whole time I was writing him down. But that's just my first book. It's not an autobiography. It's just me, Mingus. My next book will be my life in music.'

Mingus finished his lobster tails and wine and went back across the street. He telephoned his manager, Sue Ungaro, and arranged to meet her in ten minutes at a Japanese restaurant at 12th Street and 2nd Avenue. It was almost one o'clock. Mingus emptied his bottle of wine and took a cab across town. The restaurant was shut, and Mrs Ungaro was nowhere in sight.

'I better walk over to her place, maybe meet her on the way,' Mingus said. The street was deserted, but he reached into a coat pocket and took out a big East Indian knife and, removing its scabbard, held it at the ready in his left hand. 'This is the way I walk the streets at night around here. I live down on 5th Street, and we got so much crime I'm scared to be out at night.' He passed St Mark's in the Bowerie and headed west.

Mrs Ungaro was putting some trash in a garbage can in front of her building. She is a pretty, slender strawberry blonde, and she was wearing blue jeans, clogs, and a short, beat-up raccoon coat.

'They closed,' Mingus said, pocketing his knife. Mrs Ungaro said she'd still like something to eat. They took a cab to the Blue Sea on 3rd Avenue and 24th Street. It was closed. Mingus told the driver to make a U-turn, and go down to a small bar-and-grill on 10th and 3rd. He and Sue Ungaro sat in a semicircular booth under a jukebox loudspeaker. She ordered a hamburger and salad and Mingus asked the waitress, who was wearing false eyelashes and a black knitted see-through pants suit, for a dish of black olives and some Poolly-Foos.

'Poolly what?' she said, moving her lashes up and down like a semaphore. 'I don't know. I'm just helping out tonight, because I've known these people a long time.'

The manager, a short man in shirtsleeves with gleaming glasses and a big paunch, said they had Soave Bolla. A half bottle in a straw basket was put in an ice bucket on the table. Mingus scrunched it down in the bucket and piled ice-cubes carefully around its neck.

He looked at Sue Ungaro and smiled. 'It's been five years, baby. You know that?' She nodded and took a bite of hamburger. 'Sue wrote in for the Guggenheim I just got. I want to write a ballet with the money – an operatic ballet. I've had it in my head for years, like I had the book in my head. It'll have to do with Watts, where I was born and raised, and I want Katherine Dunham to choreograph it. I know her very well, and we've talked about it a long time. But getting the Guggenheim wasn't as easy as filling out forms. I had to carry about fifty pounds of music over for them to see. If I don't finish the ballet this year, I'll apply again.'

'Charles wants to put together a seventeen-piece band,' Sue Ungaro said. 'And he wants to use some of the Guggenheim money, but they won't allow it. It's only for composition.'

'If I do finish the ballet, I'll apply anyway so that I can write some chamber music. That's what I started out doing years and years ago, and I want to go back to it. I've been teaching all winter, one day a week, at the state university at Buffalo. The Slee Chair of Music. They invited me, and I've been teaching composition to about ten kids. They're bright, and they get their work done on time. I used some of my own pieces, showing them how to work with a melody and no chords or sets of chords, and no melody or just a pedal point, to give them a sense of freedom. But I feel sorry about jazz. The truth has been lost in the music. All the different styles and factions went to war with each other, and it hasn't done any good. Take Ornette Coleman.' Mingus sang half a chorus of 'Body and Soul' in a loud, off-key voice, drowning out the jukebox. It was an uncanny imitation. 'That's all he does. Just pushing the melody out of line here and there. Trouble is, he can't play it straight. At that little festival Max Roach and I gave in Newport in 1960, Kenny Dorham and I tried to get Ornette to play "All the Things You Are" straight, and he couldn't do it.'

Mingus took a sip of water and made a face. 'I don't know, this doesn't taste right.'

'Maybe it isn't cold enough,' Sue Ungaro said.

Mingus fished out his knife, deftly cut the straw basket off the bottle, and put the bottle back in the ice. The waitress appeared and said, 'Everything fine, honey?'

'The wine doesn't taste right. It's not cold enough.'

The waitress took three ice-cubes out of the bucket and plopped them in our glasses and splashed some wine over them.

'Hey, that'll make it all water,' Mingus said, seizing the bottle and jamming it back in the bucket.

'I'm just helping out, sir, like I said.'

'She'll make the reputation of this place,' Mingus mumbled.

'The Black Panthers have been to see Charles,' Sue Ungaro said, 'but he won't go along with them.'

'I don't need to. I'm a single movement. Anyway, I don't like to see the blacks destroying this country. It's a waste of time. The militants have nothing to sell. And that's what this country does best – sells. Makes and sells thing to the world. But the militants don't sell *nothing*. All the black pimps and black gangsters know this, because they *have* something to sell, like the king-pimp Billy Bones in my book. Man, he made millions of dollars around the world. The black people don't like themselves to begin with. You've got all these variations of colour and dialect. You've got terrific economic differences. You never hear anything from the wealthy blacks, but they don't like the militants. Some of them been working at their money seventy-five years, in real estate or whatever, and they not about to let the militants come and take it away for something called freedom. Hell, what's freedom? Nobody's free, black or white. What's going to happen is there will be one hell of a revolution and it'll be between black and black. Like the big trouble in Watts, when the blacks were ready to shoot the blacks. It all started when a truckload of militants arrived and started throwing bombs into the black stores and such. Well, man, the shop owners – and I grew up with a lot of them – got upset and came charging out with guns, and by this time the truck had moved on and the white cops had arrived and saw all these blacks standing around with guns and started shooting *them*, and that was it.'

Mingus leaned back, out of breath. The manager passed the table and Mingus asked him if he had any fresh fish. The manager went into the kitchen and came back with a handful of cherrystones. Mingus looked surprised. He ordered half a dozen on the half shell, and some vintage champagne.

'No vintage,' the manager replied. 'I got a bunch of vintage in last week and it was dead and I sent the whole mess back. I'll give you regular. Piper Heidsieck.'

The clams arrived and Mingus coated each one with lemon juice and cocktail sauce and about a teaspoonful of Tabasco. 'Hell, a while back, I took my daughter to Columbia to hear What's-His-Name, Eldridge Cleaver, and right away all I heard him saying was mother this and mother that. Well, I didn't want my daughter hearing that. That's vulgarity no matter if the man is right or wrong. I left. I took my daughter and left right away.'

Mingus looked relaxed and content. In fact, he looked as if he had finally got the world straightened around to his liking. The talk wandered easily along between jukebox selections, and Mingus and Sue Ungaro discussed astrology (Mingus: 'My birth date is four/two-two/two-two. The astrologists have never been able to get over that'), weight problems (Mingus: 'Man, I get to this size and it's painful. My arms hurt all the time up here from banging against the rest of me'), the effects on the stomach of too much vitamin C, the sorrows of drug addiction, and the fact that Mingus suddenly has more 'visible, taxable' money then ever before in his life.

The lights started to go out. It was almost four o'clock. Mingus went to the men's room, and Sue Ungaro said: 'I don't really like Charles's book, and I've told him. I think the sexual parts are too savage, and I think that Charles himself doesn't come through. It's the superficial Mingus, the flashy one, not the real one.' Mingus reappeared and the waitress let us out the door. "Night, now,' she said with a couple of semaphores. 'It's been a real pleasure serving you.'

Two nights later Mingus opened at the Village Vanguard with a sextet for a week's stand. It included Lonnie Hillyer on trumpet, Charlie McPherson on alto saxophone, Bobby Jones on tenor

saxophone, John Foster on piano, Mingus, and Virgil Day on drums.
Mingus the musician is a tonic to watch. He becomes a massive
receiver-transmitter, absorbing every note played around him and
then sending out through his bass corrective or appreciative notes.
The result is a two-way flow which lights up his musicians who, in
turn, light up his music.

Whenever he has felt out of sorts in recent years, Mingus has
taken to offering lacklustre medleys of bebop numbers or Ellington
tunes, completely ignoring his own storehouse of compositions. But
at the Vanguard he brought out refurbished versions of such
numbers as 'Celia' and 'Diane'. They were full of his trademarks –
long, roving melodies, complex, multipart forms, breaks, constantly
changing rhythms, howling ensembles, and the against-the-grain
quality he brands each of his performances with. Most of them were
also done in Mingus's customary workshop manner. When a
number would start hesitantly, he would rumble, 'No. No, no,' and
stop the music. Then the group would start again. Sometimes there
were three or four false starts. In all, there were half a dozen long
numbers in the first set, and they were exceptional. Mingus soloed
briefly just once, on a blues, but everything was there. Dressed in a
short-sleeved shirt and tie, he sat on a tall stool and played, and he
looked as serene as he had on Sunday.

At the beginning of the following week, Knopf gave a publication
party for *Beneath the Underdog*, with music. It was held in a couple of
boxlike, orange-carpeted rooms in the Random House building on
East 50th Street. It was jammed, and Mingus's sextet, with a ringer
on bass, was playing 'Celia' at close to the one-hundred-decibel
level. There were more blacks than whites, and Mingus, again
dressed in a dark suit and tie, was talking with a lady of his
proportions. It was like seeing Sidney Greenstreet and Eugene
Pallette porch to porch. Ornette Coleman, dressed in a glistening
black silk mandarin suit, said he had just completed a piece for
eighty musicians that sounded just like his playing. Nel King said
that Mingus's book had been a lot of work and that perhaps her
being a woman was a help in managing his tempestuous moods.
Max Gordon, a Mingus supporter from the early days, was standing

with Mingus and Sue Ungaro and a tall, slender youth in a beard, straw hat, and cowboy boots. Sue was still in her bluejeans and clogs. 'Meet my son, Charles, Jr.,' Mingus said. He poked Charles, Jr. in the stomach. '*He* doesn't have any weight problem. And look at his beard! I can't grow any more than what I have on my face.' Mingus asked his son if he had read his book.

'Listen, I haven't even *seen* it yet,' Charles, Jr., replied. 'Besides, I've been working on my play.'

A man who had joined the group said that one of the minor but unavoidable axioms of the literary life was that children never read their parents' books. Mingus grunted. Nel King approached and told him she wanted him to meet someone. She asked Mingus before she towed him away how he liked the party.

'It's strange, man,' he said.

RALPH ELLISON

On Bird, Bird-Watching and Jazz

Oddly enough, while several explanations are advanced as to how Charles Parker, Jr., became known as 'Bird' ('Yardbird', in an earlier metamorphosis), none is conclusive. There is, however, overpowering internal evidence that whatever the true circumstance of his ornithological designation, it had little to do with the chicken yard. Randy roosters and operatic hens are familiar to fans of the animated cartoons, but for all the pathetic comedy of his living – and despite the crabbed and constricted character of his style – Parker was a most inventive melodist; in bird-watcher's terminology, a true songster.

This failure in the exposition of Bird's legend is intriguing, for nicknames are indicative of a change from a given to an achieved identity, whether by rise or fall, and they tell us something of the nicknamed individual's interaction with his fellows. Thus, since we suspect that more of legend is involved in his renaming than [the title of Robert Reisner's book *Bird: The Legend of Charlie Parker*] indicates, let us at least consult Roger Tory Peterson's *Field Guide to the Birds* for a hint as to why, during a period when most jazzmen were labelled 'cats', someone hung the bird on Charlie. Let us note too that 'legend' originally meant 'the story of a saint' and that saints were often identified with symbolic animals.

Two species won our immediate attention, the goldfinch and the mockingbird – the goldfinch because the beatnik phrase 'Bird lives', which, following Parker's death, has been chalked endlessly on Village buildings and subway walls, reminds us that during the thirteenth and fourteenth centuries a symbolic goldfinch frequently appeared in European devotional paintings. An apocryphal story has it that upon being given a clay bird for a toy, the infant Jesus brought it miraculously to life as a goldfinch. Thus the small, tawny-brown bird with a bright red patch about the base of its bill and a broad yellow band across its wings became a representative of the soul, the Passion and the Sacrifice. In more worldly late-Renaissance art, the little bird became the ambiguous symbol of death and the soul's immortality. For our own purposes, however, its song poses a major problem: it is like that of a canary – which, soul or no soul, rules the goldfinch out.

The mockingbird, *Mimus polyglottos*, is more promising. Peterson informs us that its song consists of 'long successions of notes and phrases of great variety, with each phrase repeated a half-dozen times before going on to the next', that the mockingbirds are 'excellent mimics' who 'adeptly imitate a score or more species found in the neighbourhood', and that they frequently sing at night – a description which not only comes close to Parker's way with a saxophone but even hints at a trait of his character. For although he *usually* sang at night, his playing was characterized by velocity, by long-continued successions of notes and phrases, by swoops, bleats, echoes, rapidly repeated bebops – I mean rebopped bebops – by mocking mimicry of other jazzmen's styles, and by interpolations of motifs from extraneous melodies, all of which added up to a dazzling display of wit, satire, burlesque and pathos. Further, he was as expert at issuing his improvisations from the dense brush as from the extreme treetops of the harmonic landscape, and there was, without doubt, as irrepressible a mockery in his personal conduct as in his music.

Mimic thrushes, which include the catbird and brown thrasher, along with the mockingbird, are not only great virtuosi, they are the tricksters and con men of the bird world. Like Parker, who is described as a confidence man and a practical joker by several of the commentators, they take off on the songs of other birds, inflating, inverting and turning them wrong side out, and are capable of driving a prowling ('square') cat wild. Utterly irreverent and romantic, they are not beyond bugging human beings. Indeed, on summer nights in the South, when the moon hangs low, the mockingbirds sing as though determined to heat every drop of romance in the sleeping adolescent's heart to fever pitch. Their song thrills and swings the entire moonstruck night to arouse one's sense of the mystery, the promise and the frustration of being human, alive and hot in the blood. They are as delightful to eye as to ear, but sometimes a similarity of voice and appearance makes for a confusion with the shrikes, a species given to impaling insects and smaller songbirds on the points of thorns, and they are destroyed. They are fond of fruit, especially mulberries, and if there is a tree in your yard, there will be, along with the wonderful music, much chalky, blue-tinted evidence of their presence. Under such conditions be careful and heed Parker's warning to his friends – who sometimes were subjected to a shrike-like treatment – 'you must pay your dues to Bird'.

The Death of Bird

Charlie Parker died on 12 March 1955, in the New York hotel suite of his friend, the Baroness 'Nica'. The circumstances provoked some conjecture in the press. To make things worse, the delay in the announcement – the story of Parker's death did not break until three days later – upset his family and friends. The Baroness gave this account to Robert Reisner.

I'm sick of this 'shipped the body off to the morgue' business and 'laid unknown', for how long, for that is ridiculous. The doctor was there within five minutes of his dying, and he had been there a half an hour beforehand. The medical examiner was there within an hour of the doctor; and the moment the medical examiner comes, he takes over everything, and you have nothing more to say about it. All the pertinent facts were given by myself and the doctor to the medical examiner, and I saw him take them down. He had Bird's name, Charles Parker, taken down absolutely correctly; so the story of the false name-tag on Bird could not have been so. The doctor gave Bird's age as fifty-three, because that was his impression, for some reason. I didn't say, because I didn't know.

The autopsy said he died of pneumonia, when, actually, he did not have pneumonia. The doctor said it was a heart attack that killed him, but he had terrible ulcers, and advanced cirrhosis of the liver; and he had been told by doctors for years previous that he might die at any moment.

He had stopped by that evening before leaving for Boston where he had a gig at Storyville. His horn and bags were downstairs in his car. The first thing that happened which was unusual was when I offered him a drink, and he said no. I took a look at him, and I noticed he appeared quite ill. A few minutes later he began to vomit blood. I sent for my doctor, who came right away. He said that Bird could not go on any trip, and Bird, who felt better momentarily, started to argue the point and said that he had a commitment to play this gig and that he had to go. We told him that he must go to the hospital. That, he said, was the last thing he was going to do. He said he hated hospitals, that he had had enough of them. I then said to the doctor, 'Let him stay here.' We agreed on that, and my daughter and I took shifts around the clock watching and waiting upon him and bringing ice water by the gallon, which he consumed. His thirst was incredible; it couldn't be quenched. Sometimes he would bring it up with some blood, and then he lay back and had to have more water. It went on like this for a day or two. When the doctor first came, he asked Bird the routine questions and some others. 'Do you drink?' he asked. This brought a sidelong wink from Bird. 'Sometimes,' he said ironically, 'I have a sherry before dinner.'

The doctor came three times a day and any other times we would call him. The doctor knew how serious it was. Before he left the first time, he told me, 'I have to warn you that this man may die at any moment. He has an advanced cirrhosis and stomach ulcers. He must not leave, except in an ambulance.'

The doctor liked Bird, and Bird, when he wasn't racked by seizures, was in wonderful spirits. He made me swear not to tell anybody where he was. The third day he was a lot better. Dr Freymann said he might be able to leave in a little while. At first, Charlie Parker was just a name to the doctor; he didn't know of Bird's genius, nor did he know of Bird's weaknesses. Bird wanted the doctor, who had been a musician, to listen to some of his records, and the doctor developed an interest in his patient and wanted to hear Bird's work. Bird and I spent considerable time mapping out a programme. First we played the album with strings, 'Just Friends' and 'April in Paris'. The doctor was very impressed. Bird got a great charge out of that. That was on Saturday, about 7.30 p.m. Bird was so much better that the doctor agreed that he could get up and watch the Tommy Dorsey programme on TV.

We braced him up in an easy chair, with pillows and wrapped in blankets. He was enjoying what he saw of the programme. Bird was a fan of Dorsey's, and he didn't see anything strange in that. 'He's a wonderful trombonist,' he said. Then came part of the show consisting of jugglers who were throwing bricks around that were stuck together. My daughter was asking how they did it, and Bird and I were being very mysterious about it. Suddenly in the act, they dropped the bricks, and we all laughed. Bird was laughing uproariously, but then he began to choke. He rose from his chair and choked, perhaps twice, and sat back in the chair. I was on the phone immediately, calling the doctor. 'Don't worry, Mummy,' my daughter said. 'He's all right now.'

I went over and took his pulse. He had dropped back in the chair, with his head falling forward. He was unconscious. I could feel his pulse still there. Then his pulse stopped.

I didn't want to believe it. I could feel my own pulse. I tried to believe my pulse was his. But I really knew that Bird was dead.

At the moment of his going, there was a tremendous clap of thunder. I didn't think about it at the time, but I've thought about it often since; how strange it was.

It happened on a Saturday night. At one o'clock in the morning they took him away, and, from then on, it was out of my hands. I said nothing to the papers, because my first concern was for Chan, his wife. I did not want her to hear it over the radio or read it in the papers. I wanted to get to her first. I had attempted to find out where she was when Bird was at my place, but he said she had just moved into a new house, and he did not know the address.

Some people said that I had the body 'shipped to Bellevue where no one identified it for forty-eight hours'. Actually, Bird's name, Charlie (Yardbird) Parker, was entered on the death certificate that was made out in my apartment at the Hotel Stanhope. The one thing we couldn't find was Chan's address, who was known as Bird's wife. Also, somebody wrote that I was at the Open Door, your place, where you had those bop sessions in Greenwich Village, and that I was talking to Art Blakey and other friends of Bird and I didn't tell them of Bird's death. Actually, I wanted to find Chan before she got the news from the radio or the press, and I went to the Open Door to see if anybody there knew her address. Finally, I thought of Teddy Wilson, and his lawyer, it so happened, had the address of Chan's mother. Chan was finally contacted Monday evening and was told.

I did not know Bird too many years, but we did have a wonderful friendship going, nothing romantic. He always dropped in unexpectedly anytime during the day or night. He was a relaxed type of person, and you sometimes hardly knew he was around. He liked to play peggity with my daughter. That game actually superseded his love of chess. We'd talk about everything under the sun. Bird knew about everything, and then some.

I'd sit around and play him records. He loved Eddie Heywood's 'Begin the Beguine'. It fascinated him; he used to play it ten times around. Another thing he loved was Billie Holiday doing 'You're My Thrill'.

For all the adulation heaped upon him by fans and musicians, he was lonely. I saw him standing in front of Birdland in a pouring rain. I was horrified, and I asked him why, and he said he just had no place to go. He was wont to frequent a few of his friends' pads and just go to sleep in an armchair. This night he couldn't find anybody home. He said, when this happened, he would ride the subways all night. He would ride a train to the end of a line; then, when he was ordered out, he would go to another train and ride back.

Bird was a very trusting person with friends. He'd put himself completely in the hands of the people he loved. In sparing his wife the shock of a public announcement of his death, I felt I was carrying out something he would have wanted.

Following is a statement from Dr Freymann, who was attending Bird at the Baroness's apartment: I refused to sign the death certificate. He had been definitely off the drugs, I could see by his eyes. He had no veins left to inject anyway – all had been used up. To me he looked to be in his early sixties. When he died, the hotel wanted him taken away quickly. I saw him for three or four days. The second day he was in terrible pain. I gave him penicillin, and then he seemed to improve. No temperature. We begged him to go to hospital, but he would not have it.

BORIS VIAN

Round About Close to Midnight

A Fairly Fairy Tale

'Yodel . . . yodel . . . yodel . . . yodel . . .'
(Gillespie, *Collected Works*)

'What is this bipop?'
(Paul Boubal, *Poetic Anthology*)

The doorbell rang like a fast Brownian lick. I listened more carefully. There was no doubt. Somebody was imitating the trumpet solo on Ray Brown's 'One Bass Hit'.

Sluggish with sleep, I got out of bed, slipped into my pants and a sweater and went to open the door. Who could it be at this hour? I tried to get my head together. Maybe a policeman had come to arrest me for outraging public decency under the covers of jazz magazines.

I opened the door. A man walked right in. He was small and shrivelled, about fifty years old at first sight. He looked familiar except for his bulging stomach. He raised his right arm in the Nazi salute: 'Heil Gillespie!'

He clicked his heels twice up-tempo like those two brass chords in 'Stay on It'. ('That must be hard to do,' I muttered to nobody in particular.)

'Heil Parker!' I responded automatically.

'Permit me to introduce myself,' he said. 'Goebbels – special propaganda delegate to the UN Musical Commission, Jazzband Department.'

'Goebbels?' The name was familiar. I searched my memory. 'You used to be thinner,' I said finally. 'Didn't they hang you?'

'And Ilse Koch?' he asked with a big smile. 'Did they hang her too?'

'What? . . .'

'I did the same thing she did,' he said, lowering his head, blushing. 'I got pregnant in prison. The Americans freed me. I get along rather well with Americans, especially after they heard my "Flight of the Bumblebee Rag" played by the Moscow Railroadman Jazz Band. When they needed a bebropagandist, I was the obvious choice.'

'And Goering?' I asked. 'What about Goering? Is he obviously anything?'

'He plays bongos in the UN bop combo.'

We were still standing in my vestibule. 'Come in,' I said. 'We obviously have important Things to Come together.'

He lifted a glass of elixir of cannabis and toasted: 'To our beloved Birdland.' After eating a small opium cookie, he continued: 'I'll explain why I've come for your help.'

'But I'm not qualified to help you,' I said.

'On the contrary,' Goebbels answered, 'nobody takes you seriously. That's Handy. It's a perfect cover. We must be prepared to spy for Herr Gillespie!'

He got up and clicked his heels like those two chords again: 'All for bebop!' he exclaimed, sitting back down. 'And now let's talk Buzzyness. Look at this, you will see how others have set an example . . .'

He handed me a piece of paper. It was a tract signed by the French Plumbers Union. It read: 'The union requests all its members, as of January 1st, 1949, to replace brass and steel screws with Zincleton. Vive Zutty! Long live Plumbers! Vive Mezzrow! Vive le Republic-o-reeny! Smrt fasizmu! Svoboda narodu.'

'But this is Sabbytage!' I exclaimed, Furioso. I should have known it.

'Just camouflage, baby,' Goebbels said. 'And did you Getz the code at the end?'

'No. What's it all about?'

He laughed. (Bop.)* 'You'll see. Let's cut out and scarf some frim-fram sauce.'

*

* (Editor's note)

We sat down in a Chinese restaurant. 'The do-re-mi of bebropaganda,' he began, 'is to infiltrate the language with our own jive. Dig!'

He called the waiter and ordered wild Reece with Steamin' peabop soup. Getting the idea, I asked for a pot of Tea-lonious. The waiter almost fainted. Goebbels pointed to him and shook my hand with a Spring of Joy: 'That cat will remember this night for the rest of his life. Get the Groove, Holmes?'

'It seems obvious,' I said.

'Maybe for you,' replied Goebbels. 'You've already Serged Miles Ahead. But for them, the squares, the straight studs . . . do you realize the Richies and Powell we can have?'

The waiter was writhing in agony on the floor. He did not seem well at all. I Lewist my appetite.

'Let's go someplace else,' I suggested. 'How about the Bolling alley in Phil Woods?'

'Fine. But first a bottle of Dexter Corton, 1942.'

'I think I'd prefer soda-bop,' I said. 'I'm not feeling Wallington enough to go bar-bopping. I'd Rodney Stitt down for a while. Anyway we're getting Carneyd away. Let's try and be reasonnyble.'

'No. The more unreasonnyble the better,' he replied. We went outside: 'You don't have a Basie understanding of propaganda. Aren't there people who have never understood one word in any article ever written by André Hodeir? Of course there are. But Hodeir writes books about jazz, they're published by Larousse, a very serious company. And people who read his books generally consider him one of the best jazz critics. That's only one example.'

'Zoot alors!' I exclaimed.

'There's no shortage of ideas in the UN Musical Commission, Jazzband Department. We plan to publish a book about Urbie Greenbelts entitled *Megabopoli*. Colonel Tom Parker is changing his name to Charlie. Jimmy Carter, a young politician in Georgia, will change his to Ron. Through our sophisticated long-term infiltration techniques, we are grooming Charlie's piano player Al Haig for Secretary of State. Dizzy Gillespie has decided to run for president so he can sing "Salt Peanuts" in the White House. Now's the Time to get going before it Petersons out.'

*

Approaching Boulevard Saint-Germain, we Passed a bookstore.

'Let's go in here,' said Goebbels.

'I would like the complete works of Leon B. Bopp,' he said to the clerk.

'I'm sorry, we don't stock that,' the clerk replied, puffing on a musician's cigarette. 'But may I suggest *Vian with the Wind* by George Mitchell instead?'

'No,' said Goebbels, 'and don't Purdie me on.'

We left Pretty fast.

'Did you see him bebogarting that Roach?' Goebbels axed. 'He's counter-revolutionary. We must brainMarsh him to the Max.'

'Don't fight windmills,' I advised. 'Let's not make enemies in Groovin' High places. I get along quite well with the Archiedemie Française and they have agreed to replace the syllable "van" by my name. It won't cost them much, and I need the publicity. We both need the publicity.'

'That's not the problem,' he replied, worried. 'That book was written by *Blue* Mitchell, not George. Wait! Who's that Duking out the door?'

I recognized the bookseller. He was in a Rushing.

'Wow!' said Goebbels. 'He's Something Else. He's Flyin' Home. We've got to find out what's Hamptoning.'

'What if we take a Shorty cut?' I proposed. 'It might be Tough, but . . .'

'Shorty?! White West Coast Shorty *Rogers*?' Goebbels looked at me, paling with anger. 'And did I hear you say Tough? *Dave* Tough? Rhymes with Stuff? Another chalk-faced impostor.'

I turned white with fear – Whitey Mitchell white . . . whiter, white as Stan Kenton. 'Dave Tough's not all that Whiteman,' I said.

Goebbels reached into the pocket of his Black, Brown and Beige jacket. He pulled a metal object far-out and then there was a loud 'CLICK!'

The receiver clicked as I picked it up. The phone must have been ringing for five minutes. I came out of my round-Midnightmare and mumbled: 'HiLow. Sleepy John Estes here.'

'Hello,' I heard. 'It's Hodeir . . . Hello?'

'Hodeir? Which Hodeir? The Hodeir that rhymes with Brubeck?'

'What's wrong with you? It's André. Did you Wright your editorial for the Christmas issue?'

'No. You'd better do it this year,' I sighed, awake by now. 'My Dickie doesn't feel very Wells. I can't Garner enough strength.'

'Come on,' Hodeir laughed. 'It's too late for you and me to change Erroles.'

1948; freely translated by Mike Zwerin.

NAT HENTOFF

In the Studio with Miles and Louis

Part of the background for jazz is the recording studio. Records are still the basic self-instruction tools for the musician, and they are the quickest way his reputation is made with the jazz audience. To provide some indication of the way jazz recordings are made, I've selected two sessions – an informal Dixieland date with Louis Armstrong and a complex, carefully rehearsed modern jazz experiment with Miles Davis. In both, as in all record dates, there are intersecting pressures on and by the musicians, the a&r (artists and repertory) director, and the silently critical engineers.

The Armstrong record, made in the spring of 1960, was issued as *Louis and the Dukes of Dixieland*. The Davis album, recorded toward the end of 1959, is *Sketches of Spain*.

I – *'Place It Where You Want, Dolling!'*

Louis Armstrong was forty-five minutes late for the first session of an album he was to make with the Dukes of Dixieland for Audio Fidelity. Sid Frey, the label's voluble, intense owner, was not disturbed at Louis's tardiness. 'It takes him half a day to get up,' Frey explained to a bystander while waving at Armstrong. 'Then it takes him a couple of hours for the lipsalves and checking the horn. He lives his life for that horn.'

When he arrived, Louis, who had gained some weight in recent months, was in buoyant spirits. He greeted the Dukes, a white Dixieland combo, warmly, and they treated him with marked deference. Louis was in sport shirt and slacks, as were the other players and Mr Frey. The latter prowled the studio, checking microphones.

Frey moved in on Louis, who was gently unpacking his horn.

'Louis, have you decided whether you'll do that Bert Williams tune, "Nobody"?'

Louis looked up, grinned, and shook his head negatively. 'Well, Mr Glaser thinks the NAACP wouldn't like that.'

Mr Glaser is the shrewd, apoplectic Joe Glaser, Louis's personal manager and head of the Associated Booking Corporation, the most powerful agency in the jazz field. Glaser has the final veto over Armstrong's personnel, repertory, and nearly everything else concerning the band.

Frey shook his head disgruntledly and walked away. 'I don't believe it,' he muttered. 'I think Glaser is saving that song for an all-Bert Williams album for another label.'

The huge Webster Hall studio meanwhile was clangingly alive in a jangle of trombone blasts, shouts from Frey in the control room to 'turn that mike a little', a spiraling trumpet, and general disjointed noise. Webster Hall, on New York's lower East Side, occasionally doubles as a site for local neighbourhood functions but is most often in use for RCA-Victor's pop recordings. When time is available, a number of independent entrepreneurs such as Frey use the hall and generally also employ RCA staff engineers.

By three o'clock, an hour and a half after the session had been scheduled to start, Frey was moderately satisfied with the way he had set up his forces. The Dukes and Louis were arranged as a large triangle. To the right of the control room, young trumpeter Frank Assunto and tuba player Rich Mateson were stationed. To the left of the booth were Frank's brother, Fred, on trombone, and clarinettist Jerry Fuller who had joined the Dukes after five years with Jack Teagarden. In the centre of the triangle's base was Louis Armstrong.

At the apex of the triangle sat drummer Mo Mahoney. Between Mahoney and the trumpet-tuba corner was pianist Stan Mendelson. Between Mahoney and the trombone-clarinet position was Jac Assunto, father of Frank and Fred. Jac doubles on banjo and trombone.

Armstrong's wife, Lucille, a woman of great charm and total devotion to her husband, brought Louis a cup of coffee. In the control room, RCA staff engineer Ray Hall, a young man for whom New York jazz musicians have particular respect, was saying softly to Frey, 'We should spend some time with the clarinet. It's the only instrument that's peaking.'

Frey agreed. The stocky, bustling Frey is the man who stampeded the record business into stereo by first releasing a 'Stereodisc' to the industry in November 1957, and then making stereo recordings available to the public the following February. A compulsive lecturer, Frey was vehemently indoctrinating a visitor as Armstrong continued warming up. 'We record with very little reverberation,' Frey declared. 'There's already enough in the room. Maybe a little bit too much. And we get all the presence, intimacy and warmth of sound we can so that the listener can identify with what's going on. Louis, for example, leaves me emotionally exhausted; but until we cut him, he hadn't been recorded right so that record buyers could get his full impact.'

Audio Fidelity had already released *Satchmo Plays King Oliver*, and had recorded but not released a June 1959 meeting between Armstrong and the Dukes of Dixieland. The latter was being held up because Louis used some tunes in it that he had recorded for Decca a few years ago and was not supposed to record again for five years. For both last year's session and the new album with the Dukes, Frey had paid Armstrong $40,000.

Louis meanwhile was producing vibrantly full, round tones in his warm-up. At sixty, Armstrong continues to play with the most richly plangent tone in jazz; and at his best, his solos are still models of economy and passionate order.

'Pops,' Frey spoke into the control-room microphone in his customary roar, 'could you stand more in front of the mike?'

Louis did, and decided to warm up the band as well as himself in 'Indiana', a tune he usually plays at the beginning of a night-club or concert date.

Added to the high command in the control room was Joe Delaney, manager of the Dukes of Dixieland. A Louisiana lawyer with extensive experience in the record business, Delaney is tall, relaxed, and alert. Although his crew-cut hair is greying, Delaney has a perennial innocence of mien.

As 'Indiana' ended, the restless Frey said to no one in particular, 'This is a typical Audio Fidelity session. They're doing a number we're not going to record.'

'Pops,' Frey shouted, 'will you want to face in any particular direction?'

Louis turned toward the control room. 'No, you place it where you want, dolling,' and broke into laughter.

'Pops, I want you to be comfortable,' Frey persisted.

'No,' Louis said seriously, 'you fix it. I don't know anything about microphones. You put it where you want, and I'll play there.'

Louis and the Dukes began to discuss the routining of 'Avalon', the first number to be actually recorded for the album.

Louis looked at the control room and grinned. 'Anyone in there know the lyrics to "Avalon"?'

No one did. Louis began to sing what he remembered:

> 'I found my love in Avalon
> Beside the bay . . .'

He stopped, 'Well, there's no sense telling them all we did there,' and chuckled.

'Want to let them run it down once,' asked Ray Hall, 'before we make it?'

'No,' said Delaney, 'let's try our luck.'

'We're rolling,' Frey's voice shot out into the hall. 'Take one!'

The take broke down when Louis slipped: 'I left . . . I mean I found my girl . . .'

'Louis,' said Frey, 'sing into the same mike you play into. And take it easy on the drums behind the vocal.'

'All right,' Frey turned to Hall. 'Rewind the tape.'

'We can't erase today,' said Hall.

'That's nice,' Frey grimaced. 'I'd like to have the tape concession here.'

The next try worked out well. Louis improvised on the lyrics:

> 'I found my girl in Avalon,
> Beside the bay.
> Oh, she was so nice in Avalon,
> Hmmmmmmmmm, I'll say.
> But now we up in Harlem,
> And oh boy, hey, hey,
> She's not down in Avalon, folks,

She's right here in the studio –
Today!'

Frey decided to ask for another take, and went out into the hall to adjust Armstrong's microphone. 'You see what I mean by the "Frey Curtain of Sound"?' Frey rhetorically asked a visitor in the control room as he came back in. 'It's not at all ping-pong. I like broad panorama of sound so that each one of the elements is placed – and heard – according to where he'd actually be standing in a performance.'

The next 'Avalon' was superb with a thrilling highnote ending by Louis. The musicians relaxed, and listened to the playback . . .

The break was over. Frey asked for 'Avalon' once more. Armstrong, sitting down and warming up, asked Frankie Assunto, 'What key, baby, is that again?'

'F,' said Assunto.

'What's here Thursday?' Frey was asking Ray Hall. 'We may need more sessions than I'd counted on.'

'A beefsteak party at four o'clock,' said Hall, deadpan.

'Hmph,' Frey commented.

By the time he reached the vocal in the new version, Louis had changed the words again:

> 'Yes, I found my love in Avalon,
> Beside the sea.
> Oh, she was awful nice in Avalon,
> She was cute as can be.
> But now we in Harlem, Lord,
> And boy, you know,
> She knocks me out in Avalon,
> And she's here with me today.'

Louis followed the vocal with a climbing, explosive solo. Frankie Assunto, sitting on a stool with trumpet in his lap, gazed trance-like at Louis, and smiled seraphically. Louis tore the trumpet from his lips at the end of the solo, laughed in satisfaction, and walked away from the mike.

The tune ended, but Frey held up his arm dramatically for silence. At the end of ten seconds, he put it down.

'We must get those ten seconds of cymbal ring,' he explained. 'It's a natural sound.'

During the playback, Louis was talking with grey-haired 'Papa' Jac Assunto. Assunto had brought up the subject of famous New Orleans restaurants. Louis was guarded. He is bitter about discrimination in his home town, and no longer enjoys playing there.

'They still have Antoine's and all them places?' Louis finally warmed a little to the discussion.

'Yes,' Assunto assured him.

The musicians had been confident that the previous take was the final one, but Frey strode out into the hall. 'I heard an engineer,' he announced, 'who said he could do better on another shot.'

'Were you the engineer?' a suspicious onlooker whispered to Frey.

'No, no,' said Frey, 'Ray really wants to do another. He says he knows what he wants to do now.' . . .

'Dixie' was proposed as the next tune. Louis began to read the lyrics, but stopped, chuckling. 'No, I can't sing that. The coloured cats would put me down.'

'You know,' said Ray Hall, a Negro, 'I always thought he was an Uncle Tom. But he's not. And such a cooperative guy.'

Several friends of Louis had come into the hall – greying Gene Krupa and trumpeter Max Kaminsky among them. Armstrong and Krupa embraced, and then Louis caught sight of a Long Island neighbour, Dizzy Gillespie. Dizzy, though a key representative of the modern jazz that Louis once contemptuously called 'Chinese music', is an admirer of Armstrong; and the two have become friends.

'I was in his house just yesterday,' Dizzy was saying to a jazz writer. Dizzy listened for a few minutes to the playback of 'Avalon'. 'He sure can play, can't he?'

'Dixie' was shelved, and 'Wolverine Blues' took its place. Wordlessly, Louis sang the way he wanted the ending to go. 'You see what I mean,' he said to Frankie Assunto, 'you got to watch it close.'

'I think we're ready for a take,' Frey boomed from the control room; but photographers from the *Daily News*, oblivious of Frey, were shooting Louis, Krupa and Gillespie for promotion pictures in connection with a jazz concert the paper was sponsoring.

'I'll be glad when those photographers get out of here,' Frey said
to Delaney.

Max Kaminsky, whose jazz renown has faded in recent years,
stood against the wall, watching the picture-taking.

'Hey,' a sensitive friend of Louis shouted to the photographers.
'There's Maxie. Get him in there too.' Kaminsky was duly included
in the next set of pictures.

'Gentlemen,' said Frey icily, 'may we proceed – please?'

The picture-taking stopped.

'I want all the spectators,' Frey's voice cannonaded from
the control room, 'to be as quiet as possible. The mikes are wide
open.'

'It's getting to look like a Sinatra recording session,' Joe Delaney
pointed to the crowd outside the booth.

'Yes,' said Frey, 'and I don't like it.'

After the first take, Frey expressed dissatisfaction with the opening. 'The beginning is always the most important part of a record.
Let's do it again.'

By 4.15 a take on 'Wolverine Blues' had been tentatively
approved. Armstrong had played excellently, but he wasn't satisfied.
He and the Dukes began discussing changes.

'This is the way we play it,' Frankie was saying.

'Yeah,' answered Louis, 'I'll listen and find a little part for myself.'

The Dukes, standing around the seated Louis, started to play.
Louis fingered his horn, and finally joined in.

'Now,' Louis said to Frankie, 'when you finish that chorus, I'll
take over and play the obbligation to your solo.'

The Dukes laughed at Louis's play on the word.

'I', Frey announced to Delaney in the control room, 'would rather
have excitement and mistakes than no excitement and no mistakes.
That's why I try to get complete takes whenever I can, and I try not
to have them do too many. By the fifth or sixth time around, the
arrangement may get more polished, but the playing begins to lose
excitement.' . . .

'Now,' Frey announced with self-conscious gentleness, 'at the
end of this next take, everyone please be quiet. We're trying to catch
the cymbal to the very last ring.'

During the take Louis stood, arms wide apart, stomach out,

enjoying the music. He then unleashed a brilliant stop-time solo (a solo in which the rhythm section does not play continuously).

The take was approved, and Louis and the Dukes began to work out an instrumental version of 'Dixie'. Louis started to walk around the hall, playing without accompaniment, until he found the tempo he wanted. The Dukes soon fell into the same groove. . . .

II – 'What's to Understand? Play Them!'

On a grey November Sunday afternoon, Miles Davis, arranger-conductor Gil Evans and nineteen other musicians were scheduled at Columbia's huge 30th Street studios on New York's East Side. They were to record a unique album concept – Spanish themes re-scored by Evans and improvised on by Davis.

The instrumentation was Davis, four trumpets, tuba, three French horns, two trombones, bass, drums, percussion, harp, five wood-winds. Davis and Evans had already collaborated for Columbia on two brilliantly integrated orchestral albums, *Miles Ahead* and *Porgy and Bess*. Both had sold well, especially the broodingly dramatic intensification of the Gershwin score.

By 2.15 nearly all the musicians had arrived at the studios, which had once been a church, then a brewery, and were now in constant use by Columbia. The majority of the musicians were dressed in sports clothes. The one woman was slender, auburn-haired harpist Janet Putnam. Miles, short and wiry, is somewhat of a stylesetter sartorially as well as musically among the younger jazz musicians and on that afternoon he wore a green Italian sweater, grey polo shirt, green and red silk scarf and tapered chino pants. He looked, however, as if he'd rather be at home swearing at television, a continuing avocation of his.

Miles moved wearily into the control room. The effects of a recent attack of flu lingered. 'I'm breaking up,' he said in his croaking hoarse voice. 'I'm breaking into pieces.'

The a&r man, Teo Macero, a composer and erstwhile experimental jazz musician, was briskly giving instructions to engineer Fred Plaut and Plaut's assistant, Lou Belok.

The first session had taken place unsuccessfully the previous

Tuesday. Miles, even more racked by flu then, hadn't arrived until more than half the date was over, and the three hours had been spent mostly on the orchestra's finding the right tempos for the main piece in the album, Evans's re-arrangement of the middle section of the *Concierto de Aranjuez* for Guitar and Orchestra by the contemporary Spanish composer, Joaquin Rodrigo. As planned, it would take up one album side.

Miles had first heard the work several months ago on the West Coast when a friend gave him the record. 'After listening to it for a couple of weeks,' Miles said, 'I couldn't get it out of my mind. Then when Gil and I decided to do this album, I played him the record and he liked it. As we usually do, we planned the programme first by ourselves for about two months. I work out something; he takes it home and works on it some more; and then we figure out how we're going to do it. He can read my mind and I can read his.'

Fred Plaut meanwhile was beginning to express firm ideas of his own on the best way to balance the session. Plaut, a Parisian who came to Columbia over twenty years ago, is witty, conscientious and multilingual. He engineers many classical dates, most of the Broadway shows, and a large percentage of the jazz albums. Plaut is a superb photographer and many candid shots he's taken during Columbia dates have been on exhibition and in magazines.

The balance set by Macero had the trumpets, trombones and regular jazz drums (played by Miles's regular drummer, Jimmy Cobb) on the right. On the left were woodwinds, harp, and Elvin Jones on various percussion instruments, including timpani, tambourine, and castanets. The French horns, bass, and Miles were in the middle. Teo started, checking out each section of the orchestra to hear if all the microphones were working. Nine microphones had been set up – one each for brass, harp, woodwinds, horns, Miles, castanets and percussion, drums, bass, and an opening trio of flute, trombone, and trumpet.

'We're going to cross-feed some of the instruments,' Teo explained, 'to get a true stereo picture.'

In the studio, Gil Evans was checking the parts with his characteristically preoccupied look. A lean, greying man in his late forties, Gil looks like a gently ageing diplomat who collects rare species of ferns on weekends. Though always polite, he is in firm control of his record dates and insists on hearing exactly what he has written. Now, while Evans moved to one of the spare pianos at the far end of the studio to play part of the score, Fred Plaut and Teo Macero were debating the placement of the jazz drums.

'I never put rhythm drums with brass,' said Fred. 'It's a big mistake having the drums on the right side.'

'No,' countered Teo, 'they'll wash out the woodwinds if they're on the left.'

'The drums are very bright,' Fred persisted. 'And the brasses are bright too.'

'I'd rather not move them,' said Teo.

'All right! I give up,' and Fred continued checking out the microphones.

Miles had joined Gil at the spare piano and they started discussing Miles's part which spread out, accordion-fashion, over many sheets of manuscript paper. Teo walked out into the studio from the control room, and Plaut turned to his assistant. 'I'm still sorry the jazz drums aren't on the other side.'

As each section of the orchestra was being checked out, Gil kept looking at Plaut from the studio to see if any new problems were arising.

'Remember, we want lots of bass,' Teo said over his shoulder to Plaut. 'And Fred, there's a lot of leakage in the centre.'

Miles went back in the control booth. 'I always manage to put my foot in it,' he said of the Spanish experiment. 'I always manage to try something I can't do.' The statement was mockingly self-deprecating and no one bothered with the logical rebuttal that Miles is usually able to accomplish exactly what he sets out to do, and even rarer among jazzmen, he's always clear as to what it is he does want.

'I'm going to call myself on the phone one day,' Miles continued, 'and tell myself to shut up.'

At ten minutes of three, the remaining music parts were passed out. The copyist had been late. What with further checking of equipment, elimination of a crackling noise that suddenly developed on one control-room speaker, dry runs with the orchestra, and other complications, it wasn't until half-past three that Teo said, 'Stand by, please.' And then stopped. 'All right, who has a radio on in the studio?' he snapped into the microphone. 'Please!' he ordered, and the offending French horn player put a transistor radio back in his pocket.

The take began with Miles sitting on a stool; a trio of trumpet, trombone, and flute behind him; and Gil directing in the centre of the orchestra. Evans conducts with an almost ballet-like flow of motion. He uses both arms, and keeps the beat going like a firm Poseidon calming the waves. Evans is extremely careful that all the dense textural details and markings for dynamics are performed precisely and are recorded so that all the interweaving parts emerge clearly.

At one point an hour later, Evans cut off one take and said into the microphone, 'Are you getting a blending of the three flutes? I only hear one flute out here.' Macero assured him that all three were distinctly audible in the control room. Gil went into the booth, heard for himself, and was satisfied.

Miles came in for a sip of vodka. 'I can't eat. That's what's wrong with me.' After the vodka, he chuckled as he went out, saying, 'Me and Buddy Bolden,' referring to the first quasi-legendary jazz trumpeter, a New Orleans barber with a reputation for high and hard living.

By four, the shape of the piece was becoming established. The characteristic, fiercely mournful Spanish melody was a strong one. Evans's sketch for Miles looked complex, but Miles seemed to have no difficulty improvising around it. The orchestra's function, as in other Evans scores, was to provide partly a support for and partly a commentary on Davis's solo statements. The range of colours was extensive and they changed often, sometimes subtly dissolving into slightly different shades and at other times breaking sharply from ominous cool to brighter blends. By means of more complete instrumentation and varied voicings, Evans gets an unusually full-bodied orchestral sound for jazz from the deep bottoms of the tuba and French horns to high-register woodwinds and brass. 'These look like flute parts we're playing,' lead trumpeter Ernie Royal said during one break, shaking his head in respect and exasperation.

The rhythms were complex and several of the musicians found it hard to keep their time straight. Gil stopped one take as the rhythms became tangled. 'The tempo is going to go,' he waved his arm in an arc, first to the left and then to the right, 'this way and that way. Just keep your own time and let the rhythm *go.*' He again made a slow, even wave to further illustrate his point.

As more and more takes, most of them fragmentary, were tried, Miles's confidence in his own role grew markedly. He had already demonstrated in his 'Flamenco Sketches' (*Kind of Blue*) and 'Blues for Pablo' with Gil Evans (*Miles Ahead*) a basic affinity with the Spanish musical temperament and sinuous rhythms. He played as if all by himself, his tone becoming burningly dark in the sombre passages and then cutting through with sharper loneliness as the music grew more animated.

In the control room, the visiting Hall Overton, a classical composer who has also been involved in jazz as a pianist and arranger, said, 'This is the toughest notation I've ever seen in a jazz arrangement. It could have been written more easily for the players and the result would have been the same, but Gil has to have it exactly the way it happens in the piece. Another thing that makes it tough is that he's using so many different levels. Like the little trio part at the beginning that has to be balanced with Miles on his microphone. Then the three players go back to their places and that makes for another balance problem. And that's just at the beginning. Fortunately, these guys are among the best readers in town. Two of those horn players, Jim Buffington and John Barrows, were in New Jersey last night playing a Beethoven sextet for string quartet and two horns.'

In the studio, the French horn player had his radio at his ear again. Gil, listening intently to a playback a few feet away, had his ears cupped in his hands, and shook his head sadly. 'We lost the beat.' Miles meanwhile shouted from the studio into the control room, 'Hey, Teo, it doesn't matter how loud those castanets are. It's *supposed* to be that way.' Then Miles bent over, cupping his ears in his hands, and listened.

'This,' said trombonist Frank Rehak between taking pictures of Miles and Gil during the playback, 'is a tough one. To count at all, you have to count four on every beat.'

For the rest of the afternoon, the takes continued to improve. On one, Miles began to play in the lower register with deep feeling and a fuller tone than is usual in his work. 'Beautiful,' Teo said. 'The writing there is almost Gregorian.' He turned to Overton. 'It's all diatonic.'

'Fred,' Teo said quickly, 'there'll be big brass after the next little solo if Gil doesn't stop it there.' Gil did stop it.

'Ach,' said Plaut, 'why did he cut it *there*?'

Gil was back at the piano checking chords with Miles.

'This,' said Plaut to no one in particular, 'will be *some* splicing job.'

'Gil will come up for that,' said Teo, 'and probably Miles too.'

Gil and Miles came in to listen to a playback. 'I *love* that chord,' said Miles, 'and the end of that section with the flutes way up there. That's all I could hear last night in my sleep. Hey,' he turned to Macero, 'don't forget take three. That was a good one.'

Teo asked Evans if the timpani came in too softly. 'I wanted it to be just a whisper,' said Evans, 'a little cushion of air, something to keep the thing floating. I think it's all right. The tuba is too loud, though.'

'You know,' Miles returned to the conversation, 'the melody is so strong there's nothing you have to do with it. If you tried to play bebop on it, you'd wind up being a hip cornball. The thing I have to do now is make things connect, make them mean something in what I play around it.'

'Why don't we do it from the beginning again?' said Plaut after Evans and Davis had left the control room.

'No,' said Teo, 'not unless Gil and Miles want to.'

'If you don't do it again,' said Plaut, 'you'll swear at me afterwards.'

'The trumpet was a little weak on bar thirty-three,' Teo changed the subject.

A little later, Plaut shook his head. 'I'm still sorry the jazz drums aren't on the left side. Well, anyway, there's no ping-pong.'

'This will be good stereo,' Teo agreed.

'Yes,' said Fred with more than a touch of irony. 'We're playing football now in there.'

By four-thirty, the musicians were a little more than a third of the way through. 'There's more confusion in there,' said Plaut, 'than on a Broadway show recording.'

As if in counterpoint to the engineer's comment, Gil announced to the orchestra immediately afterwards, 'It's in *three* flats,' and sat at the piano to demonstrate.

'Can you *please* put that radio away,' Teo's voice came into the studio from the control booth. 'We're picking it up.' The French horn player grimly put the radio away.

The orchestra had now reached the sixty-fifth bar, and from then on it was all new territory for them. At a break, Miles was back in the control room.

'How many copies will this sell?' he asked Teo semi-seriously.

'A hundred thousand. I guarantee it.'

'Two!' Miles laughed. 'Actually we're making it just to have a record at home we can play for ourselves.'

'I think,' said Teo, 'that's what some of the artists really do.'

A few minutes later, a take broke down, and one of the musicians said, 'I can't understand those triplets.'

'What's to understand?' said Gil. 'Play them!'

At a few minutes past five, Fred Plaut began taking pictures during a playback. So did the regular Columbia photographer and a couple of the musicians.

Several more takes were tried, and a few minutes before five-thirty, Teo rushed into the control room. 'We're going from the top of the whole thing.' Plaut smiled. 'Put on another load of tape,' Teo said to Belok, Plaut's assistant.

It was the best take of the afternoon, lasting some twelve minutes, and there was no question now that the piece was going to work. During one passage, Miles played a series of notes that made Evans spin around and smile at him.

'This,' said Plaut when the take was over, 'is a lifetime project.'

'What I like about Columbia,' Miles reached for a little more vodka, 'is they spare no expense.' As often with Miles, it was hard to separate the satire from the seriousness of his comment. 'We can have seventeen flutes playing one note – in unison. Right, Teo?' . . .

In the control room, Evans was listening to the last playback. 'Damn! Miles can play beautifully down low.' In the studio, the musicians were packing up. It was a few minutes before six. 'This,' said Gil, back in the control room, 'is where the heroine is crying for the dead bullfighter.'

'Really?' said a visitor.

'No,' Gil smiled, 'it's an old Spanish vamp.'

'I would have preferred the drums on the other side,' Fred Plaut said to Belok.

'That melody,' Miles was still marvelling at the piece, 'is so strong that the softer you play it, the stronger it gets, and the stronger you play it, the weaker it gets.'

'Yes,' said Gil, 'it's distilled melody. If you lay on it too hard, you don't have it.'

'It should take two, maybe three more sessions to finish the album,' Teo was speculating.

'When Gil and I start on an album,' Miles was relaxing, 'we don't know how it's going to wind up. It just goes on and on out there. Gil,' he turned to Evans, 'our next record date will be silence.'

'You,' said Gil, 'and your big ideas.'

1960

DIZZY GILLESPIE

Bendin' the Horn

The truth is that the shape of my horn was an accident. I could pretend that I went into the basement and thought it up, but it wasn't that way. It was an accident. Actually, I left my horn on a trumpet stand and someone kicked it over, and instead of just falling, the horn bent. I was playing at Snookie's on 45th Street, on a Monday night, 6 January 1953. I had Monday nights off, but it was my wife's birthday so we had a party and invited all the guys – Illinois Jacquet, Sarah Vaughan, Stump 'n Stumpy, and several other artists, all the people who were in show business who knew Lorraine from dancing. They were down there having a good time and the whisky was flowing. They had a cake and drinks and everything. This guy, Henry Morgan, who had his own show in New York, invited me to come on his show and be interviewed. This was really another put-on because he wasn't really interested in music. Anyway, I went out to be interviewed; he was doing the show from a hotel around the corner. My horn was still straight when I left it on one of those little trumpet stands that sticks straight up.

When I got back to the club after making this interview, Stump 'n Stumpy had been fooling around on the bandstand, and one had pushed the other, and he'd fallen back onto my horn. Instead of the horn just falling, the bell bent. Nine hundred and ninety-nine times out of a thousand if someone fell on a horn, it would bend the valves or maybe hit and bend the valve case. The horn would be dented, and the valves would stick, but this horn bent. When I got back, the bell was sticking up in the air. Illinois Jacquet had left. He said, 'I'm not going to be here when that man comes back and sees his horn sticking up at that angle. I ain't gonna be here when that crazy muthafucka gets back.'

When I came back, it was my wife's birthday and I didn't wanna be a drag. I put the horn to my mouth and started playing it. Well, when the bell bent back, it made a smaller hole because of the dent.

I couldn't get the right sound, but it was a strange sound that I got from that instrument that night. I played it, and I liked the sound. The sound had been changed and it could be played softly, very softly, not blarey. I played it like that the rest of the night, and the next day I had it straightened out again. Then I started thinking about it and said, 'Wait a minute, man, that was something else.' I remembered the way the sound had come from it, quicker to the ear – to my ear, the player. A forty-five-degree angle is much closer than ninety degrees. I contacted the Martin Company, and I had Lorraine, who's also an artist, draw me a trumpet at a forty-five-degree angle and sent it to the Martin Company. I told them, 'I want a horn like this.'

'You're crazy!' they said.

'OK,' I said, 'I'm crazy, but I want a horn like this.' They made me a trumpet and I've been playing one like that ever since. At first they made it so the bell would screw in at forty-five degrees. Now, we've developed it to where it's all in one piece. One of the things a horn like mine remedies is the problem of holding your instrument too far down when you're reading music. You can never hold this horn down low enough for the bell of it to be below the music stand. Also, in small clubs, you'd be playing right up on people, and a trumpet is a very forceful instrument. If it's played straight at you, it can bust someone's eardrum if you play a hard note in the upper register. My instrument, when you hit a note, Bam! You hear it right then, instead of waiting. It's only a split second, but that split second means a lot.

STAN GETZ

Letter to the Editor of Down Beat

21 April 1954

Dear Jack:

I have many things to say, excluding excuses, regrets, and promises. Promises from me at this point mean nothing; starting when I am released is when my actions will count.

What happened in Seattle was inevitable. Me coming to the end of my rope. I shouldn't have been withdrawing myself from narcotics while working and travelling. With the aid of barbiturates, I thought I could do it. Seattle was the eighth day of the tour and I could stand no more. (Stan, you said no excuses.) Going into this drugstore, I demanded some narcotics. I said I had a gun (didn't).

The lady behind the counter evidently didn't believe I had a gun so she told another customer. He, in turn, took a look at me and laughed, saying, 'Lady, he's kidding you. He has no gun.' I guess I didn't look the part. Having flopped at my first 'caper' (one of the terms I've learned up here), I left the store and went to my hotel. When I was in my room I decided to call the store and apologize. In doing so, the call was traced and my incarceration followed. My 'dope poisoning' was sixty grains of a long-acting barbiturate that I swallowed *en route* to jail. I'd had enough of me and my antics.

When I came out of the coma three days later, with a breathing tube inserted in my trachea, I realized that the doctors at Harbour Haven County Hospital had other ideas. God didn't want to kill me. This was his warning. Next time I'm sure he won't let me live. As I lay there alive, not wanting to live because of what I had done to my loved ones and all the people who had tried to help me, the nurse came in with a good many letters, telegrams, and phone messages – all saying the same thing. They told me not to despair, that they admired my music, that I should pray as they were praying for me, and, most important, that they forgave me.

I was never what you might call a religious person, beyond being

Bar Mitzvahed (confirmed in the Jewish faith), but those people showed me that there is a God, not above us but here on earth in the warm hearts of people.

I realize what I have done has hurt jazz music in general. To say I'm sorry is not nearly enough. I can't blame what I've done on the pressures of creative music in this country. Tell this boy from Seattle that it's pure and simple degeneracy of the mind, a lack of morals, and personality shortcomings I have that he doesn't. Tell him that the really good musicians are too smart to mess with it, and don't need it, anyway.

I have much more to write, but we are allowed only three pages a day. Will try again tomorrow.

Stan

On the Road with
Stan Kenton's Band, 1946–52

After I sniffed it that morning in Chicago, I bought up a whole bunch of heroin, got a sackful of caps. We travelled back to Los Angeles. I guess it took us three months to get back, playing all the stops in between, and at this time we had a little vacation from Stan, about a month before we had to go out again. I told Patti I had sniffed a little bit, but it was okay, it was all right. She felt bad but she went along with it. Then I ran out. I got totally depressed and my stomach hurt. My nose hurt something awful, terrible headaches; my nose started bleeding. I was getting chills. I was vomiting. And the joints in my legs hurt.

I had to go to a session so I got hold of some codeine pills and some sleeping pills and some bennies, and I got a bottle of cough syrup and drank it, and I went out to this session because I still couldn't believe I was that sick.

Everything was real clear to me. Everything was so vivid. I felt that I was seeing life for the first time. Before, the world had been clouded; now, it was like being in the desert and looking at the sky and seeing the stars after living in the city all your life. That's the way everything looked, naked, violently naked and exposed. That's the way my body felt, my nerves, my mind. There was no buffer, and it was unbearable. I thought, 'Oh my God, what am I going to do?'

I looked around the club and saw this guy there, Blinky, that I knew. He was a short, squat guy with a square face, blue eyes; he squinted all the time; when he walked he bounced; and he was always going 'Tchk! Tchk!' – moving his head in jerky little motions like he was playing the drums. Sometimes when he walked he even looked like a drum set: you could see the sock cymbal bouncing up and down and the foot pedal going and the cymbals shaking and his eyes would be moving. But it wasn't his eyes; it was that his whole body kind of blinked. He'd been a friend of mine for years and I knew he goofed around occasionally with horse, heroin, so I started talking. I said, 'Man, I really feel bad. I started sniffing stuff on the road and I ran out.' I described to him a little bit of how I felt and he said, 'Ohhhh, man!' I said, 'How long is this going to last?' He said, 'You'll feel like this for three days; it'll get worse. And then the mental part will come on after the physical leaves and you'll be suffering for over a week, unbearable agony.' I said, 'Do you know any place where I can get anything?' He said, 'Yeah, but it's a long ways away. We have to go to Compton.' We were in Glendale. At that time they didn't have the freeway system; it was a long drive but I said, 'Let's go.' We drove out to Sid's house.

As we drove I thought, 'God almighty, this is it. This is what I was afraid of.' And the thought of getting some more stuff so I wouldn't feel that way any more seemed so good to me I got scared that something would happen before we got there, that we'd have a wreck. So I started driving super cautious, but the more cautious I was the harder it seemed to be to control the car. The sounds of the car hurt me. I could feel the pain it must be feeling in the grinding of the gears and the wheels turning and the sound of the motor and the brakes. But I drove, and we made it, and we went inside, and I was shaking all over, quivering, thinking how great it would be to get something so I wouldn't feel the way I felt.

Sid was a drummer also, not a very good drummer, but he had a good feeling for time. He was a guy I'd known a long time, too, a southern type cat with a little twang of an accent. We went in and Blinky told Sid I'd started goofing around and Sid said, 'Ohhh, boy! Join the club!' He said, 'What do you want?' I said, 'I don't know. I just want some so I won't be sick.' He said, 'Where do you fix at?' I said, 'I don't fix, I just sniff it, you know, horn it.' He said, 'Oh, man, I haven't got enough for *that*!' I said, 'What do you mean?' He said, 'If you want to shoot some, great, but I'm not going to waste it. I don't have that much.' I said, 'Oh, man, you've got to, this is horrible. You've got to let me have something!' He said, 'No, I won't do it. It's wasted by sniffing it. It takes twice as much, three times as much. If you'd shoot it you could take just a little bit and keep straight.' I said, 'I don't want to shoot it. I know if I shoot it I'm lost.' And he said, 'You're lost anyway, man.' I begged him and begged him. I couldn't possibly leave that place feeling as sick as I did. I couldn't drive. I couldn't do anything. I didn't care what happened afterwards, I just had to have a taste. Finally I said, 'Okay, I'll shoot it.' He said, 'Great.'

They both fixed, and I had to wait. At last he asked me what I wanted. I asked him how they sold it. He said they sold it in grams: a gram was ten number-five caps for twenty dollars. I said to give me a gram and he said, 'Whatever you want.' I said, 'I thought you only had just a little bit.' He said, 'I only have a little bit but I got enough.' It was just the idea that he wanted me to fix. I knew that. So I'd be in the same misery as he was. He said, 'Where do you want to go?' I looked around my arms. I didn't want to go the mainline, the vein at the crook inside your arm, because that's where the police always looked, I'd heard, for marks. I asked him if he could hit me in the spot between the elbow and the wrist, the forearm.

Sid put a cap or a cap and a half of powder into the spoon. He had an eyedropper with a rubber bulb on it, but he had taken thread and wrapped it around the bulb so it would fit tight around the glass part. He had a dollar bill. Here came the dollar bill again, but this time instead of rolling it up as a funnel he tore a teeny strip off the end of it and wrapped it around the small end of the dropper so the spike would fit over it real tight. That was the 'jeep'. He put about ten drops of water on top of the powdered stuff in the spoon and took a match and put it under the spoon. I saw the powder start to fade; it cooked up. He took a little bit of cotton that he had and rolled it in a ball and dropped it in the spoon, and then he put the spoon on the table. He took the spike off the end of the dropper and squeezed the bulb, pressed the eyedropper against the cotton and let the bulb loose. When he had all the liquid in the dropper he put the spike back on the end of it and made sure it was all secure. Blinky tied me up. He took a tie he'd been wearing and wrapped it around my arm just below the elbow. He held it tight and told me to make a fist. I squeezed so the veins stood out. Sid placed the point of the needle against my vein. He tapped it until it went in and then a little drop of blood came up from the spike into the dropper and he told

Blinky to leave the tie loose and me to quit making a fist and he squeezed the bulb and the stuff went into my vein. He pulled the spike out and told me to put my finger over the hole because blood had started to drip out. I waited for about a minute or a minute and a half and then I felt the warmth – a beautiful glow came over my body and the stark reality, the nakedness, this brilliance that was so unbearable was buffered, and everything became soft. The bile stopped coming up from my stomach. My muscles and my nerves became warm. I've never felt like that again. I've approached it. I've never felt any better than that ever in my life. I looked at Blinky and at Sid and I said, 'Oh boy, there's nothing like it. This is it. This is the end. It's all over: I'm finished.' But, I said, 'Well, at least I'm going to enjoy the ride.'

After I left the house I went to a drugstore that Blinky knew. At that time you could buy spikes easy, so I got four number-twenty-six, half-inch hypodermic needles, an eyedropper that had a good, strong bulb on it, and went home. I had about nine capsules of heroin left. I walked into the house and Patti met me at the door. I went into the kitchen. I put this stuff out on the table, and she looked at it, and she said, 'Oh no!' I said, 'Yeah, this is it. You'll have to accept it.' I got a dollar bill and tore a little piece off the bottom to make the jeep. I got a glass out of the cupboard, a plastic one so it wouldn't hurt the end of the needle when I put it in to wash it out. I took a cap and put it in the spoon and put some water in it, and all this time I'm talking to Patti, trying to explain because I loved her and I wanted her to accept this. I got a tie out of the closet and asked her if she would tie me, and she wrapped it and held it and she was trying to be cool and be brave, and I stuck the thing in, and the blood popped up, and I told her, 'Leave it go. Leave it go.' I looked up, and I'll never forget the look on her face. She was transfixed by the sight of the blood, my own blood, drawn up, running into an eyedropper that I was going to shoot into my vein. It seemed so depraved to her. How could anybody do anything like that? How could anybody love her and need to do anything like that? She started crying. I took her hand away and took the tie off. I shot the stuff in, and when I finished I looked at her. She turned her head and cried hysterically. I put my arms around her and tried to tell her that everything was all right, that it was better than the drinking and the misery I'd gone through before, but I couldn't get through to her.

After I got the outfit and started fixing, that was my thing. I still drank and smoked pot, but I was a lot cooler. Things were going great for me. I was featured with the band and we played all over the country. We'd go from one state to another and the bus driver we had at the time was a beautiful cat who knew what all the liquor laws were – some states were dry – and he'd stop just before we crossed into a dry state and say, 'This is the last time you can buy alcohol until such and such a date.' We'd all run out of the bus. We'd figure out how much liquor we'd need. If we went to Canada and had to pass through an inspection station we'd take our dope, the guys that were using heroin, our outfits or pills, and give them to the bus driver to stash behind a panel. We'd go through the station and get shook down, and then he'd open the panel and give us our dope back. And wherever we'd pass through we'd buy different pot. In Colorado we'd get Light Green and in New Orleans it was Gunje or Mota. There were a lot of connoisseurs of pot who'd carry little film cans of it and pipes with screens to filter it, and when we had a rest stop we'd jump out of the bus and smoke.

Me and Andy Angelo roomed together for a long time and before that it was me and Sammy, and we each had our outfits. I had a little carrying case, like an electric razor case. I had an extra eyedropper and my needles, four or five of them. I had my little wires to clean the spike out in case it got clogged. I had a little bottle of alcohol and a sterling silver spoon that was just beautiful and a knife to scoop the stuff into the spoon. I used to carry this case in the inside pocket of my suit, just like you'd carry your cigarettes or your wallet. I even carried a little plastic glass. I would set up my outfit next to the bed in the hotel with my stuff in a condom – we used to carry our heroin in one to keep it from getting wet. I'd wake up in the morning and reach over, get my little knife, put a few knifefuls in the spoon, cook it up and fix. It was beautiful.

It was wonderful being on the road with that band. . . .

There's a thing about empathy between musicians. The great bands were the ones in which the majority of the people were good people, morally good people; I call them real people – in jail they call them regulars. Bands that are made up of more good people than bad, those are the great bands. Those are the bands like Basie's was at one time and Kenton's and Woody Herman's and Duke Ellington's were at a couple of different times.

There's so many facets to playing music. In the beginning you learn the fundamentals of whatever instrument you might play: you learn the scales and how to get a tone. But once you become proficient mechanically, so you can be a jazz musician, then a lot of other things enter into it. Then it becomes a way of life, and how you relate musically is really involved.

The selfish or shallow person might be a great musician technically, but he'll be so involved with himself that his playing will lack warmth, intensity, beauty and won't be deeply felt by the listener. He'll arbitrarily play the first solo every time. If he's backing a singer he'll play anything he wants or he'll be practising scales. A person that lets the other guy take the first solo, and when he plays behind a soloist plays only to enhance him, that's the guy that will care about his wife and children and will be courteous in his everyday contact with people.

Miles Davis is basically a good person and that's why his playing is so beautiful and pure. This is my own thinking and the older I get the more I believe I'm correct in my views. Miles is a master of the understatement and he's got an uncanny knack for finding the right note or the right phrase. He's tried to give an appearance of being something he's not. I've heard he's broken a television set when he didn't like something that was said on TV, that he's burnt connections, been really a bastard with women, and come on as a racist. The connections probably deserved to be burnt; they were assholes, animals, guys that would burn you: give you bad stuff and charge you too much, people that would turn you in to the cops if they got busted. Most of the women that hang around jazz musicians are phonies. And as for his prejudice, not wanting white people in his bands, that's what he feels he should be like. He's caught up in the way the country is, the way the people are, and he figures that's the easiest way to go. One time he did hire Bill Evans for his band, but people ranked him so badly and it was such a hassle that I think he became bitter and assumed this posture of racism and hatred. But I feel he's a good person or he couldn't play as well as he plays.

Billy Wilson plays like *he* is. When I knew him, when he was young, he was a real warm, sweet, loving person. And he plays just that way. But if you listen to his tone, it never was very strong; it's pretty and kind of cracking. It's weak. And when he was faced with prison – because he got busted for using drugs – he couldn't stand it. He couldn't go because he was afraid, and when they offered him an out by turning over on somebody he couldn't help but do it. He's a weak person. That's the way he plays. That's the way he sounds.

Stan Getz is a great technician, but he plays cold to me. I hear him as he is and he's rarely moved me. He never knocked me out like Lester Young, Zoot Sims, Coltrane.

John Coltrane was a great person, warm with no prejudice. He was a dedicated musician but he got caught up in the same thing I did. He was playing at the time when using heroin was fashionable, when the big blowers like Bird were using, and so, working in Dizzy Gillespie's band, playing lead alto, he became a junkie. But he was serious about his playing so he finally stopped using heroin and devoted all his time to practising. He became a fanatic and he reached a point where he was technically great, but he was also a good person so he played warm and real. I've talked to him, talked to him for hours, and he told me, 'Why don't you straighten up? You have so much to offer. Why don't you give the world what you can?' That's what *he* did. But success trapped him. He got so successful that everyone was expecting him to be always in the forefront. What he finally had, what he really had and wanted and had developed, he could no longer play because that wasn't new any more. He got on that treadmill and ran himself ragged trying to be new and to change. It destroyed him. It was too wearing, too draining. And he became frustrated and worried. Then he started hurting, getting pains, and he got scared. He got these pains in his back, and he got terrified. He was afraid of doctors, afraid of hospitals, afraid of audiences, afraid of bandstands. He lost his teeth. He was afraid that his sound wasn't strong enough, afraid that the new, young black kids wouldn't think he was the greatest thing that ever lived any more. And the pains got worse and worse; they got so bad he couldn't stand the pain. So they carried him to a hospital but he was too far gone. He had cirrhosis, and he died that night. Fear killed him. His life killed him. That thing killed him.

So being a musician and being great is the same as living and being a real person, an honest person, a caring person. You have to be happy with what you have and what you give and not have to be totally different and wreak havoc, not have to have everything be completely new at all times. You just have to be a part of something and have the capacity to love and to play with love. Harry Sweets Edison has done that; Zoot Sims has done that, has finally done that. Dizzy Gillespie has done that to a very strong degree. Dizzy is a very open, contented, loving person; he lives and plays the same way; he does the best he can. A lot of the *old* players were like that – Jack Teagarden, Freddie Webster – people that just played and were good people.

Jealousy has hurt jazz. Instead of trying to help each other and enjoy each other, musicians have become petty and jealous. A guy will be afraid somebody's going to play better than him and steal his job. And the black power – a lot of the blacks want jazz to be *their* music and won't have anything to do with the whites. Jazz is an art form. How can art form *belong* to one race of people? I had a group for a while – Lawrence Marable was playing drums, Curtis Counce was playing bass – and one night I got off the stand, we were at Jazz City, and a couple of friends of mine who were there said, 'Hey, man, did you realize what was happening? Those cats were ranking you while you were playing, laughing and really ranking you.' I said, 'You're *kidding*, man!' I started asking people and I started, every now and then, turning around real quick when I'd be playing. And there they were, sneering at me. Finally I just wigged out at Lawrence Marable. We went out in front of the club and I said, 'Man, what's *happening* with you?' And he said, 'Oh, fuck you! You know what I think of you, you white motherfucker?' And he spit in the dirt and stepped in it. He said, 'You can't play. None of you white punks can play!' I said, 'You lousy, stinking, black motherfucker! Why the fuck do you work for me if you feel like that?' And he said, 'Oh, we're just taking advantage of you white punk motherfuckers.' And that was it. That's what they think of me. If that's what they think of me, what am I going to think of them? I was really hurt, you know; I wanted to cry, you know; I just couldn't believe it – guys I'd given jobs to, and I find out they're talking behind my back and, not only that, laughing behind my back when I'm playing in a club!

There's people like Ray Brown that I worked with, Sonny Stitt, who I blew with, black cats that played marvellous and really were beautiful to me, so I couldn't believe it when these things started happening. But you're going to start wondering, you're going to be leery, naturally, and when you see people that you know . . . I'd go to the union and run into Benny Carter or Gerald Wilson and find myself shying away from them because I'd be wondering, 'Do they think, "Oh, there's that white asshole, that Art Pepper; that white punk can't play; *we* can only play; us black folks is the only people that can play!"?' That's how I started thinking and it destroyed everything. How can you have any harmony together or any beauty when *that's* going on? So that's what happened to jazz. That's why so many people just stopped. Buddy DeFranco, probably the greatest clarinet player who ever lived, people like that, they just got so sick of it; they just got sick to death of it; and they had to get out because it was so heartbreaking.

But all that happened later on. In 1951, musically at least, I had the world by the tail. That was the year I placed second, on alto saxophone, in the *Down Beat* jazz poll. Charlie Parker got fourteen votes more than me and came in first.

At the end of 1951 I quit Kenton's band. It was too hard being on the road, being away from Patti, and I grew tired of the band. I knew all the arrangements by memory and it was really boring. I didn't get a chance to stretch out and play the solos I wanted to play or the tunes. I kept thinking how nice it would be to play with just a rhythm section in a jazz club where I could be the whole thing and do all the creating myself. As far as the money went, the money never changed. I was one of the highest-paid guys in the band, especially among the saxophone players; Stan didn't think that sax players were the same calibre as brass players or rhythm, and we had to play exceptionally loud and work real hard because we had ten brass blowing over our heads. Also the travelling got to be unbearable. At first I enjoyed it, but after a while, being nine months out of the year on the road, one-nighters every night . . . Sometimes we'd finish a job, change clothes, get on the bus, travel all night long, get to the next town in the daytime, check in and try to get some sleep, and then go and play the job and be travelling up until the time to go to the next one. We'd have to change clothes on the bus and go right in and play.

Also I became more and more hooked and I went through some unbelievable scenes – running out of stuff on the road, not being able to score, having to play, sick, sitting on the stand spitting up bile into a big rag I kept under the music stand. I guess I looked sort of messed up. People started talking. Kenton became more and more suspicious. I imagined he knew I was doing more than drinking and smoking pot. So it seemed best that I leave the band and try to do something on my own, and I gave my notice. A lot of us quit at the same time. Shelly Manne quit. Shorty Rogers quit. . . .

Because I had my own group, I wanted to do my own material, tunes that would express my personality, not just standards. I had fooled around writing little things out when I was with Kenton. Now I tried writing seriously and found I had a talent for it. I wrote a ballad for my daughter, Patricia, probably the prettiest thing I've written to this day, and I wrote a real flag-waver, a double-fast bebop tune, very difficult, and I named it 'Straight Life'.

Everything was perfect. I bought a tract house on my GI bill. I had finally gotten to know my daughter and was just mad about her, really loved her. We had a little white poodle named Suzy, and I had a car. I had everything. I was making good money and I didn't use any of that money on my habit – I was dealing a little bit of stuff to musicians, friends of mine, to support my habit. And I felt that I wasn't doing anything wrong because I wasn't taking food out of my child's and my wife's mouths by using. But I was really strung out.

I realized I had to get away from the stuff. In the latter part of '51 there began to be newspaper stories about dope. It was beginning to hit the limelight. I realized that things weren't going to be the same, things were going to tighten up. And that meant either I had to kick or I had to go to jail. That would really ruin my career. I was thinking how nice it would be to just stop, be cool, and not pay any of the real heavy dues that you usually have to pay. So that's what my thinking was when my dad came out to the house I'd bought in Panorama City and asked me if I'd like to come and have a drink.

My mother had gone to my dad, who was living in Long Beach, and she told him I was using. I had asked her not to say anything to him because he hated junkies; he'd always told me don't ever do *that*. But he found out and came to me and said, 'Let's go out and have a drink.' He used to come with Thelma, but this time he came alone and he said he wanted to talk to me.

We went and had a drink, and then he looked at me, and he put his hand on my arm. We were in a bar in Van Nuys, a bar I later worked in with a western band. He said, 'When did you start on that stuff?' He put his arm around me and got tears in his eyes. And the way he put it to me I knew that he knew. I think at first I tried a feeble 'What do you mean?' But he grabbed my arm. I had a short-sleeved shirt on. I had marks all over my arm. He said, 'You might as well be dead.' He said, 'How did it happen?' So we talked and I tried to explain to him. I had tried to minimize the feelings I had, but it was so good to be able to tell somebody about it, to let him know how awful I felt and how really scared I was. He said, 'What are we going to do?' I said, 'Oh God, I don't know. I want to stop.' He said, 'Tell me the truth, if you don't want to stop nothing is going to do you any good.' We talked and talked. Before he'd even come to me he'd inquired and found a sanatorium in Orange County, and they said they'd take me in. He made sure the police wouldn't hear about it; I wouldn't be reported. He said, 'Will you go to this place?' I was afraid because I was afraid to kick, and I was afraid I might goof, and I didn't want to disappoint my dad. I felt miserable when I saw how miserable he felt. He said, 'Anything I can do, no matter what it costs, don't worry about it. Don't worry about anything – I'll take care of you.' That's when he started crying, and we hugged each other, and we were in this bar, and it was really strange, but I felt wonderful because after all these years I felt that I'd reached my dad and we were close. And so he asked me if I'd go to the sanatorium, and I saw that he wanted me to real bad, and so I said yes, all right, that I would go.

MICHAEL S. HARPER

Here Where Coltrane Is

Soul and race
are private dominions,
memories and modal
songs, a tenor blossoming,
which would paint suffering
a clear colour but is not in
this Victorian house
without oil in zero-degree
weather and a forty-mile-an-hour wind;
it is all a well-knit family:
a love supreme.

Oak leaves pile up on walkway
and steps, catholic as apples
in a special mist of clear white
children who love my children.
I play 'Alabama'
on a warped record player
skipping the scratches
on your faces over the fibrous
conical hairs of plastic
under the wooden floors.

Dreaming on a train from New York
to Philly, you hand out six
notes which become an anthem
to our memories of you:
oak, birch, maple,
apple, cocoa, rubber.
For this reason Martin is dead;
for this reason Malcolm is dead;

for this reason Coltrane is dead;
in the eyes of my first son are the browns
of these men and their music.

JAMES BALDWIN

Of the Sorrow Songs: The cross of redemption

Baldwin wrote this piece in 1979 for a small Scottish magazine. Ostensibly a review of James Lincoln Collier's The Making of Jazz, *it follows its own beat and becomes a sort of meditation. Collier replied (see next item), providing a rational counterpoint to Baldwin's 'justified' stridency.*

29 July 1979

I will let the date stand: but it is a false date. My typewriter has been silent since July 6th, and the piece of paper I placed in the typewriter on that day has been blank until this hour.

July 29th was – is – my baby sister's birthday. She is now thirty-six years old, is married to a beautiful cat, and they have a small son, my nephew, one of my many nephews. My baby sister was born on the day our father died: and I could not but wonder what she, or our father, or her son, my nephew, could possibly make of this compelling investigation of our lives.[1]

It is compelling indeed, like the nightmare called history: and compelling because the author is as precise as he is deluded.

Allow me, for example, to paraphrase, and parody, one of his statements, and I am not trying to be unkind:

There have been two authentic geniuses in jazz. One of them, of course, was Louis Armstrong, the much loved entertainer, striving for acceptance. The other was a sociopath named Charlie Parker, who managed . . . to destroy his career – and finally himself.

Well. Then: *There have been two authentic geniuses in art. One of*

1. *The Making of Jazz* by James Lincoln Collier (New York, 1979).

them, of course, was Michelangelo, the much beloved court jester, striving to
please the Pope. The other was a misfit named Rembrandt, who managed
. . . to destroy his career – and finally himself.

If one can believe the first statement, there is absolutely no reason
to doubt the second. Which may be why no one appears to learn
anything from history – I am beginning to suspect that no one *can*
learn anything from the nightmare called history – these are my
reasons, anyway, for attempting to report on this report from such a
dangerous point of view.

I have learned a great deal from traversing, struggling with, this
book. It is my life, my history, which is being examined – defined:
therefore, it is my obligation to attempt to clarify the record. I do not
want my nephew – or, for that matter, my Swiss godson, or my
Italian godson – to believe this 'comprehensive' history.

People cannot be studied from a distance. It is perfectly possible
that we cannot be studied at all: God's anguish, perhaps, upon being
confronted with His creation. People certainly cannot be studied
from a safe distance, or from the distance which we call safety. No
one is, or can be, the other: there is nothing in the other, from the
depths to the heights, which is not to be found in me. Of course, it
can be said that, 'objectively' speaking, I do not have the temperament of an Idi Amin, or Somoza, or Hitler, or Bokassa. Our careers
do not resemble each other, and, for that, I do thank God. Yet, I am
aware that, at some point in time and space, our aspirations may
have been very similar, or had we met, at some point in time and
space – at school, say, or looking for work, or at the corner bar – we
might have had every reason to think so. They are men, after all,
like me; mortal, like me; and all men reflect, are mirrors for, each
other. It is the most fatal of all delusions, I think, not to know this:
and the root of cowardice.

For, neither I, nor anyone else, could have known, from the
beginning, what roads we would travel, what choices we would
make, nor what the result of these choices would be: in ourselves,
in time, and space, and in that nightmare we call history. Where,
then, is placed the 'objective' speaker, who can speak only after, and
never before, the fact? Who may, or may not, have perceived (or
received) the truth, whatever the *truth* may be? What does it mean
to be *objective*? what is meant by *temperament*? and how does

temperament relate to experience? For I do not know, will never know, and neither will you, whether it is my experience which is responsible for my temperament, or my temperament which must be taken to task for my experience.

I am attacking, of course, the basis of the language – or, perhaps, the *intention* of the language – in which history is written – am speaking as the son of the Preacher-Man. This is exactly how the music called *jazz* began, and out of the same necessity: not only to redeem a history unwritten and despised, but to checkmate the European notion of the world. For, until this hour, when we speak of history, we are speaking only of how Europe saw – and sees – the world.

But there is a very great deal in the world which Europe does not, or cannot, see: in the very same way that the European musical scale cannot transcribe – cannot write down, does not understand – the notes, or the price, of this music.

Now, the author's research is meticulous. Collier has had to 'hang' in many places – has 'been there', as someone predating *jazz* might put it: but he has not, as one of my more relentless sisters might put it, 'been there and back'.

My more relentless sister is, merely, in actuality, paraphrasing, or bearing witness to, Bessie Smith: *picked up my bag, baby, and I tried it again*. And so is Billie Holiday, proclaiming – not complaining – that *my man wouldn't want me no breakfast/wouldn't give me no dinner/ squawked about my supper/and threw me out doors/had the nerve to lay/a matchbox on my clothes*.

I didn't, Billie tells us, *have so many. But I had a long, long ways to go*.

Thus, Aretha Franklin demands *respect*: having 'stolen' the song from Otis Redding. (As Otis Redding tells it: sounding strangely delighted to declare himself the victim of this sociopathological act.) Aretha dared to 'steal' the song from Otis because not many men, of any colour, are able to make the enormous confession, the tremendous recognition, contained in *try a little tenderness*.

And: if you can't get no satisfaction you may find yourself boiling a bitch's brew while waiting for someone to bring me my gin! or start walking toward the weeping willow tree or ramble where you find strange fruit – black, beige, and brown – hanging just across the tracks where it's tight like that and you do not let the sun catch you crying. It is always: *farewell to storyville*.

For this celebrated number has only the most passing, and, in truth, impertinent, reference to the red-light district of New Orleans, or to the politician for whom it was named: a certain Joseph Story. What a curious way to enter, briefly, history, only to be utterly obliterated by it: which is exactly what is happening to Henry Kissinger. If you think I am leaping, you are entirely right. Go back to Miles, Max, Dizzy, Yard-Bird, Billie, Coltrane: who were not, as the striking – not to say quaint – European phrase would have it, *improvising*: who can afford to improvise, at those prices?

By the time of *Farewell to Storyville*, and long before that time, the demolition of black quarters – for that is what they were, and are, considered – was an irreducible truth of black life. This is what Bessie Smith is telling us, in 'Back Water Blues'. This song has as much to do with a flood as 'Didn't It Rain' has to do with Noah, or as 'If I Had My Way' has to do with Samson and Delilah, and poor Samson's excess of hair. Or, if I may leap again, there is a song being born, somewhere, as I write, concerning the present 'boat-people', which will inform us, in tremendous detail, how ships are built. There is a dreadful music connecting the building of ovens with the activity of contractors, the reality of businessmen (to say nothing of business) and the reality of bankers and flags, and the European middle class, and its global progeny, and Gypsies, Jews, and soap: and profit.

The music called *jazz* came into existence as an exceedingly laconic description of black circumstances: and, as a way, by describing these circumstances, of overcoming them. It was necessary that the description be laconic: the iron necessity being that the description not be overheard. Or, as the indescribably grim remnants of the European notion of the 'nation-state' would today put it, it was absolutely necessary that the description not be 'de-coded'. It has not been 'de-coded', by the way, any more than the talking drum has been de-coded. I will try to tell you why.

I have said that people cannot be described from a distance. I will, now, contradict myself, and say that people *can* be described from a distance: the distance that they themselves have established between themselves and what we must, helplessly, here, call life. Life comes out of music, and music comes out of life: without trusting the first, it is impossible to create the second. The rock against which the European notion of the nation-state has crashed is nothing more – and absolutely nothing less – than the question of identity. *Who am I? and what am I doing here?*

This question is the very heart, and root, of the music we are discussing: and contains (if it is possible to make this distinction) not so much a moral judgment as a precise one.

The Irish, for example, as it now, astoundingly, turns out, never had the remotest desire to become English, neither do the people of Scotland, or Wales: and one can suppose that the people of Canada, trapped as they are between Alaska and Mexico, with only the heirs of the doctrine of Manifest Destiny between themselves and these two definitely unknown ports of call, distract themselves with the question of whether they are French or English only because their history has now allowed them the breathing space to find out what in God's name(!) it means to be Canadian. The Basques do not wish to be French, *or* Spanish, Kurds and Berbers do not wish to be Iranian, *or* Turkish.

If one travels from Naples, to Rome, to Torino, it can by no means be taken for granted that the *nation* – hammered into a *nation*, after all, quite recently – ever agreed, among themselves, to be that. The same is true of an equally arbitrary invention, Germany: Bavaria is not Berlin. For that matter, to be in Haifa is not at all like being in Jerusalem, and neither place resembles Nazareth. Examples abound: but, at this moment, the only nations being discussed are those which have become utilitarian but otherwise useless, Sweden, for example, or Switzerland, which is not a nation, but a bank. There are those territories which are considered to be 'restive' (Iran, Greece) or those which are 'crucial', or 'unstable' – or, incomprehensibly, both: Japan, for example, is 'crucial', *and* 'unstable'. Peru, for the moment, is merely 'unstable', though one keeps on it a nervous eye: and though we know that there's a whole lot of coffee in Brazil, we don't know who's going to drink it. Brazil threatens to become, as we quite remarkably put it, one of the 'emerging' nations, like Nigeria, because those decisions, in those places, involve not merely continents, but the globe. Leaving aside the 'crafty East' – China, and Russia – there are only embarrassments, like the British colonial outpost, named for a merciless, piratical *murderer/colonizer*: named Cecil Rhodes.

What, indeed, you may well ask, has all this to do with *The Making of Jazz*? A book concerned, innocently and earnestly enough, with the creation of black American music.

That music is produced by, and bears witness to, one of the most obscene adventures in the history of mankind. It is a music which creates, as what we call History cannot sum up the courage to do, the response to that absolutely universal question: *Who am I? what am I doing here?*

How did King Oliver, Ma Rainey, Bessie, Armstrong – a roll-call more vivid than what is called History – Bird, Dolphy, Powell, Pettiford, Coltrane, Jelly Roll Morton, The Duke – or the living, again, too long a roll-call: Miss Nina Simone, Mme Mary Lou Williams, Carmen McRae, The Count, Ray, Miles, Max – forgive me, children, for all the names I cannot call – how did they, and how *do* they, confront that question? and make of that captivity, a song?

For, the music began in captivity: and is, still, absolutely, created in captivity. So much for the European vanity: which imagines that with the single word, *history*, it controls the *past*, defines the *present*: and, therefore, cannot but suppose that the *future* will prove to be as willing to be brought into captivity as the slaves they imagine themselves to have discovered, as the *nigger* they had no choice but to invent.

Be careful of inventions: the invention describes you, and will certainly betray you. Speaking as the son of the Preacher-Man, I know that it was never intended, in any way whatever, that either the Father, or the Son, should be heard. Take that any way you will: I am trying to be precise.

If you know – as a black American *must* know, discovers at his mother's breast, and, then, in the eyes of his father – that the world which calls itself *white*: and which has the further, unspeakable cowardice of calling itself *free* – if you will dare imagine that I, speaking, now, as a black witness to the white condition, see you in a way that you cannot afford to see me: if you can see that the invention of the black condition creates the trap of the white identity; you will see that what a black man *knows* about a white man stems, inexorably, from the white man's description of who, and what, he takes to be the other: in this case, the black cat: me.

You watch this innocent criminal destroying your father, day by day, hour by hour – your *father*! – despising your mother, your brothers and your sisters; and this innocent criminal will cut you down, without any mercy, if any one of you dares to say a word about it.

And not only is he trying to kill you. He would also like you to be his accomplice – discreet and noiseless accomplice – in this friendly, democratic, and, alas, absolutely indispensable action. *I didn't*, he will tell you, *make the world*.

You think, but you don't say, to your friendly murderer, who, sincerely, means you no harm: *Well, baby, somebody better. And, in a great big hurry*.

Thus, you begin to see; so, you begin to sing and dance; for, those responsible for your captivity require of you a song. You begin the unimaginable horror of contempt and hatred; then, the horror of self-contempt, and self-hatred. *What did I do? to be so black, and blue?* If you survive – as, for example, the 'sociopath', Yard-Bird, did not, as the 'junkie', Billie Holiday, did not – you are released onto the tightrope tension of bearing in mind: every hour, every second, drunk, or sober, *in sickness*, or *in health*, those whom you must not even begin to depend on for the truth: and those to whom you must not lie.

It is hard to be black, and, therefore, officially, and lethally, despised. It is harder than that to despise so many of the people who think of themselves as white: before whose blindness you present the obligatory, historical grin.

And it is harder than that, out of this devastation – Ezekiel's valley: *Oh, Lord. Can these bones live?* – to trust life, and to live a life, to love, and be loved.

It is out of this, and much more than this, that black American music springs. This music begins on the auction-block.

Now, whoever is unable to face this – the auction-block; whoever cannot see that that auction-block is the demolition, by Europe, of all human standards: a demolition accomplished, furthermore, at that hour of the world's history, in the name of *civilization*: whoever pretends that the slave mother does not weep, until this hour, for her slaughtered son, that the son does not weep for his slaughtered father: or whoever pretends that the white father did not – literally, and knowing what he was doing – hang, and burn, and castrate, his black son: whoever cannot face this can never pay the price for the *beat* which is the key to music, and the key to life.

Music is our witness, and our ally. The *beat* is the confession which recognizes, changes, and conquers time.

Then, history becomes a garment we can wear, and share, and not a cloak in which to hide: and time becomes a friend.

JAMES LINCOLN COLLIER

Black Consciousness and the
White Jazz Fan

What the white man has to do with jazz has been a troublesome question virtually from the music's birth. Whites began playing jazz even as it was evolving out of ragtime, the blues and other earlier forms, and by accident more than chicanery, the first jazz record was made by the white Original Dixieland Jazz Band. Partly as a consequence of this, in the 1920s especially, jazz was seen by most whites and not a few blacks as a *New Orleans* music played in somewhat different styles by both blacks and whites. As recently as this decade a veteran white trumpet player told me, 'Jazz wasn't invented by blacks, it was invented by Bix Beiderbecke and those guys in the Jean Goldkette band.'

Today, of course, we know better. Jazz was basically created by blacks, and most – although not all – of the major innovations in the music have been made by blacks. None the less, the idea that jazz was a product of 'the black experience' needs a little close scrutiny. James Baldwin, in his eloquent criticism of my book, *The Making of Jazz*, has taken the line – common enough these days – that jazz is black music, and that the white man cannot really understand it, any more than he can really understand what it means to be black in America. Let us have a look at the history, if we can.

Blacks arriving in the United States over some two hundred and fifty years brought with them a music that was rooted in the interplay of two or more rhythmic patterns locking and unlocking as they ran along together. They found in the United States a European music whose effects stemmed mainly from melody and harmony, rather than rhythm, and inevitably, they began to meld the two. By at least the middle of the nineteenth century, they had created a new musical system which was neither African nor European, but a thing of its own. Blacks used this new system or practice to create a number of different forms: work-songs, ring shouts, religious songs, dance music. Eventually, there grew out of it two variants – ragtime and the blues – both of which became widely popular in the white culture. This black music of course drew heavily on European devices and, eventually, instrumentation, but there is no question that it was made entirely by blacks.

When we come to the creation of jazz itself, however, we are in a little more trouble. Jazz was born out of an amalgam of ragtime, the blues, and various march and dance forms drawn from American popular music. Its creators, however, were not only the blacks. Playing a crucial, and perhaps dominant, role was a group of people of mixed blood called black Creoles, who lived in New Orleans and its environs. The term Creole referred to the original French and Spanish settlers of the city. White Creoles often took mistresses of mixed blood, and their children went on to form a subculture lodged halfway between the white world and the black one. These black Creoles did not really share in the 'black experience'. They had never been slaves. They spoke a French patois, not English. They were Catholics, and had no connection with the ring shouts and spirituals of the sanctified church. They were not – at least until about 1890 with the imposition of stringent Jim Crow laws – day labourers, but artisans, and small businessmen. And their musical tradition had nothing to do with the slaves; it was entirely European. In sum, these black Creoles never took part in what we think of as the typical experience of the early black American – the deadly drudgery of the plantations and the pine camps, the whippings, the children sold down the river, the lynch mobs, and of course the musical forms we associate with that life. The black Creoles were far more European in their habits and attitudes than were even most white Americans, holding to a European gentility and formality of manner, in so far as they could support such attitudes in the face of diminishing economic and social status.

Inevitably, throughout the nineteenth century these black Creoles held themselves away from the broader black community, with whom they felt little connection. But by the last decades of the century they were slowly forced down into the black ghetto by the imposition of new 'Jim Crow' laws. The young people among them began to be exposed to the blues, and black music in general. Their elders objected violently to blues playing – that was for the niggers. Creoles were above all that. But the young were attracted to the music, and in their efforts to use its devices in their playing of ragtime and other popular music, they went a long way toward the creation of jazz. The question we cannot answer is whether blacks or Creoles played the major role in shaping the music. Perhaps they shared in it equally. We do know, however, that in 1923, when the first spate of real jazz records appeared, the two finest jazz musicians in the world were both Creoles – Jelly Roll Morton and Sidney Bechet, with such blacks as Louis Armstrong, Johnny Dodds and others only a step behind.

Black or Creole, the men who created jazz were without exception from New Orleans and the surrounding villages. Blacks elsewhere knew nothing about it. Indeed, those who lived in the cities knew little or nothing about the older black forms, including the blues. Just as whites did, blacks outside of the South had to learn their jazz from the New Orleans players, *black and white*. The great ragtime pianists James P. Johnson and Willie 'The Lion' Smith learned their blues from sheet music. The black Chicago trombonist Albert Wynn has said that he learned jazz trombone from the white New Orleanian George Brunis. Buster Bailey, a black clarinettist from St Louis, was first brought to the music by the records of the white Original Dixieland Jazz Band. Arthur Briggs, a black New York trumpet player, has said that as late as 1919, 'We never played the blues.' Garvin Bushell, a black clarinettist from the New York area, says, 'There wasn't an eastern performer who could really play the blues. We later absorbed how from the New Orleans musicians we heard, but it wasn't original with us. We didn't put that quarter tone to the music the way the southern musicians did. Up north we leaned to the ragtime conception.' According to the English jazz historian Chris Goddard, 'The fact that such men [eastern blacks] had almost as much difficulty as whites in acquiring the new jazz skills is a powerful indication of the importance of New Orleans as a source of the music.'

Even as late as the late 1920s blacks everywhere were imitating the white cornettist Bix Beiderbecke, even to copying his solo note for note, for the very good reason that Bix was one of the best two or three jazz musicians in America. Indeed, on the evidence of records, in the early 1920s white New Orleans bands like the New Orleans Rhythm Kings and the Arcadian Serenaders were playing better jazz than the bands of such northern blacks, soon to become famous, as Duke Ellington, Fletcher Henderson, and Bennie Moten. Ellington, we must remember, grew up in a middle-class family in Washington, DC, with no experience of ring shouts, work-songs, or even the blues. He learned about jazz from Sidney Bechet, who was in his band briefly, and the cornettist Bubber Miley, who had sat at the feet of the New Orleanian star, Joseph 'King' Oliver. Fletcher Henderson, later to have one of the most influential bands in the history of jazz, was, on the testimony of the black singer Ethel Waters, struggling to learn how to play jazz as late as 1924.

Jazz, clearly, did not grow out of 'the black experience'. It was created by a specific group of people in specific circumstances with a specific history, many of whom, as I have said, did not even belong to the larger black culture. It of course reflected the experience of the black Creoles, and to a lesser degree the whites as well. Jazz has never been the basic popular music of American blacks. That role has been filled successively by the blues in the 1920s, the big swing bands of the 1930s, the rhythm and blues of the 1940s, and since then numberless variations on rock like soul, funk, disco. None of this of course should be taken to mean that whites played more than a secondary role in the making of jazz. I am simply making the point that jazz is not, somehow, a birthright of blacks in general.

I doubt that Mr Baldwin will accept the foregoing argument. I think, however, that he is more concerned with a statement I made about the seminal alto saxophonist Charlie Parker, whom I described in *The Making of Jazz* as 'a sociopath . . . who managed . . . to destroy his career – and finally himself'. As it happens, I have been taken to task for that statement by others, among them a reviewer for the *Village Voice* and Parker's last wife, Chan. If that is all I had said about Parker it would be one thing. However, *The Making of Jazz* contains a fifteen-page discussion of his life and work. Parker was a drug addict, an alcoholic, a compulsive eater, a bigamist, and a thief. He was casually unfaithful to his wives, neglected his children, bullied his worshippers, and destroyed every relationship of importance to him, without exception. He is by any ordinary definition a sociopath.

But it is Mr Baldwin's contention – if I read him correctly – that it is simply not fair to describe a black man as a sociopath or anything similar, because the experience of being a black in the United States is so difficult that inevitably some people will crack. I will not for a minute deny the fact that blacks in the United States carry an extra burden that whites do not have to bear. None the less, most blacks do not become drug addicts, alcoholics, thieves. If Parker had, out of political or philosophic design, decided to exploit whites, we could understand, and perhaps forgive. But he exploited whites and blacks indiscriminately, in general maltreating those who loved him best – again white and black.

If anthropology has taught us anything, it is that the human psyche is at bottom the same the world around. Mr Baldwin says so himself: 'All men reflect, are mirrors for, each other. It is the most fatal of all delusions, I think, not to know this. . . . ' I willingly grant that my experience has not been the same as Charlie Parker's, nor James Baldwin's. None the less, I think that I can understand these two men, up to a point, just as I think they can understand me, for we all do indeed reflect each other.

I think that Mr Baldwin will respond that my so-called 'objective' eighteenth-century rationalism is blocking this understanding I claim to have. He likes a more passionate approach to the truth. I can only respond that he has his way of determining the truth, and I have mine, and I think I can defend it.

I wish, finally, that Mr Baldwin were not so determined to raise between us cultural boundaries. It has always seemed to me that only by escaping from the cultural walls within which each of us grows up can we even begin to approach wisdom. Mr Baldwin, I think, believes this, too. But unhappily, so long as he insists that I cannot understand him, he has put a wall between me and himself that I cannot, with the best will in the world, penetrate.

JOHN LITWEILER

Ornette Coleman Learns to Play the Saxophone

... I went out and worked, around 1944–45 – shining shoes, bus-boying in hotels, doing summer jobs like scraping paint, all kinds of little jobs. Finally, after saving up my money, my mother told me to look on the couch, and there was a horn, a gold-plated Conn. . . .

... I remember when I first got the saxophone, . . . I remember thinking, as the book said, that the first seven letters of the alphabet were the first seven letters of music, ABCDEFG.

But of course, the standard concert scale reads CDEFGAB.

So I thought my C that I was playing on the saxophone was A, like that, right? Later on I found out that it did exist thataway only because the E-flat alto, when you play C natural, it is [the standard] A [transposed]. So I was right in one way and wrong in another – I mean, sound, I was right. *Then* I started analysing why it exists thataway, and to this very day I realize more and more that all things that are designed with a strict logic only apply against something; it is not the only way it's done. In other words, if you take an instrument and you happen to feel it a way you can express yourself, it becomes its own law.

Ornette Coleman's special concern with his saxophone sound began

when I realized that you could play sharp or flat in tune. That came very early in my saxophone interest. I used to play one note all day, and I used to find how many different sounds I could get out of the mouthpiece (I'm still looking for the magic mouth-piece). That just came about from, I'd hear so many different tones and sounds. . . .

A younger generation of jazz and rhythm and blues musicians was appearing on the North Texas scene when Ornette Coleman was becoming known in the area. Saxman-bandleader Red Connors, who didn't record, was probably the most advanced, but Coleman's young Texas peers included drummer Charles Moffett, trumpeter Bobby Bradford, and saxophonists John Carter, Dewey Redman and Prince Lasha, all of whom would follow Coleman's path into the new music of the 1960s. Coleman emphasizes that in his apprentice years stylistic distinctions between jazz, R&B, bebop, dance music, pop music, meant little more to him that they did to his audiences – 'I think because of being in a little city, the people never knew the difference. Once they heard the beat, they danced or they listened' – and he quite naturally incorporated the bebop solos that he learned from records into his playing. . . .

Years of scuffling followed. He worked at menial day gigs, such as running an elevator, studied harmony and theory books (on the job yet), and took his alto sax around to clubs, hoping to sit in at night. A few musicians encouraged him, rehearsed with him, and Free jazz began with the small circle that studied the revolutionary ideas he was evolving: 'It took me a long time to get them interested in studying with me, and staying . . . because when I met Charlie [Haden] and Billy [Higgins] and Don [Cherry], they were into bebop. They got very interested in the things I was trying to write to play. So when we got together, the most interesting part is: *What do you play after you play the melody* if you don't have nothing to go with? That's where I won them over.' The new challenge of this music was that Coleman didn't give his young musicians any chord changes on which to improvise. 'Usually, when you play a melody, you have a set pattern to know just what you can do while the other person's doing a certain thing. But in this case, when we played the melody, no one knew where to go or what to do to show that he knew where he was going. I had already developed playing like that naturally. . . . ' This is most important: 'I finally got them to where they could see how to express themselves without linking up to a definite maze. . . . I think it was a case of teaching them how to feel more confident in being expressive like that for themselves.' The new jazz began when Coleman and his group began playing this new music *together*.

MIKE ZWERIN

Miles and Me

In the summer of 1949, I was in New York on vacation from the University of Miami.... In those days I played my horn like a kid skiing down a slalom, with more courage than sense. Falling on my face never occurred to me. One night I climbed up to Minton's, where bebop was born, in Harlem. A lot of white cats considered Minton's too steep a slope, but I never imagined that somebody might not like me because I was white or Jewish. I was absolutely fearless. I walked in, took out my horn and started to play 'Walkin'' with Art Blakey, then known as Abdullah Buhaina, a fearful cat, I was later to learn.

When I noticed Miles Davis standing in a dark corner, I tried harder because Miles was with Bird's band. He came over as I packed up. I slank into a cool slouch. I used to practise cool slouches. We were born wearing shades; no eyes to be seen. 'You got eyes to make a rehearsal tomorrow?' Miles asked me.

'I guess so.' I acted as though I didn't give one shit for his stupid rehearsal.

'Four.' Miles made it clear he couldn't care less if I showed up or not.

Driving home over the Triborough Bridge to the house by the tennis courts, I felt like a batboy who had been offered a try-out with the team.

The next day at four I found myself with a band that would come to be called 'The Birth of the Cool'. Gerry Mulligan, Max Roach, John Lewis, Lee Konitz, Junior Collins, Bill Barber and Al McKibbon played arrangements by Mulligan and Gil Evans, who was musical director.

Miles was ... cool. Pleasant, relaxed, diffident, it was his first time as leader and he relied on Gil. He must have picked up his famous salty act sometime later because he was sweet as his sound that summer.

It did not seem historic or legendary. A good jazz gig, but there were plenty of them then in New York. We certainly did not have the impression that those two weeks in a Broadway joint called the Royal Roost would give birth to an entire style. It was fun being on a championship team, and when Gene Krupa's entire trumpet section took a front table to hear us I was proud, but my strongest memory of those two weeks is the one we played opposite Count Basie, who then had Wardell Gray on tenor saxophone. Like a later summer spent listening to John Coltrane with Thelonious Monk at the Five Spot, Wardell with Basie is a sound that has never left my head and I will go to my grave with it.

I call that sound that stays in my head 'the Cry'. I seem to remember somebody else once talking about the Cry so if I'm stealing I apologize. Anyway, stealing is the essence of literary love. You cannot patent licks, just shove them out there and hope they are stolen. The Cry is everywhere. The Romanian pan-pipe-player Gheorge Zamfire has it – Zoot Sims, Ray Charles, Bruce Springsteen. Bob Marley had it. The blues are the classical incarnation of the Cry. You could also call it 'the Wail', a direct audial objectification of the soul. You know it when you hear it. Billie Holiday had it, to die. I wonder whether to include Mozart's operas, which might be a bit too structured to fit my definition of the Cry. The Cry must be a bit off, informal, direct, not stifled by structure or commercial consider- ations. Glenn Gould had it, Trane, Bix, Bird, Hendrix, Prez, Monk. Indian ragas have it, Flamenco singers, Milton Nascimento (all Brazilian singers seem to have it), Jewish cantors, black gospel singers. I could go on but you get the idea. Miles Davis certainly had it.

How would my life have changed had I stayed in New York to pursue the Cry after the summer of 1949 instead of going back to Miami and college like a good boy? A few months later, Miles made that 'historic' *Birth of the Cool* record with Kai Winding on trombone, and I became a footnote to jazz history. Do I have the Cry? Perhaps it is here on a few pages. Will I ever get into the body of the work?

'Have a nice day at the office, dear,' my better half said as I left for work.

'Bye bye, wifey,' I answered, pecking her cheek. 'Have fun ironing my shirts.'

We were both increasingly aware that we were stuck in roles we did not have the courage to opt out of. When I called her 'the little woman', she would pull out the blade and twist it back: 'It's a bird; it's a plane; it's BUSINESSMAN.'

We stayed home nights reading. Reading is what Eleanor does. It is her occupation, her commitment, her passion. She is still reading every day until this day. You are what you read. 'Wouldn't you hate to die while you were reading a bad novel?' she once asked me. I was in the middle of *Marjorie Morningstar* at the time. I never finished it. Flirting with the intellectual wing of the Catholic Church, Eleanor read Christopher Dawson, Simone Weil, Jacques Maritain and the entire *Summa Theologica*. We subscribed to *Commonweal* and the *Partisan Review*. We caught foreign – imported – films on weekends. I ferried babysitters home, children to dance-classes. We held hands listening to Bach, Rameau sustained us for a while. We discovered Scarlatti, who sustained us for months. We discovered Beethoven's late string quartets. Then she took the kids to Miami for a short vacation and never returned.

I could hear Fred Mann's clichés: 'Back to square one . . . it's a whole new ball game.' Finding yourself in Paris is a cliché in itself but none the less good for it for that reason, and I went there. I took mistress music out to lunch, bought her flowers, kissed her every day, moved into a musicians' hotel called the Crystal. Stéphane Grappelli practised Bach sonatas in the next room on his violin. Allen Eager could be found in the Old Navy Café. William Burroughs and Brion Gysin were cutting up words in the Beat Hotel. I practised scales, arpeggios, patterns and old Lester Young solos.

Word spread that Miles Davis was coming for a concert at the Olympia Theatre and three weeks in the Club St Germain, across Rue St Benoit from the Crystal.

But no Miles by the afternoon of the concert. Speculation focused on what kind of number he was running. Still no sign of him by the half-hour. When the curtain went up, only sidemen on stage. I've always somehow been waiting for Miles Davis. As you may have guessed by now, he's no great friend of mine, yet I've always known him and he will always be close to me. Nasty son of a bitch or not, he's touched and formed me more than many of my great friends. Like family, he may disappear and ignore me but I can count on his return. I imagine Miles slinking down dark streets, the collar of his Burberry raincoat turned up. There he goes roaring into the Malibu sunset in his Ferrari. Now he lounges days away in some pneumatic retreat, puffing an opium pipe, surrounded by perfumed and shiny things.

Recently I was with Chet Baker in the Club Dreher on Place Châtelet in Paris one afternoon, alone there, interviewing him. He stopped talking when the tape played Miles's record *The Man with the Horn*. (Note the definite articles; no false modesty there.) Chet stared at the bottles for a while and said, 'That sure is romantic music.'

And it's true. Miles Davis has in fact never played bebop, cool, fusion or funk. He has always been a flat-out upfront romantic. Miles recorded a tune called 'Willie Nelson' in the seventies and Nelson, the country music star, praises Miles. They have been rumoured to be planning a project together. What does the bad black dude have in common with the redneck picker? In addition to grainy textured voices, restrained tension, staying-power and the uncanny ability each has to transmogrify standards (compare Miles's 'If I Were a Bell' to Nelson's 'Stardust'), each of them is an incurable romantic.

That is why Miles and Coltrane made such a timeless team – the nineteenth and twentieth centuries in tandem. And like a true nineteenth-century romantic, Miles is always disappearing with a wave of his cape and a Byronic consumptive cough into the mists, on some brave, secret, lonely mission. Always to reappear just when you need him.

Meanwhile, back in the Olympia Theatre, Barney Wilen was playing the blues on his tenor saxophone; Kenny Clarke, Pierre Michelot and Rene Urtreger behind him. Milesless in Paris. But you could feel the breeze from the cape. When the blues came to the dominant on Barney's last chorus, he moved back and Miles emerged from the right wing. It took him just exactly those four bars to reach the mike and hard – not easing in, not warming up, not even very cool – he began to machine-gun the Cry.

Actually his total absence would not have been a total surprise. Miles, who James Baldwin called 'a miraculously tough and tender man', was having hard drug problems. He talked about it to a journalist named Cheryl McCall who interviewed him for *Jazz Hot* magazine: 'Max Roach put $200 in my pocket and said I looked good. This disgusted me so much I went right home to my father in St Louis. I said to myself that son of a bitch gave me $200 and said I looked good. I was strung out and he knew it. And this was my best friend, right? I died with embarrassment. I looked at myself in the mirror and I said, "Godamn it, Miles, come on."'

'Was kicking junk terrible?' she asked him.

'Yeah, it was awful . . . but I had a plan. I was going to jump out the window and break my leg and then with a little luck they'd give me a painkiller for my leg and everything would be OK. But then every day it got a little better . . . I'd had enough of seeing myself that way. I was a pimp too. I had lots of girls. I did this and that . . . I had more money than I have now. That's right, I had about seven girls. I can't even remember their names now.'

In Paris in the winter of 1957 his drug problems were obviously over. He danced there like an in-shape champ, jabbing and under-cutting notes that stung and burned. Now and then he would stand still, wiping his lip, staring, lay out for five or six measures – a long musical space – as though waiting for his opponent to tire. The Man with the Horn.

Miles has been called 'the Prince of Silence'. 'Don't play what's there, play what's not there,' he'd tell his musicians – and 'Don't play what you know, play what you don't know.' He once said, 'I have to change, it's like a curse.' He is known for caustic put-downs, turning his back on the audience, showing up late or not at all, refusing to play encores, driving fast cars, being a clothes horse, womanizing, getting in trouble with the law; his financial negotiating prowess is legendary. He can be tyrannical.

The first night at the Club St Germain, Barney Wilen came over to me at the bar, shook his head and said, 'You won't believe what Miles said to me after my last solo.' Barney was a hot young tenorman oozing confidence and he actually thought this was funny: 'He said, "Barney, why don't you stop playing those awful notes?"'

This sort of Miles line always leaves me like one of those motel massage-beds right after the money runs out. You don't know quite how to feel. On the one hand it's sensual being launched out into that still space, on the other hand it was such a disappointment when the vibrations stopped. His lines leave you hanging like that. Towards the end of John Coltrane's period with Miles, Trane was searching desperately to find his own personality. His solos were getting longer and longer, sometimes lasting for forty-five minutes in the middle of a forty-five-minute set. Miles said to him, 'Man, why don't you try playing twenty-seven choruses instead of twenty-eight?' Trane answered, 'I get involved in these things and I don't know how to stop.' Miles said, 'Try taking the saxophone out of your mouth.'

It was once said of a playboy, 'He would rather not make love to a beautiful woman and have everybody think he had than make love to her and have nobody know it.' There must be a little bit of that in every man. Even though wooing Eugenia and Ursula had produced no physical contact with either, I revelled in my big splash descending into the basement Club St Germain, one on each arm. Everyone would think I was making it with both of them at once; an entrance worthy of Allen Eager.

'Allen Reluctant' we used to call him, the granite-faced tenorman who played more like Lester Young than Lester Young. The first time someone told me about Stan Getz, he was described as 'playing even better than Allen Eager'. There were many other white Presidents – Stanley Kosow, Brew Moore, Johnny Andrews – and I had played with all of them in Brooklyn strip clubs. They had taught me tricks like running augmented arpeggios on dominant seventh chords; listening to them had been my school, but none of them had taught me more than Allen Eager. Allen was my Joe DiMaggio; I modelled my swing after his. He listened to Prokofiev, drove racing cars (once won Sebring), frequented Swiss ski resorts, lived with high fashion models (boy were they high), patronized the best English custom tailors. He could also be a nasty bastard when strung out, which was not infrequent. Miles kept trying to find out the name of Allen's tailor but Allen wasn't talking. This was no nodding-out, nose-scratching junky fixing in dirty toilets. He was always sharp, bright, on top of it. He could hold his own with poets, writers and classical musicians. He was a model to me of what hip should be. How have I survived my heroes? How I envied Allen Eager. Much later, not too many years ago, I ran into him living in a broken-down house in the black slums of Coconut Grove. He had lost his teeth, was a born-again Christian, on welfare and the food-stamp programme.

In Paris in 1957 Allen Eager was rooming with Beat poet Gregory Corso in the Beat Hotel and I was pleased to imagine myself in his image walking into the Club St Germain with Eugenia on one arm, Ursula on the other. Miles was between sets in a dark corner. I always seem to see Miles in dark corners. He put his arm around my shoulder, asked about my health and generally made it clear that he was concerned with my welfare. His smile went a long way with the ladies. A club-owner once said to him, 'The trouble with you is that everybody *likes* you, you little son of a bitch.'

He joined us after the first set. I had to take Eugenia back to her university dormitory, where there was a curfew. When I returned I found Miles and Ursula in deep eye-contact. With his best evil ray, he looked at me and asked her, 'What do you see in a dumb cat like this? He's too fat anyway.'

I could never take his salty act seriously. He was so upfront about it for one thing. They were more jabs than anything. It was not really a knock-down round, he was just sparring. He went back for another set.

'Well I guess I have a decision to make,' Ursula said. Was it possible? She was deciding between me and Miles. You can understand the nature of groupiedom from the beginning of time when I tell you I almost recommended Miles, pleased to be able to furnish him a beautiful woman. As we walked up the stairs together, Miles squinted at us from the bandstand. He looked so tragic, so Byronic, like a little lost poet as he opened up the melody of 'When I Fall in Love' like a flower.

Just How Much Did Elvis Learn from Otis Blackwell?

. . . Rock and roll was a businessman's music from the beginning. Music-publishing battles, in and out of court, over composer credits were the result of a palm-greasing environment as iniquitous as anything uncovered in the payola scandals. But that was backstage stuff: the youth-directed product was built around the lone image of the performer, pristine and unencumbered by collaborators. Which was all right with the collaborators – most of them were embarrassed by their contributions to a fad they didn't expect to outlast the decade. So a lot of stories haven't been told, a lot of credit unfairly distributed on speculation. One such story involves a relationship unlike any other I know in music: Elvis Presley, white, born in Mississippi in 1935, rock and roll's most explosively successful performer, and Otis Blackwell, black, born in Brooklyn in 1932, rock and roll's most influential songwriter. His songs include 'Don't Be Cruel', 'All Shook Up', 'Return to Sender', 'Great Balls of Fire', 'Fever', 'Hey Little Girl', 'Handy Man', 'Make Me Know It', 'Just Keep It Up', and 'Breathless'. From 1956 through the early 1960s, they fed off each other's talent, sharing a close musical affinity and, more incredibly, a vocal style so similar as to be eerie. They never once met.

I had never given any thought to Otis Blackwell until I sat across the aisle from Panama Francis on a plane. Panama had garnered impressive credentials as a jazz drummer (with Roy Eldridge, Lucky Millinder, Cab Calloway, et al.) before he rather reluctantly earned a reputation as *the* session drummer for pop records in the 1950s. From 1953 to 1963 he laid down the rhythm for numerous hits cut by La Vern Baker, Jackie Wilson, Buddy Holly, Dinah Washington, and many others. Wincing in pain at the memory, he described an afternoon when Fabian sang forty-one takes of 'Tiger' – 'and he never did get it right'. Surprised at my interest in the subject, he asked if I had ever heard of a little guy named Otis Blackwell, who made demos for Presley, which were copied, note for note, by Presley's musicians. 'If you compare the demos with the records, you'll see that Presley's vocals were practically an exact copy.' Noticing my scepticism, he promised to play one for me when he returned from a long gig out of town.

A week later the *Village Voice* had an ad for an upcoming engagement at the Other End by one 'Otis Blackwell, the Man Who Made Elvis Presley and Jerry Lee Lewis'. Intrigued, and confused as to whether the demos had been made for the publishing company or the record company, I went up to RCA to see if anyone knew anything about Blackwell. There was some disbelief at the story, but I was told that the only one who would know was Grelun Landon, now RCA's manager of press and information in Los Angeles, who had worked with the Colonel (Tom Parker, Presley's fabled manager) and the song publishers in the 1950s. A call to Landon revealed that yes, Presley's musicians had to copy the Blackwell arrangements off the demos because they couldn't read music. But did Blackwell actually influence Elvis Presley's singing? 'Well, Elvis learned how to deliver the songs from Otis.' He paused: 'I remember Otis always wore a hat and he wouldn't take it off until he warmed up to you. He was an *extreme* talent, an original. I wish I could tell you more about him; he was very much respected.'

When Blackwell opened at the Other End on a Saturday night, the place was nearly full. It was the first time in twenty years that he had sung for an audience. Barely five feet, he ascended the stage while a loud rhythm section went into 'Don't Be Cruel'. He has large round eyes and a gap-toothed smile, and moved loosely, as though each limb were tied to a marionette's string. The shock was in the voice: the high notes had Presley's cutting tenor edge; he rode the beat with broken syllables – 'We-el do-on't be-e cruel-l' – and on the longer, strained notes there was the Presleyan quiver, receding into a faint whirr. On quieter songs, like 'Return to Sender' and 'Love Me Tender', the similarity was equally apparent, and the audience seemed to respond as much to the novelty of a middle-aged black man who sounded like Elvis as to anything else. He acknowledged his friend and colleague Doc Pomus in the audience and sang a medley of Pomus songs, beginning with 'Save the Last Dance for Me'. He sang 'Handy Man', without the falsetto screeching that was Jimmy Jones's trademark. (The Jones record had actually been a Blackwell-produced demo that MGM decided to release.) In response to the ovation for his stomping 'Great Balls of Fire', he said, 'Yeah, I think I'll stay around for a while.' . . .

Otis didn't want to do an interview until after the gig, so I called Doc Pomus, a large, heavily bearded white man, confined to a wheelchair, whose songwriting activities have ranged from a blues for Ray Charles, 'Lonely Avenue', to Dion's 'Teenager in Love'. . . . Pomus and his cowriter Mort Schuman had also done demos for Presley where the arrangements were copied. 'Presley is an extraordinary talent, the first white singer to get real recognition for the blues, and he could sing *anything*. He's an original – always Presley – but on certain things – fast tempos – he comes from Otis.' As a songwriter, Pomus names Leiber and Stoller and Blackwell as influences: 'Jerry and Mike in terms of structure, and Otis in the sense of originality and spontaneity.' I asked him about the assumption, prevalent in Presley criticism, that Elvis created head arrangements on his best records, that he was in effect the producer. 'This is absolutely untrue. Elvis did not create those sounds, and I can tell you that he managed to get his name on songs he had nothing to do with writing. One thing I can assure you is that his singing was significantly influenced by Otis. If you compare the demos, you will find it incredible how close Presley copied them, especially the *sound* of Otis's voice.' . . .

In 1822, an English music-hall performer named Charles Matthews was visiting America, observing Negro music and dialect. He got the idea of blacking himself up and becoming an interpreter of 'Ethiopian' melodies. Robert C. Toll, in his instructive book *Blacking Up*, pinpoints that moment as the beginning of minstrelsy, the most widespread and influential medium for American popular culture in the nineteenth century.

Minstrelsy is said to have died at the hands of vaudeville, but it was a death in form, not spirit. Its images abound in contemporary life, from the indelible memory of Tim Moore's Kingfish to the witticisms of Earl Butz. The Aunt Jemima–Uncle Ned darky, solicitous of massa and scornful of the abolitionists who would wreck their joyful plantations, was implanted in the American mind to such an extent that even black minstrels, in the antebellum years, were expected to enact the familiar stereotypes memorialized by minstrel composers like Stephen Foster. There was triple-edged irony here: minstrelsy provided unprecedented opportunity for gifted black performers, among them Bert Williams and Ma Rainey, but only if they could adapt the ludicrous precepts of white 'Ethiopian imitators'; the blacks were so good, so 'authentic', that white minstrel troupes were soon put out of business; the minstrel form was then replaced by a new kind of entertainment nourished by Tin Pan Alley tunesmiths who had found their initial success by appropriating a black sound called ragtime.

The process of whites stealing from blacks is also the process of osmosis by which whites allowed black music to enter the commercial mainstream. In this regard, the most influential of modern minstrels have been Al Jolson, Bing Crosby, and Elvis Presley. Jolson, a protégé of minstrel Lew Dockstader, seriously believed he was bringing the Negro sound to Broadway when he crooned 'Mammy' on bended knee. He was confident enough of his authenticity to suggest that *Porgy and Bess* – an opera by the same man who had given Jolson 'Swanee' – be staged in blackface with Jolson in the lead. (Perhaps Sophie Tucker would have played Bess.) Bing Crosby's distillation of black song in the 1920s was relatively sophisticated, causing Jolson's performing brilliance to seem quite suddenly out of date. But it wasn't until the Presley revolution that Jolson's style became untenable: Jolson still sold a lot of records even in the years immediately following his death in 1950.

In Jolson, theatrical showbiz schmaltz was mated with an irresistible vitality – maudlin sentiment was the flip side of snappy eye-rolling rhythms. He had much in common with Presley: each came from lower-class, culturally alienated environments (immigrant Jewish and southern poor white); each was something of a rebel – Jolson, the son of a cantor, left home in adolescence to travel the country singing in music-halls, and Presley, also from a religious family, found himself in Negro blues. Each was an obsessive mother-lover; each chose to live in isolation at the peak of his career. In *Feel*

Like Going Home, Jerry Lee Lewis tells Peter Guralnick, 'I loved Al Jolson, I still got all of his records. Even back when I was a kid I listened to him all the time.' Elvis's first record for the Sun label, 'I Love You Because', was a thinly disguised rewrite of a melody that Jolson never recorded but that rebellious Asa Yoelson sings repeatedly during the first half hour of *The Jolson Story*, released in 1946 (when Presley was eleven), a song called 'When You Were Sweet Sixteen'. Presley remained true to Jolson's schmaltz even as his best work eclipsed that of 'the jazz singer'. What would Jolson have made of a white boy with a pompadour as high as a Negro conk, bumping like a stripper and singing 'Heartbreak Hotel' on national television? He probably would have been a lot less shocked than many of his contemporaries. For Jolson's pelvis swivelled much the same way, as can be seen in his performance of 'Toot Toot Tootsie' in the 1927 film *The Jazz Singer*.

Bing Crosby might have empathized with Presley, for they made similar leaps. True enough that Crosby chose omnipresent asexuality as his mature show-business persona, in contrast to Presley's unavailable metasexuality. But Crosby was once the carousing, would-be jazz singer of the jazz age whose ultimate success came in delivering a 'White Christmas' to every American turntable. For him, Presley's willingness to become Hollywood's teddy bear must have seemed inevitable; nor could he have been much surprised to learn of Presley's non-existent personal relationship with Blackwell, as it somewhat parallels Crosby's rather aloof relationships with his black idols, Louis Armstrong and Ethel Waters. Jolson was palatable for about thirty years (1919–50), Crosby for about thirty-five (1926–60). By palatable, I mean capable of renewing their audiences generationally rather than depending on antiquarians. Presley had been a star for over twenty years when he died on 16 August 1977; it would have been interesting to see how far he could go in the long stretch.

The nature of Presley's minstrelsy assumes particularly bizarre overtones if one imagines him secretly imitating Blackwell vocals. Imitation, however, was tempered by Presley's own considerable abilities (which were perhaps more strikingly evident on ballads than on rockers; he could put over a song like 'Loving You' with all the purring emotionalism of Edith Piaf), and by the relationship's mutual usefulness. Blackwell wrote songs ideally suited to Presley's rocking style, and Presley gave them the widest possible exposure. Since their voices and vocal styles were remarkably alike, Blackwell's demos provided Presley with delivery cues that didn't force him appreciably to alter his own impulses, while Blackwell could hear his material performed almost exactly as he imagined it. Otis twice avoided opportunities to meet Elvis, out of a superstitious fear that their working relationship might crumble if Presley did not measure up to his preconception. He estimates that Presley's records are '90 per cent exact copies' of the demos. His respect for Presley is absolute; he even hopes to record a collection of Presley tunes he *didn't* write, as homage.

Which is not to say that there weren't shady dealings. Otis's office, in what used to be known as the Brill Building, is decorated with a huge colour poster of Elvis and sheet-music covers of songs he wrote for Elvis, Del Shannon, Pat Boone, Johnnie Ray, and Jerry Lee Lewis. The Presley songs are credited to both Blackwell and the singer. There are also two plaques on the wall: one is a 'Citation of Achievement' from BMI to Otis Blackwell for 'Fever'; the other is a 'Special Citation of Achievement' from BMI to John Davenport for the same song.

Otis originally used Davenport, his stepfather's name, as the pseudonym on 'Fever' because he wrote it for Little Willie John of King Records, while contracted to another publishing company. When he got into serious tax troubles, he made a deal whereby the song was given to Henry Glover, who owned King. The BMI plaque notwithstanding, Otis's name is no longer listed on the song. The presence of Presley's name on songs like 'Don't Be Cruel' simply indicated business-as-usual in the music-publishing business. One remembers Irving Mills sharing the credit for Duke Ellington songs, Ed Kirkeby taking credit from Fats Waller, and Benny Goodman getting credit for several tunes he cheerfully admits he did not write.

Otis Blackwell started performing in amateur shows in Brooklyn in the 1940s. Willie Saunders of the *Amsterdam News* took him on one of his travelling shows with a shake dancer, and, while making the rounds, Blackwell met Doc Pomus, who was also singing the blues. (Otis names as his main influences Larry Darnell, who had a big record with 'I'll Get Along Somehow', and the better-known

Chuck Willis.) In 1949 and 1950 Otis recorded a few sides for Davis Records, including a fairly successful track called 'Daddy Rolling Stone'. They were subsequently issued as an LP, along with a few sides he made for RCA. On Christmas Eve 1955, he went to Shalimar Music with seven songs, including 'Don't Be Cruel'. A month later, the head of the company called to tell him about a guy named Elvis Presley who was going to be very big.

'Well, you know, there had to be a deal, share this and that. I said no at first, but they said Elvis is gonna turn the business around, so I said okay, and they put it on the other side of "Hound Dog". It turned out we sounded alike, had the same groove, so I began doing demos for other publishers for Presley – "Teddy Bear", "All Shook Up", "Easy Question", "Don't Drag the String Around". The cat was hot, that's why his name is on the songs. Why not? That's the way the business is anyway.' . . .

The Colonel asked Otis to appear in the Presley movie *Girls, Girls, Girls*, for which he had written 'Return to Sender', but the superstition about meeting Elvis kept him from accepting. An earlier movie offer had more significant results.

Otis was asked to choose the additional talent for a low-budget musical with the odd cast of Julius LaRosa and Count Basie. He spent a day in a Brooklyn record store listening to everything he could, until he heard Jerry Lee Lewis's 'Whole Lotta Shakin''. 'I grabbed it and ran, told them there's a cat on Sun Records who's gonna be a big man.' The record hadn't become a hit yet, but the movie people wanted only songs they could control, so Otis wrote 'Great Balls of Fire'. Lewis never appeared in the film – Otis doesn't remember the name of the movie or why – but he soon wrote a follow-up hit for Lewis, 'Breathless'. 'I thought, man, I got it made. I got a Presley and a Jerry Lee. But then he got into that trouble and they stopped playing his records.' He met Jerry Lee at one of Allen Freed's Brooklyn Paramount shows. 'You can get along with him because he boogies, man. He's beautiful people.'

Jerry Lee also copied the demo closely, but Dee Clark didn't. Otis wrote 'Just Keep It Up' and 'Hey Little Girl' for Clark, but Calvin Carter of Vee-Jay did arrangements on them. Then there were records he produced for Mahalia Jackson and Connie Francis. One assignment he brought off, despite absurd obstacles, was making a hit record for Sal Mineo. 'They said he's gonna be a big movie star, so they wanted a record. I went to his house five times to teach him. He was no singer, but he was a young, nice-looking kid and the record ["Start Movin'"] made it.'

In the mid-1960s, there were problems, first with the IRS, and then with drink. 'Everything I wrote sounded like garbage.' Otis made two albums that never got off the shelves. Now he's writing again – 'It used to take a half-hour to do a song; now it takes a couple of days' – and wants to continue singing. And when I spoke with him, he was ready, at long last, to meet Elvis. In the summer of 1976, he was in Nashville and sent Presley a telegram consisting mostly of song titles. 'The guy who reads his mail thought it was a prank and threw it away. Later Elvis wrote a letter apologizing.' Asked to assess his career, he said, 'I got a real kick out of it because it was what I wanted to do. It wasn't just the money; there were some damned good songs. I mostly enjoyed working with unknowns, because I felt there was part of me coming through, like Mineo, Jimmy Jones, Elvis. Everyone said Elvis was just a flash, but I knew he'd be around a long time because he'd try *any* kind of song that was given him. Now I'd like to meet him.' He never did. Elvis was dead within ten months of our talk.

PETER GURALNICK

Howlin' Wolf Meets the Critic

The first time I saw Howlin' Wolf he was appearing at the Club 47 in Cambridge, a small basement coffee-house which was only then beginning to make the transition from strict folk to Chicago blues and amplified music. Wolf practically forced the change all by himself. With his extravagant voice, above all that gargantuan presence he very nearly overwhelmed the club, and when he returned a year later I did a piece on him for a local newspaper. The first night I came to see him he seemed to be taking it easy, sitting down at the front of the stage and letting the band do most of the work. It was a slow night and somehow or other through his guitarist, Hubert Sumlin, we were introduced. I was the guy who had done the newspaper story on them, Sumlin explained. 'Oh yeah?' said Wolf, interrupting an account of how he had been stomped on in Alabama ('They acted like heathens down there, stomping all over my breast.') for a dozen wide-eyed listeners. 'Well, sit down.' He laid a meaty hand on my shoulder. 'Sit down, boy.' He wanted to see the article, he said. Glancing over it, he apologized that he didn't have his reading glasses. Could someone read it to him?

> Howlin' Wolf is bigger than life. He eclipses lesser performers with his size and the gusto of his performance. A bluesman like Junior Wells or James Cotton will try on different styles, will jive his audience in a shuffling attempt to ingratiate himself. Wolf rolls on the floor, he passes a broom obscenely between his legs, he appears in his farmboy's overalls – yet somehow nothing Wolf does is jive, no matter how often you've seen it before or how familiar the gesture is. The Wolf is always himself. Like James Brown his vulgarity carries with it its own conviction.

The kid who is reading looks up at me. Vulgarity? James Brown? Its own conviction? Wolf's fans are appalled. I want to sink through the floor in embarrassment, but Wolf is enjoying it, unbelievably a slow smile of appreciation creases his face. 'That's good,' he growls. 'Where'd you get that from?'

> He imitates no one, and as he prowls the stage, suddenly lurching heavily forward, leaning on a post waiting out the instrumental break, impatiently biding his time, the self-created public personality becomes the man. The mighty Wolf, he shouts, 'making his midnight creep/Hunters they can't find him/Stealing chicks wherever he goes/Then dragging his tail behind him.' He turns his back on the audience and his massive hips begin to shake. 'I'm a tail dragger . . .'

'That's the truth,' he murmurs wonderingly, explaining to his admirers in that rasping whisper. 'Chicks all dig the Wolf. They *all* dig the Wolf. Because he is mighty Wolf, he's a mountain Wolf, he wipes out his tracks,' to their impatient nods. They want to know if he knew Robert Johnson or if he could reprise 'Dust My Broom' for the second set.

> His dance is awkward and ungainly, his voice overpowers with a fierce rasping force, he proclaims himself. 'I am/A backdoor man/ Well, the men don't know/But the little girls, they understand.' His glance quizzically suggests evil. There are elements both of self-mockery and genuine self-esteem when he sings, 'Take me, baby, for your little boy/I'm three hundred pounds of heavenly joy.'

'Three hundred pounds of heavenly joy,' he repeats approvingly, savouring the phrase. 'Where'd you get that from, boy? You make it up all out of your own head?'

> It doesn't matter that off-stage he is a genial soft-spoken man, drawing on his pipe, near-sighted and blinking. It is irrelevant that off-stage his name is Chester Burnett. Onstage he is the Wolf. His legend has become himself, and when he howls it is a real howl, of frustration, of bitterness, of rage.
>
> Howlin' Wolf is nearly sixty years old. He sings of events which may have occurred forty years ago in the rough traditional style of the Mississippi Delta. Yet he is modern enough to have appeared with The Rolling Stones on *Shindig* a couple of years ago when they had a hit with his 'Little Red Rooster'. The Stones and the

> *Shindig* dancers sat reverentially at his feet as the camera came in
> for close-ups of his great sweating face, seamed and unshaven,
> while he did his elephantine dance and waggled his hips at the
> nationwide audience and leapt ponderously up and down two or
> three times, and looked as if he were about to swallow the
> microphone as he blew his harp into it . . .

Elephantine? The kid hesitated on the word and glared meaningfully
at me. When he is finished sweat is pouring down my face, and I try
to think of some way to make apology, but Wolf apparently thinks
nothing of it, in fact he is visibly pleased. At the end he pumps my
hand several times and once again expresses wonderment at my
sources.

WILLIAM FERRIS

Blues House Party

As a student at the University of Pennsylvania, William Ferris recorded the sounds from this house party in Clarksdale, Mississippi, in the mid-1960s. The main speaker and player is 'Pine Top' Johnson (P), who was considered to be one of the best piano players in the region. The other participants are Jasper Love (J), Floyd Thomas (F), Maudie Shirley (M) and Baby Sister (BS).

P *I'm gonner play that 'Pine Top Boogie Woogie' first.*

Now look, let me tell you something about that 'Pine Top Boogie Woogie'.

J *I wanta hear it.*

Now when I say stop, I mean stop.

J *That means it's good to you.*

I say git it, I mean git it.
Do like I tell you.
I say hold it, I mean hold it.
That's what I'm talking about.
Now, Red [Jasper Love], hold yourself.
Don't move a peg.
Now git it.
Now boogie.

J *Don't forgit to break down that bass.*

Now look. You see that woman with her red dress on?

J *I shore do, Pine.*

I want you to swing her right on back to me.

J   *No, I'm gonner keep her for myself.*

Don't forgit it.

J   *Aw, naw.*

I say hold it, I mean hold it.
That's what I'm talking about.
Now boogie.
Now, Red, hold yourself again.
Don't move a peg.
Now git it, boogie.
Now shake it.

P   *I'm gonner try some more blues.*
J   *Play it like you was playing it when you was ploughing them mules.*

Now tell me, Little Girl, where you stay last night.
It ain't none of your business, you know you ain't treating me
    right.
But that's all right.
I know you in love with another man, but that's all right.
Every now and then I wonder who been loving you tonight.

Now look here, Baby, see what you done done.
You done made me love you, now your man done come.
But that's all right.
I know you in love with another man, but that's all right.
Every now and then I wonder who loving you tonight.

I say tell me, Little Woman, where you stay last night.
It ain't none of your business, you ain't treating me right.
But that's all right.
I know you in love with another man, but that's all right.
Every now and then I wonder who loving you tonight.

J   *I'm gonner go git me a pint of corn-whiskey 'cause I'm thirsty.*

I got a great big woman, you know, got a little woman too.
Ain't gonner tell my big woman what my little woman do.
But that's all right.
I'm in love with another woman, but that's all right.

Every now and then I wonder who been loving you tonight.
Let's go. Shake it on out.

*

Well now I walked all night long, my forty-four in my hand.
Now I walked all night long, forty-four in my hand.
You know I was looking for my other woman, been out with
    another man.
I done wore my forty-four so long, till it made my shoulder sore.
Now if I git you where I want you, Baby, ain't gonner wear my
    forty-four no more.

It won't be the first time that forty-four blow.
Yeah, it won't be the first time that forty-four whistle blow.
You know it sound just like, Baby, ain't gonner tell the truth no
    more.

J   *Tell me why you playing them blues like that.*

Say, I got a cabin, you know my room is number forty-four.
Love, I got a cabin, my room is number forty-four
Now when I wake up every morning, Baby, I declare the wolves
    steady knocking on my door.

*

P   *This piano, she sticking on me, but I'm gonner try this country shack.*

I'm setting here a thousand miles from nowhere, in this one-room
    country shack.
I'm setting here a thousand miles from nowhere, in this one-room
    country shack.

J   *I'm here with you.*

Ain't nothing for my company but that old raggledy 'leven-foot
    wall.
I wake up every night about midnight, Love, I just can't sleep.
I wake up every night about midnight, Love, I just can't sleep.
All the crickets keep me company, you know the wind howling
    round my feet.

J	*Don't worry, Pine. Our day is coming.*
P	*I'm gonner play the blues.*
J	*Play the blues.*

I'm gonner git up early in the morning, I believe I'll git outta my bed.
I'm gonner git up early in the morning, I believe I'll git outta my bed.
I'm gonner find me a Clarksdale woman, if she blind and crippled
	and lame.
That's it, People!

*

J	*How you feeling this morning, Pine?*
P	*I'm feeling kind of down and out, man.*
J	*I know how it is. I hope we can git lucky, Pine.*
P	*Yeah. We gonner git lucky. My baby woke me up early this morning,
	and you know what she told me?*
J	*What'd she tell you?*
P	*She told me she wanted to rock one time.*
J	*Well, all right.*

Rock me, Baby, rock me all night long.
Rock me, Baby, rock me all night long.
I want you to rock me like my back don't have no bone.

Roll me, Baby, roll your wagon wheel.
Roll me, Baby, roll your wagon wheel.
I want you to roll me, Love, you don't know how it make me feel.

P	*Well, Love, I'm down in Mississippi and I got to play the blues.*
J	*I know what you mean, Pine. But soon as we git lucky, we'll cut out
	from here.*
P	*I'm telling you the truth, boy. I ain't gonner plough. I ain't gonner
	plough no mule no more.*
J	*What you think about going out in California?*
P	*Yeah.*
J	*We gonner git lucky. Play the blues for me now.*

Rock me, Baby, rock your baby child.
Rock me, Baby, like I'm your baby child.
I want you to rock me like my back don't have no bone.

Looka here, Love.
See me coming, Baby, go git your rocking chair.
See me coming, Baby, go git your rocking chair.
You know I ain't no stranger 'cause I been living round with
     you.

Play it one more time.
J *Play it good, Pine.*
P *Well, all right.*

*

J *What's on your mind this morning, Pine?*
P *Boy, I'm telling you, I'm thinking about the hard work.*
J *Hard work?*
P *Yeah.*

Love, I'm setting here a thousand miles from nowhere in this one-
     room country shack.
Yeah, now I'm setting here a thousand miles from nowhere in this
     one-room country shack.

J *Why you so lonesome, Pine?*
P *I got the blues.*
J *How come?*
P *My woman done quit me.*

You know the only thing I can confess, that old 'leven-foot raggledy
     cotton sack.

You know I wake up every night about midnight, Love, I just can't
     sleep.
I wake up every night about midnight, you know I just can't sleep.
You know all the crickets and frogs keep me company, you know
     the wind howling round my bed.

*

P *I'm out on Mr Jamison's place.*
J *Driving that tractor for three dollars a day?*
P *That's right. I'm gonner play the blues now, boy.*
J *While you playing the blues, I want to ask you a question. You talk*

about Mr Jamison. That's a big man. You mean he don't pay but three dollars a day?

P   *Two and a half.*

J   *For his best tractor driver?*

P   *The best one.*

J   *But when you was ploughing that mule, you was doing that for nothing?*

P   *Dollar and a quarter.*

J   *That's the reason why you playing them blues today?*

P   *Yeah. I left there walking.*

J   *Where you trying to make your way to?*

P   *I'm trying to go to California.*

I'm gonner git up early in the morning, I believe I'll git outta my
    bed.
I'm gonner git up early in the morning, I believe I'll git outta my
    bed.
I'm gonner find me a Clarksdale woman, if she dumb and crippled
    and blind.

J   *Play the blues now and bring me a bottle of snuff.*

P   *One more time and I gotta go.*

*

P   *I'm gonner leave here, boy.*

J   *Yeah, let's go down to Vicksburg. I was down a little bit below here, coming toward Louisiana, and I looked up the road and I see a stick I thought was across the road, but it was a black snake.*

P   *Black snake?*

J   *Yeah, and I run up there and I went to kill the snake, and you know what the snake did? He throwed up both hands and told me don't hurt him 'cause he was trying to git outta Mississippi too.*

P   *(laughs) I hear you.*

I got the blues for Vicksburg, Baby, sing 'em everywhere I go.
Now I got the blues for Vicksburg, sing 'em everywhere I go.
Now the reason I sing them blues, you know my woman don't love
    me no more.

I say Vicksburg's on a high hill, Louisiana just below,
I say Vicksburg's on a high hill, Louisiana just below.

P   *What you say, Love?*
J   *I hope we can make some money Saturday night.*
P   *Look here, Love.*
J   *Tell me about it.*

I say if you don't love me, Little Woman, why don't you tell me so?
You know I got more women, Baby, than a freight train can haul.

P   *Love, I'm gonner play the blues 'cause I'm moving on.*
J   *Tell me how they did you down in Vicksburg.*
P   *I'm going away.*

I say there ain't nothing I can do, ain't no more I can say.
There ain't nothing I can do, ain't nothing I can say.
I do all I can, Baby, you know, just to git along with you.
Good bye, Baby.

*

J   *Speaking of Vicksburg, Pine. I want to tell you something.*
P   *Yeah.*
J   *I remember when my grandmother was sold down in Decatur, Alabama.
      You know what happened?*
P   *What, boy?*
J   *They say they used to have old hymns. They would sing 'There's no
      danger in the water.' They was trying to git away then. Talking about
      that old hymn, Pine, 'There's no danger in the water', well, you know
      what they meant then?*
P   *What did they mean?*
J   *They meant that Old Boss waddn't nowhere around. It would be one
      guy done got way over there. They'd be done set it up over night. 'Well,
      we gonner leave here.'*

     *They was making up a plot to git away, you know. You would hear
      one of them way over there, one of those guys would say, 'Well, I know
      the Lord gonner help me.'*
P   *Yeah.*
J   *It meant that the other man that they was going to, he gonner meet them
      on the other side. You know what I mean? My grandmother, she was
      actually sold in that time and she brought my daddy here from down in
      Decatur. Those old people, they would sit overnight and they would talk*

and as they talked, they would have one to git away and sing a verse. Right now I might tell you, 'Well, let's us go to Chicago.'

Well, we'd all say, 'Okay. We're going to Chicago.'

But in those days the way they contacted each other was through the hymns. They would be tired of this man. This man done taken all of their earnings and they couldn't do anything about it. My old grandmother, she used to sew quilts and set down and she would tell me about it. That's really honest, you know. She would say they had those songs when they wanted to git over to each other. You know what I mean. They would start the hymns. 'Well, if the Lord don't help' or something like that. They would be giving that word to another guy way over here. They was pitching that sound backwards and forwards to one another so they could git away. You would hear one guy saying, 'Well, I'm gonner steal away.'

*

J   *What do you want do for me now?*

P   *I wanna dust my broom.*

J   *By meaning you gonner 'dust that broom', is you gonner cut out or you gonner stick around, Pine?*

P   *I'm gonner put my old lady to sweeping.*

J   *What's gonner happen to you?*

I'm gonner git up in the morning, I believe I'll dust my broom.
I'm gonner git up in the morning, I believe I'll dust my broom.
My best woman quit me and my friends can have my room.

I'm gonner write a letter, telephone every town I know.
I'm gonner write a letter, telephone every town I know.
I gotta find my woman, she be in Ethiopia, I know.

J   *Why you gonner dust your broom?*

P   *My woman left me.*

J   *Why did she leave you?*

P   *I didn't treat her right.*

J   *Why don't you just tell it like it is. You didn't have the money to give her. You couldn't afford the money.*

I don't want no woman want every downtown man she meets.
I don't want no woman want every downtown man she meets.
She's a no-good doney, they shouldn't allow her on the street.

J   *Well, I ain't worried about one thing. If I git in trouble, I know my boss*
    gonner git me out.

I'm gonner go home, I believe, I believe my time ain't long.
I believe, I believe my time ain't long.
I believe, I believe my time ain't long.
I gotta call Mr Harris, tell him please send my sow back home.

*

J   *What about my boss, J. P. Davis? He's a good man.*
P   *What you say, man?*
J   *Mr Harris is a good man.*
P   *But he don't put out no money.*
J   *Well, Davis ain't putting out none neither.*
P   *He'll loan you some, though.*
J   *Say, Pine, what happened in your child days?*
P   *Well, boy. I was ploughing a mule and cutting stalks with a kaiser*
    blade. Fifty cents a day. My daddy told me, 'Son, you can't feed yourself.'
      I say, 'Okay, Poppa. One day I'll be a man.' I left. Left the mule in
    the field and told him goodbye.
J   *Told the mule goodbye?*
P   *'Goodbye. Goodbye. I don't never want to see you no more.'*
      But that mule got his pension before I got mine. He on welfare and I
    ain't.
J   *You still fooling with the mule?*
P   *No. I'm through with the mule.*
J   *In other words, you wouldn't tell the mule to 'Git up' if he was setting*
    on your lap.
P   *If he was setting on my neck.*
J   *What would you tell him 'Move'?*
P   *'Set on down.'*
J   *Well, if he was running off with the world, what would you tell him?*
P   *'Save my part. I'll be there to reckly.'*

*

[Pine Top begins playing the tune of 'After Hours'.]

J   *On this here right now, this 'After Hours'. We got a curfew. I want you*
    to talk to me and play it and tell me about it. Other words, since the last

time I seen you, I have moved up, and I come back to find out what was happening. I been to California and I'm doing pretty good. They tell me you 'after hours' or something down here.

P   *Yeah. I'm running late. They don't 'low me to stay up in Clarksdale after twelve o'clock. I'm gonner give the police a little bit of this 'After Hours', you know, by Erskine Hawkins.*

J   *You mean that's why you playing that, because they don't 'low you to stay up after hours. Look here, man. It ain't but ten o'clock now. What time you have to go to bed?*

P   *I have to go to bed at twelve o'clock.*

J   *You mean you got to go to bed and you can't be up?*

P   *I got to go.*

F   *Wait a minute, man. Let's correct that. This town is open now.*

P   *I know it is now. But it didn't used to be.*

J   *You say this town's open now?*

F   *Yes sir. All night long.*

J   *But where you going, though? You can't find a drink.*

P   *Boy, you better hush talking so loud. Mr Billy's gonner hear you. It's eleven o'clock. I'm going to Nashville, where I can git with the wee wee hours. Let me play it one time.*

J   *Pine, you got a chance to go head on out to California with me if you want to.*

P   *I'm going. Put the light out.*

J   *You playing the blues, Pine, but you ain't telling me nothing about it.*

P   *I'm fixing to go now.*

J   *You mess with my woman, I'll make my butcher knife eat you up.*

*

F   *Whip out some sound, Pine.*

J   *Is I got a soul brother in the house?*

F   *Aw yeah, man. Aw yeah.*

Big Boss, don't you hear me when I call?
Big Boss, don't you hear me when I call?
Yes, you ain't all that tall, you just big, that's all.

You long-legged, you just make a fuss.
You just fucking round, trying to be someone.

Big Boss Man, don't you hear me when I call?
Yes you long and tall, you ain't gitting nowhere.

J   *Saturday night!*

Now you try to take my woman, you ain't doing no good.
Running round here talking, trying to be someone.
Now, Big Boss Man, don't you hear me when I call?
Now you ain't that strong, you just big, that's all.

P   *I'm going, Love.* [Continues playing tune.]
J   *Just before you go, I wanta tell you something.*
P   *What you wanta tell me, Love?*
J   *There was a real good-looking guy that had plenty of money and good-looking women. So a strange lady came in and she asked this other lady why this good-looking man ain't married. She say, 'Well, he ain't found nobody here he want to marry.'*

   'Aw yeah? Y'all ain't treating him right.'

   So this lady, she walked up to him and asked, 'Why you ain't married?'

   He said, 'Well, I'm looking for a lady got two of them things.'

   'Aw yeah? Me and you gonner git married.'

   He told her, 'Well, come on to the house Friday night when I git paid off.'

P   *She come over there that Friday night.*
F   *What'd she tell him?*
J   *She said, 'Well here I is.'*

   He said, 'Is you got two of 'em?'

   She told him, 'Yeah, I got two.'

   'All right. Pull off your clothes and git in the bed.'

   So she hit the bed. She gived him that on the top first, and when he got through, she turned over and turned her back on him and told him, 'Git this one.'

   He got that one too. That was on a Friday night. The same thing happened on Saturday and Sunday night. That Monday morning she told him, 'Baby, before you go to work, let's booze some.'

   He said, 'All right, baby.'

   So she gone downtown and bought some booze. She got off from the house a little piece and she looked at her money and said, 'Well, what you told me to git? I ain't got enough money. What you want me to do, sell one of them things?'

   He said, 'Yeah, baby. That's all right.'

   She walked off a little piece further and he stopped her. He called and said, 'Hey. Wait a minute, honey. I'll tell you what you do. You sell both of them sons-of-bitches 'cause I'm through with them.'

   Go 'head and play, Pine!

P *Big Boss Man!*

*

Love, I've had my fun if I don't git well no more.

J *Long as you stay in Mississippi, you never will git well.*

I have had my fun if I don't git well no more.
You know my head is killing me and I'm going down slow.

I want you to write my mother, tell her the shape I'm in.
Want you to write my mother, tell her the shape I'm in.
Tell her to pray for me, Love, forgive me for all my sins.

J *Man, you must be broke and hungry, raggledy and dirty too.*
P *I'm in bad shape.*

Tell her don't send me no doctor, doctor can't do no good.
Tell her don't send no doctor, doctor can't do no good.
You know it's all my fault, I didn't do the things that I should.

J *What about this Old Granddaddy Eighty-six [whiskey]? Will that help you any?*
P *Yeah, boy. I know one thing. I may not git well, but I am gonner try to git well.*
J *You can have a good feeling.*
P *I'm trying to tell you.*

Now on the next train south, Love, look for my clothes back home.

J *You don't wanta go south.*

On the next train south, look for my clothes back home.
If you don't see my body, Floyd, you can view my bones.

J *Tell him to go west or north, but don't go south.*

Now, Mother, don't you worry, this is all over now.
Mother, don't you worry, this is all over now.
You know your son is lost out in this world somewhere.

P   *That's all, Love.*
J   *Play it and talk to me a little bit. Man, you must be worried to play the*
    blues like that.
P   *I'm is, boy. You know one thing?*
J   *What?*
P   *The doctor said I waddn't gonner live long. So I'm trying to tell you.*

On the next train south, look for my clothes back home.
On the next train south, look for my clothes back home.
If you don't see my body, you can view my bones.
Goodbye!

*

P   *Say, Floyd.*
F   *Yeah, man.*
P   *You know one thing, boy?*
F   *What's that?*
P   *I'm drifting.*
F   *You must be going somewhere.*
J   *He's trying to drift outta Mississippi. I know what he's trying to do.*

You know I'm drifting and I'm drifting just like a ship out on the
        sea.
Well I'm drifting and I'm drifting like a ship out on the sea.
Well you know I ain't got nobody in this world to care for me.

J   *Tell me, Pine.*

If my baby only take me back again. (She done quit me, Floyd.)
If my baby only take me back again.
Well she say I ain't good, I haven't got no friend.

J   *You mean you working all day, but ain't making no money?*

I give her all my money, tell me what more can I do?
I give her all my money, tell me what more can I do?
Now you a good woman, Baby, but you just won't be true.

J   *You can't do more, man. You can't do more.*

I say bye, bye, Baby. Baby, bye, bye, bye.
Bye, bye, Baby. Tell you bye, bye, bye.
Now it gonner be too late and I'll be so far away.

J   *Play it. I don't care what happens. Play the blues all night long.*
P   *Bye, Baby.*

*

P   *I'm gonner try this old blues now.*

Let me tell you, Baby, tell what I will do.
Rob, steal and kill somebody just to git home to you.
Ain't that loving you, Baby?
Ain't that loving you, Baby?
Ain't that loving you, Baby, and you don't even know my name.

They may kill me, Baby, do me like they used to do.
My body might rise and swim to the ocean and come back home to
        you.
Ain't that loving you, Baby?
Ain't that loving you, Baby?
Ain't that loving you, Baby, and you don't even know my name.

J   *Aw yeah. That's loving all right.*
F   *Work out, Pine.*
J   *Love her in your own way.*
P   *I'm gonner play it one more time.*

*

J   *Have a Saturday night ball.*
P   *What's that, Love?*
J   *Sunday night you gotta go to sleep 'cause you gotta git up and go to work
    Monday morning.*

You know the war is over, I'm going down that sunny road.

J   *Done got tired of soldiering now.*
F   *Wait a minute, man. They still fighting in Vietnam.*

I say the war is over, I'm going down that sunny road.
I done got tired of Clarksdale, working for my room and board.

J   *I know what you mean, man.*

I say when I was making good money, you treat me like I was a king.

J   *She lied to you then.*

When I was making good money, Darling, you treat me like I was a
    king.

J   *Then what happened?*

Now you know all my money gone, and your love don't mean a
    thing.

Hey, Baby, bring me my hat and coat.
I can feel the green grass growing under your doorstep.
You know this time tomorrow I'll be way down that sunny road.

Well I done did all, I did all I could afford.
You know I done did all, I did all I could afford.
You know this time tomorrow, Baby, I'll be down that sunny road.

J   *Work that bass again for me, Pine.*
P   *What you say, Love?*
J   *I hear you now. I see you buying a ticket, man. Where you fixing to go?*
P   *I'm going to Chicago.*
J   *The West Side or the South Side?*
P   *I'm going to the South.*

Bye, bye, Baby, I did all I could for you.
Bye, bye, Baby, I did all I could for you.
You's a bad-headed woman and I don't want you no more.

J   *If you going to the South Side, you must be going over to Stoney Island*
    where it's happening at.
P   *Yeah, boy. I got my ticket.*
F   *Man, you better go on the North Side. They raising hell on the South Side.*
J   *Detroit is on fire and Chicago is burning down.*

*

P   *Let me see what I wanta do.*
J   *What's fixing to happen, Pine?*
P   *How 'bout 'Juicy Fruit'?*
J   *Go 'head. You's a free man. You ain't got nothing to worry about.*
F   *Your way or the highway.*
P   *Here I go.*
J   *Work that bass way down.*

Hello, Juicy Fruit, how do you do?
Hello, Juicy Fruit, how do you do?
You remember me? I remember you.

Hello, Juicy Fruit, how do you do?
Hello, Juicy Fruit, how do you do?
Do you remember me? I remember you.
I used to carry you by here, by the railroad too.

*

I wants to know how much longer, Baby, have I got to wait on
        you.
I wants to know how much longer, Baby, have I got to wait on
        you.
How long, how long, how much more long?

I lay down last night, I saw you in my sleep.
I lay down last night, I saw you in my sleep.
I began to wondering what do you want with me.

How long, how much more long?
How long, how much more long?
How long, now, you want your rolling done?

J   *If you should die before your time what would happen?*
P   *What you say, Love?*
J   *If you die before your time, remember she'd be ever on your mind.*

If I should die, die before my time.

J   *Well, all right.*

If I should die, die before my time.
I want you to know what will become of me.

I lay down last night, I missed you in my arms.
I lay down last night, I missed you in my arms.
I began to wonder what do you think of me.

J *Push way back and gimme some of that low bass now.*

How long, how much more long, how long?
How long, how much more long, how long?
How long, how long you want your loving done?

I wants to know how much more longer, Baby, have I got to wait
    on you.
I wants to know how much more longer, Baby, have I got to wait
    on you.
How long, now, Baby, you want your loving done?

P *What you say, Floyd?*
F *I hear you, Pine. Work out.*
P *How long!*
J *Don't stop now. Gimme one of them good road blues.*
P *Good road blues coming up. I wants to know why my baby always play
    around.*

I wonder, Baby, why don't you settle down.
I wants to know.
I wants to know.
I just got to know.

Look like you got me flunking, if I'm wrong, please tell me so.
I know I was wrong, but some day I will realize.
I wants to know.
I wants to know.
I just got to know.

I used to believe what you'd tell me.
I used to believe every word you say.
But looks like from your way, I believe you gonner put me
    down.
I wants to know.
I wants to know.

I just got to know.
Now I wants to know, Floyd.

*

P *Remember that, Love? Remember that, Buddy? Let me git another good*
   blues now. I'm gonner play the blues one more time.
J *Let me hear you, Pine Top.*
F *Work out. Work out, Pine. Let your hair down now.*

Yes, my baby love to boogie, I love to boogie too.
Say, my baby love to boogie, I love to boogie too.
I'm gonner boogie this time and I ain't gonner boogie no more.

J *Well, all right.*

You know she do that boogie and shout it down through the street.
She doos that boogie and shout it down through the street.
She howls so loud they run up and down the street.
Boogie one time.

Don't the sun look lonesome, shining down through the tree.
Don't the sun look lonesome, shining down through the tree.
Don't your hair look lovely when you put it back up for me.

[Maudie Shirley and Baby Sister enter the room.]

J *Well, all right. Look who just come in. Work out, Pine.*
F *Look like we got to shore nuff boogie now.*

I love my baby and I tell the world I do.

M *Do you really, Darling?*

I love my baby and I tell the world I do.

M *I wanta marry you.*

Well I hope she'll come to love me too.

M *I already do.*

*

Next time I see you, things won't be the same.
Next time I see you, things won't be the same.
If it hurts you, Darling, you only have yourself to blame.

[Maudie]
You know you lied, cheated, oh so long.
You know you lied, cheated, oh so long.
You just a no-good man, you only have yourself to blame.

[Maudie]
Next time you see me, things won't be the same.
Next time you see me, things won't be the same.
If it hurts you, Darling, you only have yourself to blame.

[Maudie and Pine Top]
Well you lied, cheated, oh so long.
Well you lied, cheated, oh for so long.
You just no-good, you only have yourself to blame.

M *Work out, baby.*

You drink your whiskey, I'll drink my wine.
You tend to your business, Baby, I'll tend to mine.
Next time you see me, things won't be the same.

J *What you got against the girl?*
P *She's a heartbreaker.*

[Maudie]
Yes, next time you see me, things won't be the same.
If it hurt you . . . My Darling, you only have yourself to
    blame.

*

I say God made a elephant, he made him big and stout.
Waddn't satisfied till he made his snout.
He made his snout, made it long and round.
Waddn't satisfied till he made his tail.
He made his tail, made it to fan the fly.
Waddn't satisfied till he made his eye.
He made his eye, made it to look on the grass.

Waddn't satisfied till he made his ass.
He made his ass so he could stick in his dick.
Waddn't satisfied till he made his prick.
He made his prick, made it hard as a rock.
His nuts would crack when he coughed a lot.
He's a dirty little man.
He's a dirty little man.
Dirty little man.

Children round the house having a fit.
Your mother in the house making jam outta shit.
She's a nasty little woman.
She's a nasty little woman.
Dirty little woman as you'll find.

I want all you women, want you to fall in line.
I want you to shake it like I shake mine.
Shake it quick, Baby, shake it fast.
If you can't shake it quick, shake your little black ass.
You a dirty little woman.
Dirty little woman to me.

I had your momma, your sister too.
I throwed a brick at your old man too.
He's a running old man.
He's a running old man.
He's a running old man, running old man.

I want all you women, want you to fall in line.
I want you to shake like I shake mine.
Shake it quick, Baby, shake it fast.
If you can't shake it quick, shake your little black ass.
Shake your little ass.
You a shaking little woman, shaking little woman.

Sitting round the house and tote that brick.
Your momma in the kitchen making jam outta shit.
She's a nasty little woman.
She's a nasty little woman.
She's a nasty little woman, nasty little woman to me.

P　*I'm fixing to put 'Running Wild' on there.*
M　*Aw, Baby. I got words for you. You gonner run wild?*
P　*Running wild.*
M　*I know you ain't gonna run wild all your life. I'll slow you down one of these days.*

Listen here, Woman, where'd you stay last night?
It ain't none of your business.
You know you ain't treating me right.
Aw, Woman, Baby, you steady running wild.
Now the baby I'm loving, she don't treat me right.

M　*You got the nerve to tell me I'm running wild?*
P　*What you say?*

[Maudie]
When I stay at home every day, trying to treat you right,
You come home late at night, jump on me and there's a fight.
Baby, you know, you know that ain't right.

P　*What say, Baby?*
M　*You heard me.*

Say, I work hard every day, bring home my pay.
You tell me, Baby, I got nowhere to stay.
Now looka here, Baby, you know you running wild.
You just running round, Baby, Baby, you ain't no good.

M　*Yeah, Baby, I know just what you mean. You must think I'm a fool, don't you?*
P　*Naw. I don't.*
M　*Yeah, I know you think I'm a fool.*
P　*I love you, Baby.*
M　*I don't love you, Darling.*
P　*Why, Baby?*
M　*'Cause you always doing me wrong.*
P　*Ha ha!*

Now tell me, Woman, what you got on your mind.
Tell me, Woman, what you got on your mind.

M　*Nothing but loving, Baby.*

The way you treat me, you just running wild.

J   *Better see me then.*

[Maudie]
Well I'll tell you this one thing, Baby.
If you love me, Darling, I'll do anything you say.
If you love me, Darling, I'll do anything you say.
But as long as you messing up, Baby, I don't have no say.

I'm gonner tell you now, Baby, ain't gonner tell you no more.
I'm gonner tell you now, Baby, ain't gonner tell you no more.
Well you running wild, Baby, you just got to go.

P   *What you say about that, Baby?*
M   *Well you got your womens, why can't I have my mens?*
P   *I don't like that.*
M   *Neither do I.*
P   *You oughta not do that. I'm gonner finish up.*
J   *That's just like a woman.*
M   *Let me tell you one thing.*
P   *What you say, Honey?*
M   *Baby, you know I love you.*
P   *I love you too, Honey.*
M   *Don't worry, Darling. We'll make it.*
P   *Goodbye, Baby.*
M   *See you later, Sugar.*

GEOFF DYER

Tradition, Influence and Innovation

In his book *Real Presences* George Steiner asks us to 'imagine a society in which all talk about the arts, music and literature is prohibited'. In such a society there would be no more essays on whether Hamlet was mad or only pretending to be, no reviews of the latest exhibitions or novels, no profiles of writers or artists. There would be no secondary, or parasitic, discussion – let alone tertiary: commentary on commentary. We would have, instead, a 'republic for writers and readers' with no cushion of professional opinion-makers to come between creators and audience. While the Sunday papers presently serve as a substitute for the experiencing of the actual exhibition or book, in Steiner's imagined republic the review pages would be turned into listings: catalogues and guides to what is about to open, be published or released.

What would this republic be like? Would the arts suffer from the obliteration of this ozone of comment? Certainly not, says Steiner, for each performance of a Mahler symphony (to stick for a moment to his own preferred terrain) is also a critique of that symphony. Unlike the reviewer, however, the performer 'invests his own being in the process of interpretation'. Such interpretation is automatically *responsible* because the performer is answerable to the work in a way that even the most scrupulous reviewer is not.

Although most obviously, it is not only the case for drama and music; all art is also criticism. This is most clearly so when a writer or composer quotes or re-works material from another writer or composer. All literature, music and art *embody an expository reflection on, a value judgement of, the inheritance and context to which they pertain* (my italics). In other words it is not only in their letters, essays or conversation that writers like Henry James reveal themselves also to be the best critics; rather, *The Portrait of a Lady* is itself, among other things, a commentary on and a critique of *Middlemarch*. 'The best readings of art are art.'

No sooner has Steiner summoned this imaginary republic into existence than he sighs, 'the fantasy I have sketched is only that.' Well, it's not. It is a real place and for much of the century it has provided a global home for millions of people. It is a republic with a simple name: jazz.

Jazz, as everyone knows, grew out of the blues. From the beginning it developed through the shared participation of a community of audiences and performers. Those like Charlie Parker who went to hear Lester Young and Coleman Hawkins in Kansas City in the 1930s got a chance to blow with them at after-hours jam sessions later the next morning. Miles Davis and Max Roach served their apprenticeship first by listening to and then by sitting in with Parker at Minton's and the 52nd Street clubs, learning as they went along. In their turn John Coltrane, Herbie Hancock, Jackie McLean and dozens of others who went on to school many of the leading players of the 1970s and 1980s learnt their trade, as McLean put it, 'in the university of Miles Davis'.

Because jazz has continued evolving in this way, it has remained uniquely in touch with the animating force of its origins. From time to time in his solos a saxophonist may quote from other musicians, but every time he picks up his horn he cannot avoid commenting, automatically, on the tradition that has laid this music at his feet. At its worst this involves simple repetition (those interminable Coltrane imitations); sometimes it involves exploring possibilities that were previously only touched upon. At its best it expands the possibilities of the form.

The focus of these endeavours is frequently one of a number of tunes which have served jazz, throughout its history, as springboards for improvisation. Often these tunes have inauspicious origins as light pop songs. Alternatively, original compositions become standards (in what other medium would a classic be a standard?). Thelonious Monk's 'Round Midnight' has probably been played by every jazz musician on earth; each subsequent version tests it, finds out if there is still anything that can be done with it. Successive versions add up to what Steiner calls a 'syllabus of enacted criticism'.

Ideally, a new version of an old song is virtually a re-composition and this labile relation between composition and improvisation is one of the sources of jazz's ability to constantly replenish itself. Writing on the 'Appassionata' piano sonata op. 57, Theodor Adorno notes that 'it makes sense to think that what occurred to Beethoven first was not the main theme as it appears in the exposition but that all-important variant of it in the coda, and that he, as it were, retrospectively derived the primary theme from its variation'. Something similar happens frequently in jazz: in the course of a solo a musician touches momentarily and almost accidentally on a phrase which may become the basis for a new tune which will also be improvised on – and these solos may in turn yield another phrase to be developed into a composition. Duke Ellington's musicians frequently grumbled that some lick they'd played in a solo had been noted by Duke and built into a tune published under his name – though they were quick to concede that only someone with Ellington's genius could have grasped the potential of that phrase and made as much out of it as he did.

Since he is the most fertile source, we can begin with Ellington in a more explicit illustration of the way in which the music offers the best commentary on itself. Ellington wrote 'Take the Coltrane' for the great tenor player; Charles Mingus's 'Open Letter to Duke' is a musical essay on Ellington; it has since been followed by the Art Ensemble of Chicago's 'Charlie M'. In years to come this chain will almost certainly be lengthened by a homage to Art Ensemble saxophonist 'Joseph J' or an 'Open Letter to Roscoe' (Mitchell).

This kind of party game could be continued indefinitely, taking various names as our starting-point. Thelonious Monk or Louis Armstrong are especially fruitful places to begin but there are literally hundreds of musicians who have had one or two songs written for them. If we drew lines between all available songs in a kind of flow diagram of homages and tributes the paper would soon become impenetrably black, the meaning of the diagram obscured by the quantity of information it would have to convey.

A less explicit strand in the ongoing process of enacted criticism is at work in the evolution of jazz musicians' individual styles. To have a sound and style that are unmistakably your own is a prerequisite of greatness in jazz. Here, as is often the case in jazz, an apparent paradox is at work: to sound like themselves musicians begin by

trying to sound like someone else. Looking back to his early years
Dizzy Gillespie said, 'Each musician is based on someone who went
before, and eventually you get enough of your own things in your
playing, and you get a style of your own.' Miles Davis in turn tried
to sound like Gillespie, and countless trumpeters after him – Wynton
Marsalis most recently – have tried to sound like Miles. Often
musicians arrive at their own sound by default. Gillespie again: 'All
I ever did was try to play like [Roy Eldridge], but I never quite made
it. I'd get all messed up 'cause I couldn't get it. So I tried something
else. That has developed into what became known as bop.' Miles
Davis's lonely, chillingly beautiful sound came about as a result of
his inability to sustain the high register leaps that were Gillespie's
trademark.

There are two apparently contradictory ways in which the ante-
cedent's voice makes itself heard. Some musical personalities are so
strong, so closely associated with a certain sound that they colonize
a whole area of expression, and others can encroach on it only at
the price of surrendering their individuality. The personality of one
musician can so pervade a certain style that it only seems possible to
imitate that style, never adequately to absorb or transcend it. It is
now almost impossible for a trumpeter to play a ballad with a
harmon mute and not sound as if he is imitating Miles Davis.

Alternatively, there are rare instances of musicians assimilating
their predominant influences to such an extent that they seem at
times, as Harold Bloom has said of some poets, to 'achieve a style
that captures and oddly retains priority over their precursors, so
that the tyranny of time almost is overturned, and one can believe for startled moments, that they are being *imitated by their
ancestors*'.

By the nature of its style of performance, jazz affords more
opportunities for exactly this kind of comparison than any other art
form. The distinction between a group performance and a jam
session has always been hazy (a band for a studio date is often flung
together at the last moment and even 'named' groups are temporary
shifting units, rarely demanding the exclusive commitment of any
members), and in the course of a year many different musicians will
play together in many different formats: duets, trios, quartets, big
bands. At its worst this involves a touring star player teaming up

with a new pick-up rhythm section in each town he plays; alternatively a bassist gets a steady flow of work because he can be depended on to provide solid if uninspired support with minimum rehearsal time. The great advantage of this flexible style of employment, though, is that the individual voices of jazz are heard together in an almost infinite number of permutations, each giving rise to a new collective sound. What would Gerry Mulligan and Monk sound like together? Or Coltrane and Monk? Duke Ellington and Coleman Hawkins? Johnny Dyani and Don Cherry? Don Cherry and John Coltrane? Art Pepper with Miles Davis's rhythm section? Sonny Rollins with Coltrane's? You have only to listen to the records to find out. Every different combination gives a sharper sense of the particular qualities of each musician.

One of the standard procedures of literary criticism is to juxtapose texts by different authors in order to bring out the particular qualities and relative merits of each. In jazz the constant network of cross-performances means that that task is implicit and inherent in the accumulating catalogue of the music. The performance of a given player simultaneously answers certain questions (about musicians he is playing with or who have come before, about his relation to the developing tradition) and raises other questions (about what he himself is doing, about his own worth, about the form he's working in); the musicians he works with and who come after him provide provisional answers but these answers are also questions – about the worth of *these* musicians, *their* relation to tradition. In an elaborate critical kind of circular breathing, the form is always simultaneously explaining and questioning itself.

With the music itself performing so many of the tasks normally left to commentators, it is not surprising that the contribution of critics to jazz has been relatively insignificant. Of course there are jazz critics and jazz journals. Generally, however, writing on jazz has been of such a low standard, has failed so signally to convey any sense of the animating dynamics of the music, as to be irrelevant except – and this is just as Steiner would have it – in so far as it conveys facts: who played with whom, when a given album was recorded etc. To strip the Western literary or art-historical tradition of criticism would be to decimate our cultural capital (no Berger on Picasso, no Benjamin on Baudelaire). Much of what has been written about jazz, on the other hand, could be lost without doing any but the most superficial damage to the heritage of the music.

Despite all that has been said above, jazz is anything but a hermetic form. What makes it a vital art form is its astonishing ability to absorb the history of which it is a part. If no other evidence survived, some computer of the future could probably reconstruct the whole history of black America from the jazz catalogue. I am not even thinking of explicit works like Ellington's *Black, Brown and Beige*, conceived as a tone-parallel to the history of Afro-Americans; Archie Shepp's 'Attica Blues' or 'Malcom, Malcom, Semper Malcom'; Mingus's 'Prayer for Passive Resistance'; Pharoah Sanders's 'Soledad', or Max Roach's *Freedom Now Suite*. I intend something more general, along the lines suggested by Adorno's observation that 'it is not for nothing that the newly soulful tone of the violin counts among the great innovations of the age of Descartes.' Elaborating on Adorno, Fredric Jameson comments that 'throughout its long ascendancy, indeed, the violin preserves this close identification with the emergence of individual subjectivity'. Adorno was referring to the period from the seventeenth century onwards but his words are equally applicable to the trumpet's identification with the emergence of Black American consciousness in the twentieth century, from Louis Armstrong through to Miles Davis. Since the 1940s, that identification has been rivalled and complemented by the saxophone. According to Ornette Coleman, 'the best statements Negroes have made, of what their soul is, have been on tenor saxophone.'

Although Coleman is distinguishing primarily between the tenor and alto saxophones his claim also holds true for a larger distinction between the tenor and other means of expression: literature, painting. This is important, for hand in hand with jazz's capacity to absorb its surrounding history goes its capacity to raise to the level of genius those who would otherwise have lacked a medium to express themselves. Jazz, as Eric Hobsbawm observes, 'has been able to draw upon a wider reservoir of potential artists than any other art in our century'. 'Louis Armstrong without his trumpet is a rather limited man,' notes Eric Hobsbawm. 'With it he speaks with the precision and compassion of the recording angel.'

Jazz is not exclusively a medium of expression for black experience (as the title of Ellington's *Black, Brown and Beige* indicates, the history of black Americans is inextricably tangled up with that of white America). The white band leader Stan Kenton extended the terms of debate still further, hearing in jazz the potential for expressing the anguished spirit of the age: 'I think the human race today may be going through things it never experienced before, types of nervous frustration and thwarted emotional development which traditional music is entirely incapable of not only satisfying but expressing. That's why I believe jazz is the new music that came along just in time.'

If there is something a little self-serving about Kenton's words – a tacit advertisement for his own music – we can turn instead to a figure of considerable authority who had no vested interest in music. In 1964 Dr Martin Luther King gave the Opening Address to the Berlin Jazz Festival, his presence there serving as a reminder of how the black people's struggle for civil rights was paralleled by jazz musicians' struggle to have their art recognized as such. In his speech King noted the role played by music in articulating the suffering, hopes and joys of the black experience long before the task was undertaken by writers and poets. Not only was jazz central to the lived experience of negroes, he went on, but 'in the particular struggle of the negro in America there is something akin to the universal struggle of modern man.'

This is a vital connection; once it has been made jazz becomes a medium not only representative of a people but, implicitly, of a century, a medium that expresses not simply the condition of the black American but a condition of history.

One of the reasons jazz has evolved so fast is because musicians have been obliged, if for no other reason than to earn decent money, to play night after night, two or three shows a night, six to seven nights a week. Not just to play but to improvise, to invent as they play. This has some apparently contradictory results. Rilke waited ten years for the gale of inspiration that led him to begin the *Duino Elegies* to sweep through him again and enable him to complete them. For jazz musicians there is no question of waiting for inspiration to strike. Inspired or not they have to get on with the job of making music. Paradoxically, then, the commitment to nightly improvisation, on record dates and in clubs, leads weary musicians to play safe, to rely on tried and tested formulas. Yet the demands of constant improvisation mean that jazz musicians are in a state of constant creative alert, of habitual readiness to invent. On a given night the playing of any member of a quartet can be sufficiently energetic to lift the performances of the rest of the group until a reciprocal shiver passes through audience and performers alike: suddenly the music is *happening*. The working conditions of jazz musicians, moreover, have meant that a vast amount of material has been available for recording (each year dozens of previously unheard performances by the likes of Coltrane and Mingus find their way on to disc). Much of this material sounds fairly ordinary after a couple of listenings – but even while thinking this you are struck also by how high the standard of the average is. Or rather, for the corollary of that observation is the crucial one, you are struck by how high the standards generated by this music are, how quickly you become indifferent to anything that is not touched by greatness. The feeling jazz creates when it is really happening is so subtly but unmistakably different from when the band is just swinging along that large parts of the jazz catalogue (and many live performances) pall by comparison. This knowledge – this feeling – confronts jazz musicians with a steep and daunting slope, especially when so much of what constitutes greatness in jazz lies beyond the range of technique; especially when, as all musicians have agreed, you have to put everything of yourself into your playing, when the music is dependent on your experience, on what you have to offer as a man. 'Music is your own experience, your thoughts, your wisdom,' said Charlie Parker. 'If you don't live it, it won't come out of your horn.'

By the 1950s young players found that many of Parker's innovations were within their grasp. So abundant was the expressive potential unleashed by Parker that to become fluent in the idiom he had forged was enough to establish a player's reputation.

Towards the end of the 1950s, however, bebop's capacity for nurturing its young came to an end as jazz once again entered a period of rapid transition. Prior to this, as Ted Gioia points out, players were satisfied with making a contribution to the music, finding their own sound on their instrument. By 1960 musicians began to talk as though they were responsible to the music as a whole – not only to its past, to the tradition, but to its future. Tomorrow became The Question, what mattered was The Shape of Jazz to Come. The 1960s saw the stakes raised again as two currents became apparent. Musicians began to see themselves as pushing back the frontiers of the music in an attempt to make it ever more expressive. 'I have lived more than I can express in bebop terms,' said Albert Ayler, whose music broke the back of the jazz tradition. Where they were actually trying to take the music may not have been very clear – for the other tendency in the 1960s was for musicians to let themselves be swept on by the accumulated energy of the increasingly spontaneous production of music.

The new music – as it become known – seemed all the time to be moving towards a scream, as if it had internalized the danger that had once been attendant on the production of jazz. As the Civil Rights movement gave way to Black Power and America's ghettos erupted in riots, so all the energy, violence and hope of the historical moment seemed to find their way into the music. Simultaneously the music became less a test of musicianship or, as in bebop, of experience and more a test of the soul, of the saxophone's ability to tear out the spirit within. Commenting on the new addition to his band, Pharoah Sanders, Coltrane emphasized not his playing but his 'huge spiritual reservoir. He's always trying to reach out to truth. He's trying to allow his spiritual self to be his guide.'

That Coltrane's name should come up at this point is not surprising. All of the currents mentioned above can be *heard* converging in him. The sense of danger which is inherent and inevitable in the wildfire evolution of jazz becomes audible in Coltrane. From the early 1960s until his death in 1967 Coltrane sounds as if he is both urging his music forward and being lashed on by it. He was a consummate bebop player who was constantly straining to break free of the confines of existing forms. In the five years it was together the classic quartet of Coltrane, Elvin Jones, Jimmy Garrison and McCoy Tyner hauled jazz to a pitch of expressivity that has rarely been exceeded by any other art form. It is Coltrane who takes the lead, but he is utterly dependent on the rhythm section who not only follow him through his labyrinthine improvisations with split-second responsiveness but force him on to greater exertions. An extreme exploration of the potential of the form seems barely adequate to contain the force and intensity of the spirit of the man in whom the music has its origin. In their last recordings we hear the quartet aching on the frontier of the possible, a highly evolved musical form being taken to its limit.

A key album in Coltrane's musical ascent of the spirit, *A Love Supreme*, closes with a long dream of immanence, a search for an ending that leaves the tenor drifting like smoke over the rhythm section. *First Meditations (for Quartet)*, an album recorded six months later in May 1965, *begins* with that desire to end: there is nowhere for the quartet to go but still they are forcing their way forward. The whole of one side is a painful valediction, the four members of the quartet saying farewell: to each other, to cohesion, to the idea of the quartet as a form capable of containing Coltrane's relentless spirit.

That there is a terrible beauty in the performances of *First Meditations (for Quartet)* and the similar *Sun Ship* (August 1965) is obvious on a first listening. I did not realize how terrible until I heard Pharoah Sanders playing 'Living Space' (originally recorded by Coltrane in February 1966) in a duet with pianist William Henderson. Although not quite as raw, Pharoah's sound has all the intensity and passion of Coltrane's but it is serene in a way that Coltrane never is in his last years. I wondered why (criticism, after all, is really only an attempt to articulate your emotions), and soon realized that the reason had to do with Elvin Jones. As it evolved so the quartet sound came to be dominated increasingly by what were essentially battles between Coltrane and Jones, whose drums are like a wave that never quite breaks, that never stops breaking. As early as 1961, at the close of 'Spiritual', the soprano seems about to be drowned by the weight of drums but then emerges again, floating clear of the tidal wave of percussion crashing over it. By the time of *Sun Ship*, especially on 'Dearly Beloved' and 'Attaining', Jones is murderous: it seems impossible that the saxophone can survive the pounding of the drums. Coltrane is on the cross, Jones is hammering in the nails. Prayer turns to scream. If Jones sounds as though he wants to destroy him then Coltrane certainly wanted – needed –

him to try. Indeed, Coltrane wanted Jones to go even further, and for a while he pitted himself against two drummers: Jones and Rashied Ali, who was ostensibly an even wilder player. Coltrane's last recordings were duets with Ali, but his relationship to Coltrane does not have the same sense of relentless compulsion as Jones's.

At various times Coltrane had used musicians like Eric Dolphy to supplement the core sound of the quartet. From 1965 onwards he continually added extra musicians, swamping the quartet and arriving at an almost impenetrable density of sound, rejecting the quartet version of *First Meditations* in favour of a more extreme one featuring Pharoah Sanders and Rashied Ali. Uncertain of what their own contribution could be in such a format Tyner left in December 1965, Elvin Jones three months later. 'At times I couldn't hear what I was doing – matter of fact I couldn't hear what anybody was doing!' said Jones. 'All I could hear was a lot of noise. I didn't have any feeling for the music, and when I don't have any feelings, I don't like to play.'

In much of Coltrane's last phase (the core group consisting of Garrison, Ali, Sanders and Alice Coltrane on piano) there is little beauty but much that is terrible. It is music that is both conceived and best listened to *in extremis*. While Coltrane's concerns were becoming ever more religious his music for the most part presents a violent landscape filled with chaos and shrieks. It is as if he was attempting to absorb all the violence of his times into his music in order to leave the world more peaceful. Only occasionally, as in the haunting track 'Peace on Earth', does he finally seem able to partake in the repose he hoped to create.

The long shadow of Coltrane and the question of what can still be said in the bebop idiom are part of a larger doubt facing contemporary jazz players: does any new and important work remain to be done? Although scarcely a century old the rapid evolution of jazz means that audience and performers alike share a sense of coming very late in the tradition. Whether, after Bloom, we call this 'the anxiety of influence' or generalize it further into the post-modern condition hardly matters: the important thing is that jazz is now inescapably preoccupied with its own tradition. Indeed, art critic

Robert Hughes's vision 'of a present with continuous roots in history, where an artist's every action is judged by the unwearying tribunal of the dead' is as endemic to today's jazz musicians as it is (to Hughes's immense regret) inimical to contemporary visual artists. Whereas the jazz of the radical sixties was preoccupied with breaking from tradition, the neo-classical eighties have been concerned with affirming it. But this distinction is in danger of collapsing almost as soon as it is made. Since its tradition is one of innovation and improvisation, jazz, it could be argued, is never more traditional than when it is boldly iconoclastic. The art form most devoted to its past, jazz has always been the most forward-looking, so that the most radical work is often simultaneously the most traditional (Ornette Coleman's music, offered and perceived as nothing less than the Change of the Century, was drenched in the blues he had grown up hearing in Fort Worth). Either way, revivalism of any kind is doomed – it contradicts one of the animating principles of the music – but the development of jazz is now dependent on its capacity to absorb the past, and the most adventurous music is, increasingly, that which is able to dig deepest and most widely into the tradition.

Acknowledgements

Albertson, Chris. 'The Death of Bessie Smith', an extract from *Bessie*. First published by Stein & Day, New York, 1972. Copyright © Chris Albertson, 1972. Reprinted with the permission of Madison Books.

Allen, William F. 'The Voices of the Coloured People . . .', an extract from *Slave Songs of the United States*, compiled by William F. Allen and others, New York, 1867.

Baldwin, James. 'Of the Sorrow Songs', first published in the *New Edinburgh Review*, Autumn 1979. Reprinted with the permission of the James Baldwin Estate.

Balliett, Whitney. 'Mingus at Peace', an extract from *American Musicians: 45 Portraits in Jazz*. First published by Oxford University Press, New York, 1986. Copyright © Whitney Balliett, 1986.

Boulton, David. 'Early Ideas on the Origin of the Word "Jazz"', an extract from *Jazz in Britain*. First published by W. H. Allen, 1958. Copyright © David Boulton, 1958. Reprinted with the permission of Virgin Publishing Ltd.

Brown, Sterling A. 'Southern Road', from *The Collected Poems of Sterling A. Brown* edited by Michael S. Harper. Copyright © 1932 by Harcourt, Brace & Co. Copyright renewed 1980 by Sterling Brown. Originally appeared in *Southern Road*. Reprinted by permission of HarperCollins Publishers, Inc.

Campbell, S. Brunson. 'I Was Scott Joplin's Pupil', an extract from *Ragtime: Its History, Composers and Music* edited by John Edward Hasse. Schirmer Books, New York, 1985.

Charters, Samuel B. 'Ain't No More Cane', an extract from *The Country Blues*. First published by Rinehart, 1959. Copyright © Samuel B. Charters, 1959, 1975. Reprinted with permission of the author.

Collier, James Lincoln. 'Black Consciousness and the White Jazz Fan', first published in the *New Edinburgh Review*, Winter 1979. Reprinted with the permission of the author.

Dodson, Owen. 'Guitar', from *Powerful Long Ladder*, 1946; reprinted in *Black Voices: Poetry*, 1968 by Abraham Chapman and reprinted by permission of the author (now deceased).

DuBois, W. E. B. 'Of the Sorrow Songs', an extract from *The Souls of Black Folk* by W. E. B. DuBois.

Dyer, Geoff. 'Tradition, Influence and Innovation', an extract from *But Beautiful: A Book About Jazz*. First published by Jonathan Cape, 1991. Copyright © Geoff Dyer, 1991. Reprinted with the permission of the author.

Ellison, Ralph. 'Blues People', 'Remembering Jimmy Rushing' and 'On Bird, Bird-Watching and Jazz', extracts from *Shadow and Act* by Ralph Ellison. Copyright © 1953, 1964 and renewed 1981, 1992 by Ralph Ellison. Reprinted by permission of Random House, Inc.

Feather, Leonard. 'Monk, Blindfold', an extract from *The Encyclopaedia of Jazz in the Sixties*. Copyright © Leonard Feather, 1966.

Ferris, William. 'Work-songs' and 'Blues House Party', extracts from *Blues from the Delta*. Copyright © William Ferris, 1978. Reprinted by DaCapo, New York, 1984.

Giddens, Gary. 'Just How Much Did Elvis Learn from Otis Blackwell?', an extract from *Riding on a Blue Note: Jazz and American Pop*. First published by Oxford University Press, New York. Copyright © Gary Giddens.

Gillespie, Dizzy. 'Bendin' the Horn', an extract from *To Be, or not ... to Bop. Memoirs* by Dizzy Gillespie with Al Fraser. Copyright © John Birks Gillespie and Wilmot Alfred Fraser, 1979. First published by Doubleday, 1979. Reprinted with the permission of Doubleday, a division of Bantam Doubleday Dell Publishing Group, Inc.

Gorky, Maxim. An extract from *The Music of the Degenerate*. Translated by Marie Budberg, 1929.

Guralnick, Peter. 'Howlin' Wolf Meets the Critic', an extract from *Feel Like Going Home: Portraits in Blues and Rock 'n' Roll*. Published by Harper & Row. Copyright © Peter Guralnick, 1971, 1989. Reprinted with the permission of Richard P. McDonough.

Harper, Michael S. 'Here Where Coltrane Is', an extract from *History Is Your Own Heartbeat*. First published by University of Illinois Press, 1971. Copyright © Michael S. Harper, 1971. Reprinted with the permission of the University of Illinois Press.

Hentoff, Nat. 'In The Studio with Miles and Louis', an extract from *The Jazz Life* first published by Dial, New York 1961, reprinted by DaCapo, New York 1978. Copyright © Nat Hentoff, 1961. Reprinted with the permission of International Creative Management Inc.

Higginson, Thomas W. 'Collecting Negro Spirituals', an extract from *Army Life in a Black Regiment*, Boston, 1870.

Holiday, Billie and Dufty, William F. 'Picking up Money', an extract from *Lady Sings The Blues* by Billie Holiday with William Dufty. Copyright © Eleanora Fagan and William F. Dufty, 1956. Used by permission of Doubleday, a division of Bantam Doubleday Dell Publishing Group, Inc.

Holmes, John Clellon. 'Wing', an extract from *The Horn*, published by Thunder's Mouth Press. Copyright © John Clellon Holmes, 1988.

Hughes, Langston. 'Dream Boogie', from *Montage of a Dream Deferred*. Copyright © Langston Hughes, 1951. Reprinted with the permission of David Higham Associates.

Kemble, Frances Anne. 'Slave Singers', an extract from *Journal of a Residence on a Georgia Plantation in 1838–1839*, New York, 1863.

Kerouac, Jack. 'There You Go-Orooni', an extract from *On The Road*. First published by André Deutsch 1958. Copyright © Jack Kerouac, 1955, 1957. Reprinted with the permission of Penguin Books Ltd.

Koenigswarter, Baroness de. 'The Death of Bird', an extract from *Bird: The Legend of Charlie Parker* by Robert Reisner. Copyright © Robert George Reisner, 1962. Reprinted with the permission of the Carol Publishing Group.

Larkin, Philip. 'For Sidney Bechet', from *Collected Poems*. First published by Faber and Faber Ltd. Copyright © The Estate of Philip Larkin, 1988. Reprinted by permission of Faber and Faber Ltd.

Levey, Joseph. 'Tammy' . . . 'Ida' . . . 'Dinah' . . . 'Margie' . . ., an extract from *The Jazz Experience: A Guide to Appreciation*. First published by Prentice-Hall, New Jersey. Copyright © Joseph Levey, 1983.

Litweiler, John. 'Ornette Coleman Learns to Play the Saxophone', an extract from *The Freedom Principle: Jazz after 1958*. Published by DaCapo Press Inc. Copyright © John Litweiler, 1984. Reprinted with the permission of Multimedia Product Development Inc.

Lomax, Alan. 'Prison Blues' an extract from *The Land Where the Blues Began*. Copyright © Alan Lomax, 1993. Reprinted by permission of Pantheon Books, a division of Random House, Inc.

McDonough, John. 'The Court-Martial of Lester Young', first published in *Down Beat* Magazine, January 1981.

McPartland, Marian. 'The International Sweethearts of Rhythm', an extract from *All in Good Time*. First published by Oxford University Press, New York. Copyright © Marian McPartland, 1980, 1987.

Marquis, Donald. 'Forming The Buddy Bolden Band', an extract from *In Search of Buddy Bolden: First Man of Jazz*. Copyright © Louisiana State University Press, 1978. Reprinted by permission of the publisher.

Mezzrow, Milton 'Mezz' and Wolfe, Bernard. 'Dope', an extract from *Really the Blues*. First published by Random House 1946, republished by Citadel Press, a subsidiary of Carol Publishing Group in 1990. Copyright © Random House, 1946. Reprinted with the permission of Carol Publishing Group.

Miller, Paul Edward. 'A Vocabulary of Swing Terms', an extract from *Down Beat's Yearbook of Swing*, Westport, Connecticut: Greenwood Press.

Mingus, Charles. 'Mingus and His Psychiatrist', an extract from *Beneath the Underdog*. First published by Knopf, New York, 1971. Copyright © Charles Mingus and Nel King, 1971.

Northup, Solomon. 'Music on the Plantation', an extract from *Twelve Years a Slave*, Cincinnati, 1853.

Odum, Howard W. and Johnson, Guy B. 'Woman's Blues', an extract from *Negro Workaday Songs*. Copyright © 1926 renewed 1954 by The University of North Carolina Press. Reprinted by permission of the publisher.

Oliver, Paul. 'Henry Ford Blues', an extract from *Blues Fell this Morning: Meaning in the Blues*. First published by Cassell 1960, republished by Cambridge University Press 1990. Reprinted by permission of Cambridge University Press and Paul Oliver.

Ondaatje, Michael. An extract from *Coming Through Slaughter*. First published by Marion Boyars Publishers 1979. Copyright © Michael Ondaatje, 1976, 1979. Reprinted by permission of Marion Boyars Publishers Ltd.

Pepper, Art. 'On the Road with Stan Kenton's Band, 1946–52', an extract from *Straight Life: The Story of Art Pepper* by Art and Laurie Pepper. First published by Schirmer Books 1979. Copyright © Schirmer Books, 1979. Reprinted by permission of Picador Books.

Petry, Ann. An extract from *Solo on the Drums*, published by '47 Magazine of the Year. Copyright © Ann Petry, 1947, renewed 1975. Reprinted by permission of Russell & Volkening, Inc.

Reisner, Robert. An extract from *Bird: The Legend of Charlie Parker*. Copyright © Robert George Reisner 1962. Published by arrangement with Carol Publishing Group.

Schuller, Gunther. 'Louis Armstrong: The First Great Soloist', an extract from *Early Jazz: Its Roots and Musical Development*. Oxford University Press 1968. Copyright © Oxford University Press, 1968.

Shapiro, Nat and Hentoff, Nat. 'The Swing Era – Big Bands, Big Money, and the Breakdown of Some Racial Barriers', an extract from *Hear Me Talkin' to Ya: The Story of Jazz by the Men Who Made It*, edited by Nat Shapiro and Nat Hentoff. Copyright © Nat Shapiro and Nat Hentoff, 1955, 1983. Reprinted by permission of Henry Holt and Co., Inc and Souvenir Press Ltd.

Škvorecký, Josef. 'Red Music', an extract from *Talkin' Moscow Blues* by Josef Škvorecký and edited by Sam Solecki. First published in Toronto by Lester and Orpen Dennys Ltd 1988. Copyright © Josef Škvorecký, 1988. Reprinted with the permission of Faber and Faber Ltd.

Southern, Ellen. 'Runaway', an extract from *Readings in Black American Music*, edited by Ellen Southern. First published by W. W. Norton & Co., New York, 1971.

Staats, Gregory R. 'Sexual Imagery in the Blues', an extract from *Journal of Jazz Studies* Spring/Summer 1979. Copyright © Rutgers Institute of Jazz Studies. Reprinted with the permission of Scarecrow Press Inc.

Starr, S. Frederick 'Jazz Comes to Revolutionary Russia', an extract from *Red & Hot: The Fate of Jazz in the Soviet Union 1917–1980*. Oxford University Press, New York, 1983. Copyright © Frederick S. Starr, 1983.

Sullivan, Norman. 'Real Musician', an extract of an article in *Saturday Evening Post*, 26 February 1938.

Vian, Boris. 'Jazz Chronicle' and 'Round About Close to Midnight', extracts from *Round About Close to Midnight: The Jazz Writings of Boris Vian*, translated and edited by Mike Zwerin. Published by Quartet 1988. Translation copyright © Mike Zwerin, 1988. Reprinted with the permission of Quartet Books Ltd. 'Round About Close to Midnight' originally published in *Jazz Hot*, Christmas 1948.

Vogel, Eric. 'Jazz in a Nazi Concentration Camp', from articles first published in *Down Beat* Magazine, 7 December 1961, 21 December 1961 and 4 January 1962.

Zwerin, Mike. 'Miles and Me', an extract from *Close Enough for Jazz*, published by Quartet 1983. Reprinted with the permission of Quartet Books Ltd.

The publisher has made every effort to contact the copyright holders. We will be grateful to hear of any omissions and acknowledgement will be made at the earliest opportunity.

Index

Index